Wakefield Press

Matthew Beovich

Josephine Laffin teaches Christian history for the School of Theology at Flinders University and the Adelaide College of Divinity. She is based at Catholic Theological College. Dr Laffin has a Bachelor of Theology degree from Flinders University and a Master of Arts and Doctorate in Philosophy from the University of Adelaide.

Matthew Beovich

A Biography

Josephine Laffin

Wakefield Press

Wakefield Press
1 The Parade West
Kent Town
South Australia 5067
www.wakefieldpress.com.au

First published 2008

Designed by Liz Nicholson, designBITE
Typeset by Clinton Ellicott, Wakefield Press
Printed and bound by Hyde Park Press, Adelaide

National Library of Australia
Cataloguing-in-Publication entry

Author: Laffin, J. D. (Josephine Dene).
Title: Matthew Beovich: a biography/Josephine Laffin.
ISBN: 978 1 86254 817 6 (pbk.).
Notes: Includes index.
Bibliography.
Subjects: Beovich, Matthew, 1896–1981.
Catholic Church – Australia – Bishops – Biography.
Bishops – Australia – Biography.
Adelaide (S. Aust.) – Church history – 20th century.
Dewey Number: 282.092

History Trust of south australia

Arts SA

Contents

Acknowledgements

I am indebted to many people for assistance during the writing of this biography. It began as a doctoral thesis, and I am very grateful for the guidance I received from my first supervisor, Katharine Massam, and then, when she left the University of Adelaide, from Frank McGregor. David Hilliard kindly read draft chapters and I benefited greatly from his knowledge of Australian religious history and his editorial advice. Malcolm Saunders supplied helpful comments on an early version of the chapter on the Catholic Social Studies Movement and the ALP Split, as did David Shinnick for that chapter and the one on the 1960s. Vincent Tiggeman, Matthew Beovich's secretary from 1955 to 1966, proofread the thesis in 2006, as did Joan Brewer and the late Denise Roder. The revised version was read by Eveleen and Nicholas Kerr and Helen Harrison. Monsignor Tiggeman continued his generous support by helping to prepare the index. My sincere thanks to all these people, and to Michael Bollen and the team at Wakefield Press for so expertly transforming the manuscript into a publication.

Matthew Beovich's successor as archbishop of Adelaide was the late James Gleeson. I remember with gratitude his enthusiasm for this project. It could not have been undertaken without access to the Adelaide Catholic Archdiocesan Archives (ACAA). I thank

Leonard Faulkner, now Emeritus Archbishop of Adelaide, for granting me permission to use the material in the archives. I am also very grateful to Philip Wilson for his encouragement and support since he became archbishop in 2001, and to Gregory O'Kelly SJ, Auxiliary Bishop of Adelaide since 2006.

A number of archivists assisted my research. In particular, I deeply appreciate the help I received from the custodians of the ACAA: Marie Therese Foale RSJ and, since 2003, Suzanne Ryan. It was a pleasure to work in the archives. Sister Marie's familiarity with the material in her care and understanding of Australian Catholic history was a great help. After Sr Marie retired, Suzanne's professionalism and quiet friendly presence was invaluable. Rachel Naughton (Melbourne Diocesan Historical Commission) also deserves special mention, along with Peter Dalton (Catholic Education Office Archives, East Melbourne), the late James Kelty CFC (Christian Brothers' Archives, Parkville), Joseph Lee SDB (Salesian Archives, Ascot Park), and the library staff at the Pontifical Urban University in Rome.

I am very grateful to the many people who shared their memories of Matthew Beovich with me, both in formal interviews and innumerable informal conversations. Warmest thanks are due to my colleagues at the Catholic Theological College of South Australia for their companionship and support, also to the wider community at the Adelaide College of Divinity campus, especially the ever-helpful staff at the Adelaide Theological Library. Friends provided much encouragement over the course of my research. I particularly remember my fellow post-graduate student, Anne Roder, who died in 2002 before she could complete her own thesis, and her mother Denise, who lost her battle with cancer this year on the anniversary of Anne's death. Finally I must thank my family for many years of patience and understanding.

Josephine Laffin
2008

Prologue

> There is an element of mystery in every person, depths which are seldom sounded, or being sounded, rarely revealed. Those of us who knew Matthew Beovich well knew his clear incisive mind. We experienced the depths of his learning. We knew his capacity to grasp a problem quickly and solve it wisely. We knew his fierce determination and singleness of purpose. We remember his capacity to move with lightning speed from one place to another, to appear and disappear as if by magic. In this self-effacing and shy man we divined depths of piety which remained in the privacy of his heart and mind ...
>
> Bishop Philip Kennedy, Requiem Mass for Matthew Beovich, 29 October 1981

Matthew Beovich liked reading biographies. His eclectic book collection included volumes on saints and sportsmen, popes and politicians. However, as Philip Kennedy perceived, he was both shy and self-effacing. 'You know how I detest anything that savors of self-advertisement,' he wrote to his mother from Rome in 1921, after he was identified as the author of an article in a Melbourne Catholic newspaper, 'I felt like hiding myself under a haystack.'[1] Modesty and humility were virtues which he valued and faithfully demonstrated throughout his life, so it is unlikely that he would have relished being the subject of a biography. This fate has befallen him because he was the Catholic archbishop of Adelaide from 1939 to 1971.

I did not know Matthew Beovich personally, and as I did not join the Catholic Church until 1994; I have no childhood memories of his appearance at church functions. The first Catholic bishop I encountered was James Gleeson, who succeeded Beovich as archbishop of Adelaide from 1971 to 1985. He was one of the participants on a retreat I attended at St Joseph's House of Prayer at Aldgate in the Adelaide Hills. Although we met as a group for meals, there was no conversation for eight days – the enforced silence designed to facilitate private prayer. In the dining room I succumbed to distractions and was amused by the way some religious sisters unsuccessfully tried to wait on the elderly bishop. He jumped up and down during meals, fetching bread and butter and passing drinks around, and as soon as anyone had finished eating, he would whisk their dishes and cutlery out to the scullery. Happily wielding a tea towel, he was, very obviously, no 'prince bishop'. I was struck one day by how much the Catholic Church had changed during his lifetime, and how his life story would make a good 'prism of history'.[2]

After the retreat finished, I visited Archbishop Gleeson at his home at Medindie and discussed my search for a topic for a doctoral thesis. Could I write his biography? No, was the firm reply. He had a better idea. The most significant changes in the Catholic Church in the twentieth century had occurred during the term of his predecessor, for whom there was much more plentiful documentary evidence in the Adelaide archdiocesan archives – including a diary. I went to the archives, opened Matthew Beovich's diary, and realised that I had found my topic, or rather, it had found me.

It is impossible for biographers to remain indifferent to their subjects, even if they start that way, as I did. My affection for Matthew Beovich grew as I read his diary. One of the least mediated forms of contact possible to have with a deceased person, a diary can engender a sense of intimacy and friendship. That was my experience as I worked through the volumes which the young 'Matt' Beovich wrote as a student in Rome from 1917 to 1923. The diary which he kept from 1939 until the 1970s, when he gradually stopped writing, is less personal. As a busy archbishop, Beovich often jotted brief notes which would have jogged his memory years later but unfortunately did not have the same effect on me.

However, when it came to important events such as the Second Vatican Council in the 1960s, he was more reflective, and recorded his observations in mercifully legible handwriting. He was interested in history and appreciated the importance of keeping such records.

As I worked on the biography, in a number of interviews and many more informal conversations I asked people to describe Matthew Beovich to me. The two most common words which I heard in response were 'austere' and 'remote'. How could such an aloof figure develop from the friendly young author of the 1917–1923 diary? With the help of the diary, and other sources listed in the bibliography, I realised that I could shed some light on this very private individual, but writing a psychological study was always going to be beyond my competence.

I thought I would be on safer ground taking the 'prism of history' approach. In my case, this initially meant offering Matthew Beovich's life story as a supplement to the general histories of Australian Catholicism. The books of Patrick O'Farrell, Edmund Campion and Naomi Turner are an important starting point for anyone interested in Australian Catholic history, but these authors, based in the eastern states, rarely if ever mention South Australia.[3]

I quickly discovered a problem with using a bishop's story as a prism for viewing twentieth-century Australian Catholicism. Even if I managed to avoid what Wilfrid Prest describes as the 'occupational tendency' of biographers – the exaggeration of the significance of the subject's influence on the course of events[4] – the result was inevitably going to be what Campion calls 'head office history'.[5] It would go against the grain of recent attempts by historians like Campion, Turner and Katharine Massam to devote more attention to lay Catholics, an understandable reaction to older histories in which the laity scarcely appeared at all.[6] In defence, I could use O'Farrell's response to the criticism that the first edition of his history of the Catholic Church in Australia concentrated too much on the hierarchy and clergy. The Catholic Church is still a hierarchical and clerically controlled institution; therefore exploring how the institution has functioned and how particular leaders have exercised their authority surely remains an important task for historians.[7]

In the end I tried to make a virtue out of necessity by focusing on the role of bishop. I am interested in what bishops actually do, and how the role has changed over time. As a participant in the recent dialogue between Australian Lutheran and Roman Catholic academics on episcopal ministry,[8] the logical place to start seemed to be not 11 December 1939, when Beovich was appointed archbishop of Adelaide, nor 1 April 1896, the date of his birth, but the first century when Christian ministry began.

Bishops in the Catholic Tradition

The Greek word *episkopos*, from which the term bishop is derived, is found in some of the New Testament writings, but only as one of a number of titles given to men in leadership positions in the Christian community. No clear distinction is made between *episkopos* (often translated overseer) and *presbuteros* (elder).[9] From the fragmentary evidence, it seems that bishops/presbyters had administrative, teaching and preaching responsibilities and were supposed to be men of exemplary character.[10] The Didache, one of the earliest Christian documents outside the New Testament, describes problems which were arising in connection with the itinerant ministries of apostles and prophets. It then recommends the election of a more stable local leadership team in the form of bishops and deacons, 'gentle men who are not fond of money'.[11]

The earliest evidence of the emergence of a more monarchical style of episcopacy comes from the letters of Ignatius of Antioch.[12] Writing in the early second century, Ignatius takes for granted the fact that there is one bishop in a town or city, assisted by presbyters and deacons. He maintains that nothing should be done without the bishop's permission, and he exhorts Christians to obey their bishop as if he were God. However, he also assumes that the Christian community is small enough for the bishop to know everyone by name. Concerned about divisions and false teaching, Ignatius presents the bishop as the true shepherd of his flock and a focus of unity in the local church.

As disputes continued in the second and third centuries over what constituted authentic Christian teaching, the concept of apostolic succession became important. The bishops were identified as the successors of the apostles, responsible for ensuring that the apostolic tradition was faithfully preserved and transmitted to future generations. A collegial notion of episcopacy also developed. The installation of a new bishop required the presence of other bishops to lay hands on the new leader in an ordination rite. Bishops corresponded with one another and met at councils and synods to share decision making. Although reaching a consensus was often difficult, as H. A. Drake comments, 'It is easy to underestimate the centrifugal forces that might well have kept Christians from being anything but highly diversified local sects ... The bishop is the figure who gave the movement cohesion and stability.'[13] The bishop of Rome, as the successor of St Peter, occupied a unique position of honour in the apostolic succession, but the practical consequences of this varied from region to region and were little felt in the eastern parts of the Roman Empire.

As Christian communities grew in size after Emperor Constantine embraced the Christian religion in the fourth century, the administrative duties of bishops increased and they acquired civic responsibilities. The collapse of the Roman Empire in the West exacerbated the tendency for them to become 'law and order personified' in the remaining towns and cities in Europe.[14] At best, this was balanced by a similar strengthening of their spiritual authority. In his late-sixth-century treatise on pastoral care, Pope Gregory the Great portrays bishops as, above all, spiritual directors and shepherds of souls.[15] When 'pragmatic authority' predominated, it was but a short step to the 'career bishops' or 'prince bishops' of the Middle Ages.

At worst, by the sixteenth century a bishop could owe his position – or multiple positions – in the Church to family influence or royal patronage and live an affluent, aristocratic lifestyle. However, revisionist historians caution against accepting uncritically the tirades of Catholic reformers and Protestant critics.[16] On the eve of the Reformation there were still bishops who were conscientious, pastoral and devout. Those who gathered at the Council of Trent in the mid-sixteenth century were aware of abuses and made institutional reform one of their key objectives.[17] Decrees were passed which required bishops to live in their dioceses and perform more faithfully their pastoral duties. They were to inspect parishes regularly, hold diocesan councils and synods to publish reform legislation, and establish seminaries to train priests. From the time of Pope Sixtus V (1585–1590), bishops were also expected to visit the pope every three to five years to report on the state of their dioceses. A new ideal of episcopal ministry emerged, exemplified by Carlo Borromeo, archbishop of Milan from 1564 to 1584. An austere, zealous and holy workaholic, he was canonised in 1610. Although the implementation of the decrees of the Council was a long process, the impact of this ideal on the Catholic Church throughout the next four centuries was profound.[18]

Despite the time lapse, what could be called the Tridentine model of episcopal leadership found further legislative expression in the Code of Canon Law which was promulgated in 1917 (the year that Matthew Beovich began formation for the priesthood in Rome). It spelt out that bishops were the successors of the apostles, appointed by the pope to govern their dioceses and ensure that the laws of the Church were observed. The Code set out what those laws were, and how diocesan administration should operate. It reiterated that bishops were to inspect their dioceses regularly, and once every five years (ten if they lived outside Europe) they were to make an *ad limina* visit, a pilgrimage to the tombs of the apostles Peter and Paul in Rome. On that visit they were to submit a report on the state of their dioceses to the pope.

The Code of Canon Law reflected and consolidated the increasingly prominent role of the papacy in the Catholic Church from the late nineteenth century onwards. After the incorporation of Rome into the kingdom of Italy in 1870, the papacy emerged from the loss of its temporal power with its spiritual authority much enhanced. There was a surge in devotion to the pope. Ultramontanism, literally the tendency to look 'beyond the mountains' from northern Europe to the Vatican for inspiration, was encouraged by the personal charisma of Pope Pius IX and the decree of the First Vatican Council concerning papal infallibility. Modern means of transport and communication enabled the Church to become more centralised than ever before. As the governments of Europe became more secular, they abandoned their claims to nominate bishops and the pope took over the task of appointment. Hence in the 1917 Code of Canon Law the role of diocesan bishop appears rather like that of a branch manager of an international corporation.[19]

CATHOLIC BISHOPS IN AUSTRALIA

The development of the Catholic hierarchy in Australia in the latter half of the nineteenth century coincided with the intensification of ultramontanist sentiments. Australia's first Catholic bishop, John Bede Polding, was consecrated in London in 1834. He was an English Benedictine, but most of the men appointed to govern Australian dioceses in the remainder of the century came from Ireland. In *The Roman Mould of the Australian Catholic Church*, John Molony argues that their nationality is misleading. Influenced by Cardinal Paul Cullen, archbishop of Dublin from 1852 to 1878, they were 'products of an Irish Church undergoing a thorough Romanization at the hands of prelates trained in Rome, oriented toward Rome, and consciously seeking to shape the Church both in Ireland and Australia in the Roman mould'.[20] Patrick O'Farrell counters Molony's thesis by pointing out that most of the bishops' time in Rome was spent in an Irish enclave (the Irish College), and their subsequent relations with the Vatican reveal an ambivalence toward papal authority. It was useful when it bolstered their own positions, and relatively easy to ignore when it did not. 'The fact was,' concludes O'Farrell, 'to most Australian Catholics, the papacy, its politics and pronouncements seemed remote and irrelevant.'[21]

Molony acknowledges that Daniel Mannix was one bishop who did not get caught in the ultramontane currents swirling around the Church. Mannix assumed responsibility for the archdiocese of Melbourne in 1917, the same year the Code of Canon Law was promulgated. He ignored some of its provisions, such as the requirement that a bishop regularly inspect the parishes of his diocese.[22] B. A. Santamaria claims that Mannix 'unquestioningly accepted every decision clearly made personally by the pope'. However, Santamaria adds, 'this is not the same thing as saying that he accepted every piece of advice offered in the name of the Pope by Vatican diplomats'.[23] Santamaria does not explain how Mannix discerned the difference. As he only made one formal *ad limina* visit to Rome in his half century as a bishop (in 1921), and another pilgrimage in 1925, his opportunities for direct contact with the pope were limited.

There are more biographies of Mannix than of any other Australian bishop. They range from hagiographic to iconoclastic,[24] with two of the most recent volumes promoting Mannix's forthright leadership style as an appropriate one for the Church today.[25] James Duhig, who became archbishop of Brisbane in 1917, has not attracted as much attention as Mannix, but the biography written by Thomas Boland compensates for this by being of a very high standard.[26] Unlike Mannix, Duhig studied in Rome, but he too broke free of an ultramontane mould. Boland admits:

> One discovery in the archives amused me greatly. I found the account from E. J. Dwyer for James's first copy of the Code of Canon Law, dated 1919. There were times when I felt like exclaiming: Why did you not read the thing and let that be your guide to what a bishop is? I could have produced a slim volume of biography in six months and been rid of this pervasive prelate. In fact, his refusal to conform to stereotype was his most significant ecclesiastical contribution to the Australian Catholic Church. Yet, did he have to become so involved in politics, education – all education, not just Catholic – the arts, business, agriculture, oil, mining, urban development, racial prejudice, several wars, journalism, every subject under the sun – down to, and including, baby food? His Church was the Incarnation extended in every time, in every place, in every person. That is one way of putting it; another is that he was illimitably curious.[27]

Duhig was also a patriotic Australian citizen and fervent royalist who happily climbed from his Irish peasant background to the upper echelons of Queensland society. In 1959 his service to church and state was rewarded with a knighthood from the queen, the first given to an Australian Catholic bishop. The famously more confrontational Mannix did not receive any such honour, and probably would not have accepted it if it had been offered. Within a few years of his arrival in Australia he had become 'arguably the most revered and reviled figure in Australian history' after locking horns with the prime minister over the issue of military conscription.[28] Yet, in their very different ways, both Mannix and Duhig exemplify the importance of the bishop's public role, an aspect of episcopal ministry that is virtually passed over in the 1917 Code of Canon Law. Through force of character, they achieved celebrity status as Christian leaders. Perhaps that is why so little has been written of the other Australian bishops, who seem to pale in comparison with them.[29]

Thanks to their longevity as well as their personalities, Mannix and Duhig were the venerable elder statesmen of the Australian hierarchy in the mid-twentieth century. Mannix died in 1963 a few months short of his hundredth birthday; Duhig in 1965 at the age of ninety-three. A new generation of bishops was appointed in the 1930s. The newcomers had not been imported from Ireland or drawn from the ranks of the Irish-born clergy. They had not even trained for the priesthood in Ireland, a development which was welcomed by some as a sign of the increasing maturity of the Australian Catholic Church, but resented by others as a slight on Ireland. When Matthew Beovich became archbishop-elect of Adelaide in December 1939 he was technically the first Australian-born head of a metropolitan see, but Norman Gilroy had already been appointed coadjutor archbishop of the more prestigious diocese of Sydney in 1937. He assumed responsibility for it after Michael Kelly's death in March 1940, a few weeks before Beovich's consecration. Six years later he became the first Australian-born cardinal.

Like Beovich, Gilroy began formation for the priesthood in Rome when the Code of Canon Law was coming into effect, and his biographer, John Luttrell, comments that 'one can imagine that it was given due attention by his lecturers'.[30] He clearly approached his appointment to Sydney much more in the spirit of a loyal branch manager than Mannix or Duhig. However, he also had to assume a public role. As canon law provided little guidance, and the older bishops offered conflicting role models, he had to work this out for himself. Luttrell identifies the better integration of Catholics into Australian society as one of Gilroy's overriding concerns.[31] A measure of his success in implementing this policy is the fact that he was made a Knight Commander of the British Empire in 1969 and 'Australian of the Year' in 1970, shortly before his retirement in 1971.

The increase in the size and influence of the Catholic Church in the mid-twentieth century was not unique to Australia. James O'Toole argues that in almost every diocese in the United States, the following pattern can be seen.[32] A pioneering, missionary bishop, usually from Ireland, is followed by a number of successors who struggle to build up the young diocese. In the early twentieth century, a native-born bishop emerges, a 'consolidator who brings the local church to organizational maturity and superintends its expanding impact in the community at large'.[33] This 'consolidator' is not noted for outstanding holiness or intellectual ability. He is primarily a builder and organiser. He is a far greater centraliser than his predecessors, more firmly linked to the pope and the Roman curia, and inclined, as his efforts bear fruit, to succumb to triumphalism.

Was this also the case in Australia? There are echoes of O'Toole's stereotype in William McCarthy's account of 'James the Builder' O'Collins, bishop of Geraldton from 1930 to 1941 and of Ballarat from 1941 to 1971.[34] They become louder in Boland's study of Duhig, who was also nicknamed 'James the Builder'. Although Boland rejects the title as inadequate, it is easy for someone who never experienced the warmth of Duhig's personality to agree with Patrick O'Farrell's caustic comment that it does in fact convey the essence of his achievements as a bishop.[35]

At best, Duhig emerges from the pages of Boland's biography as a friendly, kind, benevolent shepherd/statesman. However, Boland also reveals that the archbishop of Brisbane was supremely egotistical, financially irresponsible and prone to 'doctrinal howlers'. O'Farrell is disturbed by the lack of evidence of a profound faith. Boland highlights Duhig's ideal of people living in faith and charity, good Christians and good citizens, a genial kind of Christian humanism which 'explains why to many he seemed not to have a spirituality – it was his whole life',[36] but is that adequate in a bishop? Biographers of the enigmatic Daniel Mannix have also struggled to write more than a few sentences about their bishop's interior life. Averse to 'posterity analysing my soul', he simply refused to discuss it.[37] The result, as Massam observes in her study of Catholic spirituality, is that 'central dimensions of religious experience ... have been beyond the story of bishops and buildings that constitutes so much of the study of religion in Australia'.[38]

Does a 'head office' history of the Catholic Church have to bypass the heart and matters of faith and devotion? Was Matthew Beovich a 'consolidator', a builder and an administrator rather than a pastor? Did his Croatian heritage set him apart from his contemporaries, who were nearly all descended from Irish migrants? How did he respond to the changes in church and society during his life time? These were some of the questions which I was pondering when I began investigating his life story.

One
'A Real Australian' Growing up in Melbourne, 1896–1917

> 'A real Australian, with a gentle personality and a quiet and dignified manner', was the description applied to Monsignor Beovich by Brother C. A. Mogg, vice-principal of Rostrevor College, who was at school with him ...
>
> *Advertiser*, 13 December 1939

On holiday in Melbourne in the 1960s, an Adelaide diocesan priest was having his hair cut. Chatting as he worked, the barber revealed that he used to cut 'Father Bevick's' hair. One day another customer had come into the shop, sat down next to Beovich, and exclaimed: 'Dago Bevick!' They had been to school together.[1] Perhaps that is why Brother Mogg felt it necessary in 1939 to reassure Adelaide's Catholic community that they were getting 'a real Australian' as their new bishop. Beovich's appointment as archbishop of Adelaide was hailed as the beginning of a new era because he was the first bishop who had been born in Australia rather than Ireland. Other Australian dioceses also received their first native bishops in the 1930s, but they at least bore names which reflected their Irish ancestry. Matthew Beovich stands out as a rare exception, so it is appropriate that we begin with the father who passed on the name.

Family

Mate Beović was born on the rugged island of Brač off the Croatian coast in 1861.[2] Brač then had crowded villages but no roads. Donkeys were the main form of transport, clambering up and down steep slopes to olive orchards and grape vines. Mate's father tended vines. In his early twenties, Mate joined the exodus of young people who hoped for a better life in America or Australia. Mate chose the Australian colony of Victoria where a number of Croatians had already ventured, probably lured by the discovery of gold in 1851.[3] His journey came to an end in Melbourne in 1884.

'Marvellous Melbourne': the term was coined by a late nineteenth-century traveller and in the 1880s there was much to justify it.[4] The village settlement of 1835 had evolved into a bustling, thriving metropolis. Cable trams rumbled along city streets, gas-lit at night and lined with an ever-growing number of multi-storey shops and offices. Grand public buildings, such as the neo-classical public lending library, asserted the city's claim to be a cultural as well as a commercial centre, while a network of railway lines reached out into the expanding suburbs. The population nearly doubled in a decade, rising to almost half a million in 1891, and unemployment was low.

A few years after his arrival, Mate Beović started a restaurant, probably one of the many cheap eateries clustered around Bourke Street in the centre of the city. It was a casualty of the devastating depression of the 1890s. Mate then made a living as a fruiterer, with a stall at the Queen Victoria Market. In the minor boom after the First World War he built two small shops on Sydney Road, Coburg, and, with income from the rented shops coming in, he retired in 1928. From 1901 'Charles Mat Beovich' was officially a citizen of his adopted country.

A photograph taken in Melbourne in 1893 reveals a dapper-looking man with receding dark hair and a glossy black moustache. The son of a friend later recalled in a letter to Matthew Beovich: 'Whatever your beloved father may have done in the early years of his manhood and strength, in his declining years he was to be found – fresh, brisk and magnificent – in the Victoria Market.'[5] Mate's eldest grandson has fond memories of 'a jolly man who played with his grandchildren and "sneaked" us boiled lollies'.[6]

He collapsed at Mass on Sunday, 2 July 1933, dying within minutes from a heart attack.[7]

It is tempting to trace Archbishop Matthew Beovich's shrewdness, tenacity and habitual briskness back to his peasant-businessman father. Certainly his concern for Catholic migrants after the Second World War was enhanced by the knowledge that he was a migrant's son. However, nothing more can be said for certain as the father has faded into the shadows of his son's life. All the remaining evidence points to Elizabeth Beovich as the dominant influence on the future archbishop – and Elizabeth was born Elizabeth Mary Kenny.

Thomas Kenny and Margaret Nihill were married in 1854 in the church (now cathedral) dedicated to Saints Peter and Paul in Ennis, a market town at the heart of County Clare in Ireland.[8] Towering over the square in the centre of the town is a statue of Daniel O'Connell. While many Irish towns have monuments to 'the Liberator', Ennis has a special claim to him as it was his victory in the Clare by-election of 1828, despite the fact that he could not sit in the British Parliament as he was Catholic, which was the trigger for Catholic emancipation. The statue was erected in 1867. Young Matthew Beovich saw it when he visited Ennis in 1923, but not his grandparents as they emigrated to Australia soon after their marriage.

Caught up in the gold rushes, Thomas and Margaret went to Bendigo in the colony of Victoria. They subsequently settled on a farm in the district. Elizabeth Mary was born in Bendigo on 16 June 1864, the sixth of eleven children (the three immediately before her and the one after did not survive infancy). There was no nearby Catholic school for her to attend, but this did not hinder her faith development. 'I may be biased in this, but I have rarely met a lay woman as well versed in her faith as my mother,' Matthew Beovich reflected in a speech in 1967 on the importance of family life.[9] He made the same point in an interview in 1980: 'I think there would be few people with more knowledge of the faith than my mother.'[10] He attributed this to her parents, and to the catechism, Catholic newspapers and sermons, a staple diet of orthodoxy and piety.

What drew Elizabeth Kenny from Bendigo to Melbourne

has been lost with the passage of time. She may have met Mate Beović through the church. Croatian Catholics tended to congregate around their local Catholic churches as there were no formal Croatian societies or organisations at that time.[11] Mate's closest church was St Francis's Church in Lonsdale Street. He and Elizabeth were married there on 26 April 1893. In the late nineteenth century, the 'usual occupation' section on the marriage register was often either left blank for the bride or she was assigned a label such as 'domestic'.[12] Elizabeth was described as a 'lady'; her husband was a 'caterer'. The photograph taken to commemorate the occasion shows an attractive woman, with an upright, slim figure, standing slightly behind her seated husband with a hand resting on his shoulder. In keeping with the style of the time, her expression is severe. Her eyes stare resolutely ahead.

In the autumn of 1893, as Elizabeth and Mate were getting married, thirteen Australian banking companies closed their doors. Most were based in Melbourne. They were casualties of an economic depression that 'not only caused terrific physical distress, it inflicted a psychic wound which never healed'.[13] In these troubled times Elizabeth gave birth to Mary Margaret in February 1894, and two years later, on 1 April 1896, Mathew arrived. He became known to family and friends as Matt.

Another photograph, taken in 1899, shows a solemn Elizabeth once again standing behind her seated husband. Holding his hand is an engaging five-year-old with a pretty, plump face. Grasping his father's knee is a solemn-looking boy about three-and-a-half years old. Sadly, there were to be no more such photos. On Christmas Day 1899, Mary became seriously ill. After falling into a coma, she died on 1 January 1900 from tubercular meningitis. There is no record of the impact of Mary's death on her brother, but a hint of how Elizabeth reacted may be gleaned from a letter Matt sent to his mother in 1923: 'Indeed it is true that God deeply afflicts those He loves, and as He increases His grace to a soul He does not remove the cross, rather He increases it. All this you know so well, for I have heard it from you ...'[14] Throughout his life Matt would express the conviction that an omnipotent God was ultimately in control, so whatever happened, no matter how unpleasant, had to be somehow part of God's will. Suffering was to be stoically accepted as part of Christian discipleship.

Ten months after the death of Mary, Elizabeth gave birth to Francis John (Frank). In 1902 he was followed by Elizabeth Veronica (Vera). The young Beovichs were enveloped in a circle of Kenny grandparents, aunts, uncles and cousins. The letters which Matt sent home during his time as a student in Rome (1917 to 1923) give some insight into his family ties. In 1917 he promised to write to his mother once a week. He did not manage to keep this up, but almost a hundred letters remain as testimony to their close relationship. Only constant reassurances about his health reveal that he was writing to an anxious mother and not a friend. He assumed Elizabeth would be interested in everything from politics to football matches. Sometimes he stumbled over the words, but he knew she would understand what he meant. He would finish with 'heaps of love' or 'stacks of love to yourself, Father, Frank and Vera'.

In his diary Matt noted when 'Mother' sent cheques at Christmas and for his birthday. On 22 July 1922 he jotted: 'Safe to write now and tell Mother I shall be ordained next Christmas.' In March the following year he wrote of his voyage home: 'Mother has splendidly fixed matters. The Arch. [Archbishop Mannix] will pay the boat fare plus 20 pounds. Dad will send me 120 pounds for extra expenses.' Responding to a toast in his honour when he was welcomed back to Melbourne, he declared that 'whatever honours he had won, credit was due in the first place to his mother, who, in silence and alone, had tried to mould his character'.[15]

Reflecting on his vocation in 1980, Matthew Beovich recalled that in the years between leaving school and going to Rome, his mother would accompany him to confession each week: 'I think that was a very helpful thing.'[16] Elizabeth also went with her son to Mass. Another woman in their local parish used to reproach her son for not being more like Matt Beovich, who always accompanied his mother to the early morning Mass on Sundays.[17] Elizabeth's obituary in 1949 reported that until she was bedridden two or three years before her death, she used to walk to St Francis's Church every day for rosary and Benediction.[18]

Priests, especially those of Matthew Beovich's generation, tended to promote an idealised view of motherhood. In the poetry of the Rev. Patrick Hartigan, the 'Little Irish Mother' is the uncrowned queen of the home, the domestic custodian of Catholic faith and piety. She valiantly raises her family against the odds, her greatest triumph coming when one of her sons is ordained.[19] Patrick O'Farrell insists that Hartigan's 'Little Irish Mother' was the exception rather than the rule, but for Matt Beovich it was an exception that was grounded in reality.[20] It is one of the ironies in a church which seems so patriarchal that the matriarchal influence on clerical vocations has been so strong. Norman Gilroy once said of his parents, 'My mother was a very pious woman, coming from a very pious family. My father was not quite so pious ...'[21]

While the elderly Elizabeth could bask in the glory of being the mother of an archbishop, she had what she and Matt interpreted as a 'cross to bear'. When he knelt in front of the altar encasing the tomb of St Monica in 1923, Matt was reminded of his mother,[22] for St Monica had pursued her wayward son Augustine with relentless tears and prayers until his conversion. Elizabeth's problem son was Frank, who was handsome, talented and more outgoing than his elder brother. He commenced an Arts/Law degree at Melbourne University but was unable to earn a scholarship or reconcile his parents to the expense of his education at a time when they were building the new shops on Sydney Road and sending money to Matt in Rome.

Forced to leave university, Frank became an English teacher in the state education system. He studied at night to obtain a Bachelor of Education and Master of Arts degree. He discovered that the convivial environment of a hotel, where he would be given free drinks in return for playing the piano, was preferable to his pious home, where Elizabeth went to bed at an early hour and frowned on his friends. Thus was born a habit of heavy drinking which continued until his death in 1961. He married Kathleen Hutchinson, another school teacher, but the marriage did not last. They had a daughter and two sons before separating in 1944–1945. Thereafter, Kathleen and the children had little contact with the Beovich family. Matthew John (Jack), the grandson who remembers Mate Beovich as a 'jolly man', found Elizabeth 'cold and austere', and dreaded the ordeal of having to play 'Danny Boy' to her on his violin. It was also embarrassing to have a grandmother who would march around state schools praying for the 'poor pagan children' within. Jack's first remembered contact with his uncle Matt came when, as inspector of religious instruction in Catholic schools in the 1930s, Father Beovich visited a class and asked the religious sister in charge to point out his relative.[23] His sister Joan had a similar experience.[24] At the Requiem Mass for Archbishop James Gleeson in March 2000, one of Gleeson's nieces put a Christmas tea towel on the coffin, a symbol of her uncle's participation in joyous family gatherings and insistence on doing the washing up afterwards. Such a gesture would have been unthinkable at Beovich's funeral in 1981.

The chief mourner in 1981 was Matt Beovich's sister Vera, dressed in the habit of a Sister of St Joseph. She joined the Josephites in Melbourne in 1920, taking the name 'Sister Matthew'. Intelligent and capable, she taught in primary schools in Victoria from 1922 to 1959. Then, after five years as the superior of the orphanage for boys at Surrey Hills, she began a series of administrative appointments, culminating in the position of procuratrix-general or bursar of the mother house of the Sisters of St Joseph in Sydney. After her death in 1991, her obituary highlighted her great faith and trust in God's will and divine providence, as well as her integrity and sense of justice, all qualities she shared with the brother she adored. 'Brother Matthew was very special and much loved by his Josephite sister,' the obituary recorded, '"My brother, the Arch.," she would say with pride.'[25] She was very much Elizabeth's daughter.

Home, School and Work

Matt Beovich grew up in the industrial working-class suburbs of northern Melbourne. His first home was in the inner suburb of Carlton, which then had rather shabby terrace houses and cramped cottages. At some stage during his childhood the family moved a few suburbs north to Moreland, near Brunswick. By the time Matt went to Rome the family home was on the corner of Moore Street and Sydney Road, Coburg. There was a quarry at the end of Moore Street, and Sydney Road, as its name implies, was the major thoroughfare through Melbourne for traffic heading north toward New South Wales. On Sydney Road, complained the *Coburg*

Leader in 1911, 'there is one continued tooting of horns, one constant whirl of dust and one pervading odour of petrol'.[26]

The Beovichs lived in an old weatherboard cottage, built circa 1870 and transported to the site sometime afterwards. It had four main rooms, a kitchen and bathroom tacked on, and a washhouse and lavatory in the back yard. The floors were uneven and the internal walls, lined with hessian and paper, sagged. The front garden and the hedge which screened the house from the road were sacrificed to make way for the two shops Mate built in the early 1920s. The property received a bleak assessment when Mate's estate was valued after his death in 1933, and after Elizabeth died in 1949 it was condemned by the local council.[27]

Catholics were well represented in Melbourne's industrial northern suburbs. One contemporary critic observed of late nineteenth-century Victoria: 'Irish Roman Catholics seldom rise above lower levels, and never as a class represent the mercantile, banking and squatting interests.'[28] Some statistical evidence bears this out. The census of 1901 reveals that in New South Wales only 8.2 per cent of 'white collar' banking and finance workers were Catholic, compared to 40.2 per cent of those 'blue collar' men who laboured on roads, railways, earthworks and such like.[29] Throughout the century the figures would gradually level out as more Catholics entered the middle class. This upward mobility was facilitated by Catholic schools, such as those run by the Christian Brothers.

Edmund Rice founded the Christian Brothers in 1802 to teach poor boys in Ireland. In 1868 four brothers emigrated to Victoria, the beginning of the Brothers' extensive involvement in Catholic education in Australia. In 1903 they took charge of the parish primary school (St George's) in Drummond Street, Carlton, and opened a secondary school, Christian Brothers' College in Queensbury Street, North Melbourne (also known as 'St Joseph's College').[30] The latter, set amongst factories and labourers' cottages, was a risky venture as the cost of building the school was substantial, and the fees which the Brothers charged, while modest by the standards of Protestant colleges, still made secondary education a luxury for many families. School retention rates were notoriously low, especially for children whose fathers ran small businesses like Mate Beovich's fruit and vegetable stall at the Queen

Victoria Market. They were usually expected to contribute their labour at the earliest possible age.[31]

Matt Beovich was saved from the market by the intervention of Brother Matthew Ambrose Geoghegan. In 1969 he recalled:

> As a youngster in the 5th class of St George's Christian Brothers' School, Carlton, I was told one day by Brother Marriner that the Principal of St Joseph's wished to see me.
>
> I duly arrived at St Joseph's and was told to wait in the reception room. After a short time in came an imposing figure dressed in soutane and wearing a biretta.
>
> This was Brother M. A. Geoghegan.
>
> He asked me some questions. I have forgotten both questions and answers. Then he told me he was granting me a scholarship for twelve months and that I was to enrol at St Joseph's in the beginning of July.[32]

That was July 1909, six months after Matt had received top prize for the fifth grade at St George's.[33]

St Joseph's offered a basic academic curriculum with a clear focus: passing examinations. The first goal was the Primary Public Examination which Matt passed in June 1910. His scholarship then at an end, his parents managed to find sufficient money to enable him to remain at school to prepare for the Junior Public Examination (1911) and the Federal Public Service Examination (1912).

For the boys of St Joseph's, the most accessible white-collar jobs were in the public service. As a politician, Parker Molony, said in his address at St Joseph's prize-giving ceremony in December 1911, the growing powers of the new federal parliament (then located in Melbourne) and the development of the Commonwealth Public Service provided great opportunities for the school's students.[34] After working in the public service, Matt's class mate and close friend, Arthur Calwell, went on to become a Labor member of federal parliament from 1940 to 1971, and leader of the opposition from 1960 to 1967. Only the narrowest of margins in the 1961 election prevented him becoming prime minister. He recalled in his autobiography:

> The possibility of a university education was beyond the reach of almost every one of us ... For most of us, the ideal was a place in the public

> service. Much as I dislike mentioning it at this time of toleration and ecumenism, it was very difficult for any boy who went to a Catholic school to secure a permanent position in a bank or in commercial life.[35]

'We could not pretend that we were first-class citizens,' Matthew Beovich commented in 1976. The public service seemed the only alternative to being 'hewers of wood and drawers of water'.[36] Ironically, it was not a career which his father supported. 'Whatever you do, make sure you work for yourself,' was his advice.[37] Disregarding this, in mid-1912 Matt became a clerk in the correspondence branch of the Post and Telegraph Department, working in the imposing General Post Office building on the corner of Bourke and Elizabeth streets.

As he later admitted, the 'thought of becoming a priest' had occurred to Matt from the time when he was about eleven or twelve, but financial considerations once again came into play.[38] Although archdiocesan support was sometimes available, parents were expected to bear much if not all of the cost of their son's education at the only seminaries in Australia: St Columba's, the new junior seminary in Springwood in the Blue Mountains, which opened in 1910 and took students to matriculation level; and then at St Patrick's College at Manly. As a result, seminarians tended to come from middle-class backgrounds.[39] With his father unable (or unwilling) to finance further study, Matt began work at the GPO. Once again, Brother Geoghegan came to the rescue, and made it possible for him to study British history and English literature at night. He duly passed the matriculation exam in 1913.[40]

Matt was very conscious of the debt he owed Geoghegan. Before he left to prepare for the priesthood in Rome in 1917 there was a farewell function at St Joseph's:

> He exhorted the boys to be loyal to their college, and never to do or say anything that would tend to lower their colours, the purple and the white. Ever through life they should be grateful for two things – for the great sacrifices their parents were making to give them a Catholic education, and, secondly, to the Christian Brothers, who were working so zealously and so successfully for their spiritual and temporal welfare.[41]

These were not just the sentiments of a pious young priest-to-be. Arthur Calwell wrote in 1951 that 'I owe everything I have in life, under Almighty God and next to my parents, to the Christian Brothers'.[42] Calwell's and Beovich's gratitude for an education that now seems so basic and utilitarian indicates how deeply conscious they were of their working-class backgrounds and lack of alternatives. It is also a tribute to their teachers who inspired affection and respect.

The Christian Brothers

Matthew Geoghegan was thirty-two years old when Matt Beovich first met him, a zealous workaholic with a militant faith tempered by kindness, compassion and a sense of humour.[43] Calwell later described him as a 'spiritual dynamo'.[44] Beovich thought he was a 'born teacher'. He was certainly dedicated to his job. From February to June 1910, when the primary examination was held, school would break up at 4 pm each week day, but the boys would be expected to return in the evening from 6 to 9 pm.[45]

The exam out of the way, the boys spent the remainder of the year in the care of an older Brother who was, one of his confreres later admitted, 'losing his grip'.[46] This interlude came to an end in 1911 when Brother Jeremiah McSweeny took over. 'Brother Jerry' or 'Brother Mac', as he was sometimes called, was twenty-eight years of age, tall, athletic and enthusiastic. Well aware of the lapse of discipline under his predecessor, he deliberately swung the pendulum in the opposite direction.[47] After his death in 1952, Beovich recalled that 'he was something of a slave-driver with an irascible temper which led him occasionally to practice handball in the classroom with delinquent or slow-witted pupils for a ball. He was strong and ambidextrous which made it worse for his victims.'[48]

The Christian Brothers' reputation for administering severe corporal punishment is well known. In their defence, it has been pointed out that physical punishment was not uncommon in this period, and the Brothers were under pressure to ensure that their deprived, working-class pupils successfully passed examinations.[49] Beovich realised this in 1952 when he was reflecting on his old teacher: 'even then we seemed to recognise that this occasional irascibility was caused by his great anxiety to help us.'[50] Calwell also remembered McSweeny's 'occasional exercises in muscular Christianity' with affection rather than resentment.[51]

Beovich revealed that the 'chink in his [McSweeny's] armour' was his love of sport. The students discovered that they could easily distract him from a dry lesson with a question about the tactics for the next Saturday's game (he was the coach of the college football team).[52] In fact, he was notoriously disorganised, often ran late and could not stick to a timetable. This was a problem at subsequent schools where different teachers were allocated fixed periods, but at St Joseph's McSweeny was the sole teacher responsible for all the senior and junior subjects, so he could get away with his unconventional methods. The examination results were outstanding – 100 per cent of his students passed.[53]

While academic and sporting success was important, above all, a Christian Brothers' school was expected to inculcate Catholic faith. Boys enrolled after 1918 would have had much of their religious education based on Michael Sheehan's *Apologetics and Christian Doctrine*.[54] This presented a rational, argumentative defence of the Catholic faith, encouraging a typically 'masculine' style of spirituality.[55] At school before *Apologetics* was published, Beovich enjoyed a more informal style of religious instruction. Writing for students of St Joseph's in 1969, he recalled that in a relaxed atmosphere, on Friday afternoons, the Brothers would speak about 'the truths of our Faith and the love of God and neighbour and the beloved Mother of God'. Speaking at the school's golden jubilee, Beovich commented that 'gradually, falteringly, sooner or later, we came to realise that [the Friday afternoon talks] were leading to a practical programme: a programme based on humility, charity, and acceptance of God's will'.[56] He would strive throughout his life to remain faithful to those tenets.

Beovich also remembered how the boys contributed money from their limited means so a statue of the Blessed Virgin Mary could be purchased, and they installed it on the wall of the class room. Perhaps the greatest contribution which Geoghegan and McSweeney made to Matt Beovich's religious development was that they both provided a role model of 'a vigorous type of truly Christian man', one who did not consider it unmanly to engage in the traditional devotional practices which are sometimes associated with a 'feminine' style of piety.[57]

Associations and Parish Life

After leaving school, Matt Beovich and Arthur Calwell remained close friends. They were two of the most active members of the North Melbourne Past Pupils' Association, formed at Geoghegan's instigation in 1913. In 1916 they were both elected to the organising committee.[58] The following year Calwell became president. The association was designed to help former students maintain contact with each other, the college, and the practice of their religion. Its activities included sporting competitions, debating and literary evenings, an annual ball and an annual Communion breakfast. At this event, members of the association (almost 200 in 1917) gathered for Mass, received Communion, then adjourned to the college for breakfast and an address by a guest speaker. When he left for Rome in 1917, Matt was praised for his 'indomitable energy in promoting the interests of the Past Pupils' Association'.[59]

Matt was also a member of the North Brunswick branch of the Catholic Young Men's Society (CYMS). It has been said that the CYMS, which began in Melbourne in 1885, was little more than a social club,[60] but while it sponsored sport and other recreational activities, it had a strong educational thrust. It provided extra polish for young men negotiating their way out of the working class. Matt took part in elocution competitions which may have been why, on New Year's Day, 1915, he copied poetry into a notebook, and again on 1 April 1915, his birthday.[61] Even by the standards of the day, the poems he chose were sentimental and old fashioned. They reflect the process of social transformation which was underway as Australian Catholics strove to catch up to the Protestant establishment. They also give an insight into the competing cultures of Matt Beovich's youth: Irish, English, a dash of American influence, and the gradual emergence of something that could be called Australian, albeit it was a bush tradition remote from the industrialised suburbs of northern Melbourne.[62]

Nostalgic sentimentality was also manifest in the Knighthood of Our Lady of the Southern Cross, established in 1906.[63] One of the pet projects of Archbishop Carr, the 'knighthood' was intended to inspire young men with chivalrous ideals. With Mary as their patron, they were:

> 1. to practise in public and in private, at home and abroad, the virtues of the knightly office;
> 2. to promote the faithful fulfilment of the duties of the married state;
> 3. to shield from harm and stain the dignity and purity of women;
> 4. to suppress by every legitimate means all indecency in word and action;
> 5. to exhibit towards all, male and female, a chivalrous courtesy.[64]

One of Carr's unlikely looking knights, a slim, dark-haired youth with spectacles, was Matt Beovich. He joined the branch in his local parish and dutifully went to the annual rally at the cathedral to hear an address given by Carr.[65] The knighthood failed to take strong root in Australian soil and did not last long after Carr's death in 1917.

A more militant organisation which Matt Beovich joined was the Australian Catholic Federation (ACF). Inaugurated in Melbourne in 1911, it attempted to unify Catholics into an effective lobby group. The main issue of concern was the great education grievance: Catholics paid taxes which supported the state school system, but did not get any government funding for their own schools. Although it claimed to have over 40,000 members in parish-based branches in 1913, the ACF did not succeed in changing government policy. It did, however, reinforce Catholics' sense of grievance, contribute to sectarian rancour, and trouble Catholic members of the Australian Labor Party who were caught between their church and a political party committed to education that was free, compulsory and secular.[66]

In May 1915 a new conference of the St Vincent de Paul Society was established in St Matthew's parish, North Brunswick. Matt Beovich was elected secretary.[67] If this followed the pattern established by the society's founder, Frederick Ozanam, members would have met weekly for prayer, spiritual reflection under the guidance of their parish priest, and discussion of local needs and how members could respond. A leather-bound, written tribute presented to Matt when he left for Rome, extolled the way he had been 'a good Samaritan, displaying zeal and energy in assisting God's poor by pouring the balm of charity into stricken hearts and helping those depressed by misfortune to rise again to further effort'.[68] In addition, he was president of the Altar Boys' Society at North Brunswick, and when one hundred children and thirty adults were confirmed at St Matthew's Church in 1916, he was the sponsor for the boys and men.[69] At a farewell social held in his honour in August 1917, a representative of the parishioners 'spoke in eulogistic terms of the good work which he had performed in the parish'. The parish priest, John O'Connell, supported the remarks, expressing particular appreciation for his work for the Altar Boys' Society, and 'referring to his devout habits and the edifying influence which he exercised generally'.[70]

In a sermon in 1970, Matthew Beovich commented:

> Looking back to our youthful years, we remember the time when we first thought of the priesthood. To some of us the thought came suddenly, to others by degrees and, perhaps, not always willingly. We didn't talk about it, but we prayed a good deal. We trustfully confided in Our Blessed Lady, the mother of priests. We sought the advice of a priest friend ...[71]

It is highly likely that it was John O'Connell who was young Matt Beovich's 'priest friend'. Born in Ireland in 1876, O'Connell trained for the priesthood at All Hallows College in Dublin and then at the Irish College in Rome before emigrating to Australia in 1901 to work in the Melbourne archdiocese. After his death in 1929 he was hailed as a most zealous, efficient and saintly priest, a real 'man's man' who had exercised a remarkable influence over the young Catholic men of the Brunswick district since his appointment as parish priest in 1915.[72] It was certainly O'Connell who wrote in 1916 on his young parishioner's behalf to John McCarthy, Archbishop Carr's secretary and vicar-general, paving the way for an introduction to Carr.[73]

Archbishop Thomas Carr

Thomas Carr was Matthew Beovich's first episcopal role model. Born in 1839, he was raised in affluent gentility in County Galway as a member of a large and apparently happy family.[74] After completing his studies at St Patrick's College, Maynooth, he was ordained in 1866. The first two years of his priesthood were devoted to pastoral work as a curate in the town of Westport. Four more were spent on the staff of the cathedral at Tuam. He returned to Maynooth for ten years as a teacher and administrator, then spent three years as bishop of Galway and Kilmacduagh before being appointed archbishop of Melbourne in 1886.

Carr's predecessor, James Alipius Goold, had arrived in Melbourne in 1848 to find that his diocese consisted of about nine thousand Catholics, six schools, three priests, and two churches. Coming toward the end of the 'Marvellous Melbourne' boom years, Carr inherited about 150,000 Catholics, 80 priests, almost 100 schools, 100 churches, and a half-finished, neo-Gothic cathedral. In spite of the depression, St Patrick's Cathedral was opened in 1897, and after a lull in the 1890s the diocese slowly began expanding again. Nevertheless, Catholics made up less than a quarter of the population and, as already noted, many were from Irish-Australian working-class backgrounds. The middle class in Victoria was predominantly Protestant. Evangelicalism was strong, and liberalism on the rise.[75] Both ends of the Protestant spectrum were inclined to be anti-Catholic.

Carr was well suited to this colonial world. Wise, conscientious, diplomatic and kind, he ruled his archdiocese as a benevolent autocrat while moving with ease in the highest echelons of Victorian society. When he deemed it necessary, he vigorously defended Catholic teaching, most notably crossing swords with the Anglican Bishop Goe of Melbourne and the Presbyterian Dr Rentoul in a series of public lectures in 1895 and 1896.[76] He emerged from the fray with an enhanced reputation for erudite debate. Yet Thomas Boland concludes that 'his overriding principle was harmony in the Church and society'.[77] This greatly helped Irish-Australian Catholics become better integrated into the wider community and enjoy increasing respectability. Even the governor of Victoria and (after 1901) the governor-general of Australia attended significant Catholic functions, including the most important annual event in the Catholic social calendar, the St Patrick's Day parade. Tens of thousands of Catholics converged on the centre of Melbourne (100,000 is the estimate for 1908) on 17 March.

Irish nationalism and loyalty to the British Empire merged as the procession paused by the federal parliament house in Melbourne while 'God Save the King' was played.[78] Clara Geoghegan recounts the story that the wife of the governor was asked, when she returned to England, her opinion of gentlemen in Australia. Lady Hopetoun replied that she had met them both – her husband and Archbishop Carr.[79] The story may be apocryphal but Carr was certainly a friend of the Hopetouns and a 'gentleman', and this contributed to his success as a bishop.

Boland also maintains that 'the characteristic note of his [Carr's] episcopate was pastoral intimacy'.[80] In particular, Carr enjoyed a close relationship with 'a group of talented laymen who found it a privilege as well as a joy, to advise him and to serve him'. He dined in their homes, befriended their wives, and played with their children. He had a naturally warm and affectionate disposition, a 'personal magnetism' which ensured that he was loved and not merely respected as a church leader. However, as Boland admits elsewhere, the members of Carr's 'intimate circle' came from the wealthy and professional classes.[81] Matt Beovich probably did not see this side of him, but he benefited from Carr's patronage of the numerous Catholic societies in Melbourne, and the encouragement he gave priests to befriend their parishioners.[82]

Although the young Matt Beovich had little direct contact with Carr, he was virtually the ideal product of Carr's episcopate: devout, dedicated, intelligent, refined – a 'gentleman' from a working-class background. In 1916 the elderly archbishop was so impressed that, instead of sending Matt to St Patrick's College at Manly in Sydney, he offered him one of the Melbourne archdiocese's free places at the Pontifical Urban College of Propaganda Fide in Rome. This was a rare privilege as the college was regarded as 'the seminary for the elite of the clergy from the missions'.[83] Carr did not live to see the result, as he died three months before Matt left for Rome in 1917.

Archbishop Daniel Mannix

On Easter Sunday, 23 March 1913, Matt Beovich went to Spencer Street Station. Prime Minister Andrew Fisher stood with Thomas Carr on the platform to greet the latter's coadjutor (bishop with right of succession). It was the kind of welcome now reserved for sporting heroes and celebrities. The ascetic, introverted, forty-nine-year-old cleric who descended from the train was an unlikely candidate for hero status. Yet, while courtesy or curiosity might have drawn the crowd to Spencer Street that Easter Sunday, and to the liturgical reception in the cathedral later in the day, Mannix did become a hero for many Australian Catholics in the years ahead. His gaunt features, so different from those of the amiable, rotund Carr, would stare down from framed photographs on the walls of innumerable Catholic homes. Children were named after him.[83]

Mannix came to Australia with no previous experience as a bishop or parish priest. His entire adult life had been spent at Maynooth College, first as a student, then as a member of the faculty, and from 1903 as president. In Melbourne, Dr Mannix, as he was usually called, became what he was best equipped to be: the intellectual leader of the Catholic community.[85] His first years (and Carr's last) were troubled ones. The First World War began in 1914 and the Easter Rising of 1916 and its brutal suppression crushed hopes of a peaceful transition to Home Rule in Ireland. In Australia, the war brought economic hardship, industrial unrest and an intensely bitter debate over whether compulsory military service should be introduced. Mannix entered the fray[86]. He criticised the British government's handling of the situation in Ireland, supported the right of workers to go on strike when this was denied them by the Australian government, and vigorously opposed the introduction of military conscription. This brought him into conflict with Prime Minister Billy Hughes. Both men indulged in inflammatory rhetoric. In particular, in a speech in Matt Beovich's Brunswick parish on 28 January 1917, Mannix referred to the war as – according to the Catholic newspapers – 'an ordinary trade war'.[87] One of Melbourne's secular daily papers, the *Argus*, reported the next day that he had said that it was 'simply a sordid trade war'. The version in the *Age* on 29 January was 'simply an ordinary, sordid trade war'.

Whatever the exact wording of the Brunswick speech, it was a major departure from most Australian clergymen's public responses to the world tragedy. The almost universal patriotic enthusiasm of 1914 had given way to more sober reflection by

1917, but it was still startling to hear a church leader belittle the reasons for the conflict which was costing so many Australian lives. The final tally, well on the way to being reached in 1917, was about 59,000 dead and 167,000 wounded. For Protestant patriots, Mannix's speech was evidence of unforgivable Irish Catholic disloyalty at a time of national crisis. 'Venomous snakes of treason', claimed a prominent South Australian Methodist in December 1917, had lifted their heads 'in many parts of our far-flung empire, but their warmest, most crowded nests were in Ireland and Australia.'[88]

The Catholic community itself was polarised. A 'sizeable minority' may well have voted 'yes' in the conscription referenda.[89] Although many Catholics were clearly proud of their fiery new bishop, others, especially those who had risen to positions of affluence and respectability under Thomas Carr, were aghast. A prominent lay Catholic from New South Wales, Justice C. G. Heydon, denounced Mannix for leading 'his flock along the paths of sedition'. Mannix retaliated with a personal attack on Heydon, accusing him of being a 'second or third class judge' who could not get enough followers to fill a lolly shop.[90]

Mannix's defenders argue that he was a leader who was in tune with the working-class members of the Irish-Catholic community. He became their great champion, articulated their opposition to conscription, and boosted their morale at a time when they felt isolated and oppressed by the predominantly Protestant establishment.[91] That a church leader should support the underprivileged is commendable, but Mannix's scornful denunciation of his opponents damaged the unity of his church.

Mannix has also been praised for subjecting the allies' war aims to moral scrutiny.[92] However, what caught the attention of the Australian public in 1917 was not critical analysis but biting sarcasm and witty jibes. A less positive assessment of Mannix is that he was a demagogue who 'fed the excitement of the crowds who flocked to hear him, and in turn was nourished by their reaction. He was the captive of his own wit ... He played to the gallery at the expense of the cause'.[93] It was not only what Mannix said but the way he said it which inflamed controversy.[94] Mannix claimed to speak out on the conscription issue as a private individual and not as a church leader, but inevitably the line between religion and politics was blurred. He became a lightning rod for sectarian and class bitterness – and seemed to relish that. He was a dangerous role model.

Matt Beovich in 1917

On 7 May 1917 Mannix was the guest of honour at the annual Communion breakfast for the past pupils of St Joseph's College, North Melbourne. Matt Beovich proposed the toast to 'the hierarchy and the clergy'. He first paid tribute to Thomas Carr who lay on his death bed:

> Archbishop Carr had been their spiritual director and guide, and under his benign sway the Church had prospered in Victoria exceedingly. The many colleges, presbyteries, churches and schools which they saw on all sides, were eloquent memorials of his rule. With his cultured mind and many gifts, it had well been said of His Grace that he was a king amongst men.

'Benign' and 'cultured' were good words to describe Thomas Carr. The archdiocese had indeed expanded during his time at the helm (Beovich had personally benefited from the new school at North Melbourne and new parish at North Brunswick) but this was an indirect pastoral legacy which probably would have happened regardless of who was bishop.

Having paid his respects to Carr, Beovich turned to the man who would soon take over the running of the archdiocese:

> Dr Mannix was not only a great prelate, but a statesman, champion of the Church and a fearless leader. (Applause) ... In these momentous times Dr Mannix had demonstrated his statesmanship by his fearless advocacy of what he considered best for Australia. (Applause) ... Some Catholics, perhaps, could not see eye to eye with His Grace, but fortunately their number was infinitesimal. (Applause)

Note the difference in episcopal style. Whereas Carr had been a 'spiritual director and guide', Mannix was a 'statesman', 'champion', 'fearless leader' and advocate for what he considered best for the country as a whole, not just his archdiocese, and not just with regard to spiritual matters. The only appropriate response for Catholics was to fall into line behind their new archbishop.

Beovich then referred to the adulation Mannix was receiving from many Catholics. He attributed it to more than Mannix's aggressive leadership style: 'The tumultuous applause that greeted the Archbishop and clergy on every occasion … was a striking demonstration of that bond of union between the clergy and the people – a marvellous tie.' He invited his audience to turn again to the past, this time to the 'history of their ancestors' when Ireland was ravaged by English invaders:

> Every attempt was made to rob Ireland of her priceless heritage – her faith. (Applause) In the forefront of the Irish were the priests of Ireland, who comforted the people in their hour of desolation and terrible tragedy. The priests died for the people but the faith remained deep and strong …[95]

That was a myth. Like all good myths, it contained truth, but it was a myth nonetheless. It failed to do justice to the complexity of the relationship between the institutional church and the people in Ireland over the centuries, the many times when church leaders had compromised with British rule, and the fact that indifference to religion had not been uncommon among the laity, especially before Cardinal Paul Cullen's energetic campaign to revive Irish Catholicism in the latter half of the nineteenth century.

Beovich not only used the myth of holy, persecuted Ireland as a convenient rallying cry in 1917. From his diary entries in 1918 and 1919, it seems that he actually believed it, that he had absorbed to the full a romantic attachment to the land of his maternal forebears. In this he was not unique. At the whirl of farewell functions before he left for Rome in August 1917, 'God Save Ireland' was 'sung with great enthusiasm'.[96] In one speech, Beovich declared that he was 'proud of his faith, proud of his association with the Christian Brothers, and proud of his Irish blood'.[97] His mother, parish priest and school teachers could congratulate themselves on producing an apparently exemplary Irish-Australian Catholic. This could lead to the conclusion that, in spite of the Croatian surname, the new archbishop of Adelaide in 1939 was just as much a product of the Irish-dominated Australian church as his future episcopal colleagues and friends, James O'Collins and Norman Gilroy. However, like them, he left that church for six years to prepare for the priesthood in Rome, and it is to that crucial period that we now turn.

Two

'The Centre of Christianity'

Rome, 1917–1923

> Every priest had a great love and devotion to the Holy Father; some priests by virtue of the circumstances that enabled them to study in Rome had an opportunity of gaining a still greater devotion to the Holy See.
>
> Matthew Beovich, 7 April 1940

In 1917 Daniel Mannix's devoted young disciple travelled to Rome to study at the Urban College of Propaganda Fide. Pope Gregory XV founded the Sacred Congregation for the Propagation of the Faith in 1622.[1] As the world beyond Europe opened up, 'Propaganda Fide' assumed responsibility for the disparate Catholic missionary enterprises that were so often beset by nationalism and rivalry between different religious orders. Its international college, named after Gregory's successor Urban VIII, was established in 1627 to prepare secular priests (i.e., not members of religious orders) for the mission fields, with special emphasis on candidates from the mission countries themselves.

For four centuries alumni from Propaganda have dutifully fulfilled the expectation that they should become leaders in their local churches. They have been particularly prominent in the Catholic Church in Australia, which was under the jurisdiction of the Congregation for the Propagation of the Faith until 1976. John Molony focuses on the nineteenth century in the *Roman Mould of the Australian Catholic Church*, but he supports his argument by pointing out that the majority of Australian bishops in the 1960s, including all seven archbishops, were Propaganda graduates. These bishops, he suggests:

> imbibed the papal system with their spaghetti and vino, they became eager lieutenants of the Pope, anticipating his wishes and obeying his commands to the letter; they learned to love the Roman way of doing things and looking at things, so that throughout their lives their proudest boast would be what they called their Romanità.[2]

One of those men was Matthew Beovich.

The Journey to Rome

Beovich left Melbourne on Saturday, 11 August 1917. Standing with him on the deck of the *Katoomba* as it steamed out of Port Philip Bay were Arthur Leydon and Michael (Mick) O'Sullivan, also bound for priestly formation in Rome. Their first destination was Sydney. Beovich loved the harbour but was disappointed in St Mary's Cathedral. In fact, he would find few churches on his way to Rome which he liked more than Melbourne's St Patrick's. 'Sheer bias of course,' he later conceded in a margin note in his diary.[3] He met the students who were training to be priests at St Patrick's College, Manly, and cast a wistful glance at the stately sandstone seminary. 'Rome surpasseth all,' however.[4]

After a week in Sydney, the friends embarked on the *Ventura* for the journey across the Pacific.[5] On the first day they ran into bad weather. Leydon was sea sick, but Beovich revelled in the magnificent sight of the raging sea. As the days grew warmer and the sea calmer, the trio sat on the upper deck in the evenings praying the rosary. During the day Beovich read the fifteenth-century classic attributed to Thomas à Kempis, *The Imitation of Christ*.[6] Its admonitions reinforced the course upon which he was already set: a 'way of the cross' involving humility, obedience, self-denial, patient acceptance of suffering and devotion to the presence of Christ in the Eucharist.

Beovich also read a novel by his favourite author, the Irish priest Patrick Sheehan, whose books were popular in Ireland and throughout the Irish diaspora. Sheehan wove together stories of parish life, Irish politics, spirituality and romance. The one which captivated Beovich on the *Ventura* was *The Blindness of Dr Grey*. Grey was an elderly priest, legalistic and proud, who had to cope with the arrival in his parish of an idealistic young curate. As the novel progresses, the latter matures as Grey mellows. Beovich jotted in his diary after he finished the story: 'I do not lay one of his [Sheehan's] books down without feeling refreshed, spiritually and physically. Maybe it is because I love to dwell on his line of thought. Anyway, I'll back his books against all comers.'[7]

While he enjoyed reading and sitting on the deck watching the sun rise and set, Beovich was no solitary recluse like Dr Grey. He chatted to other passengers, and with Leydon and O'Sullivan enthusiastically explored Pago Pago in American Samoa and Honolulu.[8] On 9 September the *Ventura* sailed into San Francisco, and two days later the three young friends began their journey across the United States by train. They spent a night at Salt Lake City and visited the Mormon temple: Beovich did not record his reaction in his diary. Not far from Chicago, he lost his wallet with all his tickets and money. 'I lost count of the number of Hail Marys I said to Our Lady, the Little Flower [Thérèse of Lisieux] and St Anthony,' he later wrote to his mother. The next day the wallet, with all its contents, was returned to him by a clerk at the station, confirming his conviction that the Blessed Virgin was bestowing special protection on the journey.[9]

After a detour to Niagara Falls (not quite so spectacular as anticipated), the travellers arrived in New York on 20 September. They had sailed across the harbour at San Francisco on the largest ferry in the world, visited the largest shop (the Marshall Field Store in Chicago), and now, to get to Brooklyn, they crossed the largest bridge. 'America seems to have the largest of everything,' Beovich wrote wearily in his diary.[10] They had to wait over a fortnight for a berth on a ship to Europe, but they made the most of their time, visiting museums, art galleries, parks and, naturally, churches (the verdict on St Patrick's Cathedral was that it was beautiful but not as large as their St Patrick's).[11] Relatives of friends in Melbourne befriended them and they enjoyed visits to the theatre and the cinema. A walk down Wall Street was not so pleasant. Beovich was sickened by the crowds, noise and atmosphere of anxiety and greed. He was struck by a remark made by a character in his latest Sheehan novel, *Geoffrey Austin, Student*: 'Peace comes not with fulfillment, but with the quenching of desire. Self-denial is the watchword!'[12] No one would ever be able to accuse him of materialism.

On 6 October the Australian trio boarded the *Isla de Panay*. Unlike the *Ventura*, which had sailed in darkness, its portholes closed and covered, the *Isla de Panay* crossed the Atlantic in a blaze of lights, flying the flag of neutral Spain as prominently as possible. While it was hoped that submarines would therefore hold their fire, mines could not be expected to be so discriminating. 'Through God's grace we make a safe journey,' Beovich recorded in his diary.[13] After two days anchored at Cadiz, the *Isla de Panay* safely reached Barcelona on 23 October.

From Barcelona, the trio intended to travel by train to Rome. However, at Caporetto in northern Italy, the Italian army was suffering its worst defeat in the war. As the friends waited in Barcelona, Austrian and German divisions advanced toward Venice and Allied troops were rushed across the French border to reinforce the front. The British consul in Barcelona was sympathetic to the Australians' plight but his French counterpart did not like the Croatian name and refused to give Beovich a visa.[14] The wait was frustrating and expensive (they had to cable Mannix to ask for more money), but they threw themselves into sightseeing. Beovich was captivated by Spain, its people, its scenery and the manifestations of Catholic piety. He was particularly impressed by the respect shown to the dead on 2 November, All Souls' Day, when crowds flocked to the cemeteries and graves were decked with flowers. Many years later he would try to encourage that practice in Adelaide. The one aspect of Spanish culture which 'thoroughly disgusted' him was the national sport – witnessing one bull fight was more than enough. He was manly enough to record in his diary a detailed account of 'a stand up real Australian fight' at a soccer match, but too sensitive to enjoy the sight of a bewildered animal being tormented and finally slaughtered.[15]

At last, on 27 November, Beovich and his friends boarded the *Morden*, 'a miserable vessel, certainly, yet I think that even the Israelites did not look with greater thankfulness on the Promised

Land than I did on that ship'. Not everyone would have been so thrilled, for submarines and mines were known to be lurking in the Mediterranean around the Italian coast. As a concession to the threat of attack, Beovich kept his socks and underclothes on when he went to bed, but he slept soundly. The next day he found that the *Morden* was hugging the coast – a delightful view of the French Rivera was, therefore, consolation for 'a little danger'. At Villefranche the *Morden* joined a convoy escorted by two destroyers and a light cruiser. On 1 December Beovich was chatting to O'Sullivan in the saloon after breakfast when he heard a sharp order from the deck:

> Rushed up to the bridge and saw that the light cruiser, distant from our ship about 200 yards, had been struck by a torpedo in the bow ... The warship sank quickly, her crew jumping into the water and being picked up by lifeboats as quickly as possible. In four minutes all that remained were two feet of mast sticking above the water. In the meantime one destroyer threw out a net which protected our ship, and then rushed about to locate the submarine. But no trace was left ... Had a splendid view of the whole affair ... Certainly a most exciting morning.

He spent the rest of the day admiring the beautiful Italian coast.

At 5 pm the *Morden* berthed in Genoa. The friends spent 2 December 1917 sightseeing and then boarded the night train for Rome. They arrived at nine the following morning. Rome was shrouded in dense fog, but the trio left their bags at the station and dashed to the Vatican to see St Peter's and the Sistine Chapel.[16] The last few hours of freedom passed quickly and at 6 pm, with only a few small coins left in their pockets, they knocked on the door of the Urban College of Propaganda Fide.[17]

The 'Seminary of the Universal Church'

When Beovich arrived, the college was still in its original location, a triangular-shaped palazzo designed by the two most famous Baroque architects of seventeenth-century Rome, Bernini and Borromini. In the heart of Rome, the building faces the Piazza di Spagna near the Spanish Steps.[18] The immediate post-war years were good ones for the college. As travel became easier, the number of students increased from 100 in 1918 to 152 in 1919, although it dropped back to 120 the following year as those who had studied during the war returned home. In 1920 the students came from twenty-seven different countries, so the college was entitled to consider itself 'the seminary of the universal church', as well as 'the seminary for the elite of the clergy from the missions'.[19]

As there were students from the Syrian, Maronite, Malabar, Melkite, Chaldean and Armenian churches in communion with Rome, Beovich was introduced to the Eastern rites. Nevertheless, most students (99 out of 120 in 1920) belonged to the Latin rite, and two countries were represented more than any other. Twenty-seven students were from Ireland, most intending to work in Australia, and sixteen were from Australia itself. In equal third place were 'America' (presumably the United States), Romania, Switzerland and Albania with six each. There were two students each from China, Japan and Korea, and one from India. The number of students from Asia and Africa would increase significantly in the years ahead, but not until after Beovich left.

Academic Studies

The college's academic year began in early November. Nineteen other Roman seminaries sent students to classes at Propaganda, including the Irish, American and German colleges, so there could be over 500 students in the lecture halls.[20] Five days a week there were two hours of lectures each morning (8 am to 10 am), and two each afternoon (2 pm to 4 pm), with two hours of private study from 10 am to noon.[21] Owing to the delay in Barcelona, Beovich missed the first month. He was given no time to settle in. The afternoon after his arrival he attended his first lectures: one hour of Greek followed by logic. The latter was in Latin and it seemed as though Professor Dante 'rattled out the Latin about three times as fast as we speak English'. The following day he began mathematics ('very elementary, but in Italian'). He must have quickly surmounted the language difficulties as he satisfactorily passed the exams at the beginning of February in these subjects, as well as in zoology, chemistry and geology.[22] By the end of June 1918 he had completed the requirements for a Bachelor of Philosophy degree.[23] The following year's subjects included physics, mechanics, ethics, philosophy and history, and resulted in a Licentiate and Doctorate in Philosophy (1919).[24] His year group was the last to complete philosophy degrees in two years. In 1918 it was decided that the programme was too gruelling for students and should be spread over three years.[25]

Subjects like zoology might seem an odd preparation for the priesthood but, while secular universities were moving toward greater specialisation of fields of study, leading Roman churchmen in the early twentieth century still stressed the need for future priests to be given a good general education, beyond that of most of the laity. A model priest was 'an educated gentleman fitted for public life' who could speak with authority and win the respect of Catholics and non-Catholics alike.[26] In his third year (1919–1920) Beovich began studying church history, fundamental theology, canon law, liturgy and Hebrew for his Bachelor of Divinity (1920).[27] Then came his Licentiate (1922) and Doctorate in Divinity (1923), the culmination of three further years studying scripture, church history, science of missions, and dogmatic, moral and sacramental theology.[28]

The system was clearly designed to produce apologists rather than scholars, men who could defend the teaching of the Church rather than push forward the boundaries of knowledge. When Beovich reached Propaganda in 1917, it was only a decade after Pius X had thundered in the anti-Modernist encyclical *Pascendi*: 'May the spirit of innovation be far, far removed from the priesthood.' While Pius had good reason to be concerned about the way 'modern' currents in biblical and theological scholarship could undermine traditional Catholic teaching, the repressive reaction generated a climate of fear and zealotry, especially in seminaries. This began to abate when the more moderate Benedict XV became pope in 1914, but the Propaganda lecturers could be forgiven for still following an essentially cautious and defensive path in 1920. Training priests to promote and defend the faith had been a vital part of the college's mission long before the bitter Modernist controversy.[29]

It has been said of Propaganda during James Duhig's years in Rome in the 1890s that 'the students were devout and they studied Theology; but it was merely a mental discipline; their Christian life was not influenced by their Christian doctrine'.[30] Little had changed thirty years later. Beovich never jotted in his diary any significant insights which he gained from his academic studies, only the occasional comment about his lecturers. Di Somma, the philosophy professor, fared the best: 'His lecture is almost an oration, it is a choice between taking notes & missing the beauty of the lecture, or neglecting notes & enjoying his Ciceronian style.'[31] On one occasion, Sacco, the Hebrew professor, 'was as funny as a blanky circus. Nearly burst my breeches laughing.'[32] Not all classes were so enjoyable: 'Solieri [canon law] was as dry as bone dust ... dead sleepy during the afternoon hour ... Ruffini's class [scripture] was damn awful, that is, the material. Came out with a headache ...'[33]

Like most students, Beovich also moaned about the pressure of exams. One of the worst years was 1919 when preparation for the final exams in June coincided with a heat wave: 'Weather hot as blazes ... Phew, what with heat & study I feel like a grease spot ...'[34] After the written exams came the ordeal of the oral examination when, one by one, the students had to face the academic faculty. As in the lectures, philosophical and theological ideas were stated in thesis form. The candidate was then required to defend the thesis and answer any objections.[35] Beovich reported in his diary on 1 July 1919:

> Slept fairly well. Heard Cardinal not coming: good. Afternoon cooled up the blood with ice cream: walked the corridors feeling pretty confident, whether through ice cream or otherwise? Bell rings: entered the dread precincts. A big room, big table, big everything except the culprit. Rector presiding. Prof. Dante opened the ball. 'De origine idearum, falsis systematis'. Things going fine till he whacked in the difficulties, then a case of steady with your eye. The proximate danger past. Prof. Coloana took a hand ... my luck was in, things going well when his time bell rang. Prof. Fabiani then had a shot at Maths, & Colon. followed up with Ethics ... his difficulties are not deep like Dante's & easily answered. In short here I am, at the end of 50 minutes outside the room, not knowing whether on my head or heels, & then the Rector comes out with the verdict. Have been made a doctor in philosophy.

He wrote to his mother: 'Having to live up to the title, I could not turn somersaults or stick an umbrella through my hat or turn the fire hose on, instead tried to bluff and look unconcerned as if such things are a passing occurrence.'[36]

The annual graduation/prize-giving ceremony was held in November. At the first distribution of prizes Beovich attended, 'no miracles happened so I got nothing', although he was numbered among the top students in Gregorian chant. While Pius X is best remembered as the reactionary anti-Modernist pope, he also took a great interest in liturgical reform, including the revival of Gregorian chant, so Propaganda students were trained in the latest theory and practice.[37] Beovich's academic efforts were rewarded the following year when, to his great surprise, he received first prize in physics ('bolted up for the medal looking a bit silly').[38] He explained to his mother that he had 'tied with a chap from the Irish College, and got the medal by lot'.[39] As Boland comments in his biography of Duhig, the Roman system of prize distribution bore resemblance to a lottery.[40] In 1920 Beovich received the top prizes in church history and sacred archaeology.[41] Despite the peculiarities of the system, this was very gratifying. It was not only reported in the Melbourne Catholic papers. On 12 February 1921 Beovich was surprised to receive a cutting from the *Birmingham Catholic Times*. An article on Archbishop Mannix (then travelling through Britain) included a reference to his Propaganda student's prizes. 'Feel as pleased as punch. O vanity: read it through a dozen times & in Lent!' After he successfully defended a thesis in the scripture class, 'Sully couldn't hold it in, must blurt out if I wanted a column report in the *Tribune*?'[42]

There were lows as well as highs. Only a month after the clipping from Birmingham arrived, Beovich was lamenting the fact that he had been 'solemnly botched' in Professor Borgongini-Duca's dogmatic theology class.[43] He confessed to his mother that 'I came a cropper and didn't get through the mid-year exams' in what was 'perhaps the most important subject',[44] but he did receive full marks for scripture and science of missions.[45] His final year brought better results for dogmatic theology (8¾ out of 10) but only a bare pass for scripture (6/10), 'a hit in the eye'. His best results were in sacramental theology (9½) and moral theology (10).[46] He fared better with his written thesis for the doctorate in divinity than the oral exam which was 'an awful strain'.[47] Clearly, he was a very good student, among the best in his year to judge from the class lists, but he had to work hard.

Beovich's thesis was a defence of the sacrament of confession.[48] He pointed to Matthew's gospel where Jesus gave Peter the keys to the kingdom of heaven, the authority to bind or to loose. Making no concessions to the historical development of the sacrament or recent biblical scholarship, he argued that anyone who entered a Catholic church and saw a penitent whispering his sins to a priest witnessed this gospel passage come alive. The universal Roman Church had preserved unchanged the sacrament of secret, auricular confession and penance since the time of the apostles.

The list of twelve theological works in Beovich's bibliography was led, inevitably, by Thomas Aquinas's *Summa Theologica*. It was followed by Louis Billot's *De Poenitentia* (Rome, 1922). The leading Thomist scholar of the late nineteenth and early twentieth centuries, Billot, was noted for resisting the development of historical criticism in the study of the Bible and Christian doctrines; dogmas, he insisted, have no history.[49] Beovich challenged Protestant views of penance but did not actually consult any Protestant theologians. He concluded with a quotation from G. K. Chesterton's *Apologia*. A recent convert to Catholicism, Chesteron wrote with romantic fervour: 'The other religions are like indecisive and haphazard imitations of a forgotten melody. The Catholic Church is this very melody, which one had recognised from its first measures, and whose memory haunted the soul the more one departed from it.'[50] By Roman standards Beovich's thesis was well-researched and reflected the best current scholarship, but it would not have earned him a doctorate in a secular university.

After he had finished typing the thesis, Beovich submitted it for examination on 31 January 1923. He exclaimed in his diary: 'That's a load off my mind; hope Prof Tardini and Padre Aggy won't be in a very critical mood.' 'Aggy' was Gregory Agagianian. Only a year older than Beovich, he was still a student when Beovich arrived at Propaganda in 1917. He befriended the newcomer and showed him around the college, and on Christmas Eve Beovich attended his ordination.[51] Forty-one years later, as the Cardinal Prefect of Propaganda Fide, Agagianian was regarded as the most serious rival to Angelo Roncalli in the conclave after the death of Pope Pius XII.[52] Domenico Tardini also had a distinguished career in the Vatican bureaucracy. After working closely with Pius XII he was raised to the rank of cardinal and became John XXIII's secretary of state. Among the other young lecturers in Beovich's time were the future cardinals Francesco Borgongini-Duca, Pietro Ciriaci, Enrico Dante, Alfredo Ottaviani and Ernesto Ruffini. With the exception of Borgongini-Duca, who died in 1954, the rest played a major – and highly defensive – role at the Second Vatican Council. Beovich's academic studies did not merely consolidate his conservative understanding of Roman Catholic tradition. In the Propaganda lecture halls he got to know and respect men who would wield great power and influence in the Church in the years ahead.

Prayer and Discipline

The academic standard of Catholic seminaries may have been below that of many Protestant colleges, but whereas academic study tended to dominate training for ministry in mainline Protestant denominations, it was only one component of a seminary formation programme in the Catholic tradition.[53] Established in the wake of the sixteenth-century Council of Trent, the seminary, literally 'seed plot', was designed to encourage young men to sink deep roots into the desired clerical culture, to inculcate discipline, dedication, self-sacrifice and obedience.

A postcard Arthur Leydon sent Vera Beovich in April 1918 indicates some of the adjustments to daily life required of seminarians:

> Since our arrival here both Matt and I have altered in many ways. I shall tell you a few acts that Matt doesn't perform. He doesn't turn over to have another forty winks when called in the morning. He doesn't come home at all hours in the morning nor does he eat the paper while reading his breakfast. He doesn't mind shaving with cold water when there's no hot (always). He doesn't bring me out to visit his friends. I could tell you many more of his doesn'ts but I won't. Just think of what he used to do & say he doesn't do those now . . .[54]

Each day began when the bell rang at 5.30 am. By six students had to be ready for half an hour of private meditation. They were encouraged to follow the methodology of St Francis de Sales's *Introduction to the Devout Life*:

> 1st, Place yourself in the presence of God, by a lively faith that he sees and beholds you, and is most intimately present in the very centre of your soul; prostrate yourself in spirit before him ... make an offering of your whole being to him, and humbly beg his pardon for all your past treasons and sins ...

For those who found this too difficult there was a simpler alternative: prayerfully reading 'some good book'.[55]

Private prayer was followed each day by the Eucharist. The students took turns to be altar servers. There were plenty of opportunities for this as it was still the custom for priests to celebrate a private daily Mass, and Propaganda had no shortage of priests. Beovich recounted one day that he had to be 'up at 4.15 to serve Cardinal's Mass ... in addition served three other Masses this morning: Rector's, Economo's [the bursar], and Freddy Butler's'.[56] For the students as a whole, there was another visit to the chapel before dinner at noon, and again in the evening as the day drew to a close. On Sundays High Mass was added to the schedule in the morning and Vespers in the afternoon. Students were also required to go to confession once a week, receive communion frequently, pray the rosary and read inspiring spiritual books, such as Cardinal Manning's *The Eternal Priesthood* which Beovich 'read with profit' in 1917.[57]

The college community was divided into small groups known as *cameratas*. To maintain Propaganda's universalist ethos, nationalities were deliberately mingled, and twice a year the groups were changed to discourage 'particular friendships'. Opportunities to talk to students from other '*cams*' were few and far between. Even within a *camerata*, conversation was limited to specific recreation periods and had to be in Italian or Latin. At meal times, everyone listened to a reading from an edifying book. The students were not allowed to visit each other's bedrooms. They could not leave their rooms – or wherever their *camerata* was supposed to be – without permission. They could not keep food, money or unapproved books amongst their private possessions. Bedrooms had to be kept tidy and unlocked, and at all times of the day students had to be neatly dressed in the Propaganda uniform: a black soutane. They could not dispatch or receive letters without presenting them for inspection, and they could not talk to the domestic staff. The day ended at 9.30 when everyone had to retire to bed. Each *cam* had a student prefect to ensure that his fellow students kept to the rules and adhered to the timetable.[58]

After the winds of change blew through the Catholic Church in the 1960s, this pre-Vatican II style of seminary formation was subject to much criticism. It was widely accepted that the innovative developments of the sixteenth and seventeenth centuries had, by the beginning of the twentieth century, solidified into a form of training which was too introverted and out of touch with modern society. Men who were destined for ministry in the world were subjected to a lifestyle and spirituality more suited to a monastery than their future parishes.[59] Certainly the strict regime did not suit all recruits. Ill health forced Beovich's friend Arthur Leydon to leave Propaganda after just six months. Their other travelling companion in 1917, Mick O'Sullivan, returned home early in 1920, unable to endure the college's discipline any longer, although he was subsequently ordained in Melbourne. O'Sullivan's problems caused Beovich much anguish and loss of sleep.[60] However, Beovich himself adapted well to college life. Intensely proud of his strict *alma mater*, he regularly complained in his diary that his time in Rome was passing too quickly.[61]

The only college rule which seems to have caused Beovich difficulty was the one against smoking. When the influenza pandemic swept Italy in 1918 there was some hope that the students would be permitted to smoke 'as a safeguard against the disease' but, to Beovich's disappointment, the college authorities decided to distribute camphor and disinfectant instead.[62] On 30 August 1919 he was caught with a pipe and tobacco in his room and summoned to the rector's office. He could have been in serious trouble (as president of Maynooth, Mannix once dismissed a seminarian for the same offence).[63] Beovich, however, only received a dressing down. The lapse cannot have been held against him, as a year later he was appointed prefect of the sixth *cam*. Thereafter he was prefect of a succession of *cameratas* until he left Rome in mid-1923. Given the large number of potential prefects in the college, this must indicate that the rector held him in high regard. He also developed great affection and respect for 'the boss', Paul Giobbe, and enjoyed, as a prefect, the privilege of 'yarning' with him. They were only sixteen years apart in age, and as a bishop, Beovich always visited Giobbe when he was in Rome. A friend of Angelo Roncalli, Giobbe was made a cardinal by John XXIII in 1958 and became Prefect of the Congregation of Rites.[64]

Recreation

The college authorities were wise enough to include periods of recreation in the daily routine. From Beovich's diary a sense of camaraderie emerges which must have helped make the strict discipline endurable. There were times when students could – within their *camerata* groups – talk quietly and play games like chess or billiards ('D'Cruz & myself won the billiard tournament against Healy & Murdoch, we couldn't repeat such a fluke again in a month of Sundays').[65] Outside, in the very limited confines of the triangular courtyard, there were 'some ding-dong games of footy' ('Harper broke another window – our 8th!').[66] On one occasion a rare snowfall in Rome provided ammunition for a snowball fight and resulted in three more broken windows.[67]

The most common form of recreation was long walks through the streets of Rome. On school days, unless the weather was extremely bad, each *camerata* group went off in a different direction after classes finished at 4 pm. They could be away an hour, longer when there were no lectures on Sundays, Thursdays and feast days and they could leave earlier. Walking in file, in their black soutanes, cloaks and beaver hats, they were not allowed to talk to strangers or 'stare boldly about', and had to include a quarter-hour visit to the Blessed Sacrament in a church along the way.[68] Even with these restrictions, the walks gave Beovich many opportunities to explore Rome's ancient ruins, admire the picture galleries and the Sistine Chapel in the Vatican, climb to the top of the dome of St Peter's Basilica, and visit the sites where Christian saints had lived and died. Intrepid tourist as well as devout Catholic, he relished these experiences.

Unlike James Duhig, whose favourite era was the Baroque, with all its theatrical flamboyance, the more romantically inclined Beovich was drawn to the medieval period. He especially enjoyed going to the basilica of Santa Maria in Aracoeli on the Capitoline Hill. Its fifteenth-century carved bambino was displayed in a crib between Christmas and Epiphany. 'When I visit this church,' Beovich declared on 26 December 1918, 'I am transported from this 20th century (of commerce, misery and regression) to the Middle Ages (that period of religion, art, literature and progress).' He appreciated the focus on Mary and, as in Spain in 1917, was touched by the exuberant piety of the local people. 'I think that as a rule I am unemotional, but the intense devotion of people towards the Madonna moved me more than words could tell,' he reflected after returning from devotions in honour of Our Lady of Pompeii at the Church of St Lorenzo in Damaso.[69]

Beovich admitted to his mother that the most popular destination for long walks, the catacombs of St Callixtus, possessed an attraction additional to the ancient Christian burial ground. Normally forbidden to enter shops, the students were allowed to purchase chocolate from the monastery above.[70] He did not confess that brisk walkers also sometimes found they could pull ahead of the rest of the group to smoke a cigarette. Beovich was (and always would be until old age) a very brisk walker, but he confided in his diary that he found little satisfaction in sneaking around the corner of the Trevi Fountain for a cigarette 'like a naughty schoolboy'.[71] He did it anyway, at least until reprimanded by the rector in 1919.

Feast days at the college were usually 'feast days in the full sense of the word'.[72] One memorable Christmas, James (Jim) O'Collins received permission to make traditional plum puddings instead of an Italian dessert, and Beovich stayed up till 3.30 am helping cook them.[73] Before Midnight Mass on Christmas Eve there was a 'sing-song' and another concert on New Year's Eve. The 1919 concert finished before midnight and the students were not allowed to stay up to welcome in the new year. However, 'strange thing at midnight. The Prefect's bell started ringing and kept on ringing, enough to waken the dead ... Did I in a moment of ah! ecstasy, place my hand upon the button and say, "Ring out wild bells, to the wild sky ..."'[74]

Occasionally, with special permission from the rector, the Australian students were able to spend their recreation periods together ('a quarter of an hour in Australia').[75] The excuse for such gatherings was usually that a visitor from home or a new student had arrived. Although the Australians were spread throughout the *cameratas*, strong bonds of friendship were formed which would last their lifetimes. In particular, James O'Collins, fellow Melbourne student and future bishop of Geraldton and then Ballarat, reached Rome in October 1918. He was followed in November that year by Alfred Gummer from the Bathurst Diocese (destined to succeed O'Collins at Geraldton). A year later, the future archbishop of Sydney, Norman Gilroy, arrived from Lismore. Like Beovich, they came from working-class Irish-Australian families, and took to Propaganda life like ducks to water.[76] Many years later, after reminiscing about the lack of modern amenities in the old *palazzo*, which was 'freezing cold' in winter, Gilroy exclaimed, 'yet I loved every moment in the college and every facet of its life'.[77]

Castelgandolfo

As well as being cold in winter, the college could get stiflingly hot in summer. Hence, when the academic year ended in late June/early July, staff and students migrated to the Alban Hills, like generations of Roman aristocrats before them, for almost four months. The Propaganda villa was near Castelgandolfo, an hour's train journey from Rome. On his first *villeggiatura* in 1918 Beovich could sit at his bedroom window and look out over vineyards, woods and beautiful Lake Albano. Sometimes he prayed, sometimes he thought, sometimes he just sat and drank in the view. On a clear day, he could see the dome of St Peter's in the distance. Also within sight, but much closer, was the papal summer residence. Since the loss of the Papal States in 1870, the pope had not visited Castelgandolfo, but Propaganda students were allowed to wander in his garden.

The daily routine was somewhat more relaxed than in Rome.[78] There was no study, students were allowed to stay in bed for an extra half hour, and they could enjoy a siesta in the afternoon. However, there was still daily meditation and Mass (starting at

6.30 am) and regular periods set aside for examination of conscience, spiritual reading, Benediction and praying the rosary. These were interspersed with games of tennis and football and walks around the lake and surrounding countryside.

For Beovich, a highlight of the vacations was the occasional *gita*. The students would rise at 3.30 in the morning for Mass and breakfast, and then, leaving the villa before dawn, go tramping along country lanes, through woods and across fields. Their destinations varied. Sometimes they visited the Shrine of Our Lady of Good Counsel at Genzano, at other times the eleventh-century Abbey of San Nilo at Grottaferrata. They rested among the ruins of Cicero's villa, bought chocolate and wine in Frascati, and enjoyed ice-cream and coffee at Marino. One morning, dressed as always in their long, black soutanes, they covered twenty miles in seven hours, sprinting at the end in a race to be the first home. Still in their sweat-drenched soutanes, they played football that afternoon![79]

Another *villeggiatura* highlight was the annual sports day – annual since 1917. Cardinal William Van Rossum, Prefect of Propaganda Fide, stayed often at the villa and took a benevolent interest in the students' sporting activities. He firmly believed, Beovich informed his mother, in the link between a healthy body and a healthy mind. All that was further needed was the ability to pray well.[80] The cardinal later told Jim O'Collins's brother Gerald that he had nominated O'Collins for the diocese of Geraldton in 1930 because he remembered how he played soccer, and the remote country diocese needed a 'straight-ahead player'.[81] The athletic Jim O'Collins would have been more impressive on the sports field than the enthusiastic but accident-prone Matt Beovich. In 1919 Beovich smashed his spectacles and a chair during a boisterous game of musical chairs.[82] Two years later it was his leg which was broken in a football match. Three months as an invalid in the infirmary followed, but he was pleased to be able to record in his diary that after he was carried off the field, his *cam* won the match by four goals to O'Collins's *cam*'s one.[83]

Exercise of a more intellectual kind was provided by the Newman Debating Society. This began in Beovich's *camerata* in 1919. He conceded to his mother that 'the chief drawback in Prop is the want of practice in elocution and public speaking in our native tongue'.[84] The rector succumbed to this argument, no doubt because he was also under pressure from Pope Benedict XV, who was similarly concerned.[85] In 1920 he allowed English-speaking students from other *cameratas* to join the society. Beovich was very much the driving force, devoting much time to negotiating with the rector, drawing up a constitution, and meeting with other members of the Newman executive committee.[86] While some of the topics for the debates were clearly ecclesiastical (the divinity of Christ, the infallibility of the pope), others indicated an interest in society and politics. 'Is socialism an effective remedy for present economic conditions?' was the main topic in 1919. Two years later the rector asked for a debate on nationalism and Catholicism, a sensitive issue in Italy with fascism on the rise. At some meetings the participants gave impromptu speeches on topics such as immigration, the *camerata* system, corporal punishment in schools, conscription, and the movies. Beovich once had to respond to 'Should women get the franchise?' The society notebook records that: 'After six minutes preparation, Mr Beovich came forward and very eloquently proved the affirmative answer to the question ... He was somewhat hampered by lack of time.'[87]

Another development in 1919 was the publication of the first issue of the *Alma Mater*, an annual journal sent out to alumni of the college. For the next three years Beovich was on the editorial committee. He clearly enjoyed the work involved, and very regretfully accepted the rector's advice in 1922 to withdraw from the Newman Society and the *Alma Mater* to concentrate on finishing his thesis.[88]

There was no question of withdrawing from the retreat, but Beovich had no desire to do so. For a week each holidays a stricter regime of silence and prayer was enforced, and Beovich relished it: 'My word, a man wants a Retreat now and then,' he wrote on 26 October 1919, 'feel like coming out of a luxurious bath, nice warm glow.' At his first retreat the year before, the students gathered during the morning, afternoon and evening to listen to a visiting Jesuit priest. Beovich noted his instructions.[89] It was a familiar message, the need for detachment from the world and an attitude of acceptance ('If God sends us good things ... we must not forget to thank him; and likewise if He sends us afflictions, we will bow to His holy will and thank Him ...'). Paradoxically, this passive spirituality was presented in a militantly masculine style. There were terrifying warnings of the gravity of sin. Even one mortal sin, committed by a person living an otherwise good and holy life, was such 'an outrage against the infinite God of goodness; all the punishments imaginable on this world, through all the ages, added to the torments of hell, could not make recompense to God's outraged dignity'. Life was therefore a battle, the great enemies being 'the world, the flesh and the devil'. Jesus Christ was the 'captain and leader' and priests were his officers, chosen to help lead the people across the battlefield.

The retreat director stressed that, like their captain, priests had to sacrifice worldly honours and personal pleasures: 'Consider one day in His life; there is not a minute He may call His own ... His time is not His own but His people's.' The director promised, however, that priests would find consolation and support in the Eucharist, a miracle which only they could bring about. Amazingly, 'Jesus did not limit himself to Jerusalem or Rome, but throughout the whole world, wherever His minister is, there we may find Him ... What mind but God's could think out such a legacy of love. He went from us, yet He stayed amongst us'. This way of viewing the Eucharist made a deep impression on Beovich. Many years later he would use the same words in his preaching.[90]

On the retreat Beovich was forced to take stock of his spiritual life and character. 'Remember Jesus imprisoned in the tabernacle and visit him often,' exhorted the retreat director. 'God, forgive me for my innumerable distractions and dryness of spirit,' Beovich pleaded. He became conscious of other failings: he talked too much, was inclined to be stubborn and opinionated, and lacked patience with other people. He resolved to do better: after all, by prayer nothing was impossible![91]

The Outside World

Seminarians in the nineteenth and early twentieth centuries were deliberately kept apart from the modern world so that, away from distractions and temptations, they could single-mindedly prepare for admission to their most exclusive profession. Often the aloofness was enhanced by geography. St Patrick's College, Manly, for example, was built in the 1880s on what was then a remote property on Sydney's North Head. In contrast, the Urban College of Propaganda Fide was located in the bustling heart of Rome, but even though they walked almost every day along city streets, the students were far removed from family and friends and had little contact with anyone outside their immediate circle. Beovich lived in Rome during the tumultuous rise of fascism. On the day Mussolini became minister-president, 30 October 1922, Beovich wrote in his diary 'we are confined to barracks on account of the Fascisti', but life soon resumed its normal course. The Newman Society debated nationalism and Catholicism, and once Beovich had to return to Rome from Castelgandolfo by car because railway workers were on strike,[92] but overall Italy's political and economic troubles in the early 1920s seem to have had little impact on him.

Beovich did follow with great interest the closing stages of the war and the subsequent peace negotiations. He lashed out in his diary against the 'pseudo-patriots' who had campaigned for the introduction of conscription in Australia, and he castigated England for its poor treatment of Australian troops (he heard bitter stories from a chaplain on leave from the front). He had to restrain himself from clashing with some fellow students who supported France's 'unchristian desire for vengeance'.[93]

On 18 November 1918 news reached the college that an armistice had been signed. While Beovich rejoiced in what seemed an almost miraculous victory, he was weighed down by the enormity of the loss of life. He prayed for a just peace but feared (as the pope had warned in 1915) that the losing side would be humiliated and nationalist hatred would fester.[94] When the terms of the peace negotiations appeared in the press in May 1919 his worst fears were confirmed: 'there would be another war in the next thirty years.'[95]

Beovich was also interested in the situation in Ireland. 'There is not a country that I love so much after my native land Australia, nor a history that thrills me more, than Ireland and her story,' he wrote at the beginning of 1919.[96] He refused to accept the verdict of his American Jesuit confessor that the Easter Rising of 1916 was unjustified. Far from recoiling from the violent rebellion against British rule, he thought 'it needed the sacrifice and martyrdom of brave young lives to waken their countrymen from the sleep of national death'.[97] He rejoiced in the recent election victory of the republican party, Sinn Fein, and the following year exulted in the beatification of Oliver Plunkett. A former Propaganda professor and archbishop of Armagh, Plunkett was executed in England in 1681.[98] Beovich could not see the irony – that where Ireland was concerned, he succumbed to the jingoistic patriotism which he found so objectionable in others. It was a legacy of his Christian Brothers' schooling and his devotion to Daniel Mannix.

At this stage, Mannix was still the great hero. On the day he received news of the armistice, Beovich proclaimed in his diary:

> Thank God a leader was given us and at the most opportune time he saved Australia [from going down Prussia's militaristic path]. In these critical times – for although the war is fought and won and peace is almost at hand, the world is boiling like a volcano – Dr Mannix will guide and guard the people of Australia, and if for the common good, and the state of humanity and civilization, the people – Catholics, Protestants, Atheists – follow him, all will be well.[99]

Given the sectarian animosity fuelled by Mannix's intervention in the conscription debate, and the bitter divisions within the Catholic community, this was a totally unrealistic hope. Mannix further exacerbated tensions by travelling through the United States in 1920, speaking at mass meetings in support of Sinn Fein leader Eamon de Valera.[100] The British government was so concerned about Mannix's inflammatory rhetoric that it stopped him visiting Ireland. In the early hours of the morning on 9 August 1920, two British naval vessels stopped the ship which Mannix was on before it reached its destination, the Irish port of Queenstown. He was removed from it and taken to England.

On 24 March 1921 Mannix finally reached Rome for his *ad limina* visit, supposedly the reason for his overseas travel. That day Beovich's *camerata* was walking down the steps of the Armenian Church: 'Met Dr Mannix, in a shake we were down on our knees kissing his ring. He told me that I had grown and was looking a bit fatter.' In a letter to a Melbourne friend in 1918 (subsequently, to his acute embarrassment, published in the *Advocate*),[101] Beovich had boasted that 'throughout the Urban, Irish and American Colleges in Rome the name of the archbishop of Melbourne is a household word'. Now he and Jim O'Collins rushed around preparing a welcome for the visitor. Even though the rector advised them to 'cut out the frills',[102] after all the celebrations were over, Beovich proudly wrote in an article for the *Tribune* that 'within the memory of this generation, no such welcome has been extended to any visitor to Propaganda, not even to Cardinals and Patriarchs'.[103] When Mannix rose to respond to the speeches made in his honour, he revealed something of the model of episcopal leadership he presented to young students like Matt Beovich:

> He was convinced that an Australian bishop would need to maintain with his people a much closer intimacy than might be necessary perhaps to a bishop in a Catholic-hearted country such as Italy. In Australia, the people looked for leadership and guidance not only as regards purely spiritual matters, but also as regards their temporal interests and well-being. He therefore conceived it his duty as a bishop to assist the people in both directions to the best of his ability, even though such effort made for him many bitter foes.[104]

The Development of an Australian Priesthood

Mannix was not the only one with strong opinions about the nature of ministry in Australia. The Manly Union was formed by alumni of St Patrick's, Manly, at the college's silver jubilee in 1914.[105] At that time about 75 per cent of priests in Australia were Irishmen, and the Irish-born bishops continued to import more, although the percentage of Irish-born lay Catholics had declined to a mere 5 per cent.[106] In his sermon at the opening of the jubilee celebrations, Terence McGuire passionately stated what seemed obvious to many Manly priests: 'The mission of the Church in Australia is no longer to save the Irish exile, but to convert the Australian race. In the first, the Church relied principally on the Irish priest. In the second, she must rely principally on the Australian priest.'[107] With McGuire as its first president, the Manly Union began lobbying for an Australian-born clergy (and ultimately hierarchy). An article in the first volume of *Manly*, the Union's magazine, expressed the hope in 1919 that 'the more close the union between our Australian priests and our Australian people, the stronger will be the influence of the priesthood'. Central to the dream was the conversion of St Patrick's to a national university for the training of priests for all the dioceses of Australia, a place where men could be 'educated in accordance with Australian ideals and Australian characteristics, the pride and safeguard of the nation'.[108] Unfortunately, the stridency of the Manly Union's campaign alienated the Irish-born hierarchy, and doubtless many of the Irish-born priests were hurt or offended by the implication that their time had passed.

The students at Propaganda were not immune from the tensions swirling in clerical circles in Australia. Terence McGuire had played a vital role in encouraging young Norman Gilroy's vocation.[109] On 16 May 1921 Beovich noted in his diary that Gilroy had arranged for the Australian students to meet and discuss a letter which had arrived from a professor at Manly, Justin Simonds. O'Collins chaired the meeting, and after 'a fair amount of discussion', Gilroy was asked to find out whether only alumni from St Patrick's could join the Manly Union. Gilroy was also deputed, along with Alf Gummer and Leo Jones, to arrange some articles for *Manly*. A few days after this Beovich had a chat to Frank Kissane who had spent some time at Manly:

> Learned some more of the Manly Spirit, confirmation that the Aussie spirit here in Prop. is some 50% better than in Manly! Also of two camps: 'Irish' – 'Anti-Irish'! The trouble is I'll end by having a poor opinion of our chief (and only) seminary.[110]

On 1 June 1921 Beovich confided to Gilroy that he had some concerns about the articles for *Manly*. Gilroy tried to reassure him: 'His suggestion that private articles of a possibly contentious nature will also be "seen" by a few "prudent" guys will about solve the difficulty.'[111] Beovich duly went ahead and wrote a piece on the nationalisation of Manly. On 5 June Patrick Phelan, Irish-born bishop of Sale in Victoria, visited Propaganda. Beovich reported in his diary:

> Things passed off well, Deo Gratias. The rumour had got about that Dr Phelan had no time for Australian priests, and trouble brewed; fortunately got wind of the affair in time and persuaded Gilroy, Gummer and Jones to come down. Matters have come to a head and evidently

> these three gentlemen might form an opposition camp and cause damage. A long talk with Jim [O'Collins]; result he saw the Rector ...

Three days later the rector summoned Beovich, Gilroy and O'Collins to his room and they 'thrashed the matter out'. Paul Giobbe stressed that while he did not want to become involved in the internal issues of the Australian Church, he did want to prevent 'party strife' entering Propaganda. He was particularly concerned about the Irishmen who were preparing for ministry in Australia. Beovich thought his position wise: 'At all events it will definitely prevent any Irish and anti-Irish or "Australianism" camps among the Aussies at Prop.' Another outcome of the meeting was that Beovich told Gilroy that he did not want his article submitted to *Manly* after all, 'chiefly because of its inability to effect any positive good'.[112]

At the meeting on 8 June the rector also revealed he had consulted Bonaventura Cerretti, apostolic delegate to Australia from 1914 to 1917. Back in Rome, Cerretti had become one of the most important and influential officials of Benedict XV. He had 'expressed great surprise when he heard that there was only one seminary in Australia' because he had told Mannix to open one in Melbourne.[113] A couple of weeks later Cerretti himself visited Propaganda and met the young Australians: 'Touched on THE question, and hinted at the possibility of an increase in seminaries: in fact he was fishing and we were fishing – and both parties seemed satisfied.'[114] On 30 January 1923 Beovich received the 'great news' that a seminary was to be established in Melbourne. This effectively ended the Manly Union's quest for St Patrick's to become the national seminary. At the same time, it was a significant step forward in the campaign for an Australian-born priesthood.

The whole affair was an excellent initiation for Beovich into political undercurrents within the Australian church and the Roman curia. At some stage during his student days, according to an Adelaide priest who worked with him in the 1960s, he learnt that Vatican officials regarded Mannix with suspicion, even as a possible schismatic.[115] There is no confirmation of this in Beovich's own writings, but there is also, after 1921, no further evidence of slavish devotion, although fondness and respect would continue.

Thanks to the internationalist ethos at Propaganda, he could see Mannix from a broader perspective. He had also developed a passionate allegiance to a higher authority than his archbishop.

The Pope

It has been said that 'the first pope a person sees remains "the pope" for the rest of his life'.[116] Beovich's first pope was the man dubbed 'the unknown pope', Benedict XV. They were similar in temperament. The modest, shy Giacomo Della Chiesa had only been a cardinal for four months when he was elected in September 1914 as the world went to war. He walked the tightrope of neutrality, with each side accusing him of favouring the other. Although his diplomatic efforts bore little if any fruit, he courageously championed the cause of peace and sponsored much humanitarian relief work. Within the Church he curbed the anti-Modernist zealots, while remaining utterly loyal to traditional Catholic teaching. Unlike his predecessor, Pius X, he was a man of quiet piety rather than heroic sanctity. His besetting sin, which he frequently repented of, was a tendency to irritability, but he also demonstrated great kindness and charity.[117]

Three weeks after Beovich arrived in Rome in 1917 there were celebrations to mark the third anniversary of Benedict's coronation. The Propaganda students went to St Peter's Square and Beovich had his first glimpse of 'a man very small in stature, with a prominent Roman nose, clear eyes, a face rather thin, surmounted by black hair'. Although he had just a few moments to see the pope, he wrote to his mother: 'I literally feasted my eyes on him: the father and ruler of the Christian world.'[118] A greater treat was in store. On 11 February 1918 the students left Propaganda before sunrise and walked to the Vatican for Mass in the pope's private chapel. To his amazement, Beovich found himself in the front row. At the conclusion of the service the students were escorted to the pope's study (Beovich was impressed by the simplicity of the papal apartments), introduced to Benedict and allowed to kiss his ring. Benedict then asked them to gather closely around: 'He looked so very small, but his face so mystical; and when he spoke ... his voice was strong and eloquent, and his enthusiasm and inspiration were beautiful to see and receive.' He pointed out that it was the anniversary of the first appearance of the Marian apparition at Lourdes in 1858, and he linked this to the students' future ministry. Beovich later wrote in his diary what he remembered of the address:

> When Christianity was contending against heretics and unbelievers; when the faith of the people was lessening, when charity was half spent and hope seemed lost, the Virgin Immaculate appeared to little Bernadette in the grotto at Lourdes. By the miracles she worked ... faith revived ... charity toward our neighbours was increased, and hope was again enkindled. From the four corners of the world came petitions imploring the Divine Compassion through the Intercession of Our Lady.
>
> And in our day, we alumni of Propaganda Fide would prepare in our course and acquire, with the help of Mary Immaculate, those three graces: Fede, Speranza, Carita ... and going forth to the different nations spread the glorious Faith ...
>
> Such was the substance of the address of His Holiness. When he spoke of the glorious Faith, his face lighted up, and he half rose in his chair, so enrapt was he. What inspiration and enthusiasm he enkindled in our hearts![119]

On 9 January 1919 the Propaganda students had another early morning walk through the dark and deserted streets of Rome. As dawn was breaking they reached the Vatican and were ushered into the pope's private chapel: 'There in the stillness we, eighty favored ones, assisted at the Mass of the Father of Christendom, the ruler of 300 million loving hearts ... before our eyes God and His Vicar were speaking, even as He and Moses spoke on Mount Sinai.' Benedict's address this time focused on the faith and courage of the Magi who overcame all doubts and difficulties in their journey to find the Christ-child. He exhorted the Propaganda students to have similar hope and perseverance on their own Christian journey.

Beovich loved visiting St Peter's Basilica. He commented on 31 December 1917 that each visit made 'the Cathedral of the World' seem 'grander and more sublime'. He was reminded of lines from Byron's 'Childe Harold's Pilgrimage':

But thou, of temple old or altars new,
Standest alone, with nothing like to thee –
Worthiest of God, the holy and the true.
                                        ... Majesty,
Power, Glory, Strength and Beauty all are aisled
In this eternal ark of worship undefiled.

Enter: its grandeur overwhelms thee not;
And why? It is not lessen'd; but thy mind,
Expanded by the genius of the spot,
Has grown colossal, and can only find
A fit abode wherein appear enshrined
Thy hopes of immortality ...

On 9 May 1920 Beovich saw, for the first time, the pope preside at a ceremony in the basilica ('Truly St Peter's is not complete without the Vicar of Christ'). The occasion was the beatification of Louise de Marillac, co-founder with St Vincent de Paul of the Sisters of Charity. Four days later (13 May) came the canonisation of Margaret Mary Alacoque, who promoted devotion to the Sacred Heart of Jesus, and Gabriel Possenti, noted for his devotion to the Sorrows of Mary. The account which Beovich wrote of the ceremony in his diary is over thirteen pages long. He was exultant:

> One looking down on the scene from high up can see a magnificent sight: the Cathedral is crowded with over 60,000 people, near the Confessionals are tiers of special stands for specially privileged visitors; the papal soldiery keep admirable order, there is no struggling or unnecessary pushing: the Tribune is a blaze of lights, and here there is a sight once seen, never forgotten: the Pope is seated on his throne ... here in the centre of Christendom, the Vicar of Jesus Christ is presiding over the bishops in solemn conclave. The glory and greatness of the Catholic Church is manifested: all proclaim it, the people, the rulers, the Pope; the very walls of the mighty Cathedral speak its firmness, its depth and its solidity.

The choir's singing was magnificent. It ranged from majestic full volume to almost a whisper, so that 'the hymn seemed an echo from the choirs of angels'. Meanwhile:

> the great crowds of people either at their prayers, or those far off from the altar speaking of other matters, sent up a droning murmur that swept and eddied through the Basilica. But now it was the most solemn part of the Mass: the Pope placed his hands over the Chalice; the officers commanding the guards shouted an order; the soldiers dropped on one knee and saluted; the action warned the worshippers, on the instant there was perfect silence; one could almost hear a pin drop in the great church. The Pope pronounced the words of Consecration 'Hoc est enim Corpus Meum' and over the bowed heads of those tens of thousands he raised the Creator and Saviour of the World; from the Cupola at first faintly, then increasing in volume, came the peal of silver trumpets; a welcome to the hidden God.

By the time the ceremony ended Beovich had been in St Peter's for six and a half hours, but it was not until after the pope left that he felt tired and hungry.

Not all seminarians were so enraptured with pontifical pomp. Anthony Kenny decided after his first visit to St Peter's that 'it was a cold, oppressive, vulgar, unchristian building, and I did not much care whether I saw it again'.[120] For Kenny, a student at the English College in the 1950s:

> Attendance at papal ceremonies was not much more than a hobby, a religious hobby no doubt, but away from the main course of our religious life ... Hearing Mass, of course, was a serious business; but from a strictly religious point of view the Pope's Mass was no different from any Mass said in a side chapel in the most down-at-heel suburban church. The hours amid the pageantry at St Peter's did not take one any nearer to Heaven.[121]

Clearly, attending a ceremony in St Peter's was, for Matthew Beovich, a much more intense religious experience. In this he epitomises the most extreme form of *Romanità*. It is hardly surprising that he went on to become a bishop, while Kenny eventually left the priesthood.

Beovich and Kenny did, however, have one thing in common. They both became adept at finding good positions in St Peter's. On 16 May 1920 Joan of Arc was canonised. Determined to get as close as possible to the altar, Beovich and seven other Propaganda students tried to slip into the sanctuary to sit with the distinguished guests. An 'officious' Master of Ceremonies ejected them. Undeterred, Beovich and two others made a second attempt and succeeded in gaining entrance to the area reserved for bishops' and cardinals' secretaries.[122] A week later they were back in St Peter's for the beatification of Oliver Plunkett. On 6 June twenty-two martyrs of Uganda were also beatified, as were four Sisters of Charity and eleven Ursuline Sisters on 12 June. On the latter occasion, 'as it was the last of the great ceremonies, [we were] determined to have a good place, so Harper and self dodged the door keepers ... and the rest was easy; stalked by the Swiss Guards as if we were bishops at least, and found ourselves in the sanctuary: we easily had one of the best possies in St Peter's.' Kenny reports similar strategies for getting a good position in the basilica: 'Many of the more sober students disapproved of this kind of activity, and would frown as we St Peter's buffs boasted of our exploits at a late lunch after a canonization.'[123]

Beovich's fifth audience with Benedict XV took place on 12 January 1922. He thought that Holy Father 'was looking well, but his discourse lacked its accustomed fire and energy'. On 19 January he reported in his diary that the pope was confined to bed with influenza. By the next day it was clear that Benedict was 'very ill, dangerously so'. He died at 6 am on 22 January. In the afternoon Beovich went to the papal apartments and joined the queue which filed past the pope's mortal remains. On 26 January, thanks to Cardinal Van Rossum, he was able to attend the pope's private burial, a sad and sombre ceremony. Many years later Gilroy commented that 'we [felt we] had lost a personal friend'.[124]

Sorrow over Benedict's death soon merged with speculation about the next pope. 'Great excitement: everyone is giving tips,' Beovich wrote on 2 February 1922. Cardinal Laurenti, secretary of the Congregation for the Propagation of the Faith, was *papabile*, a possible candidate. Beovich was delighted at the prospect but not overly optimistic: 'there are about six names in the running, and talk of Dutch and German Popes!' After the conclave began, on 3 February, he went to St Peter's Square and eagerly watched the narrow chimney above the Sistine Chapel, but the smoke, when it eventually appeared, was black. Next day the smoke at first seemed white, but on closer inspection was again black. On the way back to the college Beovich encountered two of Cardinal Laurenti's sisters in tears at the thought that he might become pope. 'They wanted me to pray that he would return to them. Of course I promised to pray for what would be the will of God.'

Unfortunately for those charged with discerning it, the will of God was proving somewhat elusive. Another day passed and still the smoke was black. Yet Beovich found the waiting in St Peter's Square a deeply moving experience: 'A marvellous sight – that sea of faces. And when the smoke told us the Pope was not yet elected, the crowd quietly ... melted away ... Even in externals how great does the Papacy appear. A marvellous – a divine power.'[125] February 6 was a wet day, but the crowd once again waited patiently and thousands of umbrellas were a 'novel sight'. This time patience was rewarded. At 11.30 am the chimney emitted the longed-for plume of white smoke. Beovich took up a position directly in front of the balcony from which the new pope would appear. An hour later the anxious wait was over. Cardinal Achille Ratti walked onto the balcony as Pope Pius XI. An 'indescribable enthusiasm seized the crowd'; Beovich felt sure that he would never forget the moment. The 'magnificent' Mass and coronation on 12 February was likewise 'a sight I shall never forget'.

The new pope, a much larger man than Benedict XV, was energetic, scholarly and authoritarian. Gilroy remembered him as 'a fearless leader, never on the defensive but always on the offensive'.[126] Yet although he took the name Pius instead of Benedict, he did not lead a conservative reaction to Benedict XV's rule. He largely followed his predecessor's policies, albeit in his own style.[127] Three months after his election, he presided over the international Eucharistic congress in Rome. Beovich attended the opening on 24 May 1922. 'Great enthusiasm,' he reported, 'the Holy Father's voice carries well, and we could hear his speech distinctly.' The next day the pope celebrated Mass at St Peter's. It was the best ceremony Beovich had attended in the basilica. He was very tired after standing for five hours (the leg broken in the football match at Castelgandolfo had still not fully healed) but, 'Ah it was a day of Triumph: of Jesus in the Blessed Sacrament, and his Vicar, the sweet Christ on earth whose tabernacle is the Vatican'. On 26 May the Blessed Sacrament was carried through the streets of Rome where it was raised in Benediction from the balconies of the major basilicas and the Arch of Constantine near the Coliseum. Propaganda students were among about 5000 seminarians who took part in the procession: 'Our greatest day in Rome was the verdict.'

On 11 June 1922 the students went to the Vatican for Mass and an audience with Pius XI. His message to them was simple and practical. Beovich (the future director of Catholic Education in Melbourne) summarised it succinctly: 'Look after the children, through them we can reach their parents.' On 5 June 1923, when Beovich was preparing to leave Rome, the rector took him and twenty-three other recently ordained Propaganda graduates on a final visit to the Vatican:

> His Holiness spoke to us of the great privilege that was ours in being called to study in Rome: the centre of Christianity. He blessed us and our future labours in the propagation of the faith. We received in word our direct commission from the Vicar of Jesus Christ to go teach all nations.

The evening before they left Propaganda, Beovich and Alf Gummer visited Cardinal Laurenti. The cardinal 'gave us a little spiff. Three things to inculcate: the Eucharist, the Madonna, il Papa'.[128] The advice was unnecessary. Laurenti was preaching to the converted.

Priesthood

The climax of Beovich's studies in Rome came in 1922 when he was ordained. After five Propaganda students were ordained at Easter 1920 Beovich wrote to his mother that 'among the great ceremonies of the Church, there is none so inspiring, and more beautiful than the ordination to the Priesthood' (he had not then attended a canonisation liturgy). He revealed that

> I felt its solemnity and awful majesty most when the five aspirants were lying prostrate before the altar, and again when the cardinal and the assistant priests extended their hands over the kneeling group ... But most of all my feelings were stirred when at the end

> the choir thundered out: 'Thou art a priest forever' and again and again 'forever'.[129]

The importance of the priesthood in the Catholic Church can scarcely be overestimated. In 1922, in one of his first letters as pope, Pius XI declared:

> Of all the sacred duties which the supreme pontificate includes, there is none more important or of more far-reaching significance than the responsibility of ensuring that the Church has a sufficient number of worthy ministers to enable her to discharge her divine mission.
>
> Upon this depend the dignity, the effective action and the very life of the Church; it is of the greatest importance for the salvation of the human race, because the immense blessings won for the world by the Redeemer, Jesus Christ, are communicated to men only through the ministers of Christ and the dispensers of the mysteries of God.[130]

This was an enormous responsibility for men like Beovich who took it seriously.

Such an exalted view of the priesthood owed much to the so-called 'French school of spirituality' of the seventeenth century, when men like Pierre de Berulle, Vincent de Paul and Jean-Jacques Olier rescued secular priests from the shadows cast by the religious orders. Yet while they exalted the role of the priest, they demanded great self-abnegation in those who chose it. The ideal was that priests were to be 'living sacrifices' who would strive so completely to empty themselves of self that Christ could act through them, especially during the celebration of the Eucharist.[131] Beovich fully realised and willingly accepted this. When he was ordained to the subdiaconate on 9 July 1922 he wrote in his diary: 'Body and soul I am consecrated to God, and I resolved, lying prostrate on the ground, that I would spend all my energies in the service of my Lord who called me to leave all things and follow him.'

The subdiaconate was the point at which Beovich irrevocably committed himself to celibacy. There is no evidence in his diary or elsewhere that this step caused him any anguish. After his ordination, as he proudly wrote to his mother, he was also bound to the daily recitation of the breviary. A month later, on 6 August 1922, he was ordained a deacon in the Church of St Anthony. One of the privileges of a deacon was that he could participate in the service of Benediction. Wearing a surplice which his mother had made, Beovich exposed the Blessed Sacrament for veneration the evening of his ordination. The following week he reported: 'I was deacon at the High Mass: an awe-full experience ... It's great assisting at the Altar so close to the Priest and almost touching the Precious Body and Blood of Our Lord.'

Beovich was ordained to the priesthood on 23 December 1922. Appropriately, the ceremony took place in the basilica of St John Lateran, the cathedral of the bishop of Rome. Its central nave is dominated by towering statues of the apostles, a reminder of the ancient tradition that priests receive holy orders by the laying on of hands in an unbroken chain going back to the apostles. Beovich was perhaps too exhausted after it was over to write a detailed account in his diary, and the letter he wrote to his mother is missing from the collection of their correspondence. However, on other occasions Beovich noted that some newly ordained priests broke down while celebrating their first Eucharist, overcome with awe and emotion. His friend James O'Collins, who was ordained alongside him, stumbled over some of the words.[132] To judge from the brief diary note, Beovich's own first Mass, celebrated in the college chapel at 12.30 am on Christmas Day, passed without mishaps. The following day he went to St Peter's and celebrated Mass above St Peter's tomb.

Travelling Through Europe

Matt Beovich left his beloved Rome on 30 June 1923, assuming he would never have the opportunity to see it again. One consolation was that instead of going straight home, he could spend two months exploring Europe, with funds provided by his father at his mother's urging.[133] With Alf Gummer, he travelled north by train, stopping in Florence, Venice and Milan. For a few days he appreciated the beauty of the Swiss Alps, but confessed to feeling 'Romesick'.[134] The troubled post-war condition of Austria and Germany made travel east or north problematic, so he relinquished his desire to see his father's native land and headed west to Paris. Using Paris as a base, Beovich and Gummer made three pilgrimages.

The first journey was to what had become the most popular pilgrimage destination of all: Lourdes.[135] On 18 July Beovich wrote to his mother that, in spite of the 'vulgarities of the tourists', Lourdes was 'a marvellous place, nowhere, not even in Rome have I seen and felt such an atmosphere of spirituality, the natural and the supernatural meeting'. Although he went armed with a letter of introduction from Cardinal Laurenti to the local bishop, he did not expect that this would achieve the desired result. He was wrong. On 19 July he was allowed to celebrate Mass in the famous Grotto where, to the initial disbelief and disquiet of church authorities, the young peasant girl Bernadette Soubirous reported seeing apparitions of Mary in 1858. Beovich distributed Communion for almost an hour afterwards, and then stayed in the Grotto to pray:

> While there a big commotion, a miracle had been effected and the happy person was being brought to thank the Madonna: a great excited crowd of people followed her. The young lady helped by a priest, evidently her brother, stepped from her chair, then without any help walked to the altar of the Grotto: the previous scenes of the pilgrimage had moved me but none as much as this: the pilgrims burst into the Magnificat, a canticle of joy and praise to the Blessed Virgin. I could not restrain my tears. I believed and here in the presence of the supernatural how much more did I believe.

He later went to the medical bureau and copied down details of the case. The young woman had been suffering from tuberculosis in the spine and had been unable to walk. Five doctors examined her and pored over her medical records and x-ray photographs. Their verdict: the spine had been diseased, and its instantaneous cure could not be attributed to a natural cause.[136]

The next pilgrimage was to the small village of Paray-le-Monial.[137] Beovich and Gummer said Mass in the chapel of the Visitation Convent where Margaret Mary Alacoque had experienced visions of Christ in the 1670s. In their wake, she promoted devotion to the 'Sacred Heart', an image of Jesus which encouraged worshippers to dwell on his suffering, love and gentleness. Despite the initial reluctance of Church authorities, this Christocentric cult became very popular in the nineteenth and twentieth centuries. It was particularly important to Pius XI.[138] As noted above, Beovich attended Margaret Mary's canonisation in 1920. After his ordination in 1922 he chose to say his second Mass at the Sacred Heart altar in the Propaganda College chapel.[139]

The third pilgrimage was to Lisieux where Beovich and Gummer said Mass near the tomb of Thérèse Martin and visited her family home, seeing the toys which she played with as a child.[140] Thérèse was no saint from times remote. She had died, aged only twenty-four, the year after Beovich was born. Beovich attended her beatification in April 1923 and in June attributed his doctorate in divinity in part to her intercession.[141] Thérèse's *Story of a Soul*, first published in 1898, encouraged Catholics to cast off fear and scruples and approach God with confidence and love. She maintained that exceptionally heroic deeds were not the only path to sanctity: small efforts and sacrifices done for the love of God would equally please him, just as a parent delights in the humble gifts of a child. It was a wholesome message for a young priest inclined to asceticism, and Thérèse's frank acknowledgement that she battled doubts and temptations and experienced a 'dark night of the soul' added a healthy note of realism to her story.[142]

Resuming their journey home, on 28 July 1923 Beovich and Gummer left Paris and headed toward the English Channel. They stopped to say Mass in the cathedral in Amiens for the Australian soldiers who had died during the war. The anger Beovich felt when he thought of the war did not extend to the soldiers who had lost their lives on the battlefields. The following day they reached London. They visited the usual tourist attractions. Beovich thought Westminster Abbey 'ridiculously packed with monuments', and a debate in the House of Commons was 'dull … and most uninspiring'.[143] On 3 August they travelled to Ireland where they met up with Jim O'Collins.

Did Ireland live up to expectations? The diary account is curiously bland. The Irish Free State was still recovering from its bloody civil war, but apart from the inconvenience of having to break a train journey because a bridge had been destroyed, Beovich made no mention of this. He visited St Patrick's College at Maynooth. The students were away on holidays and their rooms smelt.[144] He witnessed a hurling match but thought it brought out the worst qualities of Irishmen, with accidents and bad feeling common.[145] He enjoyed scenic drives through the Wicklow Mountains and Connemara, but failed to find any relatives in Ennis.[146] In Venice he had become acquainted with three travelling Australians, a Mr and Mrs O'Connor and a Miss Ryan.[147] They met again in Milan and Lucerne (it is not clear whether this was by design or not).[148] Unexpectedly their paths crossed in Limerick, and Beovich went sightseeing with them and visited their relatives while Gummer tracked down his family connections.[149] For a few days Beovich also travelled with John O'Connell, his parish priest from Melbourne.[150] It is dangerous to try to read between the lines of the diary, but Ireland seems to have been an anti-climax after Rome. As a youth Beovich had been passionately attached to an idealised Ireland of saints and martyrs. He visited the real Ireland in 1923, but he visited it as a tourist. It was not a homecoming.

Beovich and Gummer returned to London in time to board the *Khymber* on 31 August. Beovich then stopped writing in his diary. The great adventure was coming to an end, and it was time to rest on the long sea voyage in preparation for the busy life ahead.

The Impact of Rome

How had Beovich changed during the six years that he had been away from Melbourne? He had come to know a church which was more universal in its reach, more *catholic*, than the Irish-Australian institution of his childhood.[151] He had experienced the liturgical richness of eastern Christian traditions, embraced a more disciplined and self-sacrificing way of life, learnt the Italian language and honed his organisational, speaking, writing and leadership skills. He had formed new (and in some cases life-long) friendships, and become a member of a formidable 'old boys' network. Yet, although he returned to Australia bearing what he described as 'no small burden', a doctoral degree in theology,[152] his academic studies did little more than consolidate the faith of his childhood. His personal piety – including his devotion to Mary the Mother of God, the Sacred Heart of Jesus, and Thérèse of Lisieux – probably remained little different from that of his mother and Josephite sister.

The greatest change was that between 1917 and 1923 the centre of Beovich's world shifted. While he did not express himself as melodramatically as Jim O'Collins, who wrote in his diary on 8 June 1923, 'Thus I said goodbye to Rome, the home of my heart for the rest of my life',[153] the 'Romesick' Matt Beovich clearly found the return to Melbourne a bittersweet experience. He had developed the most acute form of *Romanità*. Deference to the papacy had grown, through personal contact with Benedict XV and Pius XI, into intense devotion. Loyalty to Urban College, the Congregation of Propaganda Fide, and the wider papal curia had become deeply ingrained, and the splendour of St Peter's and the great liturgical ceremonies held within its walls had reinforced his confidence in the Catholic Church and in its ultimate triumph in an often hostile world. In short, Matthew Beovich definitely returned to Australia a *Roman* Catholic priest.

Three
'Propagating the Faith' Melbourne, 1923–1939

More than any other single factor, the schools are the key to understanding the religious life of Australian Catholics. From the first decades of the twentieth century the majority of Catholics were products of parish schools. What religion they imbibed there became the standard and foundation of whatever else followed.

Edmund Campion, *Australian Catholics*

Matthew Beovich returned to Melbourne on Thursday, 11 October 1923. Although he had warned his mother that he did not want any fuss made,[1] the parishioners of North Brunswick were not going to let him slip back that easily, nor the teachers at his old school.[2] As he stopped keeping a diary, there is no record of his private reaction to the round of social engagements, but after being away for six years he doubtless noticed many changes, not least the new church in the North Brunswick parish. It was one of about forty Catholic churches built in Melbourne between 1918 and 1930.[3] Beovich probably read in the *Advocate* the week he returned home an account of the recent opening ceremony at St John's Church at Clifton Hill. In his address on that occasion, the Rev. J. J. Malone triumphantly described the 'astounding progress' which had been made during the first hundred years of Catholicism in Australia, and confidently predicted that the Church was moving into an even more glorious future.[4]

Large congregations at Mass, innumerable parish societies, and the never-ending round of fundraising fetes, picnics, balls and concerts reported in the *Advocate* and the *Tribune* point to a vibrant Catholic community in 1923 enjoying a post-war boom. Under the surface, however, there were more disturbing signs. The increase in the number of Catholics in Melbourne did not keep pace with general population growth,[5] and in spite of the fact that Catholics were warned it was a serious sin to miss Mass, about half did so anyway.[6]

For a few months Beovich confronted this problem directly. In January 1924 he was appointed assistant priest of St Brigid's Church in North Fitzroy, an inner working-class suburb not far from North Brunswick.[7] One of his main duties was visiting lapsed Catholics to encourage them to return to Mass.[8] This proved to be his only experience, after ordination, of suburban parochial life. It did not last long. On 8 May 1924 the *Advocate* reported that Dr Matthew Beovich had been appointed diocesan inspector of religious instruction for the archdiocese of Melbourne.

Inspector of Religious Instruction

As Edmund Campion points out, it is difficult to exaggerate the significance of Catholic schools in the history of Australian Catholicism.[9] How effectively the schools have propagated the faith is a more complex matter, however. Naomi Turner's verdict on the period 1889–1939 is damning:

> The emphasis in the schools ... was on passive and unquestioning obedience: questions about the faith were not usually encouraged because they smacked of blasphemy and pride. Obedience and respect were due to the clergy simply because they were clergy. In this way it was an inflexible and repressive system. Religion was presented mostly in question-and-answer style and information learnt by rote. It is no wonder that some children rebelled and left the Church simultaneously with leaving school.[10]

Turner singles out clerical inspectors for particular criticism, commenting that they usually had little training or aptitude for the work and could only offer minimal leadership and inspiration.[11]

Beovich seems to have embraced his new role with enthusiasm.

In 1930, in a triennial report to the cardinal prefect of Propaganda Fide in Rome, he revealed that he found it even more 'congenial' as the years passed and he gained experience.[12] Inspection reports for individual schools indicate that he wanted to hear more than merely the correct answers to questions in the catechism. He encouraged children to explain what the answers meant, and he gently probed their knowledge of church history and Bible stories.[13] His counterpart in Perth, John McMahon, was frustrated by the tendency of teachers to coach students immediately prior to his visit.[14] To 'safeguard the children against the "cramming" habit', Beovich initiated surprise inspections. It is easy to imagine the dismay of teachers at the sudden appearance of the inspector in the classroom, but Beovich reported they displayed 'a generous cooperation' in the inspection process.[15] One retired teacher remembers him as 'a friendly presence in the classroom',[16] while some former students also have happy memories of his visits to their school. His habit of awarding half-day holidays is recalled with particular gratitude.[17]

The catechism in use in Australian Catholic schools in the 1920s was often known as the 'Green Catechism' or 'Penny Catechism'. Based on the 1875 Maynooth Catechism, it was approved by the Third Plenary Council of the Australian Hierarchy in 1905, after being amended by Cardinal Moran. Much criticised since the 1960s,[18] the catechism was also under fire in the 1920s. In a series of articles in the clerical journal, the *Australasian Catholic Record*, M. B. Hanrahan and Arthur O'Brien argued that, however admirable it was as a logical arrangement of Christian doctrine, it was unsuitable for children. Apart from anything else, it was contrary to the example of Jesus, who had told vivid stories instead of forcing children to recite abstract truths parrot-fashion.[19]

Sensitive to complaints about poor teaching of the catechism, but unwilling to abandon it, in 1928 Beovich arranged a series of 'Conferences on the Catechism' for teachers. They were encouraged to use the 'synthetic' method of teaching: memorisation of catechism answers only after they had been built up by explanation and illustration using Bible stories. In the wake of the 1928 gatherings he produced short leaflets to give guidance on how to teach certain subjects ('Creation – Infants'; 'Sin – Grade III'; 'Faith – Grade VII'; 'The Mass – Grade VIII' and so on).[20]

In keeping with the general practice in government and private schools at the time, Beovich relied on examinations to monitor students' progress.[21] Discovering that some teachers found it difficult to set examination papers, Beovich decided in 1929 to send out the questions himself.[22] If students were to receive the same questions, they had to be taught the same topics. Beovich first issued a syllabus of religious instruction for secondary schools in 1925, setting out which gospel was to be studied each year, and which chapters from MacCaffrey's *History of the Church* and Sheehan's *Apologetics and Christian Doctrine*. A revised edition in 1929 gave more detailed instructions on liturgical and theological topics for study.[23] Another initiative in 1929 was the introduction of lessons on Gregorian chant for students from grades six to eight. Beovich arranged a summer school for teachers in 1930 to equip them to teach it.[24]

The Catholic school system in the 1920s was hardly a system at all, but a loose collection of parochial and order-owned schools. The former were parish primary schools, some offering secondary classes as well. Staffed mainly by religious sisters and brothers, they were under the control of parish priests, and ultimately therefore under the bishop's jurisdiction. The latter were run and owned by religious orders.[25] They usually offered secondary education (for higher fees than the parochial schools) and were labelled 'colleges'. Beovich was very much aware that each order tended to operate in isolation.[26] To help overcome this, in 1925 he established a Catholic Teachers' Association.[27] Various meetings and seminars provided opportunities for teachers from different orders and schools to gather together and share ideas. Another development, probably also initiated by Beovich, was an annual Mass for all teachers at the beginning of the school year in St Patrick's Cathedral.

Beovich's confidence in teachers and support for them emerges strongly from the surviving circulars and reports. Unlike McMahon, who castigated schools for allowing elderly priests and nuns unfit for anything else to teach religion,[28] Beovich paid glowing tributes to teachers in his reports to Cardinal Van Rossum, prefect of the Congregation for the Propagation of the Faith, and Archbishop Mannix.[29] However, he could assume what McMahon could not: that all teachers had met at least minimum training requirements, mandatory in Victoria since 1905. Many of them had been trained at one of Melbourne's two Catholic teachers' colleges.

Despite Beovich's efforts, traditions of independence were hard to overcome.[30] This was particularly true of the Christian Brothers who ran most of the secondary schools for boys. They were technically accountable not to Mannix but to their Sydney-based provincial leader, who sent his own inspector to visit schools. As a result, the Brothers were exempt from diocesan inspection of 'secular' teaching. However, on the grounds that the archbishop was the one ultimately responsible for the religious education of all Catholic children in his diocese, Beovich insisted on inspecting the teaching of Christian doctrine. He was not always welcomed by the Brothers. A note of frustration entered one of his reports:

> This school is an example of the difficulty in handling Christian Brothers' schools. Admittedly the standard of teaching is very good ... But it requires a deal of tact and coaxing to get the teachers to follow instructions and at the same time to encourage them in their good work.[31]

Beovich chose the path of diplomacy rather than confrontation, keeping in contact with the Christian Brothers' provincial and the inspector he appointed. One year he compared notes with Brother Reidy, the Christian Brothers' inspector, and was pleased to find that their criticisms were very similar and that Reidy had already taken action to rectify the 'unsatisfactory' standard at several schools.[32] The unnamed failings were not reported to Van Rossum or Mannix. Beovich revealed in an interview in 1980 that he 'believed that only positive remarks concerning schools needed to be passed on, he saw little value in communicating problems which the Archbishop would be unable or even expected to solve'.[33] Someone, however, had to deal with them, and that person increasingly became Beovich himself.

The Catholic Education Office

Beovich was initially appointed diocesan inspector of religious instruction. A layman, Charles O'Driscoll, had been diocesan inspector of secular knowledge since 1911. Gradually Mannix seems to have delegated all educational matters to Beovich. In 1932 the first Catholic Education Office (CEO) was established in Melbourne. In theory, the archbishop was the 'director', Beovich was 'deputy director' and O'Driscoll was an employee. At some point in the next four years Beovich's title was upgraded to 'director', a reflection of Mannix's minimal involvement in the CEO.

In her study of Catholic education in Victoria, Anne O'Brien presents Mannix as a supreme monarch who 'decided educational policy, regardless of who was in the Catholic Education Office'.[34] However, while Beovich always passed the credit for developments in Catholic education to his archbishop, modesty was a virtue which he cultivated. He also exploited Mannix's authority, issuing circulars to teachers in Mannix's name on issues where he was likely to face opposition. Overall, it is likely that he initiated the changes and Mannix merely approved them.[35] It was one of the chief characteristics of Mannix's leadership that he allowed priests, members of religious orders, and leading lay Catholics such as B. A. Santamaria, a considerable degree of latitude. 'A thoroughbred,' he is reported to have said, 'always runs best if allowed to have his head.'[36] Santamaria testified that the strength of Mannix's 'light rein' policy was that it encouraged personal initiative and high morale.[37] The main weakness was that parishes and Catholic schools tended to be run as separate fiefdoms. Santamaria acknowledged that what little central administration existed in the diocese in the 1920s and 1930s was largely in the overburdened hands of two priests: one who occupied simultaneously the positions of vicar general, administrator of St Patrick's Cathedral and personal secretary to the archbishop; and the other who was responsible for overseeing the Catholic schools – Matthew Beovich.[38]

In comparison with the bureaucracy which developed in the 1960s and 1970s, and now occupies a multi-storey building on Victoria Parade, the CEO of the 1930s was a very small affair. It was first located in St Patrick's Cathedral presbytery, in Beovich's bedroom. Files covered his bed during the day. At night they were stored under the bed.[39] In 1936 Beovich was given the use of an office in the Bank of Australia building in Collins Street, but he did not have exclusive possession. He had to share it, and a secretary, with Theresa Wardell, the chief executive of the Catholic Welfare Bureau. He was, however, allocated another assistant, in addition to O'Driscoll. This was Daniel Conquest, a young priest of the archdiocese of Melbourne. Significantly, Conquest went to Mercy Teachers' College and undertook a teacher training course, an indication of the importance Beovich placed on appropriate professional training.[40]

Coordinating the Catholic School System

Building and maintaining Catholic primary schools was a priority for Thomas Carr during his time as archbishop of Melbourne.[41] Mannix flagged a new agenda in his inaugural address in St Patrick's Cathedral in 1913: the need for more Catholic university graduates. To enter university, students required more than basic primary schooling. Demand for secondary education was not strong in the general community at this time. As late as 1938, only 15 per cent of Victorian children attending state schools advanced beyond primary level,[42] and financial pressures may have made working-class Catholic parents even more resistant to further education for their offspring. Mannix fanned the flames of Irish nationalism to raise Catholics' educational aspirations. What W. A. Greening has called 'the Mannix thesis in Catholic education', was not free secondary education for all, but sufficient opportunity for children of genuine academic ability to progress to higher education regardless of class background.[43] In 1930 Mannix told the crowd at the opening of a new school that 'if those who could pay for high school education did so, much more could be done for talented children of poor people', while 'children who possessed ordinary talents could be satisfactorily educated in the primary schools'.[44] Beovich faithfully echoed his archbishop's opinions when in 1931 he gave evidence at a state government board of inquiry into the cost of secondary education and called for the provision of more scholarships.[45]

In 1928 the state government offered thirty-nine scholarships which were tenable for four years at any approved secondary school. Catholic students gained thirty-six of them. In spite of this success, a circular signed by Mannix but written in Beovich's style was sent to 'The Teacher in Charge' on 11 February 1929. It explained a major change in the way children would be prepared for state scholarship examinations. Teachers in parish primary schools, whose time was already 'fully occupied' (a typical Beovich sop to their dignity), would no longer do such coaching. Instead, from January 1930 two 'central schools' in the inner suburb of Fitzroy would specialise in the work: St Colman's for boys and St Ita's for girls.

Beovich turned a former two-room parochial school in Young Street, Fitzroy, into St Colman's. Its sole teacher was a Christian Brother, Paul Bowler.[46] He became one of Beovich's most trusted friends and confidants, virtually an unofficial member of the staff at the CEO.[47] St Ita's was attached to St Brigid's School which was run by Good Samaritan Sisters. The parish priest allowed the scholarship class to meet in the old billiards room behind the stage in the parish hall.[48] Emilian McLaughlan was principal for the first sixteen years, and, like Bowler, is remembered by a former student as 'a strict disciplinarian but full of love and energy'.[49] She and Beovich became good friends and he visited the school so frequently that it was sometimes referred to as 'Dr Beovich's school'.[50] He assisted in subtle ways. One former student, whose father was unemployed in 1934, remembers her mother arranging for her to go to the cathedral presbytery each term to collect the money for her tram fares from a 'very kind and courteous Dr Beovich'.[51]

Free tuition for a year at St Colman's or St Ita's was provided to winners of forty 'archbishop's scholarships'. These were awarded on the basis of results in an annual examination, held a few weeks before that for the merit certificate and of equal standard. Beovich, helped by O'Driscoll, Bowler and eventually Conquest, set the questions and marked the papers. When the state government increased the number of secondary school scholarships on offer in 1939, Beovich rushed to establish six new 'central classes', negotiating with parish priests to provide classrooms and religious orders to provide the teachers.[52] As a result, 200 more free places were offered. While educationalists would later rue the emphasis on competitive examinations, and numerous students must have missed out on scholarships, the central schools/classes were a 'gate way to the professions' for many young Catholics who might not have been able to progress beyond a basic education.[53]

Boys with more practical inclinations were not forgotten, at least after 1929 when an apprenticeship commission ruled that before a boy could be apprenticed to a trade such as carpentry, electrical engineering or plumbing, he had to spend two years in a registered junior technical school. Mannix's response was swift: 'With his characteristic zeal and determination ... he determined that we should have our own technical schools.'[54] The formal decision may have been taken by Mannix, but it was probably Beovich who 'sold it to him',[55] and it was certainly Beovich who worked rapidly with a committee of priests and Christian Brothers to develop Catholic technical schools at Abbotsford and South Melbourne.[56] These opened in 1930. Seven years later Beovich claimed that about 1400 boys from 65 parishes had passed through Abbotsford and South Melbourne, many of them able to avoid unemployment during the Great Depression as a result.[57]

The equivalent to technical education for girls was home-craft and commercial work. Beovich sent a circular to schools in May 1929 asking whether they had commercial and/or cookery classes. The following year, a commercial class was established at St Brigid's, Fitzroy.[58] What else happened is not clear. Beovich admitted in 1931 that this branch of the Catholic education system was not yet fully coordinated.[59] However, by 1939 the archdiocese of Melbourne had, in addition to 160 primary schools and 41 secondary schools, four business colleges, two domestic arts schools, and one agricultural college.[60]

At the bottom rung of the Catholic education system were the kindergartens, which increased in number from six in 1930 to eleven in 1939. Beovich was ambivalent about this development, believing that ideally the training of infants should be left to families, but he accepted that an increasing number of mothers had to enter the workforce for economic reasons.[61] He was involved in the establishment of the Catholic Kindergarten Union and a model kindergarten connected to Mercy Teachers' College at Flemington.[62]

In 1940 Daniel Mannix told the clergy of the archdiocese of Adelaide that Beovich had 'brought about a revolution in the Catholic schools of Melbourne'. 'Revolution' is a strong term, but the development of the CEO was a major challenge to the virtually autonomous way that Catholic schools had been run in the past. Significantly, Mannix also paid tribute to the 'quiet, tactful way' that Beovich operated. The director of Catholic education had to be diplomatic as he could neither offer a funding carrot nor wield a disciplinary stick. This is evident from Beovich's correspondence with the Christian Brothers' provincial, Brother Hanrahan.[63] Beovich could ask for additional teachers to be sent to certain schools, but if Hanrahan replied that no men were available, there was nothing that Beovich could do. He was sympathetic to the staffing difficulties which Hanrahan faced, and the overall tone of the correspondence is friendly. While some of the Brothers in Melbourne grumbled about the new arrangements in education, there is no evidence of the conflict with the 'wilful' Brothers which Helen Praetz believes marred Conquest's time as director in the 1940s.[64]

Praetz also queries the effectiveness of the 1937 regulations which Beovich issued regarding corporal punishment, pointing out that after 'numerous complaints' from parents and inspectors, Conquest had to remind teachers to 'read and meditate' on them in 1945.[65] However, Beovich did not forbid corporal punishment in Catholic schools in 1937 (he could not have enforced a ban). Instead he tried to shame teachers into changing their disciplinary habits ('In the best schools it is rarely if ever used; frequent recourse to it is always a sign of ineffective discipline or unskillful methods'), and he encouraged them to reflect on how they could improve their teaching skills.[66]

Representing the Catholic School System

Daniel Conquest believes that Beovich's most important and innovative responsibility as director of Catholic Education was to represent Catholic schools in negotiations with state education authorities.[67] The tension generated by the increasing secularisation of education in the late nineteenth century and the withdrawal of government funding from Catholic schools had eased during Carr's benign rule.[68] It reawakened when the more forthright Mannix took over.[69] Beovich was, therefore, caught between his strong-minded archbishop and the secular state authorities.

In 1932 Beovich was appointed to the Council of Public Education, the body which oversaw the registration of non-government schools and teachers and provided advice to the Victorian minister of education. In July 1938 he became the Council's vice-president. Writing in December 1939 to express felicitations on Beovich's appointment as archbishop of Adelaide, the president and registrar recalled that while there had been strong differences of opinion at some of their meetings, there had been no ill feeling, and they appreciated Beovich's tact and courtesy.[70]

Records do not survive to indicate what caused the differences at council meetings, but there were a number of contentious issues in the late 1920s and 1930s. In 1929 M. P. Hanson, the state director of education, began advocating the termination of primary school education at the end of the sixth year of schooling and the abolition of the merit certificate at the end of year eight. Such changes would have had a dramatic impact on the Catholic system, as parish schools were geared to take students until they sat the state examination for the merit certificate. Most students then left school. Beovich called a meeting of representatives from the Catholic teaching orders to inform them of the proposal and discuss the Catholic response.[71] The outcome of the meeting is not known, but Beovich was not in favour of costly changes, arguing that before they were made it would be best to see how the experiment fared in England.[72] In 1938 an Education Reform Association was formed, under the control of the Victorian Teachers' Union. It began lobbying for a reduction in class sizes and an increase in the minimum school-leaving age. Knowing what a struggle it was to finance the existing Catholic system, Beovich was not sympathetic.[73]

There was also pressure in this period to reform the curriculum. As Catholic schools in Victoria followed the state curriculum for secular subjects, any changes made by the Department of Public Instruction immediately affected them. In 1932 Catholic teachers were invited to participate in a committee set up to revise the primary curriculum. Beovich reported in 1933 that 'the invitation was appreciated, and for the first time Catholic school teachers sat with state school teachers on the Central Committee and various sub-committees entrusted with the work of revision'. Twelve Catholic schools took part in a trial of the new curriculum in 1933 and it was judged a great success.[74] A major concession was granted: that Catholic schools could follow their own history syllabus which would highlight the role of the Church in history. No textbook was needed because articles on history subjects were included in a new Catholic paper, the *Children's World*, which Beovich published in Melbourne from 1934. It was approved by the Department of Public Instruction for use in place of the department's own paper.[75]

On the vexed issue of government funding for Catholic schools, Beovich could celebrate a few minor victories in the 1930s. During the Depression years the state government agreed to provide textbooks for students whose parents were in 'necessitous circumstances' and to subsidise the distribution of milk to students attending Catholic schools in industrial suburbs.[76] In 1937 children attending Catholic schools were granted four pence per day as a travelling allowance if they lived a certain distance from the nearest school. Previously the allowance had been paid only to students enrolled in state schools.[77]

Religious Education

Religious education remained one of Beovich's major concerns in the 1930s. He realised that the 'Green Catechism' was too advanced and technical for young children, and so in 1930 he obtained permission from Mannix to draft a simpler one for children up to grade three. A year later he sent a copy of the draft to a Loreto sister, Ellen (Mother Patrick) Callanan, for her comments. In a covering letter, he explained that he envisaged classes studying each question and answer, but memorising only those in large type. Children in grade one would be expected to memorise sixteen answers, instead of the current forty-two; children in grade two would memorise eight more (a total of twenty-four instead of sixty); and in grade three there would be forty (instead of ninety-seven). After each chapter appropriate scripture readings were suggested, so that teachers could illustrate the catechism answers with stories from the Bible.[78]

The final version of the 'primer catechism' was distributed to teachers in 1933. It was accompanied by strict instructions in bold capitals that 'NO MEMORISING SHOULD BE ATTEMPTED UNTIL THE MEANING OF AN ANSWER IS GRASPED by the children'. To help this happen, Beovich recommended that teachers use the book *And Forbid Them Not!*. Its anonymous author (Ellen Callanan) provided advice on how to secure a child's attention, along with stories and pictures to illustrate Christian doctrines, questions to stimulate class discussions and activities to reinforce learning. Above all, Callanan reminded teachers that their aim in the Christian doctrine class was more profound than simply imparting knowledge:

> Each Christian doctrine lesson is a going apart with God for a time, a withdrawing of the children from the ordinary school work to learn about God and how interested He is in each one of them. It is also an appeal to the children to be enthusiastic about Christ, who so loves them. It is a bringing the child to know Christ, which is quite different from knowing about Him ...[79]

As well as the primer catechism, at the beginning of 1933 schools received copies of a new draft syllabus of religious instruction for all primary and secondary classes. In her sociological study of the Catholic school system in Victoria in the 1940s and 1950s, Praetz finds that Catholic teachers were inclined to be conservative and resistant to change.[80] The introduction of a syllabus was a major development for those teachers who had hitherto enjoyed considerable independence but Beovich was diplomatic in the way he imposed it. The syllabus was produced with the help of a Catholic Education Advisory Committee which he set up in 1932 with representatives from the various religious orders involved in education. The draft went out in January 1933 with the promise that feedback would be sought later in the year. After modifications were made, the final version was issued in 1934. The syllabus provided clear guidance on what topics should be taught to what grades, and how religious education periods (sixty minutes a day in primary schools and forty minutes a day in secondary schools) could be structured so that there was time each week for prayer, the catechism, doctrine, Scripture, history, and so on. Some matters were still left to each teacher's discretion, and the pill was sugar-coated with praise for the excellent standard of education in the diocese.[81]

The new syllabus came out at the same time as a new religious education textbook, *A Child's Book of Religion*. The author was Michael Sheehan, coadjutor archbishop of Sydney from 1922 to 1937, whose *Apologetics and Christian Doctrine* was widely used in senior classes. Shortly before his return to Ireland in 1937 he wrote:

> At a meeting of the Bishops of Australia and New Zealand, held soon after my coming to Sydney, I was commissioned by them to produce a book which would take the place of the Catechism then in general use. They said that the Catechism, as it was, was too difficult for children, and that something simpler should be substituted.[82]

A Child's Book of Religion was duly published in 1934, although not with the official backing of the hierarchy. Sheehan reversed the traditional form of the catechism, so that children could ask the questions not the teacher, and included maps and pictures to stimulate interest.

To Beovich's dismay, in his preface Sheehan frankly observed that as the average teacher or parent would not have the professional knowledge required to explain catechism answers, he had tried to produce a book which children could use themselves with very little assistance. In notes probably prepared for Mannix, Beovich maintained that, unless his judgement was very much at fault, this was not the case in Melbourne, even if the teachers might 'not yet have reached perfection in these matters'. Although children were supposed to be able to use the book with little or no help from adults, Beovich pointed out that those below grade three would probably not have the skills to read it, while those in senior grades would hardly relish being given a 'child's book'. It was also expensive. Even if it was distributed only to children from grades four to eight, the cost to the Melbourne archdiocese would be a staggering £10,000 in the first year. Beovich went to Sydney in

April 1933 to witness demonstration lessons based on the book and was not overly impressed. When he returned he recommended it only be used as a reference text for teachers, and that the catechism be retained, but in a more attractive format.[83]

The Catholic Education Congress, 1936

Not all educators shared Beovich's concerns about *A Child's Book of Religion*. It received warm praise from a number of speakers at the Catholic Education Congress in Adelaide in 1936.[84] Hanrahan concluded that there were no sound arguments for supplementing it with a catechism. If children were to memorise anything, it would be 'vastly better' for them to learn texts from Scripture, hymns and prayers.[85]

In response, Beovich insisted that 'defective teaching by some poorly trained teachers should not be advanced as a valid argument against the proven usefulness of an excellent book'. However, the main theme of his paper at the congress was that religious education should not be limited to fixed periods. Quoting from Pius XI's encyclical *The Christian Education of Youth* (1929), he maintained that 'every other subject taught should be permeated with the spirit of Christian piety'. How could this be done? Beovich highlighted the crucial role of teachers. Long after most students forgot information learnt at school, they would remember their teachers and be inspired by their 'deep, vivid faith' and 'kindliness, courtesy, self-control, sincerity and honesty'. While he acknowledged the 'splendid work' of lay teachers, he was grateful that the majority of Catholic teachers came from religious orders: 'For, as the Catholic philosophy of life is fully given expression to by discipline and self-denial, who can better inculcate that philosophy by the force of example than religious teachers?'[86]

Beovich did not address the consequences if teachers failed to live up to his high ideals: he simply maintained that such men and women were in a small minority. He did, nevertheless, help organise a meeting of sixteen priests and inspectors in charge of Catholic education which was held as part of the congress.[87] The issue of poor teaching must have arisen because, after the meeting, one of the recommendations which went to the Australian bishops was that, in accordance with the Decree of the Sacred

Congregation of Religious (November 1930), 'religious be required to revise, during their novitiate, their knowledge of Christian Doctrine, adding thereto a study of the methods of teaching religion, and be required to satisfy the Bishop or his delegate that they are competent before being admitted to the schools'. Another recommendation was that an official catechism be retained, but with the content revised and simplified and the format improved. Beovich was nominated as the one who would collate various suggestions and prepare a draft for the hierarchy. The bishops approved the recommendations at their national meeting later in the year.

John McMahon from the archdiocese of Perth was one of those present in 1936. Many years later he paid tribute to Beovich's 'gentle, smiling presence' at such gatherings: 'He added a pleasant calmness to our discussions. He believed in the soft word that sweetened the tone of discussions, and satisfied the battling zeal of the enthusiasts. Humour, that same medicine, bubbled from him and disarmed the persistent argument.'[88] In other words, Beovich usually got his own way, although he did not always succeed in effectively implementing the decisions of such meetings. The authority structures of the Catholic Church did not favour a national approach. There was no national primate, and individual bishops guarded their independence. The new catechism became a casualty of that attitude.

The 'Red Catechism'

Beovich began work on the new catechism in 1937. After contacting teachers and inspectors of religious instruction in every state for suggestions and advice, he sent them the first draft in the middle of the year.[89] Almost simultaneously, an article by Michael Sheehan was published in the *Australasian Catholic Record* entitled 'Some Remarks on the Catechism Problem'. In his parting shot to the Australian Church, Sheehan insisted:

> It is my conviction, based on representations from the teachers, that a technical Catechism, that is, a Catechism, wholly or mainly in the technical language of theology, will always be a stumbling-block to children. No leading-up tactics will ever be satisfactory; they have been tried and have been found wanting. The children will move along gaily

> through the pleasant warmth of easy explanations and pretty legends, but will suddenly find themselves numbed by the icy water of technical definitions.[90]

To those who insisted memorising the catechism was valuable because Catholics remembered it throughout their lives, Sheehan argued that, in his experience, even candidates for the priesthood at Maynooth had difficulty recalling catechism answers. To further prove his point, he arranged for a number of adult Australian Catholics who had learnt the catechism at school to be surveyed. The results were dismal for defenders of the catechism.[91]

Sheehan had returned to Ireland by the time his former episcopal colleagues gathered in Sydney in September 1937 for the Fourth Plenary Council. They decreed that one catechism should be used in all dioceses (canon 616) and 'it was understood that that the Catechism in process of composition would be the one'.[92] A committee of bishops was appointed to supervise the work: Daniel Mannix, Justin Simonds (archbishop of Hobart), and Norman Gilroy (who had just replaced Sheehan as coadjutor archbishop of Sydney).

Mannix took an interest in the project. Beovich recalled: 'We went through each question and answer together in a big number of sessions. He had a genius for simplicity of language and the Catechism shows this (as far as one can have simplicity of language and preserve orthodoxy at the same time).'[93] A comparison between the draft and the final version reveals that the latter also has greater theological precision and, typical of Mannix, takes a more rigorous stand against Protestantism.[94]

The other members of the hierarchy were given an opportunity to comment on the draft. The responses which Beovich received in late 1937 and early 1938 were mixed.[95] A particularly scathing one came from Joseph Dwyer of Wagga Wagga:

> I can't understand the mentality of people who write catechisms for children and use words archaic or poetic when common Australian would be better. Why call a grave a tomb – no Australian youngster ever hears such a word ... Even its theology has me bamboozled. It asserts that all sacraments give Sanctifying Grace. What on earth is Sanctifying Grace? ... Telling youths up to 18 years of age about

> Christ's mystical body is not likely to make any definite impression on them ... If this is going to be rushed into print as an approved standard for Australia – I am sorry.[96]

On the other hand, Terence McGuire of Townsville sent Mannix 'very hearty congratulations on this notable attempt to write a catechism for children instead of one for learned theologians as we have had previously'.[97] Romuald Hayes of Rockhampton provided more reassurance: 'I admire the new catechism very much. It is shorter than the former one and this is an advantage. It is clear; it is accurate, and it contains all the essentials.'[98]

At the end of January 1938 Archbishop Kelly of Sydney notified Mannix that he hoped the new catechism would not cost more than two pence and that no diocese would claim copyright.[99] An old dispute still rankled. Who could publish the 'Green Catechism' had been a source of contention between Melbourne and Sydney until Kelly passed copyright to the Australian Catholic Truth Society.[100] It does not appear that Kelly had any other objections to the new catechism. Yet in May 1938, Edmund Gleeson of Maitland informed Mannix that the bishops of New South Wales had decided at their annual meeting in April to continue to use the old catechism until a new one was approved by the bishops of Australia, and that they wanted any new catechism to 'differ as little as possible' from its predecessor.[101]

Meanwhile, the scholarly and pastoral Justin Simonds, former professor of philosophy at St Patrick's College, Manly, was correcting the proofs of the new catechism. He returned them to Beovich at the end of May with the comment: 'It is a very great improvement on the old catechism, and I think it will be acceptable to all concerned.'[102] He was wrong. A month later Gilroy wrote to Beovich:

> The draft of the proposed catechism ... is a great improvement on the original draft. Many of the questions and answers are admirable & are better than those of the old Catechism. Even still the Catechism is inferior in my judgment to the green covered catechism. I could not, in conscience, recommend its adoption.[103]

In the end a new edition of the *Catechism of Christian Doctrine Adapted for Australia by the Second and Third Plenary Councils* was published in Sydney under the imprimatur of Norman Gilroy, and teachers and priests in the Sydney archdiocese were given strict instructions that it was the only one which they could use.[104] Simultaneously, the Advocate Press in Melbourne published the *Catechism for General Use in Australia Issued with Episcopal Authority on the Occasion of the Fourth Plenary Council 1937*, under the imprimatur of Daniel Mannix. It was Beovich's first experience of how difficult it was to get the Australian Catholic bishops to act in unison. The affair does not seem to have strained his relations with Gilroy, but it may have been the beginning of what would become a close friendship with Simonds.

Campion, who grew up with the 'Green Catechism', recommends a study of the catechism to any historian who wants to understand Australian Catholicism as 'it may fairly be called the single most influential document in Australian Catholic history'.[105] Much the same could be said about its Melbourne rival. With its bright red cover, better quality paper and clearer subdivisions, it has a more appealing format than the Green Catechism, but still the same legalistic and defensive thrust. Theological doctrines like the Incarnation and Redemption are rushed over, far more space being devoted to the rules and regulations of the Church. To quote Campion again, 'Here was the concrete and steel of doctrine which lay under the airy constructions of popular piety'.[106]

In 1938 Beovich also wrote and published the *Companion to the Catechism*. He tried to do for students in grades six to nine what Callanan had done for infant classes in *And Forbid Them Not!*: set the study of the catechism amidst Bible readings, class discussions and various activities. The *Companion* provides little relief for those who might find the 'steel' of the catechism too rigid. The doctrinal unity, discipline and authority structures of the Catholic Church are proudly presented as marks of the 'true Church'. For Richard Selleck, the *Companion* illustrates the 'massive and slightly frightening certainty about Catholic teachings' which is a characteristic of this period. He believes this was an Irish legacy: 'It is easy to understand how religious beliefs preserved in Ireland through times of persecution came to have a hard and unrelenting quality;

but it is a pity those beliefs drifted in less difficult times into an obstinate dogmatism.'[107] In fact, Beovich was much more influenced by *Romanità*. It has been said of cultured English Catholics in the 1930s, including some of the great intellectuals of the 'Chesterbelloc' era, that:

> In a critical sense they were rather ahistorical and atheological: that is to say they accepted the current Roman Catholic position in doctrine and practice as almost unquestioningly right in all its details, and argued accordingly. Its very authoritativeness was what appealed. They found in it a sure framework for spiritual progress, literary creativity and political stability, but also for an ordered and coherent view of the world to replace the increasing intellectual and ideological confusion evident outside the walls.[108]

This was also very true of Matthew Beovich. As a result, the major weakness of the *Companion* is that it gives few theological and historical explanations. Doctrines like the Trinity are simply presented as mysteries which have to be accepted. In spite of Dwyer's insistence that students would not understand it, the term 'sanctifying grace' was retained in the catechism. Dwyer would hardly have been satisfied by the elaboration in the *Companion*:

> Each Sacrament gives two kinds of grace:
> 1. Sanctifying grace, which is either first given, restored or increased.
> 2. Sacramental grace, by which is meant the right to special actual graces proper to each Sacrament.[109]

Callanan advised teachers to encourage children to reflect on their experiences. Beovich also included 'discussion questions' but many have only one right answer or the students are clearly steered in a certain direction. Overall, the *Companion* lacks the warmth of *And Forbid Them Not!*, although this was in part deliberate. As Beovich explained in his paper at the 1936 Catholic Education Congress, in the junior grades religious education should be aimed primarily at the heart, while older students could approach it from a more intellectual perspective.

The best chapters of the *Companion* are those at the end where Beovich departed from the catechism text. In the penultimate chapter he explained the meaning of the word 'liturgy' and described the liturgical year with its different seasons and feast days. In keeping with more advanced contemporary liturgical scholarship, he emphasised that the Mass was not a time for Catholics to engage in private devotions; rather, it was the public offering of worship by the whole Catholic community and therefore required active participation. United in prayer with the priest and one another, Catholics could join with Christ in offering themselves – including their hopes, joys and sorrows – to the Father. Catholicism as a religion of the heart as well as law began to emerge again.

The final chapter reveals that Beovich was also familiar with the latest developments in the Church's social teaching. In Melbourne Catholic intellectual circles the concept of 'Catholic Action' became popular in the 1930s. As its leading proponent B. A. Santamaria eventually conceded, it was never possible to define exactly what Catholic Action meant because there were two main variants in Europe.[110] In Italy the concept principally implied defending the interests of the Church. Clerical control and traditional devotional practices loomed large, although this was largely determined by the political situation. Catholics in fascist Italy were obviously limited in what 'action' they could undertake. As part of the negotiations with Mussolini's government which led to the Lateran Treaties of 1929, Pius XI affirmed the purely religious character of Catholic Action and its dependence on the hierarchy.[111] Yet he also approved a rather different brand of Catholic Action. In Belgium in the mid-1920s a Catholic priest, Joseph Cardijn, founded the Young Christian Workers (Jeunnesse Oeuvriere Chretienne or JOC) and the Young Christian Students (Jeunnesse Etudiante Chretienne or JEC). These movements soon spread, encouraging young workers and students to meet in study groups to 'See' (analyse their life situations), 'Judge' (consider, in relation to the gospel, what needed to be done to bring them more into line with Christian values) and 'Act' (take initiatives to bring about change). The Jocist model encouraged a form of discipleship which went beyond the traditional blend of good works and piety of most Catholic organisations. Integral to it was a vision of ongoing adult faith formation taking place as faith was put into action. It was this model which took strongest root in Melbourne, albeit not without some difficulty.[112]

In his chapter on Catholic Action at the end of the *Companion*, Beovich gave the standard definition of Pius XI: 'Catholic Action is the participation of the laity in the apostolate of the Church's Hierarchy.' He explained that this 'simply means that Catholics, under the guidance of their spiritual rulers, would help their neighbours in particular and members of society in general to know, love and serve God', a piously vague statement in keeping with the Italian model. However, Beovich then moved to a more radical notion: 'All are called to be apostles of Catholic Action ... the pope wishes that the apostles of children would be children; the apostles of workmen would be workmen; the apostles of seamen would be seamen ...' In the questions for discussion at the end of the chapter, he encouraged the children to reflect on ways they could be apostles to other children. As a project, they were asked to 'form a special study group ... Appoint a chairman, secretary, etc. The Teacher may be present, but will be there merely to help you, not to take charge of your meetings.' Some, at least, of the Jocist method was getting through.

Publisher, Radio Broadcaster, Public Speaker and Cathedral Priest

Beovich's mission to propagate the faith was not confined to children. In April 1925 Mannix, as president, appointed Beovich secretary/editor of the Australian Catholic Truth Society (ACTS). Modelled on similar societies overseas, the ACTS had been founded in 1904 to publish 'a very cheap literature of first-class quality, which, while counteracting the influence of anti-Catholic and anti-Christian writings, will help build up a more enlightened and more fervent Catholic spirit'.[113] Beovich took over the running of the ACTS at a time when it was experiencing deep financial difficulties and had almost ceased to exist. He embarked on a 'Forward Movement' to increase the number of pamphlets in circulation, with the help of another newcomer to the ACTS executive, Frank Moynihan, editor of the *Advocate*. Moynihan proclaimed in an editorial in 1925 that 'it would be difficult to find anywhere the equal of the little two-penny pamphlets which the Society publishes ... [each] is a little treasure-house of Catholic Truth, whose gems may be extracted by the least learned reader'.[114]

The Forward Movement soon produced results. During the quarter which ended on 31 August 1925 a record 50,000 pamphlets were sold in Australia and New Zealand.[115] Overall, in 1925 annual subscribers and life members received thirty new pamphlets.[116] Beovich met this goal again in 1926 and 1927, and while he published only twenty-eight in 1928 (plus six reprints) the actual number of pamphlets sold in that year had increased from 178,671 in 1925 to 358,143 (a figure which does not include 62,500 sales of the catechism and prayer book which the ACTS was also responsible for publishing).[117]

In contrast to the practice in the early years of the society, many of Beovich's pamphlets were written by Australian authors, not reprinted from British and Irish Truth Society publications. Popular children's author Agatha Le Breton contributed stories such as the one about 'Father Tom' who became a priest in spite of falling into scrapes as a child and not liking vegetables.[118] A considerable number of pamphlets were directed at non-Catholics and controversial aspects of Catholic doctrine. Thus Marian devotion was explained lest the misunderstanding persist that Catholics worshipped Mary as they did God.[119] A convert from Methodism shared the dread she experienced at the thought of confessing her sins to a priest, and the comfort and strength which she subsequently derived from the sacrament.[120] Albert Power, the first rector of Corpus Christi College, the Victorian seminary, assured potential converts that Catholics did not blindly follow Church teaching, as was sometimes alleged, but based their convictions on evidence, reliable testimony and reasonable arguments.[121] Henry Johnson, the second rector of Corpus Christi, extolled the advantages which the Catholic Church possessed over Protestant 'sects': its world-wide spread, its unity, its doctrinal stability and its New Testament foundations.[122]

As well as increased sales in pamphlets in the mid-1920s, another gratifying trend was the rise in annual membership from 1784 in 1925 to 6030 in 1928. Most of the four thousand new members were enrolled after Beovich and a fellow priest, Bernard Geoghegan, conducted a 'membership drive' in 1927 and 1928 which involved visiting twenty-eight parishes in the archdiocese of Melbourne.[123] There was a further slight increase in sales and membership in 1929, the year the ACTS celebrated its twenty-fifth anniversary.[124] From then on the Depression began to bite. In 1933 more than a quarter of Catholic working men were unemployed.[125] The number of pamphlets sold dropped to almost half the 1928 figure, and membership went down to 2697. However, even though printing costs had risen, the price of the pamphlets had not, and income just exceeded expenditure. This was considered 'most satisfactory' in the circumstances.[126]

A number of pamphlets addressed the economic crisis. Beovich published one by the American Jesuit Daniel Lord. He attributed the collapse of the economy to pride, arrogance and idolatry. Spoilt children have to be chastised, and 'even a catastrophe like this may be only His [God's] way of reminding mankind that they are still His beloved, if wayward, children'.[127] Another pamphlet eschewed pious glosses and gave serious consideration to deficiencies in both capitalism and communism.[128] One of the last issued by Beovich attempted to convince parents of school children that even in difficult economic times so-called 'frill subjects' like music, history and drawing should not be abandoned in favour of those deemed more likely to lead to paid employment.[129]

A weakness of the ACTS was that, although it had been established as a national society, it was much stronger in the Melbourne diocese where it was based than anywhere else.[130] There was obviously a distribution problem. In a survey of Catholic literature published in the *Australasian Catholic Record* in 1930, T. A. Murphy claimed that ACTS pamphlets were only available for sale in about 40 per cent of parishes in New South Wales, and even when there were ACTS boxes in church porches, some were so carelessly maintained that it was no wonder that sales were poor.[131] Moynihan lamented in an *Advocate* editorial that even in Melbourne there were parishes without a box.[132] Beovich was aware of the problem, and removed responsibility for distributing pamphlets from the St Vincent de Paul Society and gave it to a new 'Box Tenders' Association' which he established in 1928.[133] This was not one of his better ideas. In later years he joked wryly that, having given the St Vincent de Paul Society the sack, he then had to beg for its help again.[134] Perhaps that was why Mannix singled out the Society for special praise at the 1929 annual meeting.[135]

Tributes were also paid to the secretary/editor at ACTS annual meetings. Mannix maintained in 1926 that while every member of the executive committee deserved thanks,

> the greater part of the credit for the success achieved by the society was due to Dr Beovich. (Applause). No doubt he (his Grace) could take some of the credit himself, because from many good people he had chosen Dr Beovich. Although Dr Beovich had only been a short time in office, he had proved that excellent goods were made up sometimes in small parcels.[136]

In 1927, after acknowledging the work of the writers and the members of the executive, Mannix concluded:

> If I were to select anybody for special commendation, gratitude and praise, it would be the very retiring and modest, but most efficient secretary, Dr Beovich. (Applause.) If I ever have a tendency to slacken in my devotion to the interests of the society, Dr Beovich is at hand to give me warning. (Laughter and applause.) He is always ready with some new plan to further the interests of the society, and I must say that he has never put anything before me that did not secure my commendation.[137]

One of the lay members of the executive committee, Joseph Fitzgerald, asserted at the 1928 meeting that the secretary 'did his work silently and unobtrusively, but most efficaciously. He very rarely troubled the executive, and everything that was done was practically prepared by him'.[138]

The twenty-fifth anniversary of the society in 1929 brought more praise for the secretary. The *Advocate* reflected:

> The present splendid condition of the society is due to the work during the last few years of Dr Beovich, whose quiet, unobtrusive manner cannot mask his possession of great ability and tireless energy. It is only those who know something of the work entailed in the administration of the Catholic Truth Society who can fully appreciate the very great labour that falls to Dr Beovich's lot – and it is truly a great labour.[139]

Mannix once again expressed his gratitude:

> To every member of the committee he was deeply thankful, but he was especially thankful to the most modest and most efficient member of all the committee, the Rev. Dr Beovich, the secretary of the society. Dr Beovich devoted himself to the work of the society with an energy that he did not believe he possessed, and he gave an amount of time to the duties of office that no other priest in the archdiocese could afford. In a short time Dr Beovich had achieved a success that was altogether beyond his highest expectations.[140]

An edited version of Mannix's speech was included in the pamphlet celebrating the ACTS anniversary: 'To every member of the executive committee he was deeply thankful. In a short time the executive had achieved a success that was altogether beyond his highest expectations.'[141] That is an example, no doubt, of the secretary/editor's famous modesty!

At the annual ACTS meeting in 1933 it was announced that Beovich had resigned as secretary and been succeeded by Frank Moynihan. Mannix stressed that this was not because Beovich had lost the confidence of the society, but because his other duties had become too heavy. In addition to his work in Catholic education, he now 'had a great deal to do with the Catholic Hour'.[142] This was a programme which commenced on radio station 3AW on Sunday 10 April 1932, and ran weekly from 9 to 10 pm.[143] It was divided into three sections interspersed with music. The first was devoted to general interest topics and current events; the second consisted of a lecture on an aspect of Catholic doctrine; and the third, 'the Question Box', dealt with listeners' queries on matters related to the Catholic Church. As was the case with ACTS pamphlets, non-Catholics were very much part of the target audience, along with Catholics whose faith might need some encouragement.[144] Beovich was a member of the committee responsible for running 'The Catholic Hour' and was for some time the anonymous 'Onlooker' who spoke about current affairs.[145]

Beovich's 'delightful voice' was not only heard on Sunday evenings, as he was the announcer and commentator at numerous Masses and functions which were broadcast from St Patrick's Cathedral in the 1930s. The most significant of these were the ceremonies for the Eucharistic Congress in 1934 and the celebrations to mark the centenary of the first Mass in Melbourne in 1939.[146] Beovich was also invited to be the guest speaker at a range of functions. He told Cardinal Van Rossum that whenever giving a lecture he always remembered the advice he had been given in Rome, 'to speak constantly of Our Lord in the Blessed Eucharist, on devotion to the Mother of God, and on the Papacy'.[147] His years in Rome came in very useful – he was able to deliver various versions of 'a highly interesting lecture on reminiscences of Popes Benedict XV and Pius XI', illustrated with lantern slides.[148]

As he lived in the presbytery alongside the cathedral, Beovich often assisted the cathedral priests by saying Mass and hearing confessions. Occasionally he also instructed new converts and visited the sick. The presbytery was 'a bit institutional', but the priests who lived there must have developed something like the camaraderie of the Propaganda *camerata* groups. One priest remembers Beovich as cheerful and easygoing, a willing participant in cricket matches on the asphalt yard in the adjourning St Patrick's College.[149] He never learnt to drive a car, so to get to Catholic schools he took a train, tram and/or briskly walked. No longer subject to Prop discipline, he became a chain smoker, often taking two cigarettes out of the packet at the same time (the second was wedged behind an ear ready to light from the first before it died out). He shared a keen sense of humour with his archbishop, although, to Mannix's frustration, Beovich invariably messed up the punch line of a joke.[150] Mannix lived in solitary splendour in a mansion in Kew, but he walked daily to St Patrick's so Beovich had frequent contact with him.

The hawkish bishop who soared above administrative detail and the conscientious, dove-like priest clearly made a good team. In Rome, Beovich had observed a different style of leadership from the decentralised form of administration favoured by his archbishop. However, he did not embrace a 'Roman view of the Church, in which all power was concentrated at the top and only sparingly parceled out'.[151] He had a Roman view of the essentially catholic or universal nature of the Church, and wanted Catholic school teachers, especially those from religious orders, to have a greater sense that they were part of a common enterprise. He took

Mannix's advice that it was better to ride a horse with a light rein, but tried to make sure that all the Catholic horses were on the same track and running in the same direction.

As for the children who attended Catholic schools in the archdiocese of Melbourne, no doubt a considerable number later abandoned the practice of their faith, as Turner points out; but in others the seeds which were sown in the 1920s and 1930s took strong root. A Presentation Sister still remembers fondly the excitement generated by Beovich's visit to her school in 1928, and the 'great praise' he gave her when she correctly answered a question which no one else attempted. 'I think his kindness towards me, a nervous child, really supported me,' Winefride Murphy recalls.[152] Statistical evidence from the 1960s indicates that there was a correlation between Catholic schooling and religious belief and practice:

> Those who have attended Catholic schools score more highly on religious variables than the others. More go to church regularly, more pray regularly, more believe in God, more are of the opinion that the church is appointed by God and more are likely to have had religious experiences.[153]

Beovich at least had no doubt that this was the case. In a report to Rome he proudly described the Catholic school system as 'the glory of the Catholic Church in Australia'.[154]

Given Mannix's tendency to leave priests in positions indefinitely, Beovich could well have looked forward in 1939 to many more busy and fulfilling years propagating the faith in the archdiocese of Melbourne. However, in June 1939 Archbishop Andrew Killian of Adelaide died while undergoing surgery in Melbourne. The new pope, Pius XII, had to appoint a successor. In September Beovich's former Propaganda classmate, Norman Gilroy, invited him to Sydney, supposedly to brief the apostolic delegate on education matters. Beovich went in total innocence, never suspecting that he was really attending a job interview.[155]

FOUR
'Calling God Back to the Council Chambers' Adelaide During the War

Dr Matthew Beovich is to be consecrated to the high office of Archbishop of Adelaide. The occasion seems opportune to recall to our minds the tremendous authority and dignity with which a Christian bishop is clothed, and the awful responsibility which he assumes in the sight of God and men: for, throughout the history of the Church, the story of her long battle with the world has been, to a very great extent, the story of the success or failure, courage or weakness, wisdom or unwisdom of those shepherds to whom is committed the task of feeding and guiding the flock of Christ.

Editorial, *Advocate*, 4 April 1940

On Tuesday, 12 December 1939, Matthew Beovich was marking scholarship exam papers in the Catholic Education Office in Melbourne when the telephone rang. It was Frank Moynihan, editor of the *Advocate*, with congratulations:

'What for?' 'You are appointed to Adelaide!' I assure him there must be some strange mistake ... the whole thing is absurd. Then several other rings follow: Dr Lyons, Fr Murtagh, Fr Hannan. I ask Fr Hannan to ring the Delegation & advise them of the strange rumours. He does so, then twenty minutes later the Apostolic Delegate (Dr Panico) is on the phone from Sydney. He tells me the same rumours are current in Sydney but he has received no official word. I suggest the report is impossible. He says it is not impossible but meanwhile to see no one &

> keep the report from the newspapers until he gets through to Rome. I go out on the balcony to get some fresh air & for the first time feel that 'sinking feeling'.[1]

Adelaide in 1940

In 1940 the Catholic diocese of Adelaide was just two years short of its centenary.[2] It had been formally established in 1842, only six years after the official proclamation of the colony of South Australia. Its first bishop, Francis Murphy, was consecrated in Sydney in 1844: the first episcopal consecration in Australia. His appointment was due to the distance of the new colony from Sydney – it was not a reflection of the size and affluence of the Catholic community, which consisted of about 1200 people, nearly all of them labourers and their families who met for worship in a rented warehouse. By Murphy's death in 1858 the Catholic population had grown to about 14,000 and the infant diocese had twelve missionary priests and seven chapels.[3] In 1887 the third bishop of Adelaide, Christopher Reynolds, was raised to an archbishop when a suffragan diocese was established in the north of South Australia with its headquarters at Port Augusta, but both dioceses were crippled by debt. Later the diocese of Darwin in the Northern Territory was added to the province of South Australia, but while the archbishop was entitled to precedence at any provincial meetings, he had no real jurisdictional authority outside his own diocese. In 1940 this extended along the south of the Australian continent from the Victorian border in the east to Eyre Peninsula in the west, and to the Riverland and Spalding in the mid-north.

Catholics were a small minority in nineteenth-century South Australia. Never a penal settlement, the colony was strongly influenced by English Protestant dissent. The 1901 census revealed that while the Church of England (the Anglican Church) was the largest denomination in the state, as it was elsewhere in Australia, the percentage of Anglicans (29.5) was lower than the national average (39.7), whereas the percentages for the Methodists (24.9), Baptists (6.0), Congregationalists (3.7) and Churches of Christ (1.7) were considerably higher.[4] Lutherans (7.2 per cent) were also present in unusually large numbers in the Adelaide Hills and the Barossa Valley.[5] Catholics made up the third largest religious group, with 14.4 per cent of the population, well behind the Anglicans and the Methodists and the national Catholic average (22.7). Most were of Irish descent. In the metropolitan areas, two-thirds of Catholics lived in the inner city of Adelaide and the municipalities of Port Adelaide, Hindmarsh and Thebarton, working-class suburbs on the unfashionable western side of the city where six of the ten city parishes were located.[6] The Catholic cathedral, named in honour of the sixteenth-century Jesuit missionary Francis Xavier, and built in the austere Early English Gothic style, was opened in 1858 in the centre of the city, just off Victoria Square, and extended in the late 1880s.[7] It lacked the commanding grandeur of other examples of the nineteenth-century Gothic revival in Adelaide, most notably the Anglican St Peter's Cathedral in its imposing location at the top of King William Road.

By 1940 there were signs of improvement. Further extensions to St Francis Xavier Cathedral, including a new façade and the bottom stages of a tower, were opened in 1926 (the tower was not completed until 1996). Impressive new churches at Glenelg (in classical style) and Hindmarsh (Romanesque) were also built in the 1920s. More Catholics were moving into the more affluent eastern and southern suburbs where new parishes had been created (Kingswood and Colonel Light Gardens were formed in 1923 and 1928 respectively, Dulwich, Hectorville and St Peters in 1934).[8] Twenty-four Catholic schools were offering secondary education. Those for boys included the Christian Brothers' Colleges at Rostrevor and Wakefield Street, Adelaide, and Sacred Heart College run by the Marist Brothers at Paringa Park.[9] Prominent among the convent schools for girls were those run by the Dominican Sisters at Clarence Park and North Adelaide, the Mercy Sisters in Angas Street in the city, and the Loreto Sisters at Marryatville.[10]

Some pupils from the Catholic colleges were going on to study at the University of Adelaide. By 1940 there were a number of Catholic lawyers in Adelaide, including Albert Hannan (the crown solicitor), Leo Travers, George Culshaw, Kevin McEntee and Roma Mitchell. Harry Alderman was appointed a King's Counsel in 1943. An adviser to the Commonwealth Government during the war years and confidant of Prime Minister Ben Chifley, Alderman was knighted shortly before his death in 1962. Edmund Britten Jones, who won a Rhodes scholarship in 1912 and was knighted in 1953, was a leading member of the medical profession. Dominic Paul McGuire and his wife Margaret were successful authors. Later McGuire would become a friend of Premier Thomas Playford and a personal advisor to Prime Minister Robert Menzies, and have a diplomatic career. Archie Cameron, a convert to Catholicism from rural South Australia, was a prominent member of the Country Party and later the Liberal Party. He was deputy-prime minister in 1940. There were a few affluent Catholic farmers, most notably Anthony and Lucy Sutton in the South-East and John and Mary Fennescey, originally from Yorke Peninsula.[11]

On the other hand, the 1933 census indicated that the proportion of South Australians claiming allegiance to the Catholic Church had dropped from a high of 15.4 per cent in 1871 to only 11.95 per cent, the lowest percentage of Catholics in any state in Australia (the national average in 1933 was 19.6). Two thirds of South Australians still identified themselves as either Anglican or a member of one of the nonconformist Protestant denominations. The Catholic Church remained the third largest denomination, with 69,445 adherents, but it was well behind the Methodist Church (127,978) and the Church of England (164,531). As late as the 1947 census there were still more Catholics in the inner city (22 per cent) and western suburbs like Thebarton (19 per cent) than the prestigious residential suburbs of Burnside (10.6) and Mitcham (8.8). Catholics were thinly scattered through rural districts, except for the South-East where they were slightly more numerous (22 per cent of the population of Mount Gambier in 1947).[12]

Catholics were not well represented in the state's business and professional elite. Despite the growing number of lawyers in the Catholic community, the first Catholic to be appointed a judge of the Supreme Court of South Australia was James Brazel, and that did not happen until 1959. Thomas Playford began his twenty-six years as premier in 1938, and until 1953 there were no Catholics in his Liberal and Country League government. There were some Catholics in the Australian Labor Party, but the leader of the opposition in the House of Assembly in 1940 was Robert Richards, a former mine-worker of Cornish ancestry and a Methodist lay-preacher. While the Playford era was not the Protestant golden age that it has sometimes been depicted as, in the 1940s vocal Protestant lobby groups had a considerable impact on public life, successfully restricting, for example, the availability of alcohol and gambling.[13]

Playford's background was Baptist, his real religion arguably Freemasonry.[14] Behind the scenes, the business and professional leaders who met at the Freemasons' Hall on North Terrace exerted an influence which was more subtle than that of the lobby groups but possibly even more effective. It is surely more than a coincidence that almost all the members of the judiciary were Freemasons. 'Indeed,' comments Stewart Cockburn in his biography of Playford, 'it could be said that during the first half of the twentieth century membership of a Masonic Lodge was part of the prescription of eligibility which many ambitious lawyers at the South Australian Bar would have seen as prudent to acquire along the way in their drive towards ultimate promotion.'[15] Freemasonry contained within it a current of anti-Catholicism, reciprocating the way it was loathed and feared in the Catholic community. Mannix once described it as 'a huge tumor growing upon the life and the blood of the whole of the country'.[16] Whatever the real strength of the Freemasonry network, this period is remembered by many Catholics as a time when discrimination on the grounds of religious allegiance was widespread, even if public demonstrations of bigotry were rare.

That overt sectarian bigotry was muted in Adelaide was largely due to the leadership of successive Catholic bishops. The wise and practical John O'Reily (1894–1915) established good relations with leading members of Adelaide society. The chief justice, Sir Samuel Way (a prominent Freemason and member of the Methodist Church) considered him a friend, the Anglican bishop Nutter Thomas found him lovable and kind, and the Methodist editor of the *Advertiser*, John Langdon Bonython, acknowledged his 'broadness of mind, responsible to a large extent for the excellent relationship between the two great divisions of the Christian Church'.[17] O'Reily's more reserved successor, Robert Spence (1914–1934), made a speech in Ireland in 1920 which caused a flurry of controversy in Adelaide because he condemned atrocities committed by British troops, but on political matters he usually 'kept a low profile and prudent silence'.[18] The genial and gregarious Andrew Killian (1934–1939) also focused mainly on internal diocesan administration.[19]

The 'ghetto' tendency within Catholicism in this period should not be exaggerated. As David Hilliard points out:

> The Catholic subculture was never a total or enclosed system. For the inner core of devout Catholics the church was the centre of their social world, while for others their involvement went little further than attendance at Sunday Mass. A great many Catholics – perhaps half the number of those recorded in the census – were casual about religion or had 'lapsed'.[20]

Yet while this was doubtless the case, it was the unity and distinctive beliefs of the Catholic Church which were put on display in 1936 during the highlight of Killian's reign, the National Catholic Education Congress. Although the congress was the Catholic Church's contribution to South Australia's centenary celebrations, it reflected and reinforced a sense of Catholic distinctiveness and separation from the wider, predominantly Protestant community.

On 8 November 1936 Catholic dignitaries and educationalists from around Australia, including Matthew Beovich, gathered in Adelaide for a week of lectures, rallies and associated functions.[21] There was a ball in the Palais Royal on North Terrace, a garden party at Loreto Convent, and special socials organised by the Catholic Young Men's Society and the Hibernian-Australasian Catholic Benefit Society. Catholic school children performed in a 'Thousand Voices Concert' in the new Centennial Hall in Wayville, the largest such venue in the state. The week culminated in a Eucharistic procession along King William Street from the cathedral to the university oval. Between 60,000 and 100,000 people braved inclement weather to watch or participate in the procession which took almost an hour to pass. It was a rare opportunity for the relatively small Catholic community in South Australia to indulge in a little triumphalism.

What particularly struck Beovich was the sight, as he returned to Melbourne, of a motor lorry on its way to the small country town of Pinnaroo, not far from the Victorian border. Its cargo: a parish priest with a group of Catholic men, women and children on their way home from the congress. That lorry load of Catholics enduring the discomfort of a long drive home was, he thought, an eloquent testimony to 'the bond of loyalty and cooperation between the archbishop, priests and people of Adelaide and South Australia'.[22]

By the time Andrew Killian died on 28 June 1939, there were 43 parishes in the archdiocese of Adelaide, 111 churches, 64 diocesan priests (five of them retired or on permanent sick leave), an additional 33 priests in religious orders, 48 religious brothers and 565 religious sisters. A third of the latter were Sisters of St Joseph of the Sacred Heart, the religious institute founded by Mary MacKillop and an Adelaide diocesan priest, Julian Tenison Woods, at Penola in south-eastern South Australia in 1866. There was one Catholic hospital, two orphanages, 56 parish primary schools, and 25 other schools with a combined total of 7218 primary and secondary students.[23] As it approached its centenary, the diocese was solidly established, but still small in comparison with the archdiocese of Melbourne.[24] Melbourne was, of course, a much larger city, with almost a million inhabitants. The 1933 census revealed Adelaide had just over 300,000.

Another significant difference was that the archdiocese of Melbourne had its own seminary, Corpus Christi College at Werribee, which opened in 1923. Adelaide had no such facility. Archbishops Spence and Killian preferred to recruit priests from Ireland rather than encourage local vocations. As a result, two-thirds of Adelaide's diocesan priests in 1939 (44 out of 65) were from Ireland. Only fourteen were native South Australians. Of those ordained in the 1930s, seventeen were from Ireland and only four from South Australia (Luke Roberts and Edward Smyth had studied for the priesthood at Manly; Patrick Kelly at Werribee and John Honnor at Mosgiel in New Zealand). The average age of the diocesan priests was 44, the same as their new archbishop by the time of his consecration.[25]

Archbishop Elect

The telephone call from Frank Moynihan on 12 December 1939 alerted Beovich to the rumour that he was to be the next archbishop of Adelaide. He had to wait until the next evening for the apostolic delegate, John Panico, to ring with confirmation of the news from the Vatican. The confusion had arisen because the plane carrying the papal bull of appointment had crashed into the sea near Java. The mailbag was eventually retrieved, and on 14 March 1940 Beovich received the barely decipherable document.[26]

On Thursday, 14 December 1939, Beovich travelled to Sydney to meet Panico who had been responsible for recommending his appointment to Pope Pius XII.[27] In line with Vatican policy, Panico made the development of an Australian-born hierarchy one of his particular concerns after his arrival in Australia in 1936. In the process he alienated some of the priests and bishops who had come from Ireland.[28] His relationship with Daniel Mannix was notoriously poor. In 1939 he was yet to impose a coadjutor archbishop on Mannix (the unfortunate Justin Simonds was appointed in 1942). However, Mannix resented Panico's role in the resignation of Michael Sheehan in 1937, which paved the way for Norman Gilroy's elevation to the archbishopric of Sydney,[29] and 'Panicky Jack' was already the butt of his wicked sense of humour.[30] After the second call from Panico, Beovich went to see his archbishop. Mannix expressed surprise at the appointment (he had clearly not been consulted) but he was, nevertheless, 'kindness itself'. Beovich told him that he had decided to ask the apostolic delegate to consecrate him.[31] He cannot have been unaware of Mannix's low opinion of Panico, but the apostolic delegate was the pope's representative in Australia, and that was what mattered to Beovich. He was not sure where the ceremony should be held: Melbourne or Adelaide. Mannix recommended Adelaide, wise advice as it enabled more Catholics of the Adelaide archdiocese to share in the celebration. It also ensured that Mannix was not upstaged by Panico in his own cathedral.

CONSECRATION

After a holiday in the Bathurst diocese with his friend from Propaganda days, Alf Gummer,[32] and various farewell functions,[33] Matt Beovich left Melbourne on 3 April 1940. Dan Conquest drove his car to Adelaide with a 'relaxed' Beovich beside him. A much more nervous Pat Lyons sat in the back, alongside Jim O'Collins, as the car hurtled along the Great Ocean Road. Taking the long scenic route to Adelaide, they stopped in Port Campbell and Robe before arriving in Adelaide on Friday, 5 April.[34] Lyons was the administrator of St Patrick's Cathedral in Melbourne, chancellor of the Melbourne archdiocese and Mannix's secretary. O'Collins had been bishop of Geraldton in Western Australia since 1930. He had chosen to be consecrated by Mannix in St Patrick's Cathedral, perhaps because Geraldton was too far away for most of his friends and family to visit. He had gone to his remote north-western diocese accompanied only by Matt Beovich.[35] Now, ten years later, it was fitting that he should accompany Beovich to Adelaide.

O'Collins once remarked that the only time in his life he suffered from depression was the day in June 1930 when, after a long journey from Melbourne, he reached his new frontier diocese in Western Australia. Beovich had to coax him out of the train to greet well-wishers.[36] There is no evidence that Beovich was similarly afflicted in 1940. On the contrary, he enthusiastically entered into a whirl of functions, the most important being his episcopal consecration on Sunday, 7 April 1940.

Adelaide's modest Catholic cathedral was crowded for the consecration. Loudspeakers in the cathedral grounds ensured that those who could not get a seat inside could still hear the proceedings. It was also broadcast on the radio.[37] Beovich's Propaganda classmates Gilroy and O'Collins assisted Panico, and Justin Simonds delivered the sermon. Mannix and the bishops of Ballarat, Sandhurst, Sale, Wilcannia-Forbes, Wagga Wagga, Port Augusta and Lismore were also present, along with a large contingent of Melbourne priests and fellow Propagandists from around Australia.

Appropriately, Beovich received his crozier or pastoral staff, one of the most ancient symbols of his office, on Good Shepherd Sunday. As he handed it over, Panico would have uttered the words: 'Receive this staff of the pastoral office, that in the correction of wrong-doing thou mayest temper severity with kindness, and exercise judgment without anger; and that in fostering virtue thou may soothe the minds of thy hearers, without neglecting, in thy mildness, the strictness of reproof'.[38] In his sermon, Simonds assured the Catholics of Adelaide that 'Above all, you have in your new archbishop a man of kindly and sympathetic nature, one who is not disposed to break the bruised reed'.[39] Beovich also received a ring as a symbol of his fidelity to the Church, a mitre as a 'helmet of defence and salvation', and gloves signifying the purity which was required of those dispensing the sacraments. The Book of the Gospels was held open across his shoulders, then presented to him with the instruction to 'go forth and preach it to the people committed to thee'. As the choir sang the 'Te Deum', the assistant bishops in their mitres escorted Beovich around the cathedral while he blessed the congregation, starting with his mother, brother Frank and sister Vera. A reporter from the *Advertiser* described the three-hour-long ceremony as 'a solemn, impressive ritual'.[40] To the embarrassment of her superior general, one of Beovich's friends from Melbourne, Sister Emilian McLaughlin, principal of St Ita's, Fitzroy, kept standing up on the kneeler so she did not miss anything.[41]

In 1940 episcopal consecration was understood primarily in terms of the conferral of divinely instituted powers. As Frank Moynihan explained in his editorial in the *Advocate* on 4 April 1940, when bishops gathered to lay hands on a new member of the hierarchy, in unbroken succession from the apostles, they passed on the authority to teach, rule and sanctify:

> Within that sphere – his diocese – the bishop is the veritable representative of Christ, the Good Shepherd: hence his office is of a unique importance, transcending all merely political and lay dignity ... Such is the great and holy office to which a beloved priest from our midst is to be dedicated next Sunday: and it is one which no wise mortal being would dare to undertake were he not assured that, together with the powers conferred by the act of consecration, there is also abundance of grace to strengthen the bishop for this mighty task.

In his farewell speech to the children of the Melbourne archdiocese, Beovich expressed his confidence in God's grace.[42] With or without divine intervention, that positive outlook may have helped overcome his natural shyness. Recalling his visit to Adelaide in 1940, Conquest reflected:

> My chief impression was that the consecration as a bishop changed Matt in some mysterious way. He had always been kind of diffident, you know, but after the consecration ... he was full of confidence,

> outgoing ... If somebody had said to me beforehand, 'Do you think Matt will be nervous?', I would have said, 'I think that he will'. But he didn't give the slightest impression of being nervous. He was in command of everything, and he was quite happy to be archbishop. It was wonderful![43]

Following his consecration Beovich received the pallium, the ancient symbol of the link between an archbishop and the papacy.[44] In the evening a dinner for the priests of the archdiocese and visiting members of the hierarchy and clergy was held at Cabra Dominican convent. Panico expressed his pleasure at being able to consecrate such a distinguished Australian-born and Roman-educated priest. Beovich's speech was summarised in the *Southern Cross*:

> It was his great fortune to have gone to Rome, where he came close to the Holy Father and learned in a way not possible to those who had not lived in Rome what devotion to the Vicar of Christ really meant. 'When the startling news of my appointment came my first thought was to ask His Excellency the Apostolic Delegate to do me the honour of consecrating me.'

Mannix had his revenge on Panico. He referred to his archdiocese's 'big export trade in bishops', and said that he felt sure that Melbourne could also supply an Australian-born apostolic delegate when the next vacancy occurred.[45]

Official Welcomes and First Speeches

A new bishop, especially if he comes from another diocese, can expect his first speeches to be subjected to particular scrutiny as Catholics seek clues to his leadership style and plans for their church. In his address to the priests of the Adelaide archdiocese on Sunday evening, 7 April 1940, Beovich left no doubt about his loyalty and devotion to the pope. The following day he celebrated his first Mass in St Francis Xavier Cathedral. He made clear his commitment to Catholic education by asking William Russell, the diocesan inspector of schools, to arrange for school children to be present, with the result that over two thousand pupils were crowded into the building. After the Mass, he spoke in the friendly way with which he was wont to address children:

> You know, some children are blessed by God with intelligence above the ordinary, and others have not so many talents. Personally my sympathy is with those who have fewer talents; but whether you be at the top of the class or the bottom of the class (of course, some people may be at the bottom of the class because they are lazy; I do not know if the children of South Australia are somewhat lazy; I should think not), if one does one's best and then fails in the examination, what does it matter? The point that matters is that you will not fail when we appear before the judgment seat of God.[46]

In the years ahead, parents and teachers would find that the priority of religious education over examination results would be a recurring theme in Beovich's speeches.[47]

From the Mass in the cathedral it was a short walk across Victoria Square to the Adelaide Town Hall where the lord mayor hosted a civic reception in the new archbishop's honour. In response to the lord mayor's welcome, Beovich assured the gathering that he now considered himself a citizen of South Australia, and would acquire a greater love for Adelaide and South Australia than he had for the state of his birth.[48] The next day, when he was guest of honour at the Catholic Luncheon Club, he reaffirmed his enthusiasm for his new state and flagged his intention to participate in civic life: 'I hope to contribute as best I may to the legitimate aspirations of this city and state.'[49] On the Sunday after his consecration he met the premier, Thomas Playford, at the blessing and laying of the foundation stone of the new maternity wing at Calvary Hospital. In his speech, Playford assured the new archbishop that South Australians were tolerant and willing to work together for the common good. Beovich, in turn, expressed his appreciation of 'the sympathy of the non-Catholic people. Evidently there was a fine spirit of unity between the different bodies of citizens in Adelaide, and he hoped that such harmony would remain'.[50] He clearly had no intention of confining himself to a Catholic ghetto but was prepared to engage with the wider, predominantly Protestant community.

On the evening of Monday, 8 April 1940, children from various Catholic schools presented a musical programme to the new archbishop at the Tivoli Theatre. After they finished, representatives of the Catholic laity presented him with a special address of loyalty and welcome. In response, Beovich acknowledged that he had 'an onerous position. The mantle of His Grace Archbishop Killian, so kind and gentle and patient as he was, is a difficult mantle to wear'. He appealed for the laity's prayers and cooperation. He also referred to the new Catholic Action movements which were emerging in Melbourne,[51] and said that he wished to introduce them in Adelaide as soon as possible:

> I do not know if there are any non-Catholics present this evening. Catholic Action may be misunderstood. It has nothing to do with political parties or party politics. It simply means that each individual Catholic becomes a better Catholic so that by his example and by his help he may bring other people to God ... I thank those people who have already done much in Adelaide in this matter of Catholic Action and I urge them to continue their good work.[52]

Support for what eventually became known as the lay apostolate would become one of the key features of Beovich's episcopate.

Two formal photographs taken in 1940 before Beovich left Melbourne show a slim, youthful-looking bishop. In one of these Beovich is standing in front of a bookcase, open book in hand. In another he is sitting at a desk, hands resting on a book. Both project a dignified, scholarly image. In a somewhat backhanded compliment, in his speech at the consecration dinner Mannix assured the priests of the Adelaide archdiocese that while their new bishop might not look very robust, he had never been known to take so much as a single day's sick leave in Melbourne. What he lacked in age he made up for in wisdom. 'They used to say of Lord Roberts: "He was little, but he was wise", and much the same could be said of the new Archbishop of Adelaide,' Mannix commented, adding that 'he has undoubtedly inherited the greatest charm and winsomeness from his mother':

> I express my appreciation of him for doing things which I could not possibly accomplish myself. He has a way with him of making friends all around him, and I do not think he made any enemies. I may have made some friends, but I have made many enemies. You can understand how much I feel the loss of Dr Beovich.[53]

Beovich certainly demonstrated energy, wisdom and charm during his first few days in Adelaide. He would need more of those qualities in the years ahead.

The First Six Weeks

The *Southern Cross* hailed the arrival of the first Australian-born bishop of the archdiocese of Adelaide as the dawn of a new era. The paper was published weekly, with a masthead which proclaimed that it was 'the official organ of the Catholic Church in South Australia'. The editor, one of the sixty-four diocesan priests, could have been forgiven for feeling some trepidation. After five years under the rule of the amiable and physically ailing Andrew Killian, the clergy of the archdiocese must have braced themselves for change. However, at the dinner on 7 April and the official welcome tendered by the laity the following evening in the Tivoli Theatre, Beovich disarmingly admitted that although he knew quite a lot about Catholic education, 'of the ordinary parochial matters I know little or nothing'. Therefore, he promised to do 'nothing spectacular' for some time.[54]

Beovich's first appointments reflect this cautious approach. The senior priests who, in accordance with canon law, formed the inner group of advisers to the archbishop, the diocesan consultors, remained the same as in Archbishop Killian's time; and Beovich retained the elderly Irish-born Michael Hourigan, parish priest of Goodwood, as his vicar-general. It was a diplomatic move, a reassuring sign of continuity. Eighty-one years of age in 1940, Hourigan had been a priest of the Adelaide archdiocese for almost fifty-eight years, one of the diocesan consultors since 1915, and vicar-general since 1930.[55] Another long-serving member of the diocesan administration was a layman, Darcy Woodards. He commenced work in 1912 as a clerk in charge of files and records, and in the 1920s and 1930s served as secretary to Archbishop Spence and then Archbishop Killian.[56] It was unusual for a layman to occupy that position, and he was afraid that he would lose his job when Beovich took over. Beovich did appoint one of his few young Australian-born priests, Patrick Kelly, as his 'private secretary', but he kept Woodards (who had trained as an accountant) as 'financial secretary'.[57]

After the flurry of functions to welcome the new archbishop, there was nothing unusual about Beovich's engagements in his first six weeks in office. They were typical of what lay ahead for the next thirty years. As well as blessing the foundation stone of the new maternity wing at Calvary Hospital, run by the Little Company of Mary since 1900, he blessed and opened additions to St Joseph's Orphanage at Largs Bay, and a kindergarten connected to St Joseph's School at Kingswood.[58] He went to a charity carnival at Thebarton to raise money for the institutions for homeless men and boys run by the Brothers of St John the Baptist, and he called in at the sports carnival for the Christian Brothers' colleges at Rostrevor and Wakefield Street.[59]

Beovich also attended his first meetings of some of the many Catholic organisations in the diocese. These included two charitable bodies, the women's branch of the St Vincent de Paul Society and the Catholic Braille Writers Association.[60] Two others promoted Catholic piety. The Legion of Mary originated in Dublin in 1921 and was brought to Adelaide by a young Irish priest, Philip Smith, in the 1930s. It functioned as a small but disciplined group of Catholics whose main concern was evangelism and prayer. Presiding at the Legionaries' annual consecration to Mary in the cathedral on Sunday, 12 May 1940, Beovich praised their work and thanked them for their prayers and acts of self-denial.[61] The Holy Name Society was an association for men founded by a Dominican priest, W. McEvoy, in North Adelaide in 1922. It made few practical demands on members beyond extracting a commitment to reverence the name of Jesus and to avoid blasphemy and obscenity in speech. An estimated two thousand members attended Benediction in the cathedral on Sunday, 9 May 1940, where the new archbishop exhorted them to live as 'soldiers of Christ'.[62]

An organisation of a more intellectual nature was the Catholic Guild of Social Studies. It was founded in 1932 by Paul and Margaret McGuire and Dominican priest James O'Doherty to raise awareness of Catholic social teaching. The McGuires had lived in London from 1928 to 1932 and moved in 'Chesterbelloc' literary circles, becoming acquainted with the latest Catholic social and political thinking in Europe, including Joseph Cardijn's Young Christian Workers' Movement. Beovich agreed to become patron of the Guild of Social Studies, and was guest of honour at a reception organised by Guild members at the end of May.[63]

Catholic graduates of the University of Adelaide had established the Aquinas Society in 1929. Beovich was guest speaker at the Society's annual communion breakfast on Sunday, 14 April 1940. That day was the inaugural 'Social Justice Sunday' in the Catholic Church in Australia. The first of what would become an annual series of social justice statements was issued by the hierarchy. Beovich promoted the 'Bishops' Statement on Social Justice' (drafted by B. A. Santamaria and Justin Simonds) at the communion breakfast. He reached a wider audience on Monday, 15 April 1940, via the Australian Broadcasting Commission's radio station 5CL. He made a passing reference to the old education grievance, that Catholic schools should receive 'a proportionate share of the revenue set aside for education', but tried to avoid any hint of sectarianism in affirming the Church's duty to teach 'fundamental principles concerning human rights'. He maintained, in particular, that employees had a right to receive a wage that would be sufficient for them to support a family and buy their own home, and he called for a more equitable distribution of wealth.[64]

On Anzac Day, 25 April 1940, Premier Playford joined Catholic returned soldiers who gathered for a requiem Mass in the cathedral, at which Beovich presided.[65] This solemn ceremony was followed by a more joyful one on 12 May 1940 when infants born during the previous twelve months were consecrated to Mary and received a medal from the archbishop, a custom Killian had initiated and Beovich was pleased to continue.[66] The annual Catholic Subscription Ball, 'the premier Catholic social function of the year', was held on 8 May. Forty-two debutantes dressed in white georgette and taffeta were presented to the archbishop, the stage of the Australia Hall transformed into 'flowery bower' for the occasion.[67] Most of the young women who curtsied to Beovich were destined for marriage, but the archbishop also presided at the profession ceremony for two Sisters of St Joseph at St Joseph's Convent at Kensington, and at a Carmelite sister's reception of her habit at The Carmel at Glen Osmond.[68]

Beovich joined in celebrations at the Passionist monastery at

Glen Osmond on the feast day of St Paul of the Cross, the founder of the Congregation of the Passion, and went to the Jesuit-run parish of Sevenhill to carry the Blessed Sacrament in the annual Corpus Christi procession on Sunday, 26 May 1940.[69] Before and after the trip to Sevenhill, he presided at the opening and closing of forty hours of continuous prayer before the Blessed Sacrament in the cathedral.[70] Known as Forty Hours' Adoration or Quarant' Ore, this devotion was first practiced in Milan in 1527 to invoke God's help during a time of war and plague. It was little known in Adelaide, but became common in Melbourne in the 1940s,[71] a trend Beovich was keen to foster in his new diocese. Overall, by the end of the first six weeks, the Catholics of the archdiocese of Adelaide had had many opportunities to see their new archbishop and to hear him speak. Those who missed out could read the reports in the *Southern Cross*.

Less publicly, Beovich's diary reveals that in his first six weeks as archbishop he negotiated with the apostolic delegate and Thomas McCabe, the bishop of Port Augusta, for the establishment of a seminary in Adelaide, and purchased the land near Rostrevor College on which it was subsequently built.[72] He appointed the diocese's first director of Catholic education (William Russell, the priest who had previously been diocesan inspector of schools), and inaugurated a Catholic Teachers' Association. He also arranged for the erection of a 'Diocesan Education Building' alongside the cathedral to house the Catholic Central Library, with rooms available for Catholic Action and teacher training.[73] This was a further indication that education was going to be one of the new archbishop's priorities. The building became known as Fennescey House, as retired farmers Mary and John Fennescey donated the site to the Church and the money for its construction in neo-Gothic style to match the cathedral.

In the first six weeks Beovich consolidated his status as leader of the Catholic community by visiting the governor, Sir Malcolm Barclay-Harvey, at Government House, and later having a meal with him at his residence at Marble Hill.[74] He also had lunch with Premier Playford and dined at the Adelaide Club.[75] He did not record in his diary any further details of these functions, but did note that over a meal in the Parliament House dining room he had discussed education matters with Shirley Jeffries, the state minister of education (and a prominent Methodist layman). Two issues in particular arose: the registration of teachers in non-government schools, and the teaching of religion in state schools.[76] Familiar with the situation in Victoria, where teachers had to meet certain standards to be registered to teach, Beovich had no difficulties with the former and by the end of the year had established a Diocesan Board for the Registration of Catholic Teachers to examine trainee teachers and present certificates to those who qualified.[77]

For over half a century the teaching of religion in state schools in South Australia had been a contentious subject as Protestant lobbyists had sought to make Bible reading by teachers part of the curriculum. Five bills were introduced into the state parliament between 1921 and 1934 in an attempt to amend the Education Act of 1915 to allow that to happen. Strong opposition from the Catholic Church helped ensure they were defeated. In 1940 Beovich remained opposed to government school teachers giving lessons on the Bible, but he suggested an alternative: a bill which would allow ministers of religion or their representatives the right to give thirty minutes of religious instruction a week to students belonging to their denomination. In July Beovich arranged for Catholic lawyer Harry Alderman to draft such a bill.[78] It was introduced into the House of Assembly on 18 September 1940 as a private member's bill by Robert Richards (the Labor opposition leader) and warmly endorsed by Jeffries.[79] Unlike all its predecessors, it successfully passed through the parliament. Beovich continued to maintain the superiority of the separate Catholic education system where, he said, religion was not merely another subject in the curriculum but permeated the whole school.[80] However, his support for the 'right of entry' bill was a marked departure from the policy of most bishops at the time. The same edition of the *Southern Cross* which printed his defence of the bill in September 1940 quoted Thomas McCabe saying: 'if you desire to save Christianity in our country ... you must uproot and discard the secular system of education and return to the denominational system which is the only system capable of giving the education and the environment necessary to produce Christian citizens.'[81]

That was the kind of statement Catholics were used to hearing from their bishops.

While the gestation and successful birth of the 1940 bill took place in the months after Beovich's first six weeks in office, it was undoubtedly conceived during that first meeting with Jeffries in May 1940. As he had demonstrated as director of Catholic education in Melbourne, behind-the-scenes negotiations were Beovich's preferred mode of operation. One former Catholic teacher recalls that when it was announced a Melbourne priest was to be the new archbishop of Adelaide, many teachers looked forward to Mannix-style pronouncements on controversial education matters. They were disappointed to find Beovich was convinced that persuasion was generally more effective in advancing the Catholic cause than confrontation.[82]

The First Years of the War

A sense of alienation from the sinful world pervaded much Catholic piety in the nineteenth and early twentieth centuries, as Catholics were encouraged to focus on saving their souls and achieving eternal salvation. Moynihan reflected that type of thinking in his editorial in the *Advocate* on 4 April 1940 when he referred to the bishops' key role in the Church's 'long battle with the world'. Yet in the 1930s the new Catholic Action movements promoted a rather different notion: that Catholics could achieve holiness through engagement in the secular world. Beovich tried to steer a middle way between these strands of piety. At the civic reception the day after his consecration, the lord mayor referred 'to the fine citizenship of the Catholic community'. It was not a meaningless compliment. Most of those present would have remembered the bitter sectarian divisions which had arisen during the First World War. In response, Beovich assured the gathering that good citizenship was a natural consequence of the training Catholics received: it was necessary to be a good citizen in this life to merit the glory of heaven.[83] That evening, speaking to lay Catholics, he went further. Good citizenship could not be divorced from Christian faith:

> We in these days pray for peace, but we know full well there will be no peace until the nations and the peoples return to the Lord their God,

> because without God there can be no peace. There was a time, not so distant, when men having in their minds the destinies of the nations told God to stand without the council room, and what a sorry mess they made, and we are reaping what they sowed. We shall call God back to the council chambers into His proper place.[84]

The following month Beovich returned to the Town Hall to address the Commonwealth Club. Conscious that most of his audience were not Catholics, he gave a brief history of the papacy, stressing that the pope was the visible head of the church founded by Christ, and that the neutral Vatican state was not part of Mussolini's Italy. The pope was in an ideal position to arbitrate, Beovich argued, if only the nations would listen to him and his pleas for peace. He declared that Australian Catholics were convinced that the Allies' cause was just; therefore they would pray for victory as well as peace. However, he insisted that a true and lasting peace could only be obtained if it was based on Christian principles.[85] He had taken as his episcopal motto 'Pax Christi', and throughout the war years he constantly expounded his understanding of what that meant.

One such occasion was a public lecture which was held on 28 July 1940 in the Bonython Hall at the University of Adelaide. Albert Hannan, the crown solicitor, first asked Beovich if there could be a Catholic meeting at the Town Hall 'to show solidarity for England and the war'. Beovich recoiled from the suggestion. 'Our patriotism would be judged not by speeches and flags but by enlistments and contributions to the war funds,' he wrote in his diary. Hannan 'then got another brain wave' and arranged for the university council to sponsor a series of public addresses on 'The Crisis of our Civilization'.[86] This time Beovich agreed to participate. Many were turned away as the hall (with a seating capacity of over one thousand) filled to overflowing. Beovich identified a 'grave illness' in Western civilisation: pride. This was manifest in the rejection of the authority of the Church, the secularisation of education, and an increase in divorce, abortion and use of artificial means of birth control. It was a typically Catholic diagnosis of society's ills. Beovich went on to describe the 'pagan attack on our Christian civilization' by Stalin and Hitler as 'the worst menace yet encountered in the history of Christendom'; nevertheless, 'it would be little use to conquer abroad and suffer defeat at home'.[87] In various subsequent speeches, including a new year's eve radio broadcast, he reiterated that while the Allies' cause was just, Australians should 'set our own house in order': 'The greatest enemy which the nation faced was what was called secularism, the attempt to divorce God from human society.'[88]

Such statements need to be seen in context. Prime Minister Menzies' declaration on 3 September 1939 that Australia would follow Great Britain into the war against Germany had not triggered to anywhere near the same degree the patriotic emotions of 1914, and during the early years of the conflict there was no great sense of urgency. For most Australians, life changed little. A record amount was bet on the Melbourne Cup in 1940, and a survey of public attitudes the following year highlighted the 'sense of disillusionment, futility, distrust, disgust, diffidence and indifference which so many possess with regard to politics and society in general and the war in particular'.[89] That began to change on 8 December 1941 when Japan entered the war. By the end of February 1942 Singapore had surrendered and Japanese bombs were falling on Darwin.

As the conflict drew closer, Beovich's public utterances took on a more sombre note. At the opening of a new Catholic school at Norwood on Australia Day, 26 January 1942, he called for 'wholehearted cooperation with the Commonwealth Government' in the grave crisis the nation was facing.[90] In May he launched the Catholic United Services Auxiliary (CUSA) which provided recreational facilities in Angas Street for service men and women.[91] From June 1942 the *Southern Cross* ran a regular column titled 'Catholic Patriotic Activities'. A special Mass and communion breakfast was held for troops from the United States in July 1942.[92] With their reputation for being 'over-sexed, over paid and over here', American servicemen were a mixed blessing. Beovich shared widespread concern about declining sexual morality during the war years. He did not go as far as Archbishop James Duhig of Brisbane, who advocated a curfew for girls under seventeen and a ban on marriages between Australian women and American servicemen,[93] but he and Thomas McCabe of Port Augusta issued a pastoral letter on 10 August 1942 which exhorted Catholics to withstand 'the many dangers and temptations to faith and morals' which existed in 'these difficult days'.[94] Beovich also encouraged the Catholic Women's League to provide safe accommodation for female munitions workers. He formally opened St Mary's Munitions Hostel on 25 October 1942.[95]

In April 1943 Beovich responded to Prime Minister John Curtin's appeal for prayer for Australia by declaring that 'love of the land of our birth is a virtue implanted in our hearts by God Himself', and that when the nation was in such grave danger, it was necessary to 'banish selfishness and complacency and to do what is in our power to assist our country'.[96] He promoted distinctively Catholic forms of prayer – Benediction of the Blessed Sacrament and the rosary – but was sensitive to the ecumenical difficulties which this created. Before consecrating his diocese to the Immaculate Heart of Mary in 1943, he asked his priests to remind their parishioners that Mary 'differs from her Son as the finite from the infinite, as the created from the uncreated. We do not give her that adoration which belongs to God alone'. Yet, 'as the Pope has said, we ought not to be in any way afraid of paying too much honour to Mary since the honour duly paid to her goes straight to the Blessed Trinity'.[97] The subtle nuances of this were not always obvious to Protestant critics.

The Debate on Post-War Reconstruction

By the end of 1942 the Japanese advance had been halted, and during 1943, with increasing numbers of American troops in the South-West Pacific, it became clear that the tide had turned in Australia's favour. Beovich pre-empted victory and leapt into the debate on post-war reconstruction. The reformist federal Labor government in December 1942 created a Department of Postwar Reconstruction. Ben Chifley was the minister responsible, and H. C. Coombs the director-general. Coombs later wrote that he and his colleagues were 'stimulated to believe that human communities could, by corporate action, shape the context in which the lives of their members were to be lived'.[98] They invited submissions on how this could be done. A Catholic response was provided by a committee chaired by B. A. Santamaria, assistant secretary of the Australian National Secretariat of Catholic Action. An abridged version of the submission, titled *Pattern for Peace*, was approved by the Australian Catholic Bishops' Committee on Catholic Action and issued in 1943 as the fourth of the Australian hierarchy's annual social justice statements.[99]

Beovich energetically promoted *Pattern for Peace* in a radio broadcast on ABC state radio on 11 May.[100] He called for the establishment of a basic wage which would be the same for men and women, increasing for men when they married and on the birth of each of their children. He also supported more widespread distribution of ownership in industry and the curbing of monopolies; the stabilisation of rural life through the linkage of independent farms in networks of cooperative enterprises; greater control of trading banks so that in the administration of credit the public interest alone would be considered, not private profit, and, last but not least, a fundamentally Christian education system. Yet apart from a brief mention in the newspapers, *Pattern for Peace* faded into obscurity.[101]

On 12 September 1943 Beovich gave another address, this time on ABC national radio. The theme was 'The Making of an Australian'. He outlined what he regarded as the urgent problems facing Australia: 'a declining population, a dangerous class conflict in industry, and a decline in agriculture.' He then described the ideal response:

> ... an Australian will face these serious problems by recognising that there is greater happiness and security in large families in spite of the sacrifices involved. He will not dislike foreigners but strive to understand them. He opposes racial hatred in Hitler, he will not countenance it in ourselves. He will do everything practical to welcome the immigrant, helping him to become acclimatised and absorbed into the social life of the country. He will realise that workers have a right to cooperate and share in the control of industry policy and to be treated as men and not simply as mechanical units or cogs in a machine. In striving for social justice and cooperation he will follow Christian principles because only men animated by the positive Christian ideal can discipline their selfish desires sufficiently to bear the sacrifices required to carry out national policies for the true progress of our country.[102]

He was being idealistic and he knew it. He lamented, in particular, Australians' 'insular dislike of foreign immigration'. As with similar idealism in Methodist circles, such opinions are significant not because they represent the thinking of the average person in the pew during the war years, but because they show a church leader willing to raise awareness of social and economic issues. In his history of Methodism in South Australia, Arnold D. Hunt cautions against assuming that the progressive social objectives endorsed by the local Methodist Conference would have been acceptable to the majority of Methodists.[103] A similar caveat should be borne in mind when considering Beovich's public utterances. However, given the emphasis placed on obedience to church teaching in the Catholic tradition, and the respect generally accorded to clergy in his era, Beovich may have been in a better position than Methodist leaders to influence his flock.

At the same time as he led from the front on issues such as immigration, Beovich continued to wage war on well-known Catholic targets. 'They have rationed our tea, and I suppose it is not to be wondered at if they ration the beer,' he mused in mid-1942, before going on to bemoan that things which were 'intrinsically evil' were permitted to continue: indecent literature and films, and the sale of contraceptive devices. He thought it quite odd that cars could be forced off the road due to a shortage of tyres, but rubber could still be found for twelve million condoms to be manufactured each year.[104] Methodist idealists were more worried about alcohol and gambling. For Beovich, drinking and betting did not fall into the 'intrinsically evil' category; they only became harmful when used unwisely.[105]

Confrontation

It has been said that 'the Church's quietude on the War was in direct contrast to its theoretical verbosity on how post-War Australia should be reconstructed'.[106] Beovich, however, did not remain silent when he thought that the interests of his Church were under threat. In January 1942 he heard a rumour that the buildings of Rostrevor College were going to be turned into a military hospital. He confronted the military authorities. When the report was confirmed, he demanded to know why, of all the schools in Adelaide, one of the most important Catholic colleges had been singled out. He advised the Christian Brothers not to relinquish the school, but to continue to make arrangements for the new academic year. The army backed off.[107] Not content with this victory, Beovich persuaded Mannix to write a statement protesting against the compulsory borrowing of Catholic education buildings – which had, of course, been constructed without any financial help from the government, the great education grievance – and he sent it to Gilroy to forward to the federal cabinet.[108] In Queensland Duhig adopted a much more conciliatory approach: 'Though no diocese was as badly hit as his, he led the bishops in accepting the necessity of the policy ... He wrote especially to the archbishop of Adelaide, who wanted to denounce the military authorities as acting like Nazis in Germany.'[109] Beovich was unmoved, pleased that as a result of his representations all Catholic buildings in his diocese were left undisturbed.[110]

On another issue Beovich and the archbishop of Brisbane also clashed. Horrified at the bombing of his beloved Rome by Allied forces in July 1943, Beovich contacted Mannix and Gilroy to arrange a protest.[111] Gilroy, as secretary of the standing committee of the Australian hierarchy, forwarded a cable (drafted by Mannix) to the pope, expressing sympathy at the 'outrage' which had occurred. In spite of opposition from Duhig and two other bishops, Gilroy also sent cables to Winston Churchill and Franklin Roosevelt asking for no further raids on Rome.[112] In an address in his cathedral, Duhig blamed Mussolini's fascist government for not making Rome an 'open city', and he accepted that the Allies had tried not to drop bombs on churches and places of historic interest. They had not quite succeeded, but given the number of historic sites in Rome, it would be difficult not to hit something significant. In a private letter to Gilroy, Duhig indicated that he thought the cables were imprudent, if not unpatriotic and subversive, and a cause of deep embarrassment to Catholics in the armed forces. His biographer applauds his stance:

> Others may have been more politically involved than Duhig, but no bishop – and few politicians – had a sounder instinct for what the Australian people would tolerate ... his stand confirmed his reputation

> in the minds of public and politician: the archbishop of Brisbane was a man to speak for Australia.[113]

Beovich was not interested in speaking for Australia when Rome was under attack. As bombing raids increased in intensity in March 1944, he wrote to the priests of his diocese:

> We cannot, and will not remain silent in this critical hour when the life of the Holy Father is in imminent peril and the centre of our Holy Faith is threatened with destruction ... In your love and reverence for the Holy Father you are asked, on the next three Sundays, to speak of these matters to your people and to exhort them to crowd the meeting in the Adelaide Town Hall on Easter Sunday.[114]

So many heeded the appeal that hundreds had to be turned away from the Town Hall. Those who managed to get inside were told by their emotional archbishop that 'we have come ... to grieve with the Holy Father and to show that our hearts beat in unison with his heart'.[115] A motion was unanimously passed:

> That this great meeting of Catholic citizens of South Australia ... expresses unswerving devotion to and profound sympathy with our Holy Father, Pope Pius XII: we share his anguished protest at the bombing of Rome and the State of Vatican City, and we wholeheartedly support his appeals to all the belligerents not to make a battlefield of the Holy City of our Catholic Faith.[116]

Copies of the resolution were sent to the apostolic delegate, the prime minister, the governor general, even the British prime minister and the president of the United States. Beovich exclaimed in his diary: 'It was a wonderful and inspiring meeting and I felt proud and grateful to the priests and people of Adelaide.'[117] Years later, diocesan employee Darcy Woodards recalled in his memoirs:

> I found him to be a very quiet man. He never seemed to get excited or perturbed about any difficulty that arose ... The only time I recollect seeing him excited was during the war, when we had a big meeting in the Town Hall to protest against the bombing of Rome. Well, he literally foamed at the mouth. It was the only time I ever saw him excited.[118]

Predictably, there was a reaction from South Australians who did not have such a high regard for Rome. An anonymous correspondent wrote to the *Advertiser*: 'To me, and to many other British people, Rome signifies the birthplace of Fascism in this war. It is certainly not my spiritual home. I have far greater love for London, the centre of our Empire. The reverend gentlemen who protest against the bombing of Rome were not very vocal when London was being reduced to rubble.' A week later, 'RAAF' claimed:

> The average person does not, nor do I, favor the bombing of Rome, but rather regards it as a deadly medicine for a deadly disease, viz. the cancer of Nazism which has taken root in the city. I am confident that if it should be necessary to raze Rome to the ground the spirit of Christ in the hearts of true men will still be equal to the task of building the 'brave new world' ... If it will shorten the war, or save one Allied life, then let our air fleet set course for Rome.[119]

Given the small percentage of Catholics in the state, it is likely that these views reflected a more common response than Beovich's passionate denunciation of the bombing. Ironically, while Beovich had refused Hannan's request in 1940 for a rally to show Catholic sympathy for England, he succumbed in 1944 to his own brand of exuberant patriotism.

Prisoners of War

During the war many Italians in Australia endured the trauma of being interned as enemy aliens. In addition, a considerable number of Italian soldiers captured in North Africa were sent to Australia. By December 1944 there were at least 1500 detained in South Australia.[120] Most had been baptised Catholic and John Panico, the Italian-born apostolic delegate, took a particular interest in their fate, sending them copies of an Italian prayer book. The prisoners were sent to work on South Australian farms to compensate for the scarcity of rural workers. Beovich reported to Panico on 6 June 1944 that over seven days he had travelled 843 miles, visiting prisoners of war on farms in the Mount Barker, Willunga and Mount Pleasant districts, and at the main distribution centre at Sandy Creek, where five hundred men were located. He described their living conditions as in all cases adequate, and sometimes better than what the average Australian man could expect in a farming community. Moreover, even though most of the farmers who employed the men were not Catholic, they demonstrated a lack of sectarian bigotry by taking them to the nearest Catholic church for Mass. Beovich was pleased with the religious fervour of the men. All but one took the opportunity to receive the sacrament of penance and seemed grateful for his visit. Beovich's only concern was their lack of reading matter in Italian, apart from Panico's prayer book, and he suggested that a competent person such as Jesuit priest Ugo Modotti could perhaps edit a monthly religious paper for them.[121]

On 29 September 1944 Beovich hosted an informal gathering of the Australian hierarchy after the Adelaide archdiocese's modest centenary celebrations. Ten bishops were present and Duhig presided. After Modotti recounted problems which Italian Catholics were experiencing, the bishops agreed to recommend to the next general meeting of the hierarchy that 'a missionary house might be established in Australia consisting of a number of Italian Religious priests who would be at the disposal of the bishops in giving missions and retreats to Italians in various parish centres throughout Australia'.[122] The proposal fell through, partly because Mannix, who was not present at the meeting, acted unilaterally and provided Modotti with a house to use as a base for missions in the Melbourne archdiocese.[123] The main reason, however, seems to have been opposition from Panico, who was also absent from the meeting. Anthony Cappello attributes Panico's displeasure to Modotti's close relationship with Mannix.[124] Alternatively, Panico may simply have been annoyed that his advice had not been sought by the Australian bishops on a matter on which he regarded himself an expert.[125]

The presence of the apostolic delegate at meetings of the Australian hierarchy was a sensitive issue. In 1927 the Congregation for the Propagation of the Faith ruled, against the wishes of the Australian hierarchy expressed at a meeting in 1925, that the apostolic delegate should be invited to their meetings. James O'Collins told Thomas Boland that the bishops responded by holding informal meetings when they attended each others' special functions. Boland concludes: 'If the delegate wanted to be present, he had to scramble around the continent in their dust. If he caught up with them, they could exchange polite formalities until the next funeral.'[126] Boland describes the gathering in Adelaide in 1944 as 'one of the non-meetings of the Australian hierarchy'.[127] Whatever the truth of this, Beovich genuinely respected Panico,[128] and acted more circumspectly the following year when he sought Panico's help in securing an Italian-speaking priest for the Adelaide archdiocese. As a result, Paul Zolin, a Salesian priest, arrived in Adelaide in 1946 to minister to Italian Catholics.[129]

Ecumenism

While Beovich's efforts to get the Australian bishops and the apostolic delegate to act cooperatively met with little success, there was progress on another front. In spite of his crusade to save Rome, the war years seem to have generated more ecumenical collaboration than sectarian division. One of the first South Australians to welcome the new Catholic archbishop to Adelaide was the Reverend William Harris, president of the South Australian Methodist Conference.[130] In 1941 an energetic new Anglican bishop arrived from England, Bryan Robin, and he and Beovich had a number of meetings, at least one held over lunch.[131] Both men were interested in the ecumenical initiatives taking place in England. One of the most significant developments was a letter published in *The Times* on 21 December 1940 which supported Pope Pius XII's Five Peace Points. Its signatories included the archbishop of Canterbury and the cardinal archbishop of Westminster.[132] In June 1943 Gilroy also issued a statement with his Anglican counterpart, Archbishop Mowll. Before signing the document he sent a copy to Beovich for his opinion. The cautious Beovich suggested a little more precision in the wording, but was, overall, supportive.[133] On 2 December 1943 Beovich himself sat on the platform of the Adelaide Town Hall with Robin and John C. Hughes, a prominent Methodist minister who was president of the Council of Churches in South Australia. Together they presented a joint statement calling for greater reliance on Christian principles in daily life.[134]

Despite Australia's reputation for secularism, what has been called 'civil religion' was an important element in public life in

Australia during the Second World War.[135] It was strongly influenced by Protestantism, which created a dilemma for devout Catholics. As the war drew to a close, Beovich reminded his priests that, as Catholics could not take part in Protestant religious services, they should suggest to their local civic councils that any commemorations of the victory should be such that all citizens could attend 'without any hurt to their religious convictions'.[136] He personally went to see Playford, and as a result there was a simple commemoration service outside Parliament House on Friday, 16 August 1945. There was no triumphalism. The first hymn, Catholic convert John Henry Newman's 'Lead kindly light, amid the encircling gloom', was a surprisingly mournful choice for the occasion, but one familiar to Catholics and Protestants. The premier and governor each gave a short speech and the service concluded with the hymn 'O God our help in ages past/Our hope for years to come', the Last Post and the national anthem. The crowd was then invited to go to either the Anglican or the Catholic cathedral where Robin and Beovich addressed their congregations. As James Gleeson later commented, the ecumenical initiatives of the war years 'may seem small things in our Post-Vatican II Church but, at that time, they were highly significant and quite controversial issues initiated by the first Australian-born Archbishop of Adelaide'.[137]

Pax Christi?

Alas, victory had a bitter aftertaste. In Beovich's address in St Francis Xavier Cathedral on 16 August 1945 he emphasised that peace had to be based on Christian principles of justice and charity and not 'new weapons of destruction'.[138] He was more direct a month later at the Holy Name Society communion breakfast: the atomic bomb, he declared, was 'intrinsically wrong'. Even if it had shortened the war, the end did not justify the means.[139] For once he and Duhig were in agreement.[140] Mannix also spoke out strongly against the atomic bomb.[141] The general reaction of the Australian community, however, seems to have been one of relief at the end of the war, jubilation at the victory and incomprehension of the horrors of the new weapons.[142]

Thus the shy, diffident priest from Melbourne emerged as a

confident, articulate Catholic spokesman in Adelaide during the war years. Along with challenging Australians to reflect on some of the deeper social, economic and moral issues facing their nation, Beovich had considerable success as a bridge builder between the Catholic community and the wider, predominantly Protestant society. While his passionate response to the bombing of Rome must have 'jarred the harmony of the Australian war effort',[143] there is no evidence that it did serious long-term damage, at least to his relations with the state's civic leaders and the heads of other Christian denominations. Many years later, Thomas Playford recalled his 'courtesy and cooperation' and paid tribute to his 'outstanding service' during those 'dark and trying days' when the nation was at war.[144] Moreover, within the Catholic community, Beovich's outcry at the bombing of Rome generated such an enthusiastic response that it may have helped consolidate the new bishop's status as a more traditional tribal leader. It is to his role within the Catholic community that we will now turn.

FIVE

'A Benevolent Father'
Adelaide in the 1940s

> We warn our beloved children, the clergy and people of your archdiocese, and command them in the Lord that, devoutly receiving you – their elected Archbishop – as the father and pastor of their souls and duly following and honouring you, they may obey your salutary commands, and may show reverence to you, so that you may rejoice to find them devoted children, and they may rejoice to find you a benevolent father.
>
> Pius XII to Matthew Beovich, 11 December 1939

The papal bull of appointment sent to Matthew Beovich stressed the paternalistic nature of episcopal ministry.[1] Although it reflected an unhealthy tendency for Catholic laity to be consigned to an infantile state, beneath the grating rhetoric is a more positive concept. A bishop should have a close pastoral relationship with the people of his diocese; he should not merely be its chief executive. Yet how realistic was this in even a relatively small diocese like Adelaide? Beovich struggled to remember the names of the diocesan priests, sixty-four men in 1940. Over 600 members of religious orders and 55,000 lay Catholics posed an even greater challenge. How could anyone be a 'father', benevolent or otherwise, to such a multitude?

Preacher, Teacher and Pastor

If they wished, Catholics could often encounter their archbishop in St Francis Xavier Cathedral. Beovich was at home in the pulpit giving sermons which were simple, unpretentious, 'and delivered with a heartfelt earnestness'.[2] He constantly exhorted his listeners to practise humility and charity, trust in divine providence and accept God's will – key themes which he had absorbed during his school days, and which were also present in the writings of one of his favourite saints, Thérèse of Lisieux, and Mary MacKillop, the founder of the Sisters of St Joseph, whom he much admired.

Cultivating a relationship with Christ was another constant refrain. 'Christmas is not merely the memory, the anniversary of a great event,' Beovich assured the congregation at Midnight Mass. 'It is the birth of Christ in us.' If we are to cradle the newborn Christ-child, we need to reach a point of stillness. Unfortunately, too often 'our souls are like the inns of Bethlehem, crowded and very restless'.[3]

To help overcome this problem, Beovich recommended self-discipline. Like Thérèse of Lisieux, he maintained that penance did not have to involve heroic sacrifices. Little things done for the love of God would equally please him and help 'strengthen the muscles of the will' to resist more harmful temptations. In Lent 1946 he gave a series of talks which emphasised the importance of prayer and penance in a relaxed, good-humoured way. Penance, he remarked, should never be done in a spirit of pride ('I'm doing this for Lent and that for Lent. What are you doing?'), and it should never 'make one irritable, less tolerant, less thoughtful, less kindly, a bore and a hairshirt to family and friends and fellow workers'.[4] His spirituality was definitely ascetical, but he did not encourage extreme self-denial, and any form of self-righteousness was utterly abhorrent to him.

At Easter Beovich reflected on the inevitability of suffering and linked this to Christ's death on the cross. 'He did not wipe the tears from the face of sorrow to lay sorrow by,' Beovich proclaimed one Easter Sunday, 'nor did He touch pain with a fierce redeeming beauty to have done with it. He has taken these things to Himself, and has changed them for us.' That was the mystery of the divine exchange. 'Our Divine Saviour experienced the bitterness of sorrow living our life that we might experience its splendour, living His.' Beovich reminded the congregation that Christ had not risen to create 'a material kingdom, a triumphant, prosperous, comfortable civilization based on Christianity'. Instead, his kingdom was in the human heart.[5] On the feast of Christ the King, the archbishop put forward examples from daily life to illustrate how a powerful witness to this kingdom could be made in the midst of suffering by a mother nursing a sick child, a labourer struggling to obtain justice, a young couple refusing to succumb to peer pressure to use artificial birth control, a widow mourning the loss of her husband, and a returned solider coping with the loss of an arm or leg without bitterness. This was his preferred model of Christian holiness, one which did not require outstanding virtue or heroic martyrdom but quiet, faithful discipleship. It was deceptively simple with, Beovich insisted, far-reaching implications. 'Every Christian's life, no matter how humble, has repercussions for good or ill upon present day conditions all over the world.'[6]

To reach beyond the cathedral congregation, Beovich occasionally used radio broadcasts. Having being involved in the *Catholic Hour* in Melbourne, he was so keen to utilise the new technology in Adelaide that he applied for a radio broadcasting licence in 1941. The application was not successful, but two years later the Methodist Church's Adelaide Central Mission was given permission to run radio station 5KA. One of the conditions of the licence was that free time had to be given each week to the Anglican and Catholic churches. As a result, 5KA's 'Catholic Hour' commenced on Sunday, 12 December 1943, at 9 pm.[7] Most of the responsibility for organising the programme in the early years fell on one of the diocesan priests, William Russell, secretary of the Catholic Hour Committee and director of Catholic education, but Beovich himself sometimes spoke on the programme. The Lenten talks in 1946 were delivered via 5KA.

Beovich also visited the parishes of his diocese as he was required to do by canon law. With no Melbourne precedent to draw on, as Daniel Mannix refused to go on visitation, Beovich followed the example of his former Propaganda classmate, Norman Gilroy in Sydney.[8] Like Gilroy, he had a booklet printed,

'Episcopal Visitation of Parishes'.[9] Two copies were sent to the parish priest before each visitation, one to be returned to the archbishop, and one to be kept in the parish archives. There were 115 questions related to every aspect of parish life. The parish priest had a lot of homework to do, filling in the blank spaces. Beovich was interested in everything from whether the church roof leaked to how often the priest visited the school. He was not as meticulous in his attention to detail as Gilroy, whose booklet contained almost 300 questions, but his scrutiny of parish administration was still intense.

Nevertheless, the visitations were also pastoral occasions, with time set aside for the archbishop to preach and teach and meet the Catholics of his diocese. Beovich developed a visitation regime whereby he would spent three to four days in each parish, celebrating Mass, hearing confessions, administering the sacrament of confirmation and presiding at special devotions, which usually included the rosary, Benediction of the Blessed Sacrament and a sermon.[10]

In his first year in 1940 Beovich focused on country parishes, starting with Murray Bridge in July, Balaklava in August, the Riverland in September, Yorketown and Snowtown in October, and the parishes of the South-East in November. Within three years he had completed the circuit, visiting every parish of the archdiocese. Then he began again. Each parish would receive two more visits before the decade was finished. Unable to drive himself, Beovich inherited from his predecessor, Andrew Killian, a chauffeur, the indefatigable and loquacious Keith Koen.[11] In their forty years together, Koen testified, he and Beovich covered a million and a half miles and 'wore out' fifteen cars. He particularly recalled the number of morning and afternoon teas they had to consume or politely extricate themselves from as they went from house to house, meeting elderly parishioners and invalids.[12] Once in 1942 Beovich played a game of Chinese checkers with a little girl stricken with facial palsy. He remained in her memory as a gentle, quiet man.[13]

A shrewd parish priest probably lined up as many parishioners as possible for the archbishop to meet to distract him from the formal visitation process. According to the oral history of the diocese, some priests learnt another tactic: a few good books were left lying around the presbytery where he would be sure to notice them.[14] While that may well have happened, there seems to have been very little leisure time for reading, especially on the first visitation round. Social functions such as parish concerts and, during the early years, civic receptions, were also part of the visitation experience. In his diary Beovich privately referred to these as 'an ordeal', but surviving reports indicate that he endured them with grace and good humour.[15]

After Beovich left the Maitland parish on Yorke Peninsula in September 1942, Richard Morrison, the parish priest, wrote to him: 'I am glad you liked your Maitland visit. I thought you did as you were so natural and informal.'[16] A glowing report was sent to the *Southern Cross*, probably by Morrison. The 332 known Catholics in the district were outnumbered almost ten to one by Protestants.[17] At a civic reception hosted by the mayor of Maitland, Beovich met members of the wider community, including the district's Protestant clergymen. 'Dr Beovich not only appealed to all as a charming and learned gentleman,' enthused the *Southern Cross*'s correspondent, 'but he actually charmed copious quantities of strictly rationed tea from the Maitland Catholic ladies.' His energy, zeal and enthusiasm 'held all spellbound'. His sessions with children went particularly well:

> His Grace, although lacking the years of his predecessors, does not lack anything of their dignity and courtesy, and is rich with the rare gift of sympathy. The children, keen judges, soon saw this. Rarely do children 'enjoy' examinations, but the children at Maitland and Arthurton did when the Archbishop examined them for Confirmation. Even the adults, who smiled and listened, enjoyed the examination. All could have sat interested longer than they did.

The report concluded eulogistically:

> The visit of Dr Beovich to the Maitland Parish strikes one as an epitome of Catholic life itself. It was a call to those outside the Church. It was a restless and untiring energy for God [i.e., the archbishop moved with great speed and did not stay long in any one place]. It was a submission to His Holy Will [one of the most common themes in Beovich's preaching]. It was an acceptance in a glad spirit of sacrifices great and

> small [except, apparently, forgoing rationed tea]. It was an acknowledgment that what God does or allows, though beyond understanding, is ultimately best for us here and hereafter [the common theme again].[18]

At Walkerville, later in 1942, it was reported in slightly less effusive terms that 'around their parish, and in their little church hall, His Grace was homely, without losing any of his dignity, and the people came to regard him as a true father'. The visit was 'the most important and memorable event in the short history of the parish'.[19]

Administration

The Walkerville parish was one of eight new ones which Beovich created in the 1940s by subdividing, where possible, large metropolitan parishes. He also relinquished three country parishes to the Port Augusta diocese. When Andrew Killian was bishop of Port Augusta, he wanted the boundaries between the South Australian dioceses redrawn so that Port Augusta could gain more territory. After he transferred to Adelaide, that no longer seemed so desirable and he resisted similar appeals from his successor at Port Augusta, Norman Gilroy. The day after Beovich's consecration, the issue was discussed at a meeting attended by Beovich, John Panico (the apostolic delegate), Thomas McCabe (bishop of Port Augusta), Gilroy (then archbishop of Sydney) and Francis Henschke (bishop of Wagga Wagga and former vicar-general of the Port Augusta diocese). Panico was willing to agree to changes, but Beovich successfully argued for the maintenance of the status quo until he had had a chance to get better acquainted with his diocese. A year later, having visited the parishes himself, he was willing to hand Spalding in the mid-north and Port Lincoln in the west to the northern diocese. Later he would relinquish Morgan in the Riverland as well. He was inherently cautious but not unreasonable. Moreover, as the Adelaide diocesan priests who had been serving those parishes were not part of the deal, they helped ease the clergy shortage caused by the increase in metropolitan parishes.[20]

As well as refusing to countenance changes to diocesan boundaries, Archbishop Killian had withstood his secretary Darcy

Woodards's pleas that parish priests should be required to submit regular financial statements to the central diocesan office ('Church Office'). It went against the grain of the Irish bishops' tendency to permit a great deal of local autonomy. 'None of the other bishops do it. Why should we?' Woodards remembered Killian saying to him. He found Beovich more receptive to the argument that the archbishop should know the real financial situation of his archdiocese.[21] In 1942 Beovich ordered a thorough audit of parishes and Church Office.[22] In a circular to priests in 1943 he revealed that 'the question of uniformity in parochial accounts and balance sheets has been giving me anxiety for some time'. He tried to implement a more orderly regime.

> The financial year ended on the 31st March last. I would be grateful if you prepared a balance for your parish to that date and filled in the accompanying form. When duly filled in I would ask you to bring it to the Church Office on the date mentioned hereunder, when the Diocesan Accountant will help you complete the form by giving details of insurance, rates, interest, etc. I am desirous that Mr Woodards would not have the task of preparing statements from cheque butts and other papers.[23]

Although Woodards still had trouble extracting all the information he wanted from some priests, higher standards of financial accountability gradually became the norm.

The greater professionalism which Woodards, supported by Beovich, brought to diocesan finances was an asset when Woodards approached banks for loans for the Church. Building restrictions limited what could be achieved during the war and its immediate aftermath, but Beovich encouraged what projects he could in the 1940s. Reflecting the fact that it was a time of consolidation in Australian Catholicism rather than expansion, most of the buildings were school extensions and new convents and presbyteries rather than new churches.[24] Beovich was pleased to open a new convent for the Sisters of St Joseph at Alberton in September 1940, because on his first visit to Alberton he had found six sisters sharing an attic in the old convent which was in danger of falling down. He appreciated the sisters' dedication and self-sacrifice, but thought their sleeping arrangements took this too far.[25] A new infant school run by the Sisters of Mercy opened at Millicent in 1949. The sister in charge wrote to Beovich in May 1948 to ask for permission for the building to go ahead. She had already received verbal permission at the last visitation: 'I expect you remember telling me that I should be in jail for having the children in the Infant department so crowded.'[26] Thus the visitations produced some practical results as the archbishop got to know his diocese.

The Diocesan Synod of 1945

On 5 December 1945, Beovich held a diocesan synod. According to the Code of Canon Law, this was a purely consultative body which could be convened and presided over by the bishop to consider measures for the welfare of the clergy and the people of the diocese. As the sole legislator, the bishop alone could issue statutes, and Beovich did so: fifty-four in all. What lay behind this surge in legislative activity is unclear, but Beovich was probably responding to deficiencies he perceived during his visitations.

One statute which had far-reaching consequences when building restrictions were lifted in the 1950s decreed: 'Where a reasonable number of the faithful, especially children, are unable to go to a church or place where Holy Mass is celebrated, the priest should set up a station in a convenient place where the faithful may hear Mass and the children be instructed in the Catechism.' Another statute warned any priest more inclined to denounce sin than practice mercy that one 'who publicly refuses Holy Communion, or threatens to do so, assumes a grave responsibility. More than ordinary prudence and caution are required in making a decision in this matter'. Evidently some of the Irish clergy still had a tendency toward the puritanical, Jansenist-type rigour which had infected the Church in Ireland. This did not please the archbishop, who had trained for the priesthood not long after Pope Pius X had encouraged the movement toward more frequent reception of communion.

A few statutes encouraged the introduction of pious customs such as visiting cemeteries on 2 November, All Souls' Day. In Spain in 1917 Beovich had been deeply moved by the sight of great numbers of Spaniards taking flowers to the graves of loved ones on that day.[27] He also praised the 'laudable practice' of each church holding a procession in honour of the Blessed Sacrament on the Feast of Corpus Christi. Another legacy of his Roman training was that he called for Gregorian chant, 'the supreme model for sacred music', to be introduced and fostered.

Of greater significance to priests, perhaps, were the statutes which related to financial and administrative matters. Most notably, the financial independence of parish priests was curbed. Regulations were issued for the keeping of parish account books and it was decreed that the written authorisation of the archbishop was necessary for any parish expenditure of fifty pounds or more. The salary for assistant priests was set at eight pounds per month. This was only a third of the average minimum wage rate for adult males in 1945, but at least assistant priests were guaranteed that amount, instead of being dependent on the generosity of their parish priest, and they did not have to contribute to presbytery expenses which were to be paid from a separate account.

The Archbishop and His Priests

Father William (Bill) Kelly arrived in Adelaide in 1945, a new recruit from Ireland. He was taken from the ship at Port Adelaide to meet Beovich at 'Archbishop's House', West Terrace. 'I was surprised at this energetic young bishop not much older than myself,' he recalled half a century later, 'he was so friendly and welcoming ... he treated me almost as an equal rather than as a subject.'[28] Almost an equal, but not quite. Beovich was not arrogant, but like most bishops of his generation, until his retirement he carefully kept some distance between himself and his priests. To his face, a priest would always call him 'Your Grace' (behind his back, many referred to him as 'Matty'). He would invariably call the priest 'Father'. Thomas Horgan, one of the first priests whom Beovich ordained, thought Beovich was 'most at home' in the company of priests where he could indulge in good-natured clerical banter.[29] Edward Mulvihill, who worked closely with the archbishop in the 1960s, agrees.[30] However, Horgan was amazed at Beovich's informality when visiting an acquaintance from Melbourne who was in hospital in Adelaide: 'he sat on the end of this fellow's bed and talked to him with great affection ... that was a side which we wouldn't often see.'[31] Mulvihill remembers

Beovich's 'natural graciousness – a dignity that remained unchanged equally at home in the kitchen or at a Government House reception'. Yet 'with this dignity came a certain aloofness', perhaps arising from Beovich's shyness combined with his consciousness of being a bishop.[32] As W. T. Southerwood says of Guilford Young, appointed auxiliary bishop of Canberra and Goulburn in 1948 and archbishop of Hobart in 1955, 'he never seemed ... to be completely relaxed or totally at ease'.[33]

The fact that the diocesan synod in 1945 lasted only one day indicates that little discussion can have taken place. It was the same at the 'Clergy Conferences' required by the Code of Canon Law. Beovich's successor, James Gleeson, later lamented the fact that there was so little dialogue,[34] although he also pointed out that this was typical of society generally: 'They used to say, I don't know how true it was, that when Tom Playford was premier, his ministers in the cabinet had to listen to his weekly broadcasts to find out what the government was deciding.'[35] Playford could certainly be autocratic, as the subtitle of Stewart Cockburn's biography – *Benevolent Despot* – implies. Moreover, even if the Clergy Conferences were 'largely one-directional in communication', as Gleeson admitted, they at least provided Beovich with an opportunity to meet his clergy as a group three times a year. Like the 'teacher conferences' which Beovich had organised in Melbourne, the meetings had an educative thrust. 'Junior clergy', those recently ordained, were examined on their knowledge of theology, scripture and canon law, and were required to present sermons to be dissected by their more experienced peers and the archbishop. Senior clergy did not have to submit themselves to this ordeal, but must have benefited to some extent from the process. The conferences demonstrate Beovich's interest in the continuing education of his priests as well as his commitment to fulfil the requirements of canon law.

As few parish priests in the Adelaide archdiocese enjoyed the canonical status of 'irremovable pastors', most priests were at the mercy of the archbishop when it was time to make appointments. Like an army general, he plotted his manoeuvres.[36] It is part of diocesan clerical folklore that, 'How's your health, Father?', was an ominous question when asked by Matthew Beovich. It invariably preceded news of a shift to another parish or the acquisition of additional responsibilities.[37] Yet Beovich was not as authoritarian as he could have been. He was assiduous in consulting the senior priests who formed the elite group of diocesan consultors, both formally, when moves to different parishes were being planned (usually in June, sometimes also in January), and also informally. A curate in the Woodville parish in the early 1950s, Leonard Faulkner remembers the archbishop often dropping in, unannounced, at the presbytery to see Monsignor William Russell, one of the consultors and a key adviser.[38] Thomas Horgan recalled that he was strolling in the garden at Sacred Heart College during a retreat in 1945:

> Archbishop Beovich came to me and said, 'Father Horgan, we're thinking of sending you to Mount Gambier. What do you think of that?' 'Well, you're in charge, Your Grace.' 'You're a decent man,' he said, 'you're a decent man.'[39]

'Decent' was one of the highest encomiums Beovich bestowed on those whose goodness and integrity he valued. It was when the latter was lacking that he was most likely to act imperiously. In 1955 he was so annoyed when news of parish appointments leaked after a consultors' meeting that he immediately changed them, sending a young curate destined for a country parish to a metropolitan one, and the one chosen for the city to the country.[40]

Peter Travers, Beovich's secretary in the 1960s, insists that Beovich routinely consulted parish priests on matters affecting their parishes. Presumably that was a characteristic of the 1940s and 1950s as well:

> He would never, never make a move without consulting the parish priest. It would be just unthinkable. If anything at all came up which had ramifications at parish level, the very first thing he would do would be to talk to the parish priest.[41]

Beovich was also conscious of his pastoral responsibilities towards priests. Thus, for example, when he discovered that Richard Morrison, parish priest of Maitland and amateur historian, was tired and depressed, he arranged for him to return to Adelaide and work as the diocesan archivist. Morrison was deeply grateful: 'Your belief in me has brought me back from that dangerous borderline when I was beginning "not to give a damn about anything or anyone". I never experienced such help before from any quarter and I shall try hard not to let your Grace down.'[42] Reflecting on priests' relationship with the archbishop, Bill Kelly concluded:

> He was very kind and charitable when he knew you were genuine ... On the other hand, if he thought you were trying to put something over him, he could be very severe. He liked honesty. If you were honest with him, that counted. You could have done terrible things, and gone and told him you were sorry ... he was very kind and helpful and sympathetic.[43]

As Simonds had testified at Beovich's consecration, he would not 'break the bruised reed'. Kelly did not give an example of a 'terrible thing' but misconduct by Irish priests was often related to alcohol. Beovich advocated temperance but not total abstinence,[44] and was himself a chain smoker.

Bill Kelly also recounted that when his father was dying of cancer, Beovich insisted that he return to Ireland and arranged for him to receive a cheque to help pay for the journey. Other Irish priests had similar experiences:

> I know some of the other priests who are dead now, they told me how kind he was to them when their relatives died in Ireland ... Even the ones that disagreed with him, said how kind he was to them.

Tom Horgan's father died suddenly in Adelaide in 1943. Beovich came into the sacristy before the funeral service: 'he took hold of my upper arm and gave it a little pressure, which said a lot about his feelings and his sympathy.'[45] It was a typical gesture, one which another priest interpreted as 'his shy way of reinforcing his loving concern'.[46] Another of Horgan's memories was of his ordination day, 27 July 1941. After the ceremony Beovich knelt before him for a blessing: 'It was a brotherly act that, over the years remains in memory as a symbol of his real affection for and genuine effort to understand his priests.'[47]

To Horgan, Beovich was quite approachable. 'I can only say I hope there are many bishops who can be asked by phone on Saturday night to supply Mass on Sunday in an emergency,' he remarked in 1965.[48] However, after his ordination Horgan lived with Beovich for some time at Archbishop's House, so he had a better opportunity than most to build a relationship with the archbishop – and he was 'a decent man'. Darcy Woodards testified that some of the priests who did not know Beovich well were 'a little timid of approaching the archbishop' and used to try to use Woodards as an intermediary. He personally found Beovich 'gentle and understanding, but he could be firm'. Woodards saw nothing wrong in that. With an ingrained respect for authority, and a belief that obedience was a virtue, Woodards commented simply: 'One can get through life much easier by being obedient.'[49]

Not only did Beovich also regard obedience as a virtue, it was part of his personal piety to value acts of self-sacrifice. On one occasion Tom Horgan and Pat Kelly asked, as they were obliged to do, for permission to go to see a stage show. They were told that as it was November, the time of the year when the souls of the departed were specially remembered, they should stop at home 'and offer it up for the holy souls':

> Later, when he was retired, I was talking to him about some old past things and I reminded him of that. He said, 'Did I do that to you? That was a bit tough, wasn't it?'[50]

Peter Travers had a worse experience. Working in Church Office on a swelteringly hot day, he took off his coat and clerical collar. Beovich walked into the room and noticed them hanging from a conveniently placed prong on the diocesan crest on the wall. He was not amused: 'Father Travers, we all have to practise some kind of penance. I think it would be a good idea if you put your coat on.'[51] The one consolation was that when it came to self-denial, Beovich was as tough on himself as anyone else.

The Archbishop and the Religious Orders

Almost half of the priests working in the diocese belonged to religious orders or congregations and all the Catholic schools and charitable institutions were run by religious brothers or sisters.[52] In the 1940s Beovich lured three new orders to Adelaide: the Sisters of the Good Shepherd (1941), the Salesian Fathers (1944) and the Sisters of Our Lady of the Sacred Heart (1947). It was clearly in his best interests to cultivate good relations with the orders which provided the diocese with a very cheap labour force. To judge from the tributes paid on the twenty-fifth anniversary of his consecration as archbishop of Adelaide, he was very successful. Cuthbert Hoy MSC praised the way 'his Grace has always been so gracious, humble and easy of approach ... We could not imagine any archdiocese offering more homeliness and brotherliness than that of Adelaide'.[53] Sister Mary David was equally eulogistic in depicting Matthew Beovich as 'a true father' to the religious: 'He was not a superior living in splendid isolation; he was their guide, philosopher and friend. He needed his co-workers; he sought their advice; he wanted their help; he depended on their prayers, and so God's work was done in a family spirit.'[54]

Beovich usually carried out his pastoral activities with as little publicity as possible. Hence few traces remain, but one example of his pastoral care has been recorded. In the early 1940s several Dominican sisters at Cabra Convent contracted tuberculosis and had to be isolated from the rest of the community in a special infirmary, known as Santa Sabina. The prioress asked the archbishop if the Blessed Sacrament could be reserved in a room at Santa Sabina. Beovich not only granted permission for this to happen, he also made it part of his weekly routine to celebrate Mass at Santa Sabina on Saturday mornings. 'The sisters,' wrote Helen Northey in her history of the Dominicans, 'cherished the memory of this outstanding example of pastoral concern and compassion.'[55]

Yet filial affection was undoubtedly strained at times, as the Sisters of Mercy amalgamation demonstrates. The Mount Gambier-based Mercy congregation was separate from the Adelaide congregation with its mother house in Angas Street behind the cathedral. The former had thirty-two sisters in 1940, the latter seventy-five. While he was in the South-East in November 1940, Beovich officially visited the Mercy convents as was required by canon law. It struck him as desirable that the two congregations should amalgamate. He was concerned about the poor state of the Mercy-run schools in the South-East, and he thought that a larger congregation could provide better teacher training as well as a larger pool of experienced teachers. The Mount Gambier sisters held a ballot to determine their future. Half wished to remain independent, but Beovich pushed ahead and drafted a letter for the superior to send to him, asking him to petition the apostolic delegate for the amalgamation. He tried to assuage the feelings of the older women by stressing that no sister who had made her final profession ten or more years previously should be moved from the country to the city, or vice versa, unless she wanted the change. The mother superior dutifully copied Beovich's draft and the amalgamation proceeded. However, it generated considerable unhappiness and a lingering belief that 'the Mounties' had been bullied by the archbishop.[56]

Similarly, in 1940 Beovich pressured the Sisters of St Joseph into closing their novitiate in Adelaide. He thought it preferable that young sisters be sent to Sydney where they would receive formal teacher training. While most Josephites would now see the wisdom of this development, at the time 'the older Sisters felt the closure deeply'.[57] When there were no obvious problems, Beovich came to appreciate the wisdom of non-interference. One priest recalls a classic Beovich aphorism: 'The sisters are like bees. Leave them alone and they will make good honey for God and the Church. But you give them trouble and they will sting you!'[58] No doubt he spoke from experience.

Where there were problems, however, the archbishop had a duty to act. Beovich did not shy away from making tough decisions even when this generated bitterness and criticism, as was the case with the suppression of the Institute of St John the Baptist. Begun in the late nineteenth century by John Healy, parish priest of Thebarton from 1881 until his death in 1921, the Institute was a rare example of a local foundation for men.[59] It is sometimes compared with the religious congregation established in 1866 by Mary MacKillop and Adelaide diocesan priest Julian Tenison Woods. Beovich himself made the link in a speech at a charity function to raise money for the work of the brothers in April 1940. He paid tribute to Monsignor Healy 'who had founded a religious order for brothers ... just as Father Tenison Woods had founded the Sisters of St Joseph'.[60] Yet the achievements of the brothers were much more modest than those of the Josephites. They did not spread beyond the Thebarton parish, where they taught in the parish school and ran a refuge for discharged male prisoners and a reformatory for delinquent boys. In 1940 there were just fourteen brothers living in a community wracked by dissension.[61]

Beovich was entitled to make a formal visitation of the dysfunctional institute but rather than undertake it himself, in 1941 he asked the Reverend Dr P. McCabe of the Sacred Heart Fathers to visit Adelaide. McCabe was the canonist to the apostolic delegation and superior of Sacred Heart Monastery at Kensington in Sydney. After living with the brothers for several weeks, McCabe reported that 'the Institute suffers from the lack of definite traditions of the religious life ... The fact is that the Institute is governed to a great extent by what Brothers John and Thomas [the two oldest brothers] now think is "Father Healy's spirit"'. Paradoxically, while there was a lack of discipline with regard to such an important aspect of religious life as regular times for prayer, there was rigidity over such petty matters as what hat should be worn. McCabe also observed a significant generation gap: there was at least twenty years between the youngest of the oldest brothers and the oldest of the youngest ones, and he noted that there appeared to be no one with sufficient education and leadership ability to be the superior of the community.[62]

McCabe agreed to work on a new constitution for the Institute, but in August 1942, before this had been completed, Beovich was informed of allegations that one of the brothers had been sexually abusing a number of boys in his care at the recently established orphanage at Brooklyn Park. Beovich swiftly set up a committee of inquiry consisting of two of his most senior and trusted priests, Thomas Davis, parish priest of Kingswood and one of the diocesan consultors, and Osmund Thorpe, superior of the Passionist monastery at Glen Osmond.[63] When they concluded that the allegations were credible, Beovich discussed the matter with his diocesan consultors and then descended on the brothers' residence at Brooklyn Park. Another brother also admitted he had been 'guilty of wrong practices' and Beovich issued both brothers with letters of secularisation, forcing them to sever their connections with the Institute.[64]

Concerned as well at the lack of cleanliness and discipline, and by the manifest incompetence of the brother in charge, Beovich decided in October 1942 to entrust the institution to the care of the Salesians of Don Bosco. He was familiar with the work in Melbourne of this international society which specialised in assisting underprivileged boys and young men. Most of the remaining brothers of St John the Baptist indicated that they would like to seek entry to other religious orders, and Beovich obtained permission from the apostolic delegate, John Panico, for them to do so.[65]

By 1948 only three elderly brothers were left, and at the instigation of Panico, Beovich applied to the Sacred Congregation of Religious in Rome for the suppression of the Institute of St John the Baptist.[66] He acknowledged the praiseworthy conduct of the three brothers but, given their advanced age, thought 'it would be impossible, humanly speaking, for them to train in time future leaders of an Institute, even if they had the ability'. They, however, decided to fight the suppression, complained indignantly about Beovich's treatment of them and attracted considerable sympathy. The first Salesian priest who came from Melbourne to work in Adelaide, John Biloni, was 'virtually ostracised by the local clergy'.[67] Beovich could do little to defend himself against accusations he had been unduly harsh to the Institute because he wanted to keep the troubles of 1942 secret.

In 1951 the new apostolic delegate, Paul Marella, informed Beovich that it was the wish of the Sacred Congregation of Religious that the Institute continue to engage in charitable work.[68] Beovich indicated his willingness to allow the brothers to move to another diocese.[69] By 1953 there were only two left. When Mannix gave them permission to work in the Melbourne archdiocese, they moved to Victoria but died not long afterwards. The matter dragged on until 1960 when a settlement was finally imposed by the Congregation for the Propagation of the Faith. The Institute of the Brothers of St John the Baptist was formally suppressed on the grounds that it had no surviving members, and Beovich was authorised to transfer the property at Brooklyn Park to the Salesians, and what remained in Melbourne was given to Corpus Christi Seminary.

In recent years the inadequate response of members of the Catholic hierarchy to allegations of sexual abuse by priests and religious has attracted almost as much condemnation as the abuse itself. In 1942 Beovich handled the situation with a decisiveness at odds with the current stereotype of episcopal laxity and neglect. Ironically, his own reputation suffered as a result. Unaware of the events of 1942 which led to the Institute's demise, a supporter of the brothers vehemently maintained a few years ago, 'Beovich was a pig of a man'. Such reproaches were the price the archbishop paid for endeavouring to keep his beloved Church free from scandal.

The Catholic Welfare System

When Beovich arrived in Adelaide in 1940 he found, in addition to the reformatory for boys at Brooklyn Park run by the Brothers of St John the Baptist, a refuge for unmarried mothers and 'foundlings' at Fullarton, and two orphanages. Ninety-six children were living at the Orphanage of St Vincent de Paul at Goodwood under the care of the Sisters of Mercy, and seventy-five at St Joseph's Orphanage at Largs Bay, the responsibility of the Sisters of St Joseph. There were only nine boys at Brooklyn Park.[70] Beovich decided that all the girls at Largs Bay should be sent to Goodwood; young boys from Goodwood were transferred to Largs Bay, and the institution at Brooklyn Park was transformed into an orphanage for all the senior boys.[71] An unhappy outcome, apart from the problems at Brooklyn Park, was that siblings were often separated. However, the changes did ease pressure at Goodwood and Largs Bay. The number of children at Goodwood dropped to seventy in 1942 and Largs Bay went down to fifty-seven.[72] In 1941 Beovich persuaded some Good Shepherd Sisters from Victoria to establish a home and training centre for wayward teenage girls at 'The Pines', an imposing old house on Marion Road at Plympton which Darcy Woodards bought on behalf of the diocese.[73]

The Good Shepherd Sisters developed a commercial laundry at Plympton, both to provide 'training opportunities' for the inmates and help 'The Pines' become self-supporting. The other Catholic institutions had fundraising committees. The Goodwood Orphanage Committee was particularly successful, its major fundraiser being a biennial fete.[74] In 1941 Darcy Woodards and H. J. (Bert) Savage, who were both active members of a number of Catholic organisations, suggested to the archbishop that a more coordinated approach to fundraising could be adopted. Beovich liked the idea and presided in August 1941 at a meeting of representatives from parishes and organisations which resulted in the establishment of the annual Catholic Diocesan Charities Appeal.[75] In 1942 £5500 was raised – no mean feat during the war years – and distributed to the homes at Fullarton, Brooklyn Park, Goodwood and Largs Bay. Yet despite this success, 'much heart-ache' was felt, especially by members of the long-established committee at Goodwood who were left to mourn the passing of their fete as the new committee embraced other fundraising strategies such as 'badge days' and appeals to parishes by the archbishop.[76]

Another centralising initiative in the 1940s also encountered resistance. As director of Catholic education in Melbourne, Beovich shared an office and secretary with Theresa Wardell, chief executive of the Melbourne archdiocese's Catholic Welfare Bureau. Established in 1936, this was the first such bureau in Australia. Norma Parker, an Australian graduate of the National Catholic School of Social Service in Washington, helped set it up, as well as the departments of social work in St Vincent's Hospital in Melbourne and St Vincent's Hospital in Sydney. In 1941 Beovich invited Parker to Adelaide to advise him on the establishment of a bureau in South Australia.[77] In a public address, Parker described how a bureau could coordinate the work of the various Catholic charitable institutions and provide advice to volunteers who worked in organisations such as the St Vincent de Paul Society.[78]

Beovich duly opened the Catholic Welfare Bureau in Adelaide in 1942 and appointed, as its first executive officer, twenty-five-year-old Hannah Buckley. She had just become one of the first to graduate from the University of Adelaide's new School of Social Work.[79] She was given an office and secretarial assistance but, as in Melbourne, this had to be shared with the director of Catholic education. It was not an ideal arrangement. A study in 1972 concluded:

> Her immediate problems of lack of suitable accommodation and an almost total lack of funds compounded the delicate nature of her task of introducing the concepts of the new profession of social work into organisations that were accustomed to their own well-established methods of work. In practice, coordination in any sense at all was

> restricted to two children's homes directly dependent on the bishop for their finance. But even here, the degree of intervention by the social worker in the daily running of the home was very limited.[80]

Buckley did manage to break into new fields. She helped wartime refugees and later post-war migrants, but found it difficult to get support from parish priests and religious orders. Conscious of her lack of clerical status, she recommended to Beovich that he appoint a priest to be the executive officer of the bureau, in the hope that he could wield greater authority.[81] Luke Roberts, an Australian-born priest ordained in 1938, duly took up the position in 1948, after completing a year's social work training. Nevertheless, even with a priest in charge, the bureau's coordination role was frustrated by the high degree of independence enjoyed by parish priests, the religious orders and volunteer associations.[82] Beovich did not resolve this problem. It is not clear why he was unwilling to impose a similar degree of 'heartache' to that experienced by the Goodwood fundraising committee, but as diplomacy and negotiation had been hallmarks of his own style as director of Catholic education in Melbourne, he may have expected the same from the directors of the Catholic Education Office and the Catholic Welfare Bureau in Adelaide.

In any case, Beovich accepted ultimate responsibility for Catholic welfare in his diocese. He did not allow the Catholic Welfare Bureau to become a buffer between himself and the institutions, nor the institutions to become too independent. The correspondence between the women in charge of the Goodwood and Largs Bay orphanages and the archbishop's secretary testifies to Beovich's involvement in financial matters. Everything from the purchase of a new stove and washing machine to the unblocking of the toilets was referred to him. He also closely supervised the transfer of the orphanage at Brooklyn Park from the Brothers of St John the Baptist to the Salesian Fathers. After arriving in Adelaide, John Biloni SDB wrote in his diary:

> Tuesday 19.1.43 (1) Morning in conference with His Grace. (2) Afternoon visit Boys Town with His Grace ... (3) 7pm–9 pm in conference with His Grace ... 22.1.43 (1) Morning: conference with His Grace (2) Shopping with Fr. Con McGrath (Carpets-Lino-Electric Cookers)

> (3) Afternoon conference with His Grace. Necessary initial expenses ... Sat 23.1.43 (1) All morning spent about Adelaide driving from store to store endeavoring to secure kitchen equipment. (2) His Grace again approves of any necessary expense in equipment ...[83]

Thereafter Beovich was a frequent visitor at Brooklyn Park, sometimes by prior arrangement, but often unexpectedly. He was impressed by Biloni's management of the orphanage and shocked and grieved when he was killed in a car accident in 1946.[84]

Patricia Carlson, one of the child migrants sent to Australia from Britain after the Second World War, testified to a Senate inquiry in 2001 that she had been beaten by the sister in charge of the Goodwood orphanage. She also recalled that when Archbishop Beovich was told of this, he attended a meeting at Goodwood and insisted that 'the strap was never to be used'. The sister responsible for the abuse was 'shipped back to Angas Street, with most of us cheering'.[85] 'Some of the nuns were lovely – really dedicated dear ladies,' another former inmate told Anne McLay, author of a history of the Sisters of Mercy in South Australia, 'others patently didn't like kids.' McLay does not mention the incident described by Carlson, but notes that the sister in question 'was an assertive personality and a strict disciplinarian'. Her successor had 'a softer personality'.[86]

Beovich's diary reveals that he often visited Goodwood on happier occasions, such as sports days and annual concerts. In December he shared special guest status with Father Christmas at the Christmas party. Some children even got to ride in his car when Keith Koen drove them to picnics in the Adelaide Hills.[87] Life for the children was undoubtedly highly disciplined, spartan and institutional, but efforts were made to try to make it more bearable.

The Catholic School System

Catholic orphanages were not the only focus of Beovich's attention. Although it was no longer his main responsibility, developing and coordinating the Catholic school system remained one of his major concerns. He implemented in Adelaide the changes which he had already introduced in Melbourne, most notably the development of a Catholic education office, with William Russell as director. In 1941 the parish school at Thebarton was transformed into the diocesan technical school, run initially by the Brothers of St John the Baptist.[88] When their Institute collapsed in 1942, Beovich arranged for Marist Brothers to take over the school. In the early 1940s he also encouraged the development of an agricultural college run by the Marist Brothers near Mount Gambier, and in 1944 asked the Dominican Sisters to set up a class for handicapped and retarded children in the grounds of the Dominican convent in Franklin Street. From 1951 it was St Patrick's Special School.[89] As he had done in Melbourne, Beovich limited the number of parochial schools which could offer secondary classes, preferring students of academic ability to attend 'central schools'.

Along with better coordination of the school system came a new syllabus for religious education. It was issued in 1940 and prominently featured the catechism which Beovich had developed in 1937 and the *Companion to the Catechism* which he had written. The syllabus has been described as an excessively cognitive and abstract document likely to reinforce 'a rather narrow devotional approach to prayer'.[90] Its dry bones were fleshed out in numerous teacher-training sessions. Beovich believed, as he had maintained at the Catholic Education Congress in 1936, that the key to good religious education was the teacher. 'What the teacher is matters more than what he says,' Beovich stressed at the annual Mass for teachers in the cathedral in 1942.[91] The following year he assured teachers, 'I know your difficulties ... I have visited your schools'. However, he insisted that they had to instil in children 'a high sense of their own dignity as children of God'.[92] In another address in 1945 he emphasised the difference between teaching prayers and teaching a child to pray. It was the latter which was most important. Once children understood that God loved them, and they could talk to him as easily as to their parents, prayer was easy. They could learn some set prayers, but Beovich strongly recommended that these should not be too long.[93]

For most of the 1940s the infant bureaucracy of the Catholic Education Office consisted of just William Russell and a part-time secretary. In 1948 Beovich appointed Russell parish priest of the newly created parishes of Woodville and Albert Park, in addition to his duties in Catholic education. It was a heavy workload, but Beovich supplied an assistant priest to help in the two parishes and another young priest to work in the Catholic Education Office. The latter was James Gleeson. Born in rural South Australia, Gleeson was ordained in 1945 after studying at Corpus Christi College in Melbourne. He spent the following year as an assistant priest in the cathedral parish. In 1947 Beovich sent him back to Melbourne for a year at Mercy Teachers' College.[94] When he returned to Adelaide, Gleeson worked more closely with Beovich than Russell.[95] He formally replaced Russell as director of Catholic Education in 1952.

Like Buckley and Roberts at the adjoining Catholic Welfare Bureau, Russell and Gleeson found it difficult to get the religious orders to comply with their wishes, but no matter how much they prized their independence, school principals also valued episcopal patronage. Beovich made the most of this and forged friendly ties with school communities. In his first December in Adelaide he attended a school speech night nearly every evening in the month, a pattern which he stoically maintained in subsequent years, and he was often the special guest at school concerts, sports carnivals and such like. Students in Adelaide, like their counterparts in Melbourne in the 1920s and 1930s, benefited from his habit of granting half-day holidays and many remember him fondly as a result.

St Francis Xavier Seminary

From 1942 boys who aspired to be priests could undertake secondary schooling at St Francis Xavier Seminary. Of all the diocesan projects undertaken in the 1940s, the establishment of the seminary was the one closest to Beovich's heart.[96] From the time of Pope Benedict XV (1914–1922), it was the policy of the Congregation of the Propagation of the Faith to encourage dioceses to open their own seminaries. On 10 April 1940, just three days after his consecration, Beovich met with the apostolic delegate and Bishop Thomas McCabe of Port Augusta to discuss how this could be done in Adelaide. It was agreed that a minor seminary would be built, with both South Australian dioceses contributing on a pro-rata basis (later fixed at a ratio of one-sixth for Port Augusta and five-sixths for Adelaide).[97] A little over a month after the initial meeting, on 18 May 1940, Beovich arranged with McCabe to purchase land close to the Christian Brothers' College at Rostrevor.[98]

Before building could go ahead, a permit had to be obtained from the National Security Regulations Council. Albert Hannan took one of the members of the council, James Gosse, to visit Beovich so that Beovich could put the Church's case personally. Beovich enlisted Gosse's support and the permit was forthcoming. Part of the deal was that all other building work in the diocese would be halted until the seminary was built. While this meant a delay in other projects, Catholics throughout the diocese were encouraged to embrace the seminary appeal which Beovich launched in March 1941. To the archbishop's satisfaction, a great number did so.

As the rector of their new seminary, Beovich and McCabe appointed a young Australian priest from Perth, Alan Johnston. He was a surprising choice. At twenty-eight years of age, he had been ordained only four years and had no postgraduate qualifications. However, the apostolic delegate, John Panico, had met him in Perth and warmly recommended him. On 22 May 1940 Beovich wrote to Archbishop Redmond Prendiville of Perth to ask if he could spare Johnston. Prendiville replied on 28 May 1940 that he would be 'delighted' to offer Johnston's services in 1941. In December that year Prendiville wrote again to Beovich to tell him that Johnston's move to Adelaide would be announced in the Perth diocesan paper, the *Record*, on Christmas Eve: 'I shall advise Father Johnston of this appointment on Monday, 23 December. That will allow him ten days to put his house in order! So far he knows nothing about it.' That is an example of how autocratically bishops could treat their priests. Johnston's reaction is not known, but he dutifully arrived in Adelaide in the first week of January 1941 and began touring Catholic schools to encourage vocations.[99]

There was a setback when the builder went bankrupt and the new building at Rostrevor was not ready for occupation at the beginning of 1942, as had been hoped. The Christian Brothers provided temporary accommodation at their school across the road for Johnston and the twenty-four pioneer seminarians who were aged between twelve and fourteen. The group included a future archbishop of Adelaide, Leonard Faulkner. On 1 February 1942

Beovich went to Rostrevor to give them his blessing. 'You will be studying like other boys, playing the same games,' Beovich informed them, 'but in the inner sanctuary of your soul you will be seeking perfection of the highest order.'[100]

The successful launch of the minor seminary in 1942 was followed by its gradual expansion. Nearby Stradbroke Hall was purchased in 1943, and the next year, to celebrate the centenary of the first bishop's arrival in South Australia, a fund was established to raise money for a major seminary. From 1946 students could progress from secondary schooling to philosophical studies, the latter taught by two young Australian-born priests, James Bourke from Perth and Tom Horgan from Adelaide. Those who persevered were then sent to Melbourne, Sydney or Rome to complete their theological studies and formation for the priesthood.

For the first three years Johnston was the only resident priest at the seminary. By 1946 five priests were living there.[101] On 25 March 1947 Beovich noted in his diary, 'From certain information I am not happy about the rector's position at the seminary. On one hand, Father Johnston has done good work during the past five years; on the other hand, he has not shown himself a good superior with the staff. However, in fairness to him all aspects must be carefully gone into.' Three weeks later he jotted:

> Again I have the impression – and this is shared by Dr McCabe – that Father Johnston in spite of certain good qualities has limitations which either are more apparent now or did not exist in the first period of the seminary. If our impressions are correct, the solution would be to appoint a new rector.

Johnston's obituary in 1958 perhaps hints at the problem. He was described as 'a priest of forceful character and direct speech'.[102] Margaret Press refers to him as 'mercurial' and 'irascible'[103]. Rather than dismiss Johnston outright, Beovich arranged for Prendiville to recall him and James Bourke to Perth on the face-saving pretext that there was a shortage of priests in Western Australia. Beovich was sorry to lose Bourke, but his departure was necessary if Johnston was to leave with his dignity intact. Johnston subsequently returned to Adelaide for ordinations and stayed with Beovich.[104]

Beovich kept a close eye on his seminary, visiting it at least weekly. This does not mean that he got to know the students well – stories abound of his struggle to remember their names.[105] They probably had more contact with his chauffeur, Keith Koen. David Shinnick, one of the first seminarians in 1942, recalls Koen wandering down to the milking shed every Tuesday morning while the archbishop met with the rector and other staff or prayed in the chapel. The students were under a strict obligation to remain silent while they milked the cows, but Koen cheerfully insisted, as he passed on the latest news, that the rules did not apply to him. When Shinnick went to see Beovich to tell him that he had decided not to proceed to ordination, Beovich accepted the news calmly. He did not try to persuade him to stay or offer him any kind of counselling: 'It was all very matter of fact. I had no idea what went through his mind or was in his heart.'[106]

Beovich would not have been too dismayed at Shinnick's departure because vocations to the priesthood seemed to be increasing. There were more keen young men to take his place. In spite of the inevitable teething problems, the seminary was fulfilling his hopes. He reflected in his diary on 30 November 1949:

> The seminary means everything to the diocese. Before it, there seemed to be few vocations. Since its foundation, the future looks promising. Already we have twenty-three students for the diocese in philosophy and theology ... The first student (Faulkner) will be ordained to the priesthood in Rome on 1st January next.

The tide had at last begun to flow in favour of Australian-born priests and it was no longer necessary to import men from Ireland.

Aquinas College

The other major project of the 1940s was the establishment of a Catholic residential college connected to the city's university, as was the case in Melbourne, Sydney and Brisbane.[107] The driving force behind this was Albert Hannan, one of the University of Adelaide's first Catholic graduates. He was a leading member of the Catholic graduate society, the Aquinas Society, which commenced in 1929, and he persuaded Archbishop Spence that one of the aims of the society should be to work towards a residential college. At the Catholic Education Congress in Adelaide in 1936,

Archbishop Killian announced that a Catholic college would be established. During the next two years a Catholic University College Endowment Fund Committee was set up, with Hannan as chairman. However, by the time Killian died in 1939, the committee had raised less than £2000 of the £5000 Killian considered necessary to start a project which, it was estimated, would probably exceed £10,000.

The new archbishop had barely had a chance to unpack his bags when Hannan began lobbying him.[108] Beovich's response was lukewarm. He thought that a Catholic residential college was desirable in theory, but he had other priorities: establishing the seminary and improving parochial schools. He was also conscious that most of the Catholics of the archdiocese of Adelaide were 'poorer people' who would not benefit directly from the proposed college.[109] On 26 November 1941 Beovich told the Catholic University College Fund Committee that unless the Church received a large bequest the project would have to be postponed indefinitely. He tried to soften the blow by saying that he would review the decision in ten years time.[110] Hannan was not mollified. His daughter remembers him returning home very angry. He regarded the archbishop 'as a difficult man whom you couldn't budge on things, especially money'.[111]

Yet Hannan did not have to wait ten years for Beovich to change his mind, only five. By 1946 the war had finished and the new seminary was progressing well. At a conference of the University Catholic Federation of Australia, held at the University of Adelaide on 24 January 1947, Beovich announced that a site on Mackinnon Parade near the University of Adelaide had been purchased, and that, as soon as there was sufficient funding, Aquinas College would be established. Uncomfortable with anything which smacked of elitism, he explained that it would not only be a residential college but:

> especially a spiritual centre for all the Catholic undergraduates of the university. I would hope – not for a great college whose residents might consider themselves a cut above the non-residents – but rather for a Catholic centre and power house for the university, with a rector and chapel and library catering for all our students, and then at the same

> time but secondarily, as a place where a certain number of students could reside.[112]

The appeal that Beovich launched in April 1947 exceeded all expectations. By the end of the year £16,000 had been raised. As with the seminary appeal, the bulk of the money did not come from Adelaide's social and professional elite, but from the parishes, schools and religious communities of the diocese.[113] The site on Mackinnon Parade was deemed too small, and in August 1948 Beovich authorised Hannan to submit a tender for 'one of the finest, if not the finest site in Adelaide', a nineteen-room mansion on Montefiore Hill at North Adelaide. It had been the home of a former chief justice and chancellor of the university, Sir Samuel Way.[114] To Beovich's relief, the diocese's offer of £20,500 was accepted.[115] Substantial alterations were needed, and as building restrictions were still in force, Beovich personally went to see Premier Playford with a proposal for the construction of a new wing. Playford was sympathetic and the necessary permit was obtained.[116]

Beovich also arranged with the Jesuit provincial for Father Cornelius Finn SJ to become the first rector of the college, the start of the Jesuits' fifty-year involvement with Aquinas. The formal opening of the college took place on 30 September 1951: 'Highly successful function, & a landmark in the educational history of the diocese,' the archbishop wrote with satisfaction in his diary that night.

Catholic Organisations

In the 1940s there was a multitude of Catholic groups ranging from parish sporting clubs to professional associations like the Guild of St Luke for Catholic doctors and the Assisian Guild for Catholic teachers. Beovich took a particular interest in the new Catholic Action Movements linked to the Australian National Secretariat of Catholic Action in Melbourne: the Young Christian Workers' Movement (YCW), the National Catholic Rural Movement (NCRM), the National Catholic Girls' Movement (NCGM) and the Young Christian Students' Movement (YCS). He became episcopal chairman of the YCS, which by 1950 had about

5000 members throughout Australia between the ages of fifteen and eighteen.[117]

To the annoyance of advocates of the more analytical Catholic Action approach, with its 'See, Judge, Act' methodology, Beovich invited the Ladies of the Grail to run their 1941 national summer school in Adelaide.[118] Founded in Holland after the First World War, the Grail was welcomed to Sydney by Archbishop Kelly in 1936. Instead of encouraging serious study and reflection, Grail meetings were usually joyful and folksy, with lots of singing and liturgical dancing. Frustrated by the 'Dutch folk dances' and the lack of 'solid' formation for pupils at Cabra Convent, Dominican priest James O'Doherty wrote in disgust to his friend and co-founder of the Catholic Guild of Social Studies, Margaret McGuire: 'What is needed is the butchering of a few Bishops and priests – preferably Bishops.'[119] He did not say who he had in mind, but Beovich would have been a likely candidate. Beovich also bruised some women's feelings when he forced the Junior Catholic Women's League to disband in 1947 and reform as part of the NCGM.[120]

Although this was probably a further irritation to the intellectual O'Doherty, Beovich is fondly remembered by supporters of the Therry Dramatic Society for encouraging the formation of a Catholic drama group in Adelaide.[121] George Walton, a devout layman, had produced a morality play ('Credo') for the centenary celebrations in Melbourne in 1937. Beovich was familiar with his work, and in 1943 asked Walton to establish a branch of his Melbourne-based Therry Society in Adelaide. As a result, an enthusiastic group of young adult Catholics met weekly in the Diocesan Education Building alongside the cathedral. With Walton as director and Tom Horgan as spiritual director, the society's first production was 'The Way of the Cross' in April 1944. As the society's patron, Beovich usually sat in the front row on opening nights.[122]

These new, innovative movements did not directly challenge traditional assumptions about the role of women in church and society.[123] One of the main aims of both the Grail and the NCGM was to help Catholic women become better wives and mothers. By the late 1940s there was an organisation with more explicitly feminist aims. Originally founded in England in 1911, the St Joan's Alliance provided a forum for educated career women to discuss social and political issues and press for equal rights for women. It is not clear when the Alliance was inaugurated in Adelaide, but a group was formed in Sydney in 1946 and probably in Adelaide soon afterwards. The Sydney Alliance suffered from Cardinal Gilroy's disapproval – he actively discouraged Catholic women from joining it.[124] In contrast, Beovich tolerated the Alliance in Adelaide. He allowed members to gather for an annual Mass in the cathedral with breakfast in the cathedral hall afterwards, but he did not himself attend.[125]

Beovich was undoubtedly more comfortable exhorting members of the Catholic Women's League (CWL) to model their homes on the holy house of Nazareth,[126] and praising Legionaries of Mary for their spirit of humility and self-denial.[127] He warned the Hibernian Australasian Benefit Society about the danger of a declining birth rate and the need for government support for large families,[128] and encouraged the Catholic Pharmaceutical Guild to fight against the sale of contraceptive devices.[129] While he accepted that some women had to undertake work for economic reasons, he believed, as he told the CWL in 1940, that it was God's will for most women that they be 'queens in their homes, queens of their family'.[130] His own redoubtable mother certainly seems to have fulfilled that role.

Beovich never underestimated the time and effort that many Catholics put into Catholic societies, nor the sacrifices they made to support the Catholic school system and social welfare institutions. His former secretary, Pat Kelly, recalled in 1965:

> 'People are very good, Father' – that was a favorite expression of his. How often he used to say it as a kind of spontaneous comment on something that had come to his notice ... Come to think of it, this would perhaps be the key impression that comes through after all these years: his esteem for people and his appreciation of the goodness in them in whatever way it was manifested.[131]

Beovich expressed his gratitude in short speeches at innumerable functions: a few well-chosen words of encouragement, support and pious exhortation. Nevertheless, the famous speed with which he circulated at such gatherings, culminating in 'jet-propelled getaways', indicates that while he met a great many people, few got to know him well.[132]

'The Beovich Way'

In retrospect, Darcy Woodards saw the 1940s as 'one of the most progressive periods of Archbishop Beovich's time'.[133] He thought primarily in terms of building and fundraising: the establishment of St Francis Xavier Seminary, Aquinas College, and the Diocesan Charities Appeal loomed large in his memory and they were certainly significant achievements. From their modest beginnings in the 1940s, the Catholic Education Office and the Catholic Welfare Bureau (now known as Centacare) would also assume great importance in the diocese as the years went on, while Beovich's support for the Catholic Action movements and the 'Catholic Hour' on radio 5KA is further evidence of the 'progressive' nature of his first decade as a bishop. There was a modest but steady increase in the Catholic population in this period. In his report to Rome in 1950, Beovich estimated that the number of Catholics in his diocese had risen by about 10,000 to a total of 66,500. The number of children in Catholic schools had increased by just over 2000. Eight new parishes had been created, nine new churches or Mass centres, and eight new schools. The number of diocesan priests had only risen by eleven, but the thirty-six students in residence at the seminary offered hope for the future.

Buildings, bureaus and statistics are important, but they reveal little about the personal characteristics and administrative style of the bishop. In this respect, Matthew Beovich defies easy categorisation. It is not just that people remember him differently. He seemed to contradict himself in a number of ways. For instance, he demonstrated a peculiar mixture of efficiency and disorganisation in his administration. His first secretary, Patrick Kelly, wrote in 1965:

> Thinking back one can't help recalling the Archbishop's phenomenal filing system. It was mostly in his head, but there was an impressive certainty about the way he located what he wanted. He'd dart to the particular pile of papers – whether one of the three or four on his desk or the half dozen or more on the floor and chairs – and after a little brisk shuffling come up with the required document.[134]

Twenty years after his death, important diocesan papers were still turning up in books in the study at his former home, indicating that the system did not always work. When reading, he tended to use whatever piece of paper came to hand as a bookmark. Another idiosyncrasy was that he saved paper when he was preparing sermons, addresses, and such like, by jotting notes on the backs of used envelopes and other documents. A priest who wrote to ask for his approval for some matter could receive his original letter back with a brief margin note indicating the archbishop's agreement or disagreement. Thus Beovich cleared his desk of paperwork as quickly as possibly, but no copies were kept for the archives.[135]

People who did not know Beovich well sometimes got the impression he was an impulsive man. Those who worked closely with him knew the exact opposite was true: he was innately cautious and disliked being rushed into a decision. Then, when he had made up his mind, it was difficult to convince him to change it.[136] He was impulsive only in his movements, darting here and there, and arriving and disappearing from functions with lightning speed. Few could keep up with him. Woodards wrote of one of his first encounters with the new archbishop in April 1940:

> My first duty was to take him to the manager of the Commonwealth Bank to introduce him. Under civil law the Archbishop would be the executive officer of Church finance. We set out to walk from West Terrace. It was a nice sunny day in April, but I can tell you that by the time we got to the bank I had just about had it. Not that I was a slow walker, but the Archbishop went along in a way that said – we've got a job to do and we want to get it done. Well that was carried out alright, but this characteristic of his, of going straight to whatever he had to do, characterised his whole life. I found it the same in other matters and situations. He would do what he had to do – do it well – and then away and he was gone – the job completed.[137]

The downside to this was that briskness could sometimes become brusqueness, and getting to the heart of a matter as soon as possible could mean overriding the opinions of others. Beovich made many shrewd decisions in the 1940s, but he was seldom able to implement them without some pain being felt. Of course, it would have been impossible for him to have pleased everyone, and it is to his credit that he was able to withstand considerable pressure when making decisions, even from influential Catholics like Albert Hannan. However, it does seem the charm which Mannix found so winsome in Beovich as a young priest deserted the older bishop at times, especially in his relations with subordinates. One observer reflected that Beovich was not always good at explaining the reasons for his decisions.[138] Given the hierarchical structure of the Catholic Church, and the emphasis placed on humility and obedience as virtues, he may not have seen the need to be more forthcoming. That was a flaw in the institution rather than the man. The tributes which flowed on the twenty-fifth anniversary of his consecration indicate that Beovich may actually have been more sensitive to the feelings of subordinates than many others in positions of leadership in the Catholic Church, and much more willing to consult.[139] It was clearly not arrogance which made him refrain from telling Alan Johnston the real reason for his recall to Perth. 'Deep down, beneath the sometimes brusque manner, he was a very compassionate man,' remembers one former diocesan priest.[140]

A Private Life

When Beovich arrived in Adelaide in 1940, he lived in Archbishop's House on the corner of West Terrace and Grote Street. The oldest part of the building had been constructed in 1845 as a residence for Adelaide's first bishop, Francis Murphy. In 1940 it was also the home of the five priests who served the cathedral parish, the archbishop's secretary and the central diocesan office. Two years later Mary and John Fennescey, deciding that the archbishop should have a residence away from the busy and crowded cathedral presbytery, donated money to the diocese for another dwelling to be purchased.[141] Mary chose a gracious two-storey house, built circa 1890, overlooking the parklands in the prestigious suburb of Medindie. An 'astounded' Beovich objected that it was too elegant, too far from the cathedral, staffing would be a problem, and there were other more worthy projects in the diocese which required funding.[142] Mary persisted, and Beovich eventually withdrew his objections, moving into his new home in September 1943.[143] He named it 'Ennis' after his Kenny grandparents' home town in Ireland, a reminder to the Irish-Australian Catholics of his diocese (and perhaps especially the Irish-born priests) that he also had Irish ancestry.[144]

As a status symbol, 'Ennis' demonstrated that the Catholic archbishop of Adelaide could take his place in the leading ranks of Adelaide society. When the diocese sold the property in 2004 for $3.51 million, it broke the record for Adelaide's highest-priced residential sale.[145] Behind the elegant Victorian façade, there was a large formal drawing room and dining room. A spacious lobby, lit by a vaulted skylight, contained an ornate, polished staircase which led to four imposing bedrooms. Beovich, however, chose to live in what would originally have been the servants' quarters. The smallest, plainest rooms at the rear of the house on the top floor became his bedroom, sitting room and bathroom. He also used a long narrow room on the ground floor on the western side of the house, and lined its walls with book cases and hundreds of books, but the drawing room at the front of the house was kept for formal occasions. Beovich could play the role of 'prince-bishop' when he felt that occasion demanded it, but he was never one at heart.

Ennis gave Beovich more space and greater privacy than he would have had at Archbishop's House. A significant disadvantage – although it might not have appeared so at the time – was that it removed him further from his priests. There was one exception. In 1945 Beovich invited Thomas Davis to retire from the parish of Kingswood and live at Ennis. Davis had been born in Sydney in 1872 and, like Beovich, had studied at the Urban College of Propaganda Fide and been ordained in the basilica of St John Lateran. He began his priestly ministry in Adelaide in 1895, and was one of the diocesan consultors when Beovich arrived in Adelaide. In 1945, on Beovich's recommendation, the pope appointed him to the rank of domestic prelate, with the title of 'Monsignor'. Of quiet, retiring disposition, he was an unobtrusive companion (his hobby was stamp-collecting). Until his death in 1958 at the age of eighty-six, Davis provided Beovich with gentle support and the benefit of more than fifty years experience in the diocese.[146]

There were no pet animals at Ennis – Beovich was wary of dogs.[147] He never owned a record player; nor did he spend what little leisure time he had playing sport or going to the theatre. Sometimes he listened to tennis and cricket matches on the radio.

Tom Horgan called at Ennis one New Year's Day and found the archbishop pacing in his garden – Australia was losing too many wickets and he could not bear the tension.[148] Most of all, Beovich read. His library included volumes on politics and current affairs, Agatha Christie novels for light relaxation, and almost everything published by the publishing house run by Frank Sheed and his wife Maisie Ward.[149] Sheed was a favourite author. In the 1940s he and Ward were among the foremost Catholic apologists in the English-speaking world. Adrian Hastings locates them in the 'mildly progressive centre of post-war English Catholicism' – that is, progressive as regards social thought, not theology:

> Sheed's *Theology and Sanity* represents Catholic doctrine at its clearest, most rational, most convincing, with clerical preoccupations reduced to a minimum – a layman writing for laymen. Yet it remains the most straight contemporary orthodoxy, with a hardly a hint of history in it, not a suggestion that anything might be wrong, missed out or one-sided in the current theology, canon law or institutional structure of the Church ... Sheed ... was proof of the thesis that the clergy could trust the laity, that the lay apostolate could work to perfection in unsubservient but utterly loyal terms.[150]

Beovich's copy, bought in 1948, is well thumbed.

Most Sunday evenings in the 1940s Beovich caught the train to Seacliff where the Little Company of Mary (the 'Blue Sisters' who ran Calvary Hospital) had a beach house. The Sisters set aside a bedroom and bathroom for the archbishop, and he celebrated Mass for anyone staying in the house on Monday mornings. He then spent the day on his own, returning late afternoon by train to the city.[151] His clerical friends back in Melbourne, who liked playing golf and cards, were incredulous that anyone would want to spend their day off 'watching sea gulls'.[152] Beovich, however, had never been good at sport or cards and he enjoyed solitude.

Once a year Beovich had a longer break, spending most of the month of February at Koroit near Warnambool in Victoria. Koroit was a mensal parish – a parish under the special jurisdiction of the local bishop, in this case, the bishop of Ballarat. Jim O'Collins, who transferred from Geraldton to Ballarat in 1942, invited Beovich, Pat Lyons and Justin Simonds to join him at

Koroit in February 1943. This became an annual event for Beovich for the next thirty years. Located in a fertile farming area where many Irish migrants had settled in the nineteenth century, the town was one of the most Catholic in the nation.[153] The parish church and presbytery had been designed by no less an architect than William Wardell. A pupil of the great Welby Pugin, Wardell was also responsible for St Patrick's Cathedral in Melbourne and St Mary's Cathedral in Sydney. His neo-Gothic church in Koroit was described as 'the most magnificent and costly ecclesiastical building in Western Victoria', and the adjoining two-storey, bluestone presbytery, a 'palatial mansion ... befitting the residence of a bishop'.[154] The parish history recounts:

> The annual arrival of the Bishops created the feeling that Koroit was a special parish. The curates would leave to make room or take their own holidays, and the visiting Bishops would take over Parish duties, saying Sunday masses, hearing confessions and for those five or six weeks being made very welcome by everyone in the Parish. It was not unusual to see them walking along the streets of Koroit, sometimes five abreast and often wearing their Episcopal robes of the sacred purple.[155]

Occasionally the formal attire was abandoned. O'Collins, the story goes, once ordered by telephone one of the boats which were available for hire at the beach. The next day, dressed in old slacks and a pullover, he went to collect it. The woman in charge of the boats refused to relinquish it: 'No, you can't have that one. That's for the bloody bishop!' 'I am the bloody bishop!' O'Collins retorted.[156] A bishop was a bishop, even on holidays.

Koroit was an appealing holiday destination for O'Collins because of its proximity to golf courses and beaches. Beovich did not share his friend's enthusiasm for golf and fishing. He sometimes went out on the boat with the other bishops, but often he just strolled on his own along the beach. He also took the opportunity, while in Victoria, to meet clerical friends like Dan Conquest from his Melbourne days. Conquest testifies that there 'was not the slightest change' in their relationship after Beovich became a bishop.[157] Beovich always visited his mother when he was in Melbourne until her death in 1949, and sometimes saw his sister Vera. However, he had little contact with his brother and his brother's children.

Sadly, Beovich's niece and nephews could not say of him what Laurie Bayliss said of his uncle, Norman Gilroy:

> One time at a family gathering he just started to talk and he was talking about the loneliness at the top, of how difficult it was to be at the top and not really have any friends and how much he had relied on his family for normality and the wonderful things the family had given to him and how much he loved the family.[158]

In a speech in 1941 Beovich conceded that 'the life of a priest was a lonely life, and that of a bishop even more lonely'. Unable to be truly a 'benevolent father' to the thousands of Catholics in his diocese, he, like Gilroy, was reluctant to show favouritism by singling out a few people in his diocese for special attention. One of the diocesan clergy remembers Beovich commenting that *if* he had had personal friends, Darcy Woodards would have been one of them.[159] For both Beovich and Gilroy, being a bishop brought with it 'a necessary isolation'.[160]

It is clear, nonetheless, that Beovich genuinely tried to be a pastor of souls and not just the chief executive of his diocese, and that his efforts met with considerable success. In his report to Rome in 1950, he praised the zeal, cooperation and loyalty of the priests, religious and laity of the Adelaide archdiocese.[161] The tribute seems to have been offered with genuine gratitude and to have been well deserved. Not everyone liked the archbishop or supported all of his decisions, but Beovich rarely encountered opposition. As the next chapter will show, that changed in the 1950s when he found himself mired in political controversy.

Six

'A Dangerous Experiment' The Movement

> Mr Santamaria's success in making the Movement a personal instrument is roughly proportional to the lack of political and theological sophistication of the Australian bishops. In the main, they allowed themselves to be swept along on a wave of hysteria and be so mesmerised by the Santamaria rhetoric that they could not even see clearly (or did not want to see) the theology of their own Church on the limits of Church intervention in politics ... The Movement was such a dangerous experiment, with its potential for inflaming sectarian feeling, that, in retrospect, it is surprising that the bishops could have given their unanimous approval to it.
>
> Paul Ormonde, *The Movement*

On 21 December 1953 Matthew Beovich sat at a dinner table in Sydney with Archbishop Romolo Carboni, the new apostolic delegate to Australia. In his diary later that night, Beovich recounted that he (Beovich) had praised the work of 'the Movement', the secretive anti-communist organisation led by B. A. Santamaria, and told Carboni that Mr Santamaria was 'the best Catholic lay man in Australia'. At some later date, after Carboni had become an enthusiastic supporter of Santamaria, Beovich went back to his diary entry and wrote in the margin alongside it: 'Mea Culpa.'

Between the original comment and the margin note lay one of the most divisive episodes in Australian political and religious history. On 5 October 1954, the federal leader of the Australian Labor Party (ALP), Dr H. V. Evatt, publicly denounced the Movement. This triggered a bitter schism which cost the party government in Victoria and Queensland. The ALP did not return to power in those states until 1982 and 1989 respectively, and there was no federal election victory until 1972. To Beovich's dismay, the Catholic hierarchy was also divided over its response to the situation.

There is now considerable literature on the Movement, the ALP Split and the role of the Catholic Church.[1] Explanations as to why the bishops behaved the way they did vary, but it is generally accepted that differences between Melbourne and Sydney were crucial. Patrick O'Farrell contrasts Daniel Mannix's support for lay initiatives in Melbourne with the Sydney bishops' authoritarian clericalism (Santamaria thought this a 'most perceptive summary' of the affair).[2] Bruce Duncan, on the other hand, criticises Mannix for being too indulgent toward Santamaria, and credits Sydney's Norman Gilroy and James Carroll with greater pragmatism. There was a successful Labor government in New South Wales, led by Premier J. J. Cahill, a devout Catholic, and memories of the damaging split during the 1930s were still fresh enough to curb any enthusiasm for another schism. In Victoria the climate was more volatile and ideological.[3] Whatever the merit of these arguments, they do not take into account the role of Matthew Beovich, a former Melbourne priest and a bishop in a state with a well-entrenched Liberal and Country League government. What led to his change of heart with regard to the Movement and Santamaria?

Beovich, Santamaria and the Hierarchy's Endorsement of the Movement

In their early lives, Matthew Beovich and Bartholomew Augustine (Bob) Santamaria had much in common. Their family homes were on Sydney Road in working-class Melbourne, and their migrant fathers sold fruit and vegetables to earn a living. At school they both had to endure the label 'dago'.[4] They owed much of their education to the Christian Brothers; Santamaria spent two years at St Joseph's College, North Melbourne, Beovich's old school, before matriculating at St Kevin's College in 1930–1931. Beovich was, however, nineteen years older. In contrast to the informal weekly sessions in which the Brothers shared their faith with the young Beovich, Santamaria's religious instruction was based on Michael Sheehan's *Apologetics and Christian Doctrine*, first published in 1918. He later credited this textbook with supplying 'the rational justification for my act of faith in Catholic Christianity'.[5] Edmund Campion comments that its 'argumentativeness may account for the high incidence of Catholics among Australian lawyers and philosophers'.[6] Santamaria trained as a lawyer before being appointed assistant director of the Melbourne-based Australian National Secretariat of Catholic Action (ANSCA) in 1937. He was also the secretary of one of its specialised bodies, the National Catholic Rural Movement (NCRM), from 1939.

Soon after coming into existence in 1937 with the authorisation of the Australian Catholic hierarchy, ANSCA was beset by internal and external tensions, arising in large part from the 'diverse and contradictory interpretations and misunderstandings' of what 'Catholic Action' actually meant.[7] Although Catholics were encouraged to promote the Church's social teaching in their workplaces and local communities, Popes Pius XI and Pius XII tried to draw a line between this and involvement in party politics. As the influential French philosopher Jacques Maritain maintained, the latter was acceptable as 'action of Catholics' done independently of the Church, but not under the umbrella of the various Catholic Action movements which were under the control of the hierarchy. Unfortunately, however, the difference between 'the action of Catholics as believers and the action of Catholics as citizens' was seldom clear cut.[8]

At the third state conference of the NCRM in South Australia in August 1943, Beovich welcomed Santamaria to his diocese with effusive praise, in words similar to those he would use in his conversation with the apostolic delegate ten years later: 'Without exaggeration, he would say that, so far as the preservation of Christianity and the welfare of Australia were concerned, he doubted if there was a layman in Australia who had done more than Mr Santamaria.'[9] It is likely that Beovich knew then of Santamaria's involvement in a secret anti-communist organisation, as the archbishop of Adelaide was a member of the Episcopal

Committee on Catholic Action, and there is a reference in the minutes of the committee's May 1943 meeting to Santamaria reporting 'on the special work he has been undertaking in the last six months'. 'Special work' was one of the euphemisms used for the Movement.[10] Beovich was certainly aware of its existence in 1944 when Santamaria wrote to him concerning Norman Gilroy: 'His Grace is emphatic that Sydney should work along lines of complete uniformity where the confidential work is going, and that it should be subject to the Commonwealth executive.'[11] Ironically, this letter was written on paper bearing the NCRM letterhead. Santamaria's involvement in both official Catholic Action (through the NCRM and ANSCA) and the Movement, and the fact that both were effectively run from the same office in Melbourne, would become one of the problems in the years ahead.

After the ALP Split, Santamaria argued that the Movement was essentially 'a voluntary lay organisation', encouraged but not controlled by sympathetic Catholic bishops like Daniel Mannix in Melbourne.[12] In the mid-1940s, however, he was keen to have it defined as part of Catholic Action, even though this would have placed it formally under episcopal control. In a memorandum sent to the Australian bishops before they met in Sydney in September 1945, he assured them that the Movement would, in each diocese, be 'in all things subject to the will of the bishop'.[13] Santamaria later paid tribute to the 'invaluable' support at the 1945 meeting of his 'close friends' Matthew Beovich and Francis Henschke of Wagga Wagga, the episcopal chairman of the NCRM.[14] At the insistence of Justin Simonds, coadjutor archbishop of Melbourne and chairman of another Catholic Action body, the Young Catholic Workers Movement (YCW), the new 'Catholic Social Studies Movement' was not placed under the Catholic Action umbrella. However, a motion was moved by Henschke, and seconded by Beovich, that it be controlled 'both in policy and finance' by a committee of bishops. In practice, episcopal control did not amount to much because one of the three members, Norman Gilroy, did not attend meetings, and the other two, Daniel Mannix and James O'Collins of Ballarat, were very close to Santamaria. Of greater significance was the funding. The bishops agreed to provide an initial grant of £10,000. Thereafter their dioceses were subject to an annual quota to support the national headquarters of the Movement in Melbourne. They also agreed to fund regional offices in capital cities.

In 1945 there were legitimate concerns about communist infiltration of trade unions and trades halls in Australia. During the Second World War, some of the nation's largest unions seem to have fallen under communist leadership, including the Seaman's Union, the Waterside Workers' Federation and the Miners' Federation.[15] As the Cold War intensified in the late 1940s, anti-communism became a mainstream phenomenon in western democracies. Gallop polls indicate that 67 per cent of Australians in 1948 expected another war within ten years, and 80 per cent thought that the Soviet Union wanted to dominate the world.[16] Catholics were particularly susceptible to this crisis mentality. Pope Pius XII strongly opposed communism, decreeing in 1949 that no Catholic could belong to a communist party. He also promoted the cult of Our Lady of Fatima, helping it become one of the most popular forms of Marian devotion. The prophecies associated with the apparition at Fatima in Portugal in 1917 – the year of the communist revolutions in Russia – had a sharp political edge: 'If [Mary's] requests [for prayer and penance] are heeded, Russia will be converted, and there will be peace, if not ... [Russia] will spread her errors throughout the world, causing wars and persecutions of the Church ... various nations will be annihilated.'[17] The spread of communism through Eastern Europe in the wake of the Second World War seemed to confirm this dire prediction. Throughout the 1940s and 1950s reports of the persecution of the Church in communist countries regularly dominated the front page of Catholic newspapers. Adelaide's *Southern Cross* was no exception. Post-war migrants and refugees brought to Australia personal accounts of suffering. As John Maguire comments, 'in the atmosphere of the Cold War, passionate commitment to the anti-communist cause seemed a logical consequence of one's Catholicism'.[18]

What the bishops approved in 1945 was an organisation which would take the fight against communism into the 'industrial field' using some of the communists' own tactics. Santamaria offered them 'a national organisation as strongly disciplined as the

Communist Party';[19] in other words, one in which a high degree of commitment and obedience to the leadership was expected from members.

Although Santamaria later claimed the Movement was 'about as secret as the Sydney Harbor Bridge',[20] secrecy was also very much part of its ethos.

What Santamaria received from the bishops in 1945 was an endorsement which added a strong religious dimension to the fight against communism. Thereafter devout recruits to the organisation were left in no doubt that they were fighting on God's side against the enemies of the Church.[21] Their branch meetings (referred to in the Movement's 1948 handbook *Into Thy Hands* as 'staff conferences with the Lord') began and ended with prayer, and they were assured of the hierarchy's support. Edmund Campion recalls how significant this was in the 1940s and early 1950s:

> In the Catholic imaginative world the authority of the bishops was underpinned by Christ; to deny one was to deny the other; to disobey one was to disobey the other. Thus obedience to the authority of the bishops was not a mere notional assent, it bit deep into the emotions. Those who spoke with the authority of the bishops could count on a flow-on from this obediential psychology ... Catholic critics of the organisation were told that their criticism made them disloyal to the church, at odds with 'the mind of the hierarchy', almost like traitors in wartime.[22]

The Movement was indeed 'a dangerous experiment'.[23]

The Movement in South Australia

As the Movement's regional officer in South Australia, Beovich appointed Edward (Ted) Farrell, a devout lay man who was the president of the Assisian Guild of Catholic Teachers. His task was to 'bring influence to bear on the trade union movement, on the ALP, and, by propaganda, on the community, especially the working community'. Specific aims of the Movement in South Australia were listed as follows:

1. To de-louse 4 or 5 trade unions.
2. To strengthen the local committees in Adelaide and the suburbs.

3. To extend in scope and volume propaganda both literary and viva voce.
4. To begin, by lectures and study circles, the education part of the work.[24]

'De-lousing' trade unions was to be achieved by a coordinated campaign of branch-stacking and vote canvassing. A document titled 'Suggestions for Organisation', presumably sent from the national executive in Melbourne circa 1945, recommended that small groups be established in each parish. Members were to draw up lists of the names and occupations of parishioners, from which possible trade union membership could be determined. They were to seek such information from parish census books, school rolls, parish societies, and such like. Such was the secrecy with which the Movement was shrouded that only as a last resort were they to ask the people concerned directly.[25]

It is generally agreed that the influence of the Communist Party of Australia on the trade union movement peaked around 1945 and thereafter waned.[26] The decline coincided with the development in the mid-1940s of 'Industrial Groups' to combat communist infiltration. In South Australia they were approved by the annual state convention of the ALP in 1946. In contrast to older assessments which downplay the significance of both the Industrial Groups within the ALP and the Movement's influence within the Groups,[27] Ross Fitzgerald believes that 'the Industrial Groups were the only source of consistent resistance to the Communist Party's strategy to gain control of the union movement, and Santamaria and the Movement were the intellectual force behind the Groups'.[28] Malcolm Saunders also has no doubt that 'the driving force of the Groupers was always the Movement'.[29] In South Australia, the Groupers seem to have played a major role in the overthrow in 1953 and 1954 of the left-wing leadership of two unions, the Shop Assistants' Union (SAU) and the Federated Ironworkers' Association (FIA), and they almost succeeded in gaining control of the Federated Clerks' Union.[30]

With 22 branches in 1950, the South Australian arm of the Movement was smaller than that in Victoria (74 branches), New South Wales (100) and Queensland (61).[31] An internal review written circa 1957 observed that 'amongst the several Cs [Catholics] in full-time trade union positions, there are only three who may be classified as M. [Movement] members'. Yet, 'in a voluntary capacity, many other members hold executive and delegate positions'. They owed, it was claimed, these positions to the Movement:

> In the final analysis, it is by the number of organised voters that the Communists have been defeated. It is by organising and persuading unionists to attend their meetings to vote that sound policies are pursued and the common good of members is protected. Experience over 12 years has taught that, except in isolated cases, a general appeal to the general body of Cs. has not raised union attendance unless accompanied by constant and unremitting organisation.[32]

Nevertheless, in the 1950s the Industrial Groups in South Australia operated under a significant handicap, the ALP state conference having withdrawn its support for them in 1951. Clyde Cameron and Jim Toohey exerted strong control over the state branch of the ALP, and with little evidence of a significant communist threat, were just as hostile to extreme right-wing interests in the labour movement as they were to the extreme left.[33] Santamaria himself conceded that 'while the Industrial Groups were formally established in South Australia, they enjoyed a merely formal existence until their charter was ultimately withdrawn in October 1951'.[34] This is at odds with the Group's success in the SAU and FIA, but it was almost certainly the case that 'the few enthusiastic Groupers in South Australia were constantly frustrated by the state executive's – most notably Cameron's – hostility toward them'.[35]

With limited opportunities for direct influence in the trade unions and ALP, much of regional officer Ted Farrell's time was devoted to 'the education part of the work'. His own background as a teacher, as well as Beovich's interest in education, doubtless encouraged this thrust. In 1947 Beovich asked Farrell to establish an adult education institute in the Diocesan Education Building alongside the cathedral. It formally opened in 1948 as the Newman Institute. Designed 'to equip Catholic men and women with a knowledge of industrial and economic problems based on the social teachings of the Catholic Church', it was particularly directed at the 'young, keen intelligent Catholic youth who is not afraid to think, to read and to study'.[36] Significantly, while it was a cloak for the education wing of the Movement, the Newman Institute was under Beovich's control, not Santamaria's. During the following decade 417 adults attended classes on such topics as industrial relations, capitalism and socialism, trade unions and working conditions.[37]

The national headquarters of the Movement also organised speakers to solicit funds and warn of the crisis about to befall Australia in the form of a communist revolution. A letter written by Thomas Ormonde of the Sacred Heart fathers gives an insight into the Movement's impact at parish level. In the early 1950s Ormonde was parish priest of Saddleworth-Manoora, a small rural parish in the archdiocese of Adelaide. In 1969 he wrote to his nephew, Paul, who was writing a book on the Movement:

> ... my friend Archbishop Beovich ... sent a confidential letter to certain priests saying that Father Lalor would be coming to expound to worthy and trustworthy selected Catholic men things concerning an existing peril 'to those things we hold most dear'. A list of names was given, these men were invited to this highly secret meeting, admission to be gained by production of the letter. The meeting had the atmosphere of a conspiratorial gathering ...
>
> Father Lalor's thesis was the danger of the imminent takeover of Australia by the communists. He had possession of the plans, he was aware of the locations of the communist arsenals and the machinegun ammunition. The immediate aim of the meeting was finance for the Movement. Those poor sheep cockies whose fear was not of the loss of faith but the loss of farms and fleeces took out their cheque books and wrote Santamaria £800. A neighbouring parish wrote £1300.

Ormonde disliked Lalor's methods and their result, but as Lalor came to his parish with Beovich's backing, he could not publicly oppose him. He asked his nephew not to reveal his or Beovich's involvement in the incident:

> You can understand how impossible [it is] for me to associate my name with anything critical of Archbishop Beovich. However, if these facts were transferred to Queensland, they would be true. Poor Archbishop Beovich. You can guess how he felt that [the Labor Split]. He was

> Labor by instinct, been it all his life, followed for a time the Movement line, and then retreated faster than most others.[38]

The 'Father Lalor' who addressed the meeting at Manoora was Harold Lalor, a Jesuit priest and one of Santamaria's closest associates. His fiery, apocalyptic tirades, which stressed that time was running out, earned him the nickname 'the five minutes to midnight priest'.[39] Beovich was more restrained in his anti-communism. He usually balanced his attacks on communism with condemnation of the abuses of unrestrained capitalism and – a more positive message – promotion of the Church's social justice teaching.[40] In 1948 he heard American evangelist Fulton Sheen speak in Melbourne and was struck by Sheen's remark that 'just as we hated sin but loved the sinner, so we must hate communism and any other false doctrine but love the communist'.[41] He exhorted members of the Catholic Railway Workers' Association to remember that the most effective weapons against communism were the spiritual ones recommended by Our Lady of Fatima: prayer (especially the praying of the rosary) and penance. In passing, he encouraged them to become involved in their trade union, but that was not his top priority.[42] In contrast to the bleak pessimism which pervades much of Lalor's and Santamaria's rhetoric ('hope was not prominent in his repertoire of virtues', comments Patrick Morgan of Santamaria),[43] Beovich retained the conviction that God was in control, and therefore good would ultimately triumph. There was a wide gulf between his personal piety and the policies and practices of the Movement, but it seems to have taken him some time to realise the significance of that.

Growing Tensions

Beovich still backed Santamaria when, in the late 1940s, Santamaria encountered considerable opposition from within Catholic Action circles. ANSCA had been founded in 1937 to inaugurate the Catholic Action movements. Once they were well established, some leaders wanted greater autonomy, especially those involved in the Young Christian Workers' Movement. In 1946 and 1947 the Episcopal Committee on Catholic Action (which included Beovich) affirmed the importance of coordination and unity, after lobbying from Santamaria who was in control of

ANSCA from 1946.[44] At a meeting of the Australian hierarchy in 1948, Beovich successfully presented the case for retaining the National Secretariat.[45] The following year the Episcopal Committee on Catholic Action further strengthened ANSCA's role by decreeing that between meetings of the Episcopal Committee it would be 'the final authority in all that pertains to the finances and administration of all the movements of Catholic Action, including the appointment of officials'.[46] This was a victory for Santamaria, but a pyrrhic one as much bitterness remained.[47]

Friction also arose in the latter half of the 1940s between Santamaria and some Movement officials in Sydney.[48] Compounding what Santamaria interpreted as interstate rivalry were divisions within the hierarchy and between some bishops and the apostolic delegate, John Panico. The tension generated by Panico's promotion of Australian-born priests to the episcopacy was exacerbated by Gilroy's elevation to the rank of cardinal in 1946. Beovich was delighted when he heard 'the wonderful news', and 'with a full heart' sent Gilroy a congratulatory telegram.[49] Not everyone was so thrilled, especially those who had hoped that Mannix would get to wear the 'red hat'. An elderly Irish priest in Melbourne spat out: 'So the Dago's Pup has got it after all,' a spiteful remark which sped around Melbourne clerical circles.[50] To Beovich's dismay, the matter achieved wider publicity, thanks to his old school friend Arthur Calwell who had become minister for information and minister for immigration in the Chifley federal government. Calwell dashed off a press statement which was scathingly critical of Panico, whom he blamed for the slight on Mannix.[51] Beovich wrote to Panico on 9 January 1946, deploring the 'shocking injustice' of the attack. When Gilroy made his first visit to Melbourne as a cardinal in May 1946, Mannix, a master in the use of irony, belittled Gilroy's career under the guise of flattery.[52] The incident highlights not only a lack of unity in the Catholic Church in Australia but also a lack of respect for Gilroy in Melbourne which became even more apparent in the 1950s.

Gilroy received a much warmer welcome in Adelaide a week before his visit to Melbourne. Beovich basked in the respect shown to the new cardinal not only by the Catholics of his diocese but also by the state's civic leaders and the general community.[53] His high regard for his friend from Propaganda days seems to have been reciprocated as Gilroy sought his advice on a number of occasions. The most notable in the late 1940s concerned the bank nationalisation controversy. In August 1947 Prime Minister Chifley announced that the federal Labor government would nationalise the Australian banking system. Among the many critics of the plan was the outspoken Catholic cleric Archdeacon T. J. O'Donnell of Hobart who maintained that all Christian members of the Australian Labor Party should vote against it. The front page of Adelaide's *Sunday Mail* reported his comments on 13 September 1947, with a response from Beovich. Beovich was aware that Pope Pius XII in 1944 had tried to steer a middle course on nationalisation. He had warned against an excessive concentration of power in the hands of the state, but recognised that in certain circumstances nationalisation could be in the interests of the common good.[54] Hence Beovich concluded that selective nationalisation was not contrary to the teaching of the Church, and Catholics could, with good conscience, support or oppose it.

In Sydney a draft bishops' statement was prepared which claimed, among other things, that the bill for nationalising private banks opened the way to a totalitarian state. In a hysterical tone, the statement finished up:

> We state that if this Bill is intended as a first step towards complete socialism it is an immoral measure. We state that if it is intended only as an isolated instance of nationalisation it is fraught with danger to the foundations of civil society as ordained by divine law and that, therefore, it must be declared fundamentally unsound in the moral order. ACCORDINGLY, INVOKING OUR TEACHING AUTHORITY AS BISHOPS OF THE CHURCH, WE OFFICIALLY DECLARE THAT THE BANKING BILL IS ONE WHICH NO CATHOLIC IS FREE IN CONSCIENCE TO SUPPORT.

Gilroy sent Beovich a copy. Beovich replied on 4 November 1947 that he thought it would be unwise to issue such a 'panicky and drastic condemnation'. If it forced good Catholics to leave the ALP, it would mean abandoning the party to extremists, and if there was another depression like that of the early 1930s, it would look as though the Catholic bishops had supported reactionary capitalism rather than considering the interests of poor workers. Moreover, with regard to the supposed nexus between nationalisation and totalitarianism, Beovich reminded Gilroy that there had been private banks in Hitler's Germany. It seems that Gilroy heeded Beovich's comments as the statement was quietly dropped.[55] The nationalisation bill passed through parliament but was declared invalid by the High Court, a judgement eventually upheld by the Privy Council in London.

In calling into question the support which Catholics could give to the ALP, the banking controversy foreshadowed the Movement crisis of the 1950s. It also focused attention on the decision of the ALP federal conference in Brisbane in 1921 to affirm socialisation as part of Labor's policy platform. In September 1948 the entrepreneurial James Duhig, a strong opponent of the nationalisation bill, warned in Queensland that 'socialisation is a much more plausible and subtle foe than communism'.[56] On 20 September the *Sydney Morning Herald* reported that Brian Doyle, a prominent Sydney Catholic layman, had commented that the socialisation objective threatened Catholic involvement in the ALP. Gilroy sent Beovich a copy of a letter he received from Chifley which insisted that while the Labor Party supported collective ownership when it was necessary to prevent exploitation, it did not seek to abolish private ownership when it was utilised in 'a socially useful manner and without exploitation'.[57] This was known as the 'Blackburn interpretation' as it had been moved by Maurice Blackburn at the 1921 conference. According to Clyde Cameron, Beovich intervened directly in the controversy, offering to make a 'helpful statement' if Cameron could get the ALP's federal conference in September 1948 to reaffirm the Blackburn interpretation.[58] Cameron claims he did this, although the official report of the conference reveals that he subsequently withdrew his motion and the 1921 interpretation was not formally reaffirmed.[59] Beovich, nevertheless, declared in his homily at the Labor Day Mass on 12 October 1948 that a Catholic could, in good conscience, subscribe to the present Labor platform.[60] It was a line which he would uphold throughout the 1950s.

Beovich was also a voice of moderation during the campaign leading up to the 1951 referendum to ban the Communist Party.

The Movement publication *Newsweekly* criticised Labor politicians for campaigning for a 'no' vote, but Beovich refused to direct Catholics how to respond. In fact, Duhig was the only member of the hierarchy to publicly back the 'yes' case.[61] Cameron attributes the defeat of the referendum to Evatt and the Catholic bishops, Beovich, Gilroy and Mannix.[62]

In 1949 Beovich mused in his diary that it was his 'strong opinion so far as party politics is concerned: the Church does not take sides, but she assumes a benevolent neutrality to that side which is most concerned with the workers and the poor, and the less privileged of the citizens'.[63] There is no doubt that for him that party was the ALP. His Labor sympathies were typical of many Catholics of his generation. There were a number of Catholics in the state branch of the Labor Party, including the leader of the opposition (Mick O'Halloran) and his deputy (Frank Walsh), but none in the Liberal and Country League government. Beovich, however, was not blindly partisan. He enjoyed a cordial relationship with Premier Thomas Playford, and the fact that a Catholic lawyer was pre-selected for a winnable Liberal seat in 1953 has been attributed to his influence over Playford.[64]

From Trade Unions to Party Politics

When devout Catholics assumed important roles in the trade union movement, their influence naturally extended into the ALP. David Shinnick recalls his involvement in the ALP in South Australia as an 'essential task' associated with his membership of the Movement: 'Each year, prior to state [ALP] conferences, we assembled to consider the motions before conference. For nearly all of them, we were directed by the National Office [of the Movement] how we were to vote. Only very few were left to our discretion.'[65] No longer was the fight against communism the sole focus of the Movement. With the influence of the Communist Party of Australia waning, Santamaria turned his attention to other matters.

Santamaria 'believed above all in organisations and in organised action'.[66] In an undated statement (probably late 1940s) he spelt out to the members of the Episcopal Committee on Catholic Action his concern that Catholic Action could be reduced to small groups of Catholics trying to influence their own circle of friends and performing small acts of charity:

> I will not disguise the fact that this view dooms Catholic Action to littleness and frustration ... It is, for want of a better word, 'unexciting' and does not grip the imagination. From the viewpoint of practical organisation that deficiency is fatal since any movement which fails to grip the imagination will not obtain mass support ... With few exceptions, it will simply rally a number of Catholics of the 'devotional' type ...
>
> I do not believe that the world will be transformed even by millions of individual acts of charity. The reform of social institutions is the key to the Christian situation today, and this demands large scale action on legislative, political, economic and cultural lines.[67]

This was the antithesis of one of the most common themes in Beovich's preaching – the importance of even seemingly insignificant acts of faith, hope, charity, humility and submission to the will of God – but Beovich does not seem to have challenged Santamaria at the time.

In 1951, in another submission to the bishops, Santamaria recommended that

> the Church in this country should set itself out to provide a trained, coordinated and disciplined band of citizens who will pledge themselves to what amounts to coordinated apostolic action in all civic organisations, with the express objective of securing in all of them the triumph of policies based on the common good.[68]

Through his role as secretary of the NCRM and drafter of the hierarchy's social justice statements, Santamaria had become a fount of such policies. Some were quite utopian, such as his vision for Australian rural life based on subsistence farming rather than commercial agriculture, along the lines of medieval peasant villages.[69] Santamaria himself eventually acknowledged the irony of a Melbourne-based lawyer writing rural policies.[70] In 1951 the Episcopal Committee on Catholic Action had enough sense to decline his offer to establish 'a disciplined band of citizens' as 'it could involve the Church in party politics'.[71] The minutes of the annual meeting of the hierarchy on 17–19 April 1951 record that:

> The Archbishop of Adelaide said that in setting up the Movement the Hierarchy had done a most important service to the Church and Australia by offering a very effective counter to the heresy of atheistic communism. It was essential, however, that great care be taken lest the Church and the Hierarchy be involved in purely party politics.
>
> The meeting agreed that this could be achieved and that the movement could be properly directed by frequent meetings of the 'Committee to control the Industrial Movement'.

There is no evidence that greater control was exerted. On the contrary, on 11 December 1952, after Labor's victory in the Victorian state election, Santamaria informed Mannix that 'the Social Studies Movement should within a period of five or six years be able to completely transform the leadership of the Labor Movement, and to introduce into Federal and State spheres large numbers of members who ... should be able to implement a Christian social programme'.[72] A week later, Beovich reported in his diary that he had received 'disturbing news' about the Movement becoming too party-political: 'It may be so and I have feared this. Will need careful watching.'[73] He did not record the information he received, but in 1979 he came across a document filed in one of the books in his study at Ennis. Unfortunately it is undated and unsigned. Before sending it to the diocesan archives, Beovich noted that 'there were good points in its submission'. The chief complaint was that Santamaria had shifted from fighting communism in the trade union movement to promoting 'reactionary' and 'foolish' economic and political polices:

> A gigantic confidence trick is being played upon us. It cannot be challenged because it is never affirmed. The Movement that the Australian Hierarchy blessed and promoted has been given authority to do a certain work – to safeguard the faith from bloody suppression. The authority to do this work has been fully understood and has received practical acceptance. Catholics are now being made to understand by all means short of saying it that this authority extends to the promotion of various political and economic policies which are the private ideas of individuals in these matters.

In a paper delivered to a Movement summer school in 1953, subsequently published in the *Bombay Examiner* in 1955, Santamaria attempted to maintain a difference between 'political action' (which he defined as working within a political party to promote policies based on Christian principles) and 'party political action' (supporting one political party against another). The former, he argued, was acceptable for 'an organisation effectively under the control of the hierarchy'.[74] Concern must have been expressed about this policy, as on 13 May 1953 a missive from the Movement's national headquarters was sent to the regional office in South Australia.[75] It is one of the Movement's internal communications which was once deemed so highly confidential that it was cut in half for posting to separate addresses and later stuck back together. It referred to a decision taken at a Movement meeting the previous January to mention the issue of 'our acting in the political field' in the Movement's annual report to the hierarchy 'in a manner which would appear to be incidental to the main report, but which would nevertheless raise the point at issue for determination'. Subsequently the national executive, in consultation with the sympathetic Bishop O'Collins, decided that it would be 'bad tactics' to raise the matter for discussion – it would be better to assume that such political action was valid. The outcome was 'most satisfactory'. The bishops' 'most cordial' reception of the report represented 'a unanimous vote of confidence in the show' (i.e. the Movement). The only concern which was expressed was over 'the use which some of our members and organisers make of the authority which the chiefs [i.e. the bishops] have reposed in us as a major weapon in spreading the work of the organisation, and, more important, of securing adherence to its policies'. Accordingly, it had now been ruled that:

> A. We are entitled to invoke the will and authority of the chiefs as the basis for the existence of our organisation. (However, we should not invoke the authority of the chiefs too promiscuously even in this regard, using it only when it's a matter of real necessity).
>
> B. We are not entitled to invoke the authority of the chiefs as a method of enforcing compliance with every detail of policy which we adopt as an organisation. The chiefs are strongly behind our organisation and give a general support to the major lines of policy which it adopts. They cannot be expected, however, to be held responsible for

> every small item of policy and do not wish to be quoted as backing every item of policy we adopt.

Two months later Beovich delivered a lecture on the relationship between church and state at the Newman Institute in Adelaide. The notes which he prepared for the occasion indicate that he intended to make a clear distinction between action taken by Catholics as members of Catholic Action organisations, and action taken by Catholics as private citizens: 'Every active member of Catholic Action must recall that he is speaking for the Church and that there might be a danger of compromising her if any rash decisions were taken in matters political.'[76]

By November 1953 tension between the Catholic Action movements and the Movement had escalated to the point where the bishops had to act. When the Episcopal Committee on Catholic Action met on 17 November there was open conflict between Mannix and his coadjutor archbishop over Simonds's insistence that the Movement be clearly separated from Catholic Action. Mannix refused to budge and Simonds stormed out of the meeting. Beovich attempted to steer a middle course: 'Archbishop Beovich, while praising the work of both bodies, thought there should be a definite distinction between the work of Catholic Action and the Movement.'[77] In response to a letter of complaint from chaplains of the Catholic Action movements, Beovich moved that the national chaplain of the Movement should not also be the national chaplain of Catholic Action, a 'bandaid' solution which ignored the deeper problem raised in the chaplains' memorandum that the national headquarters of both bodies were in the same building and the most senior administrative officer was the same person: Santamaria. Beovich was still, at this stage, an admirer of Santamaria, as his diary account of his meeting with Romolo Carboni in December 1953 indicates.

In his annual Newman Institute lecture in 1954, Beovich again reiterated the distinction between Catholic Action and the action of Catholics, and recommended that the students read Maritain's *The Things That Are Not Caesar's*.[78] He was uncomfortable with the proposed social justice statement on 'Commonwealth and States', which Santamaria drafted for the Australian bishops in 1954, because it seemed to bind Catholics too strongly to its viewpoints.[79]

Above, inset: Mate and Elizabeth Beovich in 1893. PHOTOGRAPH COURTESY OF BRENDAN WALKER.

Above: Mate and Elizabeth Beovich in 1899 with Mary and Matthew. *SOUTHERN CROSS*, 7 APRIL 1940.

Matt, Vera and Frank Beovich in 1904. PUBLISHED WITH PERMISSION OF THE ADELAIDE CATHOLIC ARCHDIOCESAN ARCHIVES (ACAA).

Matt Beovich in 1916. ACAA.

Archbishop Thomas Carr pictured in *Proceedings of the Third Australian Catholic Congress*, Sydney, 1910.

Archbishop Daniel Mannix pictured in *National Eucharistic Congress*, Melbourne, 1936.

St Patrick's Cathedral pictured in *National Eucharistic Congress*, Melbourne, 1936.

The Urban College of Propaganda Fide depicted in a postcard which Beovich bought in Rome. Note the group of Propaganda students in the right-hand corner going for their daily walk.

Matt Beovich in 1919. 'Actually I don't think I am as serious as I look,' he commented when sending the photograph to his mother on 15 January 1920. ACAA.

Right: Matt Beovich looking out of a window at the college, 14 May 1922. It is not his handwriting, so must have been supplied by a friend.

Making the Christmas pudding, 24 December 1920, Matt Beovich in the centre.

Snow in Rome, 8 February 1922.

A 'gita' alongside Lake Albano near Castelgandolfo.

Tennis at the villa at Castelgandolfo.

Sports Day at the villa — a game of musical chairs.

Matt Beovich in front of the Marian grotto constructed at the villa at Castelgandolfo in 1919.

Australian students with Daniel Mannix in 1921. Matthew Beovich is in the front row, second from right. First from left, James O'Collins. Second row, third from left, Norman Gilroy.

Matthew Beovich, James O'Collins and Alfred Gummer on their ordination day, 23 December 1922.

Thou art a Priest for ever.....
Ps. CIX - 4.

☧

IN HAPPY REMEMBRANCE
OF MY
ORDINATION
TO THE PRIESTHOOD
AND OF MY
FIRST HOLY MASS
ROME – CHRISTMAS 1922

MATTHEW BEOVICH

PROPAGANDA COLLEGE

« OUR LADY HELP OF CHRISTIANS,
PRAY FOR ME »

« O Jesus, Eternal Priest keep this Thy Priest within the shelter of Thy Sacred Heart, where none may harm him. Keep pure and unearthly that heart sealed with the sublime marks of Thy glorious Priesthood. Bless his labours with abundant fruit, and may they to whom he has ministered be here his joy and consolation, and in heaven his beautiful and everlasting crown, Amen. »

Holy cards Matthew Beovich gave to friends and family 'in happy remembrance of my ordination'.

Matthew Beovich in 1936.

Robert Spence, archbishop of Adelaide, 1915–1934.

Andrew Killian, archbishop of Adelaide, 1934–1939.

St Francis Xavier Cathedral in 1944.

Matthew Beovich on the day he was ordained archbishop of Adelaide in St Francis Xavier Cathedral, 7 April 1940.

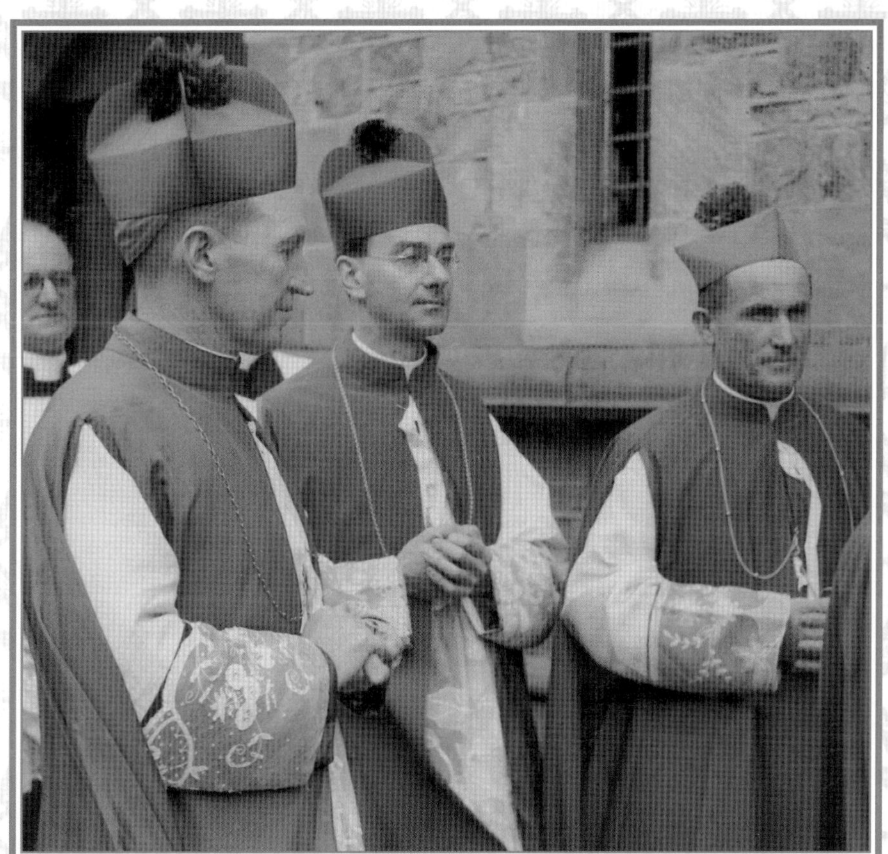

Matthew Beovich walking into St Francis Xavier Cathedral on the day of his episcopal consecration, accompanied by Norman Gilroy (left) and James O'Collins (right), 7 April 1940.

With sister Vera (Sister Matthew Beovich RSJ) at St Joseph's Convent, Kensington, 7 April 1940.

Matthew Beovich in 1940.

The clergy of the archdiocese of Adelaide and visiting members of the Australian hierarchy in the grounds of Cabra Convent, 7 April 1940.

Opposite page: Matthew Beovich with Dr Alan Britten Jones and Premier Thomas Playford at the laying of the foundation stone of the new maternity wing at Calvary Hospital, 14 April 1940.

Matthew Beovich about 1945.

Rostrevor College Sports Day at Norwood Oval.

Presenting prizes at the St Vincent de Paul Orphanage at Goodwood. SOUTHERN CROSS, 3 JUNE 1949.

The new seminary in 1942.

Seminarians at work, 1942.

'Ennis', 28 Robe Terrace, Medindie, Matthew Beovich's home from 1943 to 1981.

PHOTOGRAPH BY AUTHOR, 2003.

Record $3.5m estate will stay

RENEWAL: The Medindie mansion's new owner intends spending $1 million on restoration.

By KIM WHEATLEY

A MANSION once slept in by Pope John Paul II has become Adelaide's highest priced residential sale.

The circa-1890 Victorian residence on Robe Tce at Medindie fetched $3.51 million.

"Ennis" was owned by the Catholic Church but has been empty since Archbishop James Gleeson died in March, 2000. The new owner – a well-known Adelaide property developer, who wishes to remain anonymous – plans to spend up to $1 million on restoration.

But he told *The Advertiser* yesterday he was "absolutely not" developing any of the substantial park-like grounds, which measure 4128sq m.

The Catholic Church said all funds raised from the sale would be used for Centacare and various social welfare programs in the diocese.

ADVERTISER, 16 MARCH 2004, P. 9.

Three friends in 1943: Matthew Beovich, James O'Collins and Alfred Gummer in the same pose as on their ordination day in 1922.

Matthew Beovich addressing the state conference of the National Catholic Rural Movement, 1943.

With B. A. Santamaria in 1943.

Cardinal Gilroy in Adelaide in 1946.

The inaugural Marian procession through the grounds of St Francis Xavier Seminary in 1949.

The Marian procession reaches the seminary in 1957.

In front of the seminary at the end of the procession in 1949.

Matthew Beovich in 1950.

In Rome in 1950 with James O'Collins, Justin Simonds and Alfred Gummer.

Going to an audience with Pope Pius XII on 11 May 1955, accompanied by Leonard Faulkner (left) and Vincent Tiggeman (right), Adelaide students at the Urban College of Propaganda Fide.

James Gleeson on the day he was consecrated auxiliary bishop of Adelaide, 21 May 1957.

Matthew Beovich, James Gleeson and visiting bishops with staff and students at the opening of extensions to the seminary in May 1959.

Matthew Beovich with Cardinal Agagianian, Bishop James Gleeson and the apostolic delegate Archbishop Romolo Carboni in 1959.

Ordination day, 1961. Matthew Beovich with John Chambers, Colin Jarrett, Kevin Bartlett, Brian Taylor and Brian Schmidt.

Awarded an Order of Merit of the Italian Republic in 1962.

Blessing and laying the foundation stone of St Thérèse's Church, Colonel Light Gardens, 26 August 1962.

Bishops processing into St Peter's Basilica for the opening session of the Second Vatican Council, 11 October 1962. Matthew Beovich is looking toward the camera.

In 1962 Beovich was seated between an archbishop from Chile (right) and one from Baghdad (left), a former Propaganda classmate. The trio spoke to one another in Italian.

Inside the basilica during the Council.

The Austraian hierarchy's audience with Pope John XXIII on 11 November 1962. Beovich is the fourth bishop from John on the right.

Sailing to Rome on the *Galileo* in August 1963 with Justin Simonds (left) and Brian Gallagher of Port Pirie (right).

A meal at the Villa Lithuania where Beovich stayed for all four sessions of the Council. With him, from left to right, are Hugo Modotti SJ, Justin Simonds, Patrick Lyons and James O'Collins.

Listening to Cardinal Suenens speak on 28 October 1963, Beovich in the second row from the bottom, next to the lectern.

The Australian hierarchy's audience with Pope Paul VI on 15 November 1964. 'The Pope looked relaxed and in good health,' Beovich wrote in his diary.

Ecumenism in action. Beovich leaving St Francis Xavier Cathedral with Geoffrey Fisher, retired archbishop of Canterbury, 9 February 1964.

Another photograph of Beovich and Fisher taken on the same day, after the liturgical reception to welcome Beovich home from the second session of the Council.

The 'day of days' for Matthew Beovich: celebrating the opening Mass of the third session of the Council on 14 September 1964 with Pope Paul VI and twenty-three other bishops.

Matthew Beovich in 1965. The photograph was taken for inclusion as a print in the special edition of the *Southern Cross* on 2 April 1965 to mark the 25th anniversary of Beovich's episcopal consecration.

After the liturgical reception on 6 February 1966. Beovich with representatives of other Christian churches. Left to right: Lieutenant-Colonel R. Smith (Salvation Army), Very Rev. K. Psalios (Greek Orthodox), Rev. M. Wilmshurst (Methodist), Beovich, Right Rev. T. Reed (Anglican), Mr I. Shivell (Churches of Christ), Rev. G. Pope (Congregational Union).

Home from the Second Vatican Council. Matthew Beovich photographed leaving St Francis Xavier Cathedral after the liturgical reception on 6 February 1966.

With Premier Don Dunstan at the blessing of the Italian fishing fleet at Port Adelaide in 1967.

With Alan Commins CM, rector of St Francis Xavier Seminary, in 1969.

Matthew Beovich and James Gleeson shortly before Beovich's retirement in 1971.

With sister Vera Beovich in 1976.

With James O'Collins and Brian Gallagher in 1976.

With the Franciscan Sisters of the Sacred Heart who lived in the convent at 'Ennis' in 1977. In the background is the portrait of Beovich which was painted in Rome in 1950. It now hangs in the dining room at 'Archbishop's House', West Terrace.

Matthew Beovich in 1980.

Requiem Mass in St Francis Xavier Cathedral on 29 October 1981.

Bishop Philip Kennedy delivering the homily.

The cortege leaves St Francis Xavier Cathedral.

The grave at West Terrace Cemetery.

At the hierarchy's annual meeting in April, Beovich moved that 'the bishops confirm the principle that there is a definite distinction between Catholic Action and the Industrial Movement'. After much discussion, the motion was carried by sixteen votes to ten.[80] Beovich reported in his diary on 30 April: 'After the long discussion the Movement survives, but while the Bishops thank it for its fight against Communism, it cannot invoke the name of the Bishops to persuade its members.' He was pleased with the spirit of 'fraternal charity' among the bishops: 'Men spoke with feeling on diverse viewpoints; at the end the spirit of unity was not harmed.' Five months later, at a meeting of the Episcopal Committee on Catholic Action, Beovich successfully moved that all prior regulations of the Episcopal Committee on the legal dependence of the Catholic Action movements to ANSCA be rescinded, and the staff of the national secretariat be transferred to the national headquarters of the Catholic Social Studies Movement.[81] However, while this seemed a reasonable solution to the tension between the Movement and Catholic Action (or, to use the term which became increasingly common in the 1950s, 'the lay apostolate'), the underlying issue of the Movement's relationship to the hierarchy was not addressed and confusion persisted.[82] With the closure of ANSCA, the Movement's financial support from the bishops actually increased. The quota for the Adelaide archdiocese rose from £390 to £975 in 1955.[83]

Clyde Cameron relates how Beovich supported Brian Nash, an ardent Movement man, when he was expelled from the ALP in May 1954 for campaigning against Rex Matthews, an endorsed ALP candidate whom Nash alleged was a communist. Beovich asked to see Cameron privately, and after receiving him 'most graciously', told Cameron that 'he felt obliged to exclude all members of the South Australian executive who had been party to Nash's expulsion from future Catholic functions'.[84] Cameron recalls that he told Beovich 'that the Catholic Church in Australia was taking a grave risk of arousing the sectarian passions of the Protestant majority ... if it came to the point, many non-Catholics would rather vote Communist than allow Catholics to take over'.[85] Santamaria may have been thinking of this revelation when he alleged in his memoirs that Beovich succumbed during the Split to the fear-mongering of left-wing politicians:

> Dr Beovich had been an old and close friend, who had obviously trusted me for many years, both officially and personally. Threatened by left-wing Labor parliamentarians with campaigns in which sectarianism would play a major role, in a state in which it was easy to ferment it, he had now become an opponent. I felt the loss greatly.[86]

However, Cameron's warning had no observable effect on Beovich at the time. According to Cameron's own account, Beovich did implement a 'ban' on certain politicians: 'For a long time after that interview, none of us was ever invited to official Church functions in our respective electorates.'[87] Moreover, in August 1954 Beovich intervened publicly when seven Catholic members of the ALP in South Australia were expelled or suffered penalties after refusing to support Matthews. Without accusing Matthews of being a communist, Beovich affirmed the right of his opponents to act according to their conscience even when this meant refusing to abide by party discipline: 'An important principle is at stake and it is for that reason that I have felt it my duty to give to those who have suffered for conscience sake my public and wholehearted support.'[88] The issue of conscience versus party solidarity would soon become even more acute.

'The Split' and the Bishops' Response

The internecine struggle in the ALP which was triggered by Evatt's outburst against the Movement on 5 October 1954 is too complex to be examined here.[89] Beovich did not think highly of Evatt: 'He is splitting the Labor Party ... and thus serving the ends of the Communist Party ... As a leader he now seems a liability rather than an asset to the cause of Labor.'[90] Beovich flew to Melbourne for a meeting with O'Collins and Santamaria on 23 December 1954 and agreed that 'the orthodox thing is to close our ranks and continue the fight against atheistic communism'.[91] It was evident by then that the Sydney bishops no longer supported the national executive. After James Carroll was appointed auxiliary bishop in February 1954, Gilroy delegated Movement matters to him, and Carroll moved promptly to extricate the Movement in New South Wales from Santamaria's influence.[92] Beovich attributed this partly to 'state feeling' and partly to 'interference on a lower level (Monsignor Wallace and Calwell, etc)'.[93] This is significant because Beovich's friendship with Calwell is sometimes cited as a reason for his later opposition to Santamaria, Calwell being one of Santamaria's most bitter Catholic opponents among senior ALP figures in Victoria.[94] In fact, there is no evidence that Calwell or Wallace (another former student of North Melbourne Christian Brothers' College) influenced Beovich at all. In March 1955 Beovich was an outspoken critic of the decision of the ALP federal conference in Hobart to withdraw support from the Industrial Groups. At the opening of a new Catholic school in Goodwood on 24 March 1955, a few days after the conference ended, Beovich warned of a communist 'fifth column' in Australia 'determined to smash our liberty and make us part of the Communist empire'. He praised the 'stalwart men and women' who had, through the ALP Industrial Groups, fought to free unions from communist control, and he concluded: 'I give the warning – as one who holds in great esteem the historic Labor Party – that if the Industrial Groups are destroyed throughout Australia, the Communists will be the only gainers.'[95]

After their annual meeting in Sydney in April 1955, the Catholic bishops of Australia issued a Joint Pastoral Letter titled 'The Menace of Communism'. It praised the 'courageous campaign' which had 'saved our civil and religious freedoms when they were in grave peril' and paid 'warm tribute to all those who have engaged in the struggle'. It also condemned the disbanding of the Industrial Groups, and took a swipe at 'highly placed men, including some Catholics, [who] seem to have closed their eyes to the great issues involved ... [and] do not appear to realise that they are forwarding the interests of Communism'. While this was a remarkably strong declaration of support for the Movement, 'the campaign' was specifically identified as taking place within trade unions. The Joint Pastoral denied that the Church had any intention to intervene in party politics. It reiterated that Catholics were free to vote according to conscience for any party but a communist party, and it concluded that 'more is effected by prayer than human effort'. It was clearly a compromise document, reflecting the enthusiastic support the Movement received from bishops such as James O'Collins and Patrick Lyons, the more cautious approval of Matthew Beovich, and a little of the concern of critics like Justin

Simonds. When asked many years later to explain the Joint Pastoral, Beovich commented that the final version was more moderate than the original draft. Given their previous support for the Movement, he thought the bishops could hardly disown it: 'the Movement has been in existence, you've been helping it, you're not going to drop it like a hot potato.'[96]

Bruce Duncan describes the Joint Pastoral Letter as 'a missed opportunity for the bishops to clarify the Church's role in the Movement'.[97] They could not do that because they found it difficult to understand themselves. Beovich was a member of a working group appointed to 'study the situation more closely'. As a result of its deliberations, two motions were unanimously passed at a plenary session. One praised 'the self-sacrificing work' of the men and women of the Movement but added: 'At the next Conference of the Bishops the Committee for Social Studies will present suggestions for the future of the Social Studies Movement.' A new committee was formed, including Gilroy and Carroll as well as Mannix. The other motion affirmed that 'at all times the rights of the Bishop in his own diocese will be respected by all members of the Social Studies' Movement before any decision is implemented'.[98] The meeting of the new Committee for Social Studies on 5 May 1955 in Melbourne reached a stalemate as Mannix, the chairman, would not allow each state the right to adopt its own policies or veto decisions of the national executive, and he frustrated the attempt to reconsider the Movement's mandate by refusing to call another meeting that year.[99]

The Formation of a New Political Party

Beovich left Adelaide on 10 May 1955 with his episcopal friends James O'Collins and Patrick Lyons for an *ad limina* visit to Rome. The trio also attended the International Eucharistic Congress in Rio de Janeiro and enjoyed a vacation in Europe. As a result, Beovich did not return to Adelaide until 6 November 1955. During his absence, the Cain Labor government fell in Victoria after a bitter election campaign, helped by Movement sympathisers who had been expelled or seceded from the ALP and formed a new party, the Australian Labor Party (Anti-Communist). The day after Beovich's return from Europe, Ted Farrell and James Gleeson visited the archbishop and informed him that the Movement wished to sponsor a new party in South Australia along similar lines to the ALP (A-C) in Victoria. Farrell was still the Movement's senior official in South Australia, and Gleeson was its diocesan chaplain.

Two other full-time employees of the Movement based at the state office in Adelaide were Cyril Naughton and Brian Nash. They had attended a meeting in Melbourne the previous August and had apparently committed their region to supporting the ALP (A-C). Farrell subsequently recounted in a letter to Santamaria: 'In the absence of No. 1 [Beovich] abroad, you indicated that you were prepared to accept responsibility for this decision.'[100] Farrell himself was unenthusiastic, thinking the proposal was 'not practical', and he insisted on waiting until Beovich returned before going any further with it. He wrote to Santamaria:

> On the first morning on which No. 1 gave interviews, following his return ... I presented these recommendations as from N. H. Q. [national headquarters], No. 1 of Melbourne [Mannix] and the State Executive here. I deliberately avoided any intrusion of my own views ... No. 1 decided against the formation of such a party.[101]

In spite of Beovich's disapproval, the new party was formally established the following day, 8 November 1955, and announced in the *Advertiser* on 12 November. Like its counterpart in Victoria, it was first known as the Australian Labor Party (Anti-Communist). In June 1957 it joined the New South Wales Democratic Labor Party (DLP) and took the DLP name. Two Catholic lawyers were the driving force: Frank Moran and David O'Sullivan. Nash and Naughton became members of the party.[102]

Beovich explained the reasons why he decided not to support the party on a number of occasions.[103] He attended a meeting of the state executive of the Movement on 14 November and addressed a clergy conference on 25 November 1955. On 17 December he had a long private interview with David O'Sullivan and Stan Keon, one of the founders of the ALP (A-C) in Victoria. Presumably his explanation to O'Sullivan and Keon was similar to the one he gave the Catholic men's society, the Knights of the Southern Cross, on 21 December. He related that it was his personal opinion that the

ALP (A-C) had some legitimacy in Victoria as it had been endorsed by the old ALP executive (dissolved in controversial circumstances by the federal executive in December 1954). However, he thought a Catholic political party was 'unwise' in South Australia. He stressed that anyone who wanted to stand for parliament could do so, but they could not claim the support of the Church.[104]

Beovich's opposition to the formation of a new party was in part pragmatic. As he recounted in his diary, he realised that there was little chance of a predominantly Catholic political party 'getting any distance' in a state in which Catholics were in a minority (15.8 per cent of the population according to the 1954 census). He thought 'decent Catholics should remain in the labour movement and not leave that field to Communists and extremists'.[105] There was, nonetheless, also a matter of principle which concerned him. He accepted that Catholic electors should be free to vote according to their conscience for any party but the Communist Party. While also acknowledging this, Mannix made his own voting intentions abundantly clear in a speech published in the *Southern Cross* on 18 November 1955: 'my vote will be cast against Communists and against those who are company-keeping with Communists.'[106]

'Company keeping' or 'fellow travelling' had become one of the standard slurs used against men and women who remained in the ALP, especially in Victoria. Janet McCalman captures some of the virulence of the controversy in her history of the working-class Richmond district:

> The crusade against Communist materialism was re-opening old sectarian and class wounds. As the [Movement] crusaders became locked into a mad little world of their own, they drew on decades of class and religious grievance, tapping a vast reservoir of lower-class Catholic resentment against secular sophisticates and the Protestant establishment.[107]

However, arguably more serious than sectarianism was the gulf which emerged within the Catholic community between supporters of the old ALP and the new break-away party in Victoria. Calwell encountered so much antagonism in his local parish that he had to leave it. He claimed:

> There is not a parish in Victoria where this division in families and neighbours does not exist. Between neighbours, the hostility sometimes borders on outright hatred. Life-long friendships have been severed, calumny is widespread and detraction is now regarded as a virtue.[108]

The fall of the Gair Labor government in Queensland also took place amidst 'unparalleled bitterness'. Thomas Boland comments of the 1957 election campaign: 'Catholic accused Catholic of treason and apostasy. Priests spoke in that vein in the pulpit and some of them named parishioners.'[109]

Many years later, in a letter to Calwell's widow, Beovich commented that 'the then circumstances and heat of party politics may partly explain this lapse of charity but not excuse it'.[110] At the archdiocesan clergy conference in Adelaide on 25 November 1955, he informed his priests that they were not to give out any 'voting instructions' from the pulpit.[111] A month later, he reiterated this point to the Knights of the Southern Cross. Most priests seem to have complied. Cameron believes there were 'only a few isolated cases in which a parish priest was so overtly opposed to what the Labor Party was doing as to cause his parishioners to go to another parish for Mass'.[112] Certainly Patrick Kelly, editor of the *Southern Cross*, obediently curbed the exuberant anti-communist campaign he had been waging in the paper, and after 1955 the *Southern Cross* no longer accepted political advertisements.[113]

In its first federal election campaign in December 1955, the new anti-communist party attracted more than 35,000 votes in South Australia (8.7 per cent). Although it did not win a seat itself, by directing its preferences to the Liberal and Country parties, it prevented the ALP gaining a third Senate seat. In the 1968 state election, DLP preferences in two seats contributed to the defeat of the ALP government. Nevertheless, in terms of percentages, the 1955 result was never surpassed. In subsequent Senate elections in the 1950s and 1960s, the South Australian result was the lowest or second-lowest for the party in Australia. It slumped to 2.4 per cent in 1964. The branch never won a parliamentary seat at either state or federal level. Low membership (a peak of about eight hundred was reached in the mid 1960s) and inadequate finances inhibited the party's growth. Very few former members of the ALP joined it and no trade union chose to affiliate.[114]

Malcolm Saunders and Neil Lloyd highlight the relatively small percentage of Catholics in South Australia and Beovich's refusal to support the DLP as factors which 'do much to explain why the state branch of the Labor Party did not split in two in the mid-1950s'.[115] They also acknowledge the relatively healthy state of the local branch, largely due to the control exerted by Cameron and Toohey, and believe that memories of the bitter schism in the 1930s and a realistic hope of winning government in the not-too-distant future helped the ALP retain the allegiance of right-wing members.[116] Perhaps the strongest indication that Beovich played a significant role is the fact that the anti-communist party's best Senate result was in the 1955 election. That can be attributed to the momentum which had built up after Evatt's attack on the Movement in October 1954, helped by Beovich's denunciation of the ALP conference's decision to disband the Industrial Groups, and the enthusiastic support given to Santamaria by Patrick Kelly in the *Southern Cross*. This included extensive coverage of the 'outstanding address' which Santamaria gave to over a thousand people at the Norwood Town Hall in September 1955.[117] As they went to the polling booths in 1955, many Catholics may not have been aware that their archbishop, recently returned from overseas, had declined to endorse the new party.

The Break with Santamaria

Less than a fortnight after arriving home from Europe in November 1955, Beovich travelled to Queensland for James Duhig's episcopal golden jubilee celebrations. With so many bishops gathered in Brisbane, Gilroy took the opportunity to call a meeting of the Australian hierarchy. It was agreed that henceforth the Australian bishops would meet each year at St Patrick's College at Manly on the Tuesday preceding the last Friday in January.[118] The elderly Mannix was absent and, not intending to go to Sydney in January, wrote to all the bishops in December 1955. He stressed the importance of the Movement remaining national, and exhorted the bishops to abide by the decisions of the national executive.[119] Beovich was dismayed by Mannix's refusal to accept that the original mandate given to the Movement in 1945 was based on the assurance that in each diocese it would be 'in all things subject to the will of the bishop'. Beovich carefully prepared what he would say at the January meeting.[120] He accepted that, as the bishops had endorsed the Movement, they were responsible for it, and that its mandate needed to be reviewed. His greatest worry was the development of a predominantly Catholic political party. He stated his opposition but concluded: 'I hope I am not stubborn, and if the majority of Bishops favour the existence of a Catholic party then I shall agree with them, for I have great confidence in the collective wisdom of the hierarchy.' After the meeting he reflected in his diary that while all the bishops 'are most anxious for a strong and effective fight against the communist menace, the majority do not favour a new political party linked with the Movement'.[121] The motion that 'the Movement as an organisation is not a political party nor should it attempt to dominate any political party' was in fact carried by nineteen votes to six.[122]

In January 1956 the bishops' conference recommitted the direction of the Movement to the Episcopal Committee on Social Studies. Gilroy chaired a meeting of the committee in Melbourne on 20 March 1956. Four days later Beovich was pleased to receive the committee's decision that the Movement should confine its activities to the industrial field and education and avoid politics.[123] He thought the national executive's response – that the Movement was essentially a lay organisation and thereby free to enter the political sphere – flatly contradicted the long history of episcopal support for the Movement. He jotted in the margin of the letter he received from the executive: 'No. The Bishops are closely bound up with the Movement. They finance it in great part and gave it a specific mandate. They can hardly escape some responsibility.'[124]

By now Beovich had much more sympathy for Gilroy's and Carroll's opposition to the national executive. At the archdiocesan clergy conference in June 1956 he informed his priests of the Episcopal Committee's decision,[125] and in a private conversation with Romolo Carboni in July he commended Sydney's 'down to earth' policy: that communism could best be fought within the ALP and the trade union movement, not by forming another party.[126] His words had no apparent effect as the apostolic delegate had become a fervent admirer of Santamaria and publicly supported him at NCRM conventions and other functions.[127]

Although the national executive initially accepted the decision of the Episcopal Committee, on 18 July 1956 all the national officials of the Movement in Melbourne resigned, allegedly on the grounds that giving each bishop a right of veto over Movement activity in his diocese would result in 'the collapse of an effective organised resistance to Communism in Australia'.[128] In reality, the resignations meant little as Santamaria immediately inaugurated the Catholic Social Movement (CSM) which was virtually the same as the former Movement except that it was made clear that it was a lay organisation and that decisions of the national executive would bind all members. Beovich was displeased and refused to give the supposedly new organisation any support.[129] On 4 September 1956 he received a typewritten circular letter from Santamaria listing the names of fourteen Australian dioceses which had agreed to affiliate with the CSM. Santamaria added a handwritten note to Beovich which assured him the reconstituted national movement did not intend to establish branches in dioceses which refused to affiliate: 'I would like Your Grace to know that there is not – nor has there ever been – any suggestion that another Catholic organisation would be set up in Adelaide.'[130]

Nevertheless, within a few weeks Beovich heard that the CSM was indeed operating in his diocese. As Santamaria eventually acknowledged in his memoirs, 'two of the three lay officials [of the Movement in South Australia] stayed with the national body'.[131] He was referring to Nash and Naughton. Farrell remained closely allied to Beovich. When Beovich wrote to Santamaria on 12 October 1956 to complain about the CSM's activities in Adelaide, Santamaria glibly replied that while no 'specifically Catholic' organisation would be set up in the Adelaide archdiocese, the CSM could not allow a vacuum to occur in the fight against communism. Hence it was supporting a 'broad' anti-communist organisation whose policies were 'in harmony' with its own.[132] The episode must have further undermined Santamaria's credibility in Beovich's eyes.

Beovich was now, like the Sydney bishops, in the awkward position of trying to suppress a supposedly lay organisation at the same time as the apostolic delegate was publicly championing Santamaria's contention that such an organisation should be free from episcopal interference. Jack Kane, one of the founders of the DLP in New South Wales, insists that 'the real reason for the New South Wales bishops' stand ... was because the Movement was under the control, not of the bishops, but of a layman, Bob Santamaria. That is what certain New South Wales bishops could not stomach – an official and influential Catholic body was not under their control'.[133] Although Patrick O'Farrell supports this verdict,[134] as Gilroy pointed out in 1956, with understandable frustration, the real problem was that:

> Laymen whose frequently repeated claim of episcopal support previously gave rise to some anxiety, now would disclaim episcopal authorization altogether ... [yet] the men in question cannot be considered independent of the Church, in the light of their activities on behalf of the Church up to date, their well-known association with it, and their frequently repeated claim of support from the hierarchy. Moreover, they propose to carry the Catholic name. Surely their decisions and activities would commit the Church and its hierarchy, even though, in point of fact, they would have no right to speak on behalf of the Church.[135]

In September 1957 the two men 'who stayed with the national body', Nash and Naughton, wrote to Carboni complaining that the new auxiliary bishop in Adelaide, James Gleeson, had told a clergy conference that they were not authorised by Beovich and should not receive financial support from parishes.[136] When Carboni passed the complaint to Beovich,[137] the archbishop sent him a report on the activities of Nash and Naughton. It concluded:

> It might be possible for Messrs. Nash and Naughton to claim now that they are working simply as citizens. It is undeniable that they have previously acted and spoken as officials of a Catholic organisation with very special claims upon Catholics both financially and personally. It is no further exaggeration to state that they have, probably with no malice and with good intentions, fostered a spirit of disregard for the teaching authority of the Ordinary [the bishop] and also a spirit of division between priests and lay people.

> It is the considered opinion of a large number of experienced lay men ... that the plan of fighting Communism envisaged and promoted by Messrs. Naughton and Nash is not only ineffective in the present situation but positively harmful because it is not uniting Catholics and non-Catholics but rather isolating the Catholics and rendering them open to sectarian attack.[138]

Supporters of the CSM were embittered by the archbishop's refusal to support their cause. According to Margret Mills (Naughton's daughter-in-law), Beovich's 'assumption of control over lay Catholic Action groups' led to 'a polarising, political upheaval that bred resentment and hostility, much of which was suppressed under a façade of unity'.[139] A ludicrous claim was still being made in 2005 (with apparent sincerity) that 'the late Dr Beovich was an implant into the Roman Catholic seminary as per KGB policy of the 1930s'.[140] It is impossible to ascertain the extent of this undercurrent of antipathy toward Beovich. On the whole, the archdiocese of Adelaide seems to have escaped lightly in comparison with the more overt bitterness which infected the Church in the eastern states.

While tension between the archbishop and some lay Catholics continued, it eased on another front. Federal Liberal politician Archie Cameron died on 9 August 1956 and a state funeral was held in his honour. As he was a convert to Catholicism, this took place in St Francis Xavier Cathedral. Clyde Cameron attended the requiem Mass as a representative of the federal leadership of the ALP:

> Archbishop Beovich came up, shook hands and said, 'Well, it's a long time since we've seen you at our functions, Mr Cameron.' I replied, in a friendly way, that he knew why that was. He agreed and asked whether I would come to the next one. I said I would, and so the ban was lifted.[141]

The Split in the Hierarchy and the Appeal to Rome

The following month, on 6 September 1956, Gilroy called an emergency meeting of the Australian hierarchy to discuss the Movement. Beovich spent several weeks in Calvary Hospital in

Adelaide being treated for an abscessed appendix. In October the diagnosis changed from appendicitis to diverticulitis, a chronic illness which could not be resolved by surgery.[142] That it flared up at this time may be some indication of the stress he was experiencing. Yet despite his illness he travelled to Sydney for the meeting on 2 October. Only fifteen of the thirty-three bishops who had been invited were present.[143] The rest, 'those favouring the new set up' [the CSM], boycotted the meeting.[144] Movement sympathisers had tried a similar tactic at both the Victorian state conference and then the federal conference of the ALP in 1955. As a result, decisions were taken to which the absentees later, unsuccessfully, objected. That was also the case in October 1956. With the division in the hierarchy so starkly manifest, those present decided to send a delegation to Rome: Gilroy, Carroll and Duhig or, as happened, his coadjutor, Patrick O'Donnell. Mannix complained to Carboni about the 'unconstitutional and invalid' meeting, and at the 'urgent request' of the apostolic delegate, a further meeting was held on 30 October to give those who had been absent on 2 October a chance to express their views. However, only one of them (Guilford Young of Hobart) chose to attend.[145] The bishops discussed a submission to be sent to Rome with the delegation, highlighting their concerns about the Movement, especially its attempt to control the ALP and its recent evolution into a supposedly independent lay organisation which continued to be closely linked to the Church.[146]

The apostolic delegate also asked for a 'personal, confidential and secret' report on the situation from each bishop, this to be forwarded to Rome.[147] Beovich stressed his concern at the development of a Catholic political party, partly because it could stir up sectarian bigotry, but above all because he did not think it could achieve any positive result: 'It was tried some twenty or thirty years ago in New South Wales to get justice in education. It effected nothing before it disappeared.'[148] Beovich suggested that a possible solution to the problem of the divisions in the hierarchy over the Movement would be for the Movement to become autonomous in each province, with the bishops advising one another on developments at their annual meetings. Carboni was unimpressed. When he addressed the next national meeting of the

Australian hierarchy in January 1957, he chided bishops who 'pursued a restricted outlook, limited to the territory of their own diocese'. He further insisted that they should not publicly reveal their differences of opinion, and warned that 'lay people should not be unduly or harmfully bothered by their spiritual fathers' in matters such as politics that were purely temporal. His only concession to Santamaria's critics was to recommend that the national headquarters of the Movement be shifted to Canberra.[149]

An Adelaide diocesan priest recalls a tart comment made by Beovich during the Movement controversy: 'the apostolic delegate is the eyes and ears of the Holy Father, but not the mouth.'[150] Bypassing Carboni, the Australian delegation to Rome obtained in May 1957 instructions from Cardinal Pietro Fumasoni-Biondi. He was the prefect of the Congregation for the Propagation of the Faith and, incidentally, one of Gilroy's and Beovich's former lecturers at Propaganda College. Clarifications requested by Gilroy were issued in July 1957.[151] The May document affirmed the laity's 'freedom of initiative' when operating under 'their own personal responsibility', and denied bishops a right of veto. However, it also maintained that it was 'not advisable that a confessional political party be created or that the Movement take political character upon itself'. The July clarifications more clearly spelt out that the Movement was to be under the authority of the local bishop with regard to 'everything which directly or indirectly concerns the Church's mission', that it was to be essentially an organisation to promote Catholic social and moral teaching, and that it should 'exclude from its program all direct or indirect action on unions or political parties'.

Gerard Henderson concludes that none of the protagonists would have been pleased by the response from Rome as it meant the Sydney hierarchy had to stop actively supporting the ALP.[152] Beovich, however, wrote with relief to Gilroy after he received copies of the documents on 3 September 1957:

> I have read them carefully, and the more I think about the matter the more I appreciate the wisdom of the Holy See both for the present and the future in Australia. Whatever about my thoughts, however, Rome has spoken and I subscribe to the instructions and clarification without doubt or argument, as, I am happy to know, do all four of us

> Bishops in this ecclesiastical province of Adelaide [Beovich, Gleeson, Gallagher of Port Pirie and O'Loughlin of Darwin].[153]

After speaking with Gilroy in Sydney on 6 September, Beovich jotted in his diary: 'We are in one mind about them.'[154] Carroll, energetically promoting the Vatican directives amongst the hierarchy, appreciated Beovich's visit. He wrote to Gleeson three days later: 'Our Chief [Gilroy] has taken quite a battering over a period and the support of your man has been a big consolation and encouragement.'[155]

Beovich's one concern with regard to the Vatican directives was that they were issued 'in forma riservata' (for the bishops only) and he wanted to share them with his priests. At some point after he received the instructions, Beovich noted on the back of an envelope a list of 'mistakes of the Movement', perhaps in preparation for the 1958 meeting of the hierarchy. In retrospect, he could see that the Movement had followed too closely the communist tactic of secret infiltration of trade unions and the ALP, and that the move from the industrial field to politics had been an inevitable development. Given the close association between the Movement and the Church, 'it followed that just as the Coms were trying to take over the nation, so it would appear, was the Church ... trying to impose itself on the nation'. He thought the instructions from the Vatican would prevent these mistakes – if the documents could be made known to the people.[156]

In the Aftermath of the Vatican Intervention

At the meeting of the Australian hierarchy in Sydney in January 1958, Beovich moved a motion which expressed gratitude to Cardinal Fumasoni-Biondi and pledged that the 'authoritative directives' would be implemented.[157] This was unanimously passed. Beovich then moved a more detailed motion, spelling out that the Movement would become 'a Catholic lay association specifically intended for the social and moral formation of its members' and that it would not be involved in any kind of industrial or political action. This passed with only one vote against. However, the issue of publicising the Vatican instructions was not resolved. At the next archdiocesan clergy conference on 12 March

1958, Beovich reported, without mentioning the confidential Vatican documents, that the Movement would be reconstructed in South Australia along the lines established by the bishops' conference.[158] In practice this simply involved an expansion of the Newman Institute which had, for almost a decade, been engaged in such work.

Later in the month Beovich went to a meeting attended by members of the Movement and informed them of the change.[159] David Shinnick was one of the men present. He had become disillusioned with the Movement's 'commitment through urgency' approach, as the national executive's predictions of communist takeover had repeatedly failed to eventuate, and it had become clear that communist involvement in the trade union movement had diminished. He was ready to try something new. He recalls:

> He [Beovich] invited the [Movement] groups which then existed to continue to meet as a lay apostolate organisation under the name of the Newman Institute of Christian Studies. The Institute already existed as a formal adult education body and the Archbishop's desire was that it would broaden its approaches to include 'the lay apostolate'. All but a few accepted the Archbishop's invitation. The adult education arm became known as the Public Lecture Branch of the Newman Institute. The Institute's leaders set about the task of trying to understand 'the lay apostolate' and what it meant in concrete terms of formation, programmes, structures, activities, etc.
>
> Parish and vocational groups formed the basic structure of the Newman Institute. In 1958 I joined the St Mary's parish branch. We were a small group but tackled a wide range of social issues with emphasis on what action we could take in our lives and parish.
>
> The inspiration for three major projects came from this group: a Lenten appeal for overseas aid, discussion programmes in homes on different aspects of Catholic faith, and a parish credit union.[160]

In Sydney, Gilroy and Carroll inaugurated a body similar to the Newman Institute known as the Paulian Association. They were helped by Ted Farrell and one of his colleagues at the Newman Institute, Bill Byrne.[161] In Melbourne, however, Mannix still maintained the rhetoric of crisis, that a 'deadly struggle' was being waged by laymen against communism in Australia. When he first received the Vatican instructions, Mannix seized on the rejection of an episcopal veto and claimed that it justified his position. He then appealed to Rome against the subsequent 'clarifications'.[162] The dismissal of his appeal was welcomed in Adelaide. 'His Grace was pleased to receive this information and it would have done you good to see the smile of satisfaction on his face,' wrote Gleeson to Carroll.[163]

Beovich's relief was short-lived. In December 1957 Santamaria found a way around the Vatican directives. He dissolved the CSM and created in its place the National Civic Council (NCC). It was, Santamaria claimed, 'designed as a purely civic body with no connection whatsoever with the Church, completely independent of the bishops'. Yet, as he later conceded, except in New South Wales and South Australia where it encountered strong episcopal opposition, 'it retained the bulk of the membership [of the former Movement] ... almost all of the old officials, and the same structures of organisation'.[164] It also continued to enjoy a high degree of support from sympathetic bishops, including generous financial assistance. The only exception in Victoria was Justin Simonds, Mannix's long-suffering coadjutor who had right of succession but, while Mannix lived, less authority in the diocese than a parish priest. A dismayed Beovich noted in his diary on 2 April 1958 that he had received a letter from Simonds recounting that 'in each parish the priests have been asked to form civic committees to aid a political party, the DLP, which is the closest approach to a confessional party one could imagine. All this Dr Simonds laments and with good reason'.[165]

The 1958 federal election campaign, the second since the Split began, brought the divisions in the hierarchy into the open. The ALP seized on a statement by Gilroy that Catholics could vote for any party but the Communist Party and, without his approval, used it in its advertising. On the eve of the election, Mannix entered the fray, issuing a press release which asserted that 'every Communist and every Communist sympathiser in Australia wants a victory for the Evatt Party'. He claimed that Gilroy's 'official attitude' could be found in the 1955 Joint Pastoral against communism, and he insisted that the 'heroic' members of the DLP were standing by the Joint Pastoral.[166] Gilroy did not respond, but

Beovich firmly reiterated that Catholics could vote for any party but the Communist Party.[167] After the election he inserted in his diary a clipping from the *Sydney Morning Herald* which attributed the poor polling of the DLP in South Australia in part to the archbishop of Adelaide, 'previously thought to have been a supporter of Archbishop Mannix'.[168] The following year, after the state election in March 1959, Beovich wrote with satisfaction that 'the DLP had not even the slightest impact on the results'.[169]

Beovich starved the NCC of Catholic support in the Adelaide archdiocese by such strategies as refusing to let Santamaria speak on church property,[170] but he was hampered by the fact that the Vatican directives were supposed to be secret. To complicate matters, Mannix had shared them with Santamaria who, by tendentious analysis and selective quotation, managed to use them to bolster the NCC.[171] Ironically, the impression was given that it was Gilroy and Beovich who were out of step with Rome, not the Victorian bishops.[172] At the archdiocesan clergy conference in March 1959 Beovich finally overcame his reluctance to breach the confidentiality of the documents: 'I took the priests into my confidence regarding the Roman directives. I made it clear I would not swerve from obedience to the Holy See.'[173] Gilroy eventually did likewise, but not until he was impelled to defend his position after the *Sydney Morning Herald* ran two articles in June 1959 depicting him as disloyal to the Vatican.[174]

In August 1959 the pro-prefect of the Congregation for the Propagation of the Faith, Cardinal Pietro Agagianian, arrived in Australia. He was aware of the turmoil in the Australian Church, as he had been briefed by his two former Propaganda students, Gilroy and Beovich. Carroll once again played a significant role in coordinating the opposition to Santamaria. Concerned that Gilroy might 'be disposed to overindulge in charity', he asked Beovich to encourage Gilroy 'to state the simple truth with clarity and forthrightness'.[175] Agagianian was diplomatic and discreet and, contrary to rumours which circulated beforehand, did not rebuke Gilroy or force Mannix to resign. He did, however, hint to Beovich that 'some good solution to our problem is in the offing'.[176] Beovich later interpreted this as a reference to the appointment of a new apostolic delegate, Maximilian de Fürstenberg, a senior and experienced Vatican diplomat whom Beovich found 'very affable and sympathetic' and – unlike Carboni – a good listener.[177] Romolo Carboni, still vigorously championing Santamaria, went off as papal nuncio to Peru.[178] That left Mannix as Santamaria's most prominent supporter. At ninety-five, he could not be expected to live much longer, and there was no doubt that when Justin Simonds finally succeeded him, the official policy of the Melbourne archdiocese would change.

After Agagianian's visit, tensions subsided, although there was a 'flare up' during a by-election for the federal seat of Bendigo in mid-1960. Beovich was in Rome at the time, but received from John Toohey, bishop of Maitland, a letter and some newspaper clippings relating to the affair. Arthur Fox, auxiliary bishop of Melbourne, had declared that no Catholic could vote for the ALP. Leslie Rumble, official spokesman for the Sydney diocese, contradicted him, whereupon Mannix attacked Rumble.[179] On learning of this unedifying public spat, Beovich exclaimed in frustration: 'It is a pity Bishop Fox does not give out Catholic teaching each Sunday instead of commenting on party political matters.'[180]

Not long after Beovich returned to Adelaide in 1960, Santamaria argued in a journal article that it was necessary for Catholics to form organised groups to effectively influence political parties, and that the NCC was such a body.[181] Beovich counter-attacked in a lecture at the Newman Institute on 4 September 1960, denouncing the NCC as contrary to the Roman directives.[182] The following year he delivered a similar address to the Knights of the Southern Cross, and sent copies to all his priests. He also showed it to the premier, Tom Playford, and to Maximilian de Fürstenberg, and noted in his diary that the apostolic delegate had commended his remarks.[183]

Although Beovich's innate wisdom and shrewdness ensured that his diocese escaped the worst of the turmoil, in the end neither side in the Movement controversy could claim a clear victory. One positive outcome was that Beovich managed to maintain his friendships with bishops on both sides of the dispute. James Gleeson once queried how Beovich and Justin Simonds could continue to take their annual holiday at Koroit with Jim O'Collins and Pat Lyons, holding as they did such divergent views on the Movement.

Beovich responded: 'Oh, we just don't talk about it. We're not going to spoil the friendship of years over a thing like this.'[184] William McCarthy makes a similar comment about O'Collins: 'he never let differences over policies intrude on his friendships. His arguments were with other people's arguments, not with the people themselves.'[185] There was eventually also a reconciliation between Santamaria and Beovich. Santamaria told a Melbourne priest he had visited Beovich a few months before his (Beovich's) death in 1981 and they 'chatted for hours'.[186] Back in 1960 Beovich's relationship with Santamaria was still fractured, but the NCC was not his only problem. The next chapter will focus on other developments in the mid-twentieth century, as the archdiocese of Adelaide rapidly expanded and the archbishop aged.

Seven
'A Flourishing Diocese' Adelaide in the 1950s

More responsibilities and more problems.

Matthew Beovich, 1956

When Matthew Beovich went to Rome for his *ad limina* visit in 1960, he was congratulated on his 'flourishing diocese'.[1] It is easy to see why Cardinal Agagianian was so impressed. The number of Catholics had almost doubled in a decade (from about 66,500 to 120,000). Seventeen new parishes had been created and 146 building projects had been completed, including 23 new churches, 22 schools and 15 'church-schools', the same building being used as a school during the week and a church at the weekend. The number of diocesan priests had increased from 75 to 95, and the arrival of five new male religious orders had helped boost the number of religious priests in the diocese from 46 to 77. Thirty-four young Australian men from St Francis Xavier Seminary had been ordained so there was no longer a need to recruit priests from Ireland.[2]

The modest religious revival of the 1950s was not unique to Beovich's diocese,[3] but it was particularly noticeable there. The steady rise in the number of Catholics in South Australia (from 12 per cent of the general population in the 1933 census to 19 per cent in 1961) occurred at a time when the percentage of adherents of the Church of England and most Protestant denominations in the state remained stable or declined. In contrast to the challenges which beset the Catholic Church from the mid-1960s onward, the remembered 1950s, extending into the early 1960s, can seem the decade 'when it all came together'.[4] 'It was good to be an English Catholic bishop in 1960,' comments Adrian Hastings in his survey of Christianity in twentieth-century England.[5] Was it also good to be the archbishop of Adelaide?

The Influx of Migrants

In part the increase in the Catholic community can be attributed to the 'baby boom' after the Second World War, but it was mainly due to the influx of migrants from overseas. Thousands of 'displaced persons' from Central and Eastern Europe travelled to Australia as a result of the federal government's post-war refugee programme, while inter-government agreements facilitated the arrival of many Western Europeans in search of better conditions and employment.[6] The expansionist policies of the Playford government, a surging economy and rapid growth in the state's manufacturing industries, ensured that South Australia received a disproportionately high share of the migrants.[7] The largest group of non-English speakers came from Italy. Between 1947 and 1961 the Italian-born community in South Australia increased from 2428 to 26,230. The great majority of these (93 per cent) identified themselves as Catholic or Roman Catholic in the 1961 census. A considerable number of Catholics were also among the 16,007 migrants from Germany (30 per cent), 12,539 from the Netherlands (42 per cent), 6939 from Poland (81 per cent), 4996 from Yugoslavia (62 per cent), 2288 from the Ukraine (47 per cent), 2881 from Latvia (11 per cent), 2713 from Hungary (70 per cent) 1431 from Lithuania (75 per cent), and 1076 from Czechoslovakia (62 per cent).[8] In his report to Rome in 1960, Beovich calculated that approximately one third of the Catholics in his diocese (40,000 out of 120,000) were migrants who had arrived in the previous twelve years, an estimate which accords with the 1961 census data.[9]

The dramatic increase in the Catholic population placed a great strain on Church resources, especially the Catholic school system. There was, however, a more subtle problem as many migrants brought with them understandings of what it meant to be

Catholic that differed from the dominant Irish style. There is widespread agreement that the Australian Catholic hierarchy did not handle this challenge well,[10] although Matthew Beovich is sometimes cited as an exception.[11]

At a practical level, a number of initiatives were taken in the Adelaide archdiocese to welcome migrants. The Catholic Welfare Bureau helped them find sponsors, accommodation and employment. In 1949 Beovich asked Luke Roberts (the priest in charge of the bureau) and H. J. Savage (a lay man who was deeply involved in many Catholic organisations) to convene a meeting to discuss what more could be done. From this gathering emerged the New Australian Catholic Organisation. 'Old' and 'new' Australians were on the organising committee which arranged discussion groups and social activities. A room in the diocesan education building alongside the cathedral was set aside for the organisation's use: it became known as the Catholic Migration Centre.[12] In 1950 Beovich joined the other Australian bishops in issuing a pastoral letter which exhorted Catholics to welcome their 'brothers in Christ',[13] and he used his addresses at innumerable functions to encourage goodwill toward the newcomers. In his 1950 Christmas sermon, for example, he reminded his congregation that Jesus, Mary and Joseph had been refugees in Egypt.[14]

Beovich's main concern was to ensure that migrants had access to the sacraments. He sent one of his most energetic young priests, James Gleeson, to the Woodside Immigration Centre, a former army camp in the Adelaide Hills. For three years Gleeson worked in the Catholic Education Office during the week and went to Woodside at weekends. Assisted by the Legion of Mary and Dominican Sisters from Cabra, he organised religious instruction for the many children who passed through Woodside.[15] Beovich himself periodically visited to administer confirmation. One December day, 'there was a regular Pentecostal scene with all the various nationalities' as forty-nine children and a few adults lined up in sweltering heat to receive the sacrament.[16]

At the first Pentecost, as recounted in the New Testament, the apostles were filled with the Holy Spirit and able to speak foreign languages. No such miracle took place in the 1950s, but Beovich was able to speak Italian and often participated in special missions to the Italian community. He assiduously recruited priests who could speak the languages of the 'new Australians'. As a result, twenty migrant priests were working in the diocese by 1960. Four came from Italy, three from the United States, two each were from Malta, Poland and Holland, and one each from England, Germany, Lithuania, Hungary, Czechoslovakia, Yugoslavia and the Ukraine.[17] One of the first to arrive was Paul Jatulis, a Lithuanian priest who had studied in Rome during the war years and been unable to return to his diocese. In 1948 he contacted Beovich who arranged for him to receive a visa to come to Australia.[18] As Jatulis spoke German and Russian as well as Lithuanian, Beovich appointed him chaplain to migrants from the Baltic region. Franciscan friars from Malta accepted Beovich's invitation to establish a house in Adelaide in 1949. They were followed a few months later by a small community of Italian Capuchins, and then by another branch of the Franciscan family, the Conventuals, in 1957. Italian Scalabrinians, whose order was founded in 1887 to care for Italian migrants, especially those in the United States, began work in Adelaide in 1961. Marian Fathers from Lithuania arrived the following year. Sisters of the Resurrection from Poland took charge of a Polish orphanage at Royal Park in 1956. A small community of Franciscan Sisters of the Sacred Heart of Jesus came to Adelaide from Malta in 1962. They moved into a small convent which was built in the back garden of Ennis, Beovich's house at Medindie, and in addition to assisting the Maltese chaplain, took charge of the domestic arrangements at Ennis.

According to Sydney priest Frank Mecham, Beovich acquired such a reputation for being supportive of migrant clergy that 'chaplains who had difficulties in other dioceses often gravitated to Adelaide'.[19] The fact that the archbishop was himself the son of a Croatian migrant helps explain his sympathy. He sometimes mentioned his father in speeches – a diocesan priest remembers Beovich telling his school speech night, circa 1949–1950, that if a young man from Dalmatia had not met an Irish-Australian woman in Melbourne, he would not be there that evening.[20] The influence of Elizabeth Beovich may be detected in her son's concern that migrant children retain the ability to speak their mother's language so they could pray traditional prayers with her.[21] 'I heard Archbishop Beovich say on more than one occasion, "If there's a good Catholic mother, then the family is also good",' Beovich's former secretary recalls, 'obviously a happy reflection on his own mother.'[22]

The ease with which Beovich related to migrant priests can also be attributed to his years at the Urban College of Propaganda Fide where he lived and studied with students from the Eastern Catholic churches in communion with Rome, churches which retained their own distinctive liturgical rites. A large group of Eastern rite Catholics came to South Australia in the post-war years from the Ukraine. Beovich negotiated with the apostolic delegate and the Australian government to ensure they were joined in 1949 by a priest, Dmytro Kaczmar.[23] Beovich then provided Kaczmar with accommodation at Archbishop's House on the corner of West Terrace and Grote Street, and made St Patrick's Church in Grote Street available for him to use for Mass according to the Ukrainian rite. Kaczmar was also able to celebrate Ukrainian liturgies in various parish churches.[24] In 1952 Beovich attended the Ukrainians' Christmas and Easter celebrations and promised 'to do all possible' to ensure that they could preserve their own liturgy.[25] He instructed his priests that Ukrainian children were to be welcomed into Catholic schools where they could receive communion according to the Latin rite, but they were not to be forced to do so: 'Ukrainian Catholics are Catholics in the full sense of the word. Not only may we not try to have them change their rite, but they cannot attempt to change without the permission of the Holy See.'[26]

In 1958 Pope Pius XII created an apostolic exarchy for Ukrainians in Australia, New Zealand and Oceania, which meant they could develop parishes under the authority of their own Melbourne-based bishop, but cooperation between the two rites continued in Adelaide. St Patrick's remained the Ukrainians' main worship centre until the Church of Our Lady of Protection was opened close to the city centre at Wayville in 1975. Beovich's support was appreciated and he is remembered 'with some reverence' by the Ukrainian refugees who settled in South Australia in the early 1950s.[27]

Migrants from countries where the Latin rite predominated were not given permission by the Australian hierarchy to establish their own national parishes, even though this was recommended in the Apostolic Constitution *Exsul Familiae* in 1952.[28] Beovich accepted the decision made at the 1953 bishops' conference, but effectively circumvented it by encouraging migrants to develop their own community centres with chapels attached. He appointed chaplains to serve the chapels, thus ensuring that a close connection could be maintained between religious practice and cultural identity, and that migrants could at least go to confession to a priest who could understand their language.[29] Beovich also gave the new religious orders which arrived in Adelaide responsibility for territorial parishes in areas where there was a high concentration of migrants. Thus the Maltese Franciscans assumed responsibility for Lockleys in 1952, the Franciscan Conventuals for Ottoway in 1957, the Oblates of Mary Immaculate for Hillcrest in 1957, the Capuchins for Campbelltown/Newton in 1961, and the Scalabrinians for Gleneagles/Seaton in 1961. These were all new parishes which Beovich created by subdividing larger ones.

It was desirable to have smaller parishes, given the rapid growth taking place in the Catholic population. However, Beovich was also keen to alleviate tension between migrant chaplains and parish priests. Although the relationship between them was generally good, there were occasional disagreements when the activities of the chaplains cut across traditional parish boundaries. This was the case in the Hectorville parish in the late 1950s, where Capuchins friars had settled at Beovich's invitation. In 1953 he blessed and opened the Church of St Francis of Assisi, a multipurpose church/hall on Newton Road, Campbelltown, with an adjoining residence for the friars.[30] They initially enjoyed a good relationship with the parish priest of Hectorville, who allowed them to perform marriages and baptisms (and keep any associated income) 'without any interference'. St Francis of Assisi Church became the 'de-facto national parish' for Adelaide's Italian community, with 1600 marriages and 3300 baptisms celebrated there between 1953 and 1963.[31] A new parish priest of Hectorville, Father Louis Travers, proved to be less accommodating than his predecessor; hence 'the archbishop, in order to avoid any friction or argument, offered to cut off part of the territory and erect a parish for us'.[32] It was a typical Beovich stratagem for avoiding conflict. According to the oral history of the diocese, he also found Travers difficult. One day his chauffeur Keith Koen was, as usual, driving the archbishop from Medindie to his office on West Terrace. As they arrived at Archbishop's House, Koen pointed out that Father Travers's car was parked in front of the building. 'I am sorry, Keith, but I forgot to tell you that I am working at home today,' said Beovich, whereupon Koen turned the car around and drove back to Ennis.

Despite his dislike of confrontation, Beovich was forced into the role of mediator when tension arose within migrant communities. As patron of the Catholic Italian Welfare Association (CIWA), he became embroiled in the election of the president in 1955. With the Italian community divided, and one of the Capuchins lobbying for the position, Beovich appointed a new chaplain, Vincent Tiggeman, a young diocesan priest who had recently returned from studying in Rome and so could speak Italian, even though he did not have an Italian background.[33] There were still problems the following year. Beovich jotted in his diary on 3 August 1956: 'Went to the Italian Centre in Carrington Street, Adelaide, to make peace between the committee and the Capuchin Fathers and get them to work together in unity. The meeting was promising.' More meetings were required when disputes broke out between the Polish and Dutch chaplains and their respective communities. Gleeson, in a report on the squabble in the Dutch community, concluded that the chaplain was a 'very zealous and intense man who is not prepared to wait for people to come around to his way of thinking'. Beovich agreed that his tactlessness was a major problem, and was not sorry when he was transferred to Melbourne in 1961.[34] Whether Beovich actually requested the transfer is not clear, but it is likely that it was his solution to the problem. It is not surprising that when census figures revealed that Adelaide had received the largest increase in the percentage of Catholic migrants, Beovich wearily commented in his diary: 'more responsibilities and more problems.'[35]

The 'responsibilities' included accepting invitations to attend functions organised by the migrant communities. In the month of December the number of Christmas socials at the various community centres threatened to overtake school speech nights. One child at the Woodside Immigration Centre mistook the archbishop for Santa Claus, which was not altogether inappropriate, the *Southern Cross* explained, as St Nicholas had been a bishop.[36] During his student days in Rome, Beovich had come to respect the more exuberant aspects of Italian piety, and he willingly participated in traditional Italian religious celebrations. Most became annual events, such as the blessing of the Christmas crib at Lockleys and the blessing of the fishing fleet at Port Adelaide. The latter was started by a number of fishermen from Molfetta in south-eastern Italy. They imported a statue of their patron, Madonna dei Martiri, for St Mary's Church in Port Adelaide. It arrived in 1958 and from that year on, at the opening of the fishing season in September, a special Mass was held. The statue was then carried from the church to the wharf and placed on an altar on a fishing boat for a journey up the Port River, accompanied by important dignitaries such as the archbishop, with an enthusiastic crowd of several thousand people following.[37]

Among the many feast days celebrated in the Capuchins's parish, those in honour of Madonna di Montevergine and San Rocco were especially popular. From the mid-1950s thousands of Italians joined in long processions through the streets of Hectorville and Campbelltown. Recent studies have highlighted the importance of such events in Italian Catholicism – and the embarrassment they caused Catholics from Anglo-Irish backgrounds. Adrian Pittarello comments:

> Taking these devotions outside the church was an aspect of the Italian religiousness which Australian priests, and Catholics in general, found weird and even offensive to the Catholic religion, particularly because these devotions were displayed in front of many Protestants who could well consider them superstitious practices.[38]

Beovich's participation in the *feste* was a significant endorsement of their validity. His support was recognised in 1962 when the government of Italy awarded him an Order of Merit of the Italian Republic.[39]

Most Italian feast days had a strong local character. They

maintained links between migrants from particular villages or towns in Italy. A national and political dimension was more evident in the gatherings of the migrants whose original homelands lay behind the Iron Curtain. It even overrode denominational differences. Presiding at a special Mass in St Francis Xavier Cathedral to mark the day in 1941 when thousands of Baltic people were deported, Beovich told Catholic and Lutheran Latvians that their presence in Adelaide 'was a reminder of the diabolical nature of communism'.[40] At a Mass in the cathedral on Poland's national day, Beovich praised the Poles' bravery in the face of persecution and warned about communist 'fifth columnists' in Australia.[41] Four years later almost two thousand Poles heard Beovich lash out against communism at a memorial service in the cathedral for the workers killed during the Poznań riots: 'A paradise on earth! The oppressed industrial workers of Poznań can answer that one.'[42] In a sign of solidarity, he walked with the procession bearing the Polish flag from the cathedral to the war memorial on North Terrace, where a wreath was laid.

Even more joyful events provided the archbishop with opportunities to preach against communism. Attending a concert organised by the Hungarian community, Beovich paid tribute to the heroic resistance of Cardinal Mindszenty as 'the embodiment of the struggle for God against Satan'.[43] At Croatian gatherings Archbishop Stepinac was likely to get a similar mention.[44] Beovich recalled the heroism and faith of the Ukrainian people during a Ukrainian Christmas liturgy and, presiding at a Ukrainian Easter Mass, he linked the Ukrainians' sufferings to Christ's passion.[45] Nationalism and religion were inextricably linked, but set in the broader context of a world-wide battle for the Catholic faith against the forces of evil. Beovich was, nonetheless, confident that communism would eventually be overcome by prayer, penance and, above all, the intercession of the Blessed Virgin Mary.[46]

Marian Devotion

Like many Catholics of his generation, Matthew Beovich's devotion to the mother of Jesus was warm and personal and tended toward the 'maximalist' end of the spectrum.[47] In 1949 he initiated a procession in honour of Mary at the seminary in Adelaide. It became an annual event. The 6000 people who took part in the first procession were reminded by their archbishop that 'we do not worship Mary in the sense in which we adore Christ her Son, for adoration belongs to God alone'. Mary is not a divine being but 'stands pre-eminent among the saints of heaven, as the fairest, the most beautiful, and the most worthy of our love and devotion'.[48] There was only the finest of lines between devotion and adoration, and some Catholics strayed beyond it, such as the Dominican priest who declared at the Marian procession in 1957: 'She is the air that gives life to every cell in the Mystical Body of Christ. In her we live and breathe and have our being.'[49] Beovich was never guilty of that kind of theological aberration, but he did encourage 'a most childlike devotion to Mary, and a most ardent love for her'.[50]

On 1 November 1950 Pope Pius XII issued a definition of the dogma of the Assumption, declaring that not only Mary's soul but her human body had been 'assumed' by God into heaven. Beovich welcomed the dogma and held celebrations in Adelaide to mark its proclamation. On the evening of 1 November 1950, 15,000 people followed the archbishop and a life-sized statue of Mary in a torch-light procession around the Passionist monastery at Glen Osmond, the grounds 'transformed into a fairyland by multicoloured lights'.[51] Despite the rejoicing, Beovich realised that the dogma was a major setback to the ecumenical movement and he tried to soften the blow. He pointed out that the belief that Mary had been taken body and soul to heaven was nothing new. Catholics recalled it every time they prayed the 'glorious mysteries' of the rosary, and celebrated it every year on 15 August. The significance of the proclamation in 1950, he declared, was that amidst the confusion and materialism of modern life, 'it emphasised the truth that with us there was no uncertainty about the fact of heaven'.[52] He did not address a key Protestant complaint – that there was no reference to Mary's death in the Bible – but neither did he offend Protestant sensibilities by asserting an extreme Mariolatry.

A year after the proclamation of the Assumption, the archdiocese of Adelaide hosted Australia's first (and to date only) Marian Congress. Although rallies were a relatively common feature of Australian religious culture in the 1950s, as David Hilliard comments, 'nothing could rival the massive gatherings that were held during the post-war years to demonstrate the faith and unity of the Roman Catholic community'.[53] From 24 to 28 October 1951, the Marian Congress included a series of such events. The cathedral being too small, an altar was set up in what was then the largest auditorium in Adelaide, Centennial Hall in the Wayville Showground, so that thousands could gather for 'Women's Night', 'Men's Night' and special Masses for children and for religious sisters and brothers. The congress culminated on Sunday 28 October with a giant procession from St Francis Xavier Cathedral to Elder Park via King William Street. About twenty thousand Catholics participated, including 'new Australians' who walked in their national groups, wearing colourful costumes, bearing banners and flags, and singing their own Marian hymns. Thirty thousand more lined the route and joined in reciting the rosary as the procession passed. The statue at the centre of the celebrations was one which Beovich had commissioned on a visit to the Marian shrine at Fatima in Portugal in 1950. After the congress it toured the parishes of the diocese.[54]

While the Marian Congress helped consolidate Catholic unity and identity, integrating 'new' and 'old' Australians in magnificent displays of shared devotion, it once again highlighted how different Catholic understandings of Mary generally are from those common in Protestant traditions. To Beovich's relief, there was no surge in sectarianism. During the congress the lord mayor hosted a reception in the Adelaide Town Hall to welcome visiting members of the Catholic hierarchy. It was attended by representatives of the Anglican and major Protestant churches and the premier, Tom Playford, who tactfully described the congress as 'a gracious gesture to the State of South Australia. The Jubilee Year [it was fifty years since Federation] had been honoured by many celebrations, but all would be inadequate if there were not a serious consideration of religious and moral issues'.[55] After the congress Beovich expressed his appreciation of the 'respectful and sympathetic attitude of our brethren outside the Church, an attitude which has clearly shown the essential kindness and fair-mindedness of the South Australian public'.[56]

For Beovich, the 'tremendous success' of the congress was one of the highlights of his years as a bishop.[57] He was not greatly involved in the organisation (James Gleeson and Luke Roberts shouldered much of the burden), and he was not one of the key speakers as visiting bishops were given that honour. Nevertheless, he was intensely proud of the huge crowds, the smooth running of the congress, and the lack of sectarian rancour. It was a demonstration of the vitality of his small diocese and an affirmation of his efforts since becoming bishop to encourage both Marian devotion and more cordial relations with the wider, non-Catholic community. At a personal level, he was deeply moved by 'the goodness, enthusiasm and faith of the people'.[58] The congress was not imposed on a reluctant laity but provided an outlet for an outpouring of the most popular form of Catholic piety in the 1950s.

Catholics converged again on Elder Park in the centre of the city in 1953 – 60,000 of them, exulted the *Southern Cross* – for the Family Rosary Crusade Rally, part of American priest Patrick Peyton's world-wide campaign to encourage Catholics to commit to praying the rosary every day as a family group. His famous slogans were: 'The Family that Prays Together Stays Together' and 'A World at Prayer is a World at Peace'. Beovich also addressed the rally, giving his strong support to Peyton, 'who is but echoing a request of the Mother at God at Fatima'.[59] Demonstrating once again ecumenical sensitivity, he reminded his listeners that during the recitation of the rosary, 'the Bible itself is brought to life' as episodes in the life of Christ are recalled. In a pastoral letter he acknowledged that the family rosary pledge would not bind Catholics under pain of sin, a realistic acceptance of that fact that once the initial enthusiasm for the practice had passed, many people would find it difficult to honour their commitment.[60] With regard to Marian devotion, Beovich could perhaps be described as a moderate maximalist.

Catholic Schools

Along with the Marian Congress, Beovich took great pride in the Catholic school system: 'the glory of the Catholic Church in Australia,' he proclaimed in 1949.[61] He was pleased to report to Rome that Catholic parents did not need to be prodded to send their children to Catholic schools, they were willing to make the financial sacrifices involved: 'I sometimes think that God may spare our people from open persecution because of their loyalty and generosity in the matter of Catholic schools.'[62] Unfortunately, as the decade progressed, it became increasingly difficult to accommodate the growing number of students. Beovich noted in his diary in 1952 that the number of Catholic children in the outer suburbs of Kilburn and Enfield had risen from 50 to 540 in just three years, and most other parish schools were also 'bulging at the seams'.[63]

For twelve months in the working-class western suburb of Albert Park there literally were seams. A fortnight before the first school term was due to start in 1949, the school building was destroyed by fire. It was quickly replaced by a large marquee, a calico curtain dividing the tent into two classrooms.[64] When Beovich visited during a storm, he had to crawl under the lashed down canvas.[65] Other creative solutions were found to the shortage of classrooms in the post-war years. At Stirling in the Adelaide Hills, the Dominican Sisters began teaching in what had once been the glasshouse of the old mansion which had become their convent. As the number of students increased, they expanded into the stables. A renovated shed served as the first Catholic school in the small country town of Riverton before the Mercy nuns and their students moved into a large house. A private dwelling was transformed into a school in the new satellite city of Elizabeth, while at Tailem Bend, a railway junction on the main train line to Melbourne, the parish established a school in an old railway hostel.

As Beovich admitted to Rome in 1955, his main problem was not opening new Catholic schools, difficult though it was to finance such expansion. The greatest challenge was finding sufficient teachers.[66] Beovich lured some new religious orders to Adelaide,[67] and he persuaded existing congregations to expand their involvement in the diocese, but in spite of this the total number of religious only rose from 593 sisters and 58 brothers in 1949 to 681 sisters and 69 brothers a decade later (most but not all would have taught in Catholic schools). This 13 per cent increase was slight in comparison with the doubling in the number of students (from 9394 to 20,931),[68] and few schools could afford to pay lay teachers a reasonable salary.

Beovich regularly asked for prayer for more vocations to religious life. However, at the annual Catholic teachers' conference in 1954 he passed on some wise advice: do not talk too much about vocations, students will resent it; do not boast about the number of girls you have sent to the convent, it will put them on the defensive; do not say 'we need sisters' – that is the lowest of all motives, give the girls a supernatural motive or none at all. Beovich stressed that the criteria for a good teacher included understanding, enthusiasm and a sense of humour, and he pointed out that priesthood and religious life would be more attractive to young people if priests and religious appeared happy rather than austere and unfriendly.[69] He spoke on a similar theme at another conference in 1957, exhorting teachers 'to cultivate a spirit of joy in working for Christ, and to transmit this joy to pupils'. Exhausted teachers might well have asked how they could do that when they were being pushed close to breaking point. Beovich urged them not to underestimate the power of prayer.[70] The conviction that difficulties should be accepted patiently and 'offered up' to the Lord was an important part of his personal piety, but he was not without sympathy for the plight of teachers with very large classes. He heard first-hand accounts of what it was like from his own sister. In 1954 she had 100 students in three grades in her class in Melbourne.[71] James Gleeson, director of Catholic Education from 1952 to 1957, attributed his archbishop's reluctance to allow the Catholic Education Office to run teacher-training sessions in school holidays to Vera Beovich's influence. Beovich was not opposed to teachers' improving their skills, Gleeson recalled, but he realised that they needed a complete break.[72]

Ideally Beovich would have liked every Catholic child to attend a Catholic school, but he was realistic enough to know that this was now a pipe dream. The Australian bishops had ruled at the Fourth Plenary Council in 1937 that 'parents who, without grave cause ... allow their children to frequent non-Catholic schools, sin mortally', but it was no use fulminating against such parents when children were being turned away from overcrowded Catholics schools. Beovich admitted in 1958 that a thousand children had missed out on a place that year.[73] Other strategies had to be devised to propagate the faith. In 1952 Beovich asked the provincial and national leaders of the Sisters of St Joseph if Josephite sisters could travel around country districts where there were no Catholic schools and provide religious instruction in government schools.[74] This 'Motor Mission' was subsequently also endorsed by the Australian bishops at their annual meeting in 1953.[75] By 1957 two sisters based at Aldgate in the Adelaide Hills were engaged in the work, driving between government schools in a Holden car purchased by the Catholic Education Office with the help of the archbishop.[76] The sisters worked with groups of lay catechists. In 1958, in what the editor of the *Southern Cross* identified as an 'epoch-making call', Beovich invited lay people to volunteer their services for the love of God.[77] In February 1959 over 200 heeded the request and attended a three-day intensive course on catechetical methods.[78] At the teachers' conference that year, Beovich paid tribute to the 'help and devotion' of the volunteers.[79] They soon had an annual conference of their own. In 1963 it focused on the introduction of a new Australian catechism.[80] About 460 people, mainly women, were given guidance on how to use it.[81] Reflecting on the success of this initiative, Beovich recalled with pride how he had 'initiated the Bill' in the South Australian parliament in 1940 which allowed ministers of religion and their representatives right of entry to state schools to give religious instruction: 'This may be remembered against my deficiencies.'[82]

Beovich was also pleased to note a great improvement in the relations between the state and Catholic education systems in Adelaide since he became archbishop.[83] He gave the credit for this to his three successive directors of education, William Russell, James Gleeson and, from 1958 to 1972, Edward Mulvihill. They followed his policy of quiet negotiation rather than public protests over education grievances. Beovich consistently tried to take the sectarian sting out of the debate over the lack of government funding for Catholic schools. At the opening of a new church-school in 1958 he advocated 'one very good solution: Do not regard a child as going to a state school, or an Anglican school, or a parochial school, or what you call a college. Just regard the child as an Australian – an Australian who must be educated'. As the state government was already providing a certain amount of funding for each person in private as well as public hospitals, he thought similar per capita grants could be made to schools.[84] Premier Playford seemed sympathetic to the idea, and Beovich kept up the gentle pressure through private discussions with him,[85] and exhortations to parents to campaign for educational justice for all Australian children without discrimination.[86] He was disturbed by the widely publicised 'Goulburn strike' in July 1962, when the Catholic schools in Goulburn were closed for a week and 2000 students suddenly enrolled in the state system.[87] In retrospect, the Goulburn Strike has been seen as a significant 'milestone on the road to state aid',[88] but Beovich continued to urge patience rather than agitation.[89]

In the Office

Beovich tried to spend as little time in his office as possible. Keith Koen would drive him from Ennis to Archbishop's House on West Terrace each weekday morning at about 9.30 for several hours of paperwork and appointments, and then he would return to Ennis for lunch. Often these were 'working lunches': priests with special responsibilities, like the director of Catholic education and the editor of the *Southern Cross*, were regular guests. It was one of the ways in which Beovich kept in touch with developments in the diocese. Ennis was also the venue for many informal interviews and meetings, usually in the evening.

One priest sarcastically described bishops of this era as 'like vending machines – just dispensers of permission'.[90] They were the recipients of innumerable requests for dispensations, especially with regard to Catholic marriage laws. In line with progressive thinking in the United Kingdom and United States, Beovich softened his stance on 'mixed marriages' in 1950, indicating in a circular to priests that he was prepared to grant dispensations for marriages between Catholics and non-Catholics to be celebrated in Catholic churches, but permission still had to be sought for this.[91] Eight years later he expressed his willingness to approve the 'passive attendance' of a Catholic at a non-Catholic wedding, if the application was endorsed by the wedding guest's parish priest. He resolutely refused to allow Catholics to be bridesmaids or page boys at non-Catholic weddings, even when the request involved one of the most socially prominent Catholic families in the diocese: 'It is not easy to say no, but very necessary.'[92]

The sacrament of marriage embroiled priests not only in the complexities of canon law but also civil law, resulting in much official paperwork. Circulars were sent from Church Office reminding priests of their obligations. Tedious but important issues involving taxation and insurance also crossed Beovich's desk. As the church and school building boom gained momentum in the late 1950s, much of the archbishop's time was spent scrutinising building plans. While Beovich was pleased at the rate of expansion of his diocese, and commended priests and parishioners on their 'zealous efforts' to build new schools and Mass centres, he was concerned about finance, and reluctant to give approval for building projects until he was assured that they were financially viable. Unlike some other bishops, most notably James Duhig in Brisbane, he did not run up huge debts in property investment. He also did not share Duhig's fondness for neo-Baroque church buildings.[93] The priests who earned his highest praise were those who demonstrated practical common sense, like William Russell, parish priest of Woodville and Albert Park. At the opening of his new church in Albert Park – a Nissen hut – Beovich commented that Russell was 'following wise lines in increasing the number of Mass centres and schools – future generations can put up the grand buildings'.[94]

Beovich was initially wary of the 'Wells Way', a method of fundraising developed by the Wells Organisation in the United States to encourage parishioners to pledge weekly sums to support their church.[95] He came to see the benefits of planned giving programmes as they enabled parishes to borrow money with greater certainty that loans could be repaid.[96] Beovich's careful management of diocesan finances can also be seen in the hard bargains he drove with religious orders, which ensured that the diocese did not bear the brunt of the cost of establishing a number of new parishes.[97]

Files of circulars to priests in the archdiocesan archives testify that the archbishop was concerned with more than bricks and mortar. He placed his stamp on popular piety, exhorting priests to attend and to promote to their parishioners annual diocesan events such as the processions in honour of the Blessed Sacrament and Mary. A roster was drawn up so that the Forty Hours' Prayer could be celebrated at regular intervals throughout the parishes of the archdiocese, and priests were directed that each parish should pray a Novena before the feast of the Sacred Heart and hold

Benediction of the Blessed Sacrament on the day. Their attendance at clergy conferences and the annual retreat for diocesan clergy was also required.

Of particular concern to Beovich in the mid-1950s were the liturgical reforms proclaimed by Pope Pius XII, including the relaxation of the Church's laws on fasting before receiving communion, the introduction of evening Masses, and the restoration of the Easter vigil. In obedience to the pope, Beovich promptly implemented the changes in Adelaide and was pleased with the response from the laity, noting that many more people were coming forward for communion.[98] In August 1959 he sent priests and members of religious orders a detailed summary of instructions issued by the Sacred Congregation of Rites which encouraged greater participation by the laity in the liturgy, especially through the so-called 'dialogue Mass', in which the congregation had certain Latin responses to make. Yet in spite of the archbishop's approval, many older priests were unenthusiastic about the changes, and Beovich did not force the adoption of dialogue Masses against their will.[99]

Beovich continued to utilise modern technology in the 1950s as a tool for evangelism. He seized on the advent of television, and not only negotiated for prime time Catholic programmes on channels Nine and Seven, but purchased shares in the former television station: 'It will be useful for the Church to have an interest in this important field.'[100] A diocesan committee coordinated both the television work and the 'Catholic Hour' on radio, with a number of priests presenting programmes, including James Gleeson, Thomas Horgan and Robert Aitken. On Beovich rested 'the agonising responsibility' of deciding how much money the Church could commit to this expensive venture. In February 1960 he authorised a special collection in parishes to raise funds.[101] The appeal was launched in a fresh, new version of the diocesan weekly paper. Under the editorship from 1960 of one of the youngest of the diocesan priests, Robert Wilkinson, the *Southern Cross* had more local content, a greater focus on the lay apostolate (Wilkinson was deeply involved in the Young Christian Workers' Movement) and many more pictures. Wilkinson did not experience the kind of interference in editorial matters which his counterpart in Sydney, Kevin Hilferty, endured as editor of the *Catholic Weekly*.[102]

Wilkinson maintains that Beovich allowed him virtually free rein, only keeping a close eye on finance and expressing concern about the mounting cost of the paper.[103]

'At the office this morning ran into a problem each quarter of an hour,' Beovich lamented in his diary on 12 November 1957. 'What a day!' He did not specify what the problems were. However, if Catholics were offended by remarks made in the pulpit, or upset because their preferred priest could not perform a baptism, wedding or funeral, they could complain to the archbishop. While Beovich invariably upheld the rights of parish priests to celebrate the sacraments in their parishes, he tried to soothe tensions. He preferred to see both parties to a dispute personally rather than put his response in writing, even though this was more time-consuming: 'A day of interviews! Well, aren't they all?'[104] He exacerbated the situation by dismissing no issue as too trivial. In 1954 he received a letter from a Catholic woman who had joined the fencing club run by the Young Women's Christian Association (YWCA). She enjoyed fencing and could not play the sport anywhere else, but her conscience began to trouble her when she realised that the YWCA was a Protestant organisation. In a note on the letter, Beovich instructed his secretary to write back suggesting that she make an appointment to see him to discuss the matter.[105] A young man afflicted with schizophrenia, who sometimes believed he was Jesus, became a regular visitor to the archbishop, whom he regarded as a descendent of the apostles. No record survives of what must have been some interesting conversations, just a warm tribute to Beovich's 'patient pastoral care' from a grateful family member.[106]

John Brewer, state president of the Catholic Young Men's Society (CYMS), visited Beovich on a number of occasions to discuss problems he was facing as membership diminished. Founded in Ireland in the nineteenth century, the CYMS had reached its peak in Australia by the time it was inaugurated in Adelaide in 1927, and it faced stiff competition from the Catholic Action movements in the 1950s. By 1959 it had only 300 members spread throughout eight parish branches, in contrast to the YCW which could boast sixty branches and five hundred leaders in 1965.[107] Brewer recalls Beovich wisely remarking that organisations in the Church did not necessarily exist in perpetuity, there was a time for them to grow and flourish, and a time for them to fade as circumstances changed.[108] Brewer shifted focus to the Knights of the Southern Cross. Although now in a similar state to the CYMS, it enjoyed greater vibrancy in the 1950s and 1960s.

The most difficult problems Beovich faced involved diocesan clergy. A circular sent out to priests on 9 March 1959 recommended that they attend a public meeting organised by Alcoholics Anonymous as 'an understanding of the nature of alcoholism and a working knowledge of Alcoholics Anonymous is of considerable value in the pastoral care of souls'. The tactful wording concealed the underlying reality that alcoholism was a serious personal problem for a number of priests, especially those who had come from Ireland. In 1957 Edward Griffiths, much loved parish priest of Blackwood, was 'summarily withdrawn' from the parish.[109] It might have seemed an abrupt move to Griffiths's parishioners, but Beovich had been concerned about Griffiths's problems for some time and he eventually insisted that he join Alcoholics Anonymous before he was placed in charge of another parish.[110] Griffiths later served at three other parishes before his death in 1968. To Beovich's dismay, he did not learn that Peter McCabe and Martin Comey were alcoholics until it was too late. They both died of alcohol-related illnesses in Calvary Hospital in January 1959. McCabe was only forty years old, Comey forty-seven.[111] Their hospitalisation coincided with the annual retreat for priests at the seminary, at which several priests overindulged in liquid refreshment. In an angry outburst Beovich threatened any priest who drank outside meals with immediate suspension.[112] It was a rare loss of control which indicates how distressed he was by McCabe's and Comey's plight. One of the chief offenders on the retreat later added attending race meetings and gambling to his excessive drinking. After discussing the case with his diocesan consultors, Beovich transferred the delinquent cleric from the metropolitan area to a quieter country parish.[113]

A problem which taxed Beovich's peace-making skills was the situation at the beachside suburb of Semaphore near Port Adelaide. The parish had been ruled since 1907 by James Hanrahan. A dynamic young priest in his early years, Hanrahan became exceedingly cantankerous as he aged and made life difficult for the priests who lived with him. In a mighty clash of wills Beovich insisted that he become 'pastor emeritus' with no further involvement in parish affairs. When trouble continued, Beovich purchased a new presbytery for the administrator of the parish and his assistant. Beovich wrote in his diary that Hanrahan was 'at first inclined to argue' but eventually accepted the new situation.[114] Buying another residence was an expensive way to ease tension, but it allowed Hanrahan to keep his dignity and a modicum of independence, and ensured that the younger priests were not locked out of their home at night.

By now Beovich was conscious of his own increasing age and diminishing energy: 'It seems that the pressure of work is increasing each year but this impression may be due to my own advancing years.'[115] From the mid-1950s he battled diverticultis, a chronic illness which caused periodic outbreaks of intense pain similar to appendicitis. During a severe outbreak in September 1956 he spent several weeks in Calvary Hospital. As he was unable to fulfill his commitments to celebrate the sacrament of confirmation, James O'Collins traveled across to Adelaide from Ballarat to help out.[116] After a hectic few weeks in October and November 1956, which included several aeroplane flights, Beovich returned to Calvary with a blood clot behind the right eye. On 18 December 1956 an operation successfully reattached the retina to the eyeball, but the night before, his doctor recommended that he receive extreme unction. The situation seemed 'pretty grim'.[117] Overall, Beovich was forced to spend most of December and January in bed, doing what office work he could from his hospital room.

While in hospital in November 1956, Beovich received a visit from the apostolic delegate, Romolo Carboni, and he broached the subject of an auxiliary bishop.[118] The following March his wish was granted when the appointment of James Gleeson was announced.[119] Beovich did not, like Mannix in 1942, have to suffer the indignity of a coadjutor being appointed without consultation. 'I want to congratulate you on your decision to have an auxiliary to help you and above all upon the wisdom of your choice,' wrote Thomas McCabe, bishop of Wollongong, on 4 April 1957. 'Whatever about the final appointment, I know from our former discussions that you justly looked on him as the most suitable for episcopal responsibility.' Gleeson no doubt earned his promotion by demonstrating outstanding organisational ability, energy, zeal and loyalty as director of Catholic education and chaplain of the Young Christian Students Movement. He had also played a significant role in the management of special events such as the Marian Congress.

Beovich delegated to Gleeson the supervision of the Newman Institute and the Catholic Action movements, Catholic radio and television programmes and the Catholic Immigration Centre. Gleeson also came to preside over the Council of Sites and Architecture, the Seminary Procession Committee, and the Diocesan Charities Appeal. Beovich, however, remained firmly in control of the most important aspects of diocesan administration, including 'all matters of diocesan policy and finance', St Francis Xavier Seminary, Aquinas College, the Catholic Education Office, the Catholic Welfare Bureau, the *Southern Cross*, matters to do with liturgy and worship, permits required for acquiring sites and erecting buildings, and spiritual vocations.[120] The two men clearly worked well together and were very fond of one another ('like father and son, the way they would chat,' commented Keith Koen),[121] but Gleeson's authority was strictly limited. On at least one occasion, when he made a decision regarding the *Southern Cross* without consulting Beovich, the older man reacted sharply and Gleeson quickly apologised.[122] It was not an equal partnership.

Out And About

Beovich kept his afternoons as free as possible of appointments and often used that time for visiting convents, schools and presbyteries.[123] The seminary was his destination every Tuesday afternoon. He would spend some time in the chapel on his own and then join the faculty for afternoon tea. His sudden appearances and disappearances from the staff room, amidst a cloud of cigarette smoke, became part of seminary folklore.[124] He was also a frequent visitor at Calvary Hospital, only a few minutes' drive from his home. Nursing staff became accustomed to seeing him dart through the wards chatting to patients, trying not to get in the way of their work.[125]

There was more pomp and ceremony at the laying of foundation stones, opening of new buildings and blessing of extensions which were so characteristic of this period. It has been said of the elderly Archbishop Duhig that if he had nothing to open on a Sunday, 'he would enquire querulously what the clergy were doing'.[126] Beovich regarded the few Sundays on which he had no engagements as a rare treat.[127] In addition to the openings, which escalated in the late 1950s after building restrictions were lifted, it was not unusual for Beovich to go to several churches on a Sunday afternoon for the sacrament of confirmation. One Sunday he noted in his diary that he had confirmed 270 children at Edwardstown in two batches. The following week there were ceremonies at Goodwood and Cabra in which 320 children received the sacrament.[128] December was a particularly busy month, filled with Christmas socials and school speech nights. Beovich was relieved when he came to the end of the month in 1954, noting in his diary that he had given 'some 34 talks of various types: God help the listeners and myself'.

Not much divine aid would have been required as Beovich had mastered the art of giving short, simple exhortations with a down-to-earth touch. Thus at a nurses' graduation ceremony he said that nurses needed an understanding of the spiritual significance of pain ('unless there is a Good Friday in our lives, there will never be an Easter Sunday'), but he added that they required another very important attribute: a sense of humour so that they could see Christ in all their patients, no matter how stubborn and exacting they were.[129]

The feast day of St Joseph the Worker, celebrated for the first time on 1 May 1956, gave Beovich an opportunity to reflect on how ordinary people in their daily lives could serve God:

> Since Joseph, then, and God's choice of him, a halo has been set upon obscurity. Except in daydreams, most of us face up to the sad fact that we are not among the world shakers, the brilliant, the talented, the famous. And, facing that, we tend to get smothered in our own ordinariness. What is it that I, being what I am, can do to set the labouring world aright? Nothing, it seems ... But it is precisely this tendency of plainness to underrate itself which God condemned when He chose Joseph. You are just a plain, foot-slogging private soldier, are you? Never mind, says God ... When the world is won for God – and it will be so won – it will not be the generals who have done it, but the

> privates, the Josephs: the tram conductor with his patient, cheerful word, the policeman courteous in spite of his sore feet, the store salesgirl taking time out from commerce for common human friendliness, the housewife struggling along Rundle Street at high noon with a pram in one hand and bundles and a four-year-old in the other. These are the plain people, the privates, the Josephs, and of them – in God's plan – is earth's salvation to be moulded.[130]

In a similar vein, Beovich assured members of the St Vincent de Paul Society that 'God does not put a premium on success'. In fact, success could lead to pride rather than humility, and for Beovich, the latter was one of the most basic virtues of spiritual life.[131] At the opening of a new church he stressed the importance of 'faith, hope, charity, humility and submission to the will of God. Nothing less is sufficient in a Christian; nothing more is required in a saint'.[132] As Katharine Massam says of Thérèse of Lisieux, Beovich 'redefined heroism and put the opportunity for heroic effort firmly in the context of a God-watched daily life'.[133]

Beovich practised what he preached, never succumbing to triumphalism as his diocese expanded. What mattered most to him at the opening of a new church was not the architectural merit of the building but the faith of the people. With its west wall of blue-tinted glass and simple marble altar, the steel and cream brick Holy Name Church in the inner suburb of St Peters was described as the loveliest church in Adelaide by a leading expert on church art and architecture.[134] At the formal opening ceremony on 26 April 1959, Beovich agreed that Holy Name Church was a beautiful building and he admired its elegant simplicity. He remarked, however, that in an ideal world with perfect weather, it would be better to worship God out in the open air. Wind, rain and intense heat made a building necessary, but the best churches were those which did not distract from the worship of God.[135] Fortunately, Holy Name Church passed that test.

As Holy Name was a war memorial church, it was opened the day after Anzac Day. Beovich acknowledged, as he always did, the presence of civic dignitaries. He was pleased that the mayor, aldermen and councillors of St Peters had come in their official robes, because it underlined the important role of the Church in the local community and demonstrated how well integrated Catholics had become in a predominantly Protestant state. There was, however, a price to be paid: Beovich referred to it in his diary as 'donning the hair shirt'.[136] He was himself invited to numerous civic functions and had to mix with Adelaide's social elite. A regular guest at Government House, he went with reluctance but usually enjoyed himself once he had overcome his initial shyness. 'A very pleasant and happy party,' he wrote one night after dinner with the governor, the governor general, the premier and their wives. 'I groan in spirit when facing these functions, but the principals are so kind and friendly that my penance is worth little.'[137]

There was much to be gained from mixing with civic leaders. Apart from the gratification of seeing them at significant Catholic functions, such as the requiem Mass in St Francis Xavier Cathedral for Pope Pius XII in 1958 (attended by the governor, premier and lord mayor),[138] there were opportunities to exert quiet influence. Reg Wilson, former general secretary of the Liberal and Country League (LCL), told Thomas Playford's biographer that the premier came into his office one day in 1951 or 1952 and said:

> Reg, I've had an approach from Archbishop Beovich. He says it's time the Government recognised the influence and support the party gets from Catholics. He wants to see their numerical strength better reflected in the Parliament, in the Cabinet and in the Courts. I think he's right, Reg. I think he's right, and I think you'd better have a look at how we can pre-select some good man. You could start with that lawyer chap, Leo Travers.[139]

Travers duly became the first Catholic LCL member of Parliament in 1953, and a judge of the Supreme Court in 1962. Overcoming the longstanding anti-Catholic prejudice of Chief Justice Sir Mellis Napier, the first Catholic Supreme Court judge, J. T. Brazel, was appointed in 1959.[140]

Progress continued on the ecumenical front. Beovich noted in his diary in 1957 the 'very cordial atmosphere' at a function in the Adelaide Town Hall to farewell the Rev. J. Blanchard: 'Blanchard is an old friend from my first days in Adelaide, when he was moderator and then moderator general of the Presbyterian Assembly.'[141] Beovich also appreciated the tributes to Pius XII in

October 1958 from 'our non-Catholic friends', including a resolution unanimously passed by the standing committee of the Church of England synod.[142] However, in the same month he was annoyed by the insistence of the newly elected Anglican bishop of Adelaide, T. T. Reed, that his name go first on a joint letter issued by the Christian churches to promote the 'Put Christ back into Christmas' campaign. In retaliation, Beovich withdrew his name, and replaced it with James Gleeson's, a gesture which showed his displeasure without significantly impairing Catholic involvement in the campaign.[143] He maintained contact with his rather autocratic Anglican counterpart, going to Reed's residence, 'Bishopscourt', in the mid-1960s for a number of meetings to plan an ecumenical religious centre for the new university campus under construction at Bedford Park. Originally a campus of the University of Adelaide, it became the Flinders University of South Australia in 1966.[144]

A decade earlier, joint representation by church leaders had failed to persuade the University of Adelaide to introduce degrees in scholastic theology (for Catholics) and biblical studies ('for our non-Catholic friends').[145] However, through coordinated action the major denominations succeeded in gaining considerable funding for their residential colleges from the federal and state governments and a university-managed joint appeal.[146] It had always been Beovich's desire that Aquinas College not only provide residential facilities for students, but also be an important link between the Catholic Church and the university. Apart from some financial worries as the college expanded, he was very pleased with its progress in the 1950s. The rector, Michael Scott, moved easily in academic circles and the college was the venue for various debates, conferences, discussion groups and recollection days which were open to non-residents.[147] After presiding at the opening Mass for the academic year in 1958, Beovich expressed in his diary his 'deep satisfaction' that Aquinas had 'indeed become the spiritual centre of Catholic life in the University'.[148]

Yet for all Beovich's genuine interest in ecumenism and concern for the development of an educated Catholic laity, St Francis Xavier Seminary remained his chief pride and joy. Under the care of the Vincentian Fathers from 1952, it was upgraded to a major seminary in 1958, so students could complete their formation for the priesthood in South Australia and, except in special circumstances, not have to travel interstate or overseas. When the new theology block opened in 1959, there was accommodation for eighty-six students. Sixty-one were in residence the following year.[149] Against the backdrop of the Morialta Conservation Park, close to the city yet seemingly remote, the seminary's elegant red brick buildings lent themselves to the headline in the *Southern Cross*: 'Young Students Man a Fortress for God.'[150] At the opening of the new theology block and chapel – and the launching of an appeal to cover the remaining debt of £48,000 – Beovich proclaimed that 'No work is greater to the cause of Christ and the welfare of immortal souls than the education and preparation of young men for the priesthood'.[151] Eight bishops from interstate were present to witness the opening, and any Catholic dignitaries who passed through Adelaide were given a tour of the seminary by the enthusiastic archbishop. In 1959 the Marian procession was timed to take place during Cardinal Agagianian's visit. Twenty thousand Catholics walked from Rostrevor College to the seminary, which Beovich jubilantly hailed as 'the power house of this ecclesiastical province of Adelaide'.[152] In his diary Beovich reflected that 'the days of ordination to the Priesthood are always my happiest days' and he had many opportunities in the 1950s to enjoy the experience.[153]

In 1957 Beovich stood back and let his new auxiliary bishop have the privilege of ordaining his first priests. James Gleeson took on many other engagements, including official openings, confirmations, speech nights and debutante balls, but to Beovich's dismay, the number of functions he was expected to attend kept increasing, so his workload did not noticeably diminish.[154] There was one obligation which he passed over to Gleeson entirely: parish visitation. The travel involved had become difficult for Beovich when he was battling diverticulitis, and it gave Gleeson a chance to get to know the diocese better, but in retrospect it was not one of Beovich's wiser decisions as it deprived him of one of the best ways of getting to know his priests. Men ordained from 1957 onwards often found him a rather remote figure. Many still joke about his inability to remember their names. 'Who's that over there?' Beovich is reported to have asked at a clergy dinner. 'Oh, that's Father ... Your Grace, you ordained him last Saturday.'

Further Afield

Throughout the 1950s Beovich continued to take a vacation every February, spending three to four weeks at Koroit in Victoria with fellow bishops Jim O'Collins, Justin Simonds, Pat Lyons and Alf Gummer. He was also assiduous in his attendance at the annual bishops' meetings and special Catholic functions interstate. In addition, to fulfill his obligation according to canon law to make *ad limina* visits to Rome, he travelled overseas in 1950, 1955 and 1960. As air travel was then uncommon, he normally went by sea, returning by air for the first time in 1960.

Beovich's travelling companions in 1950 were Simonds, O'Collins and Gummer.[155] Their journey through Canada and the United States was like a study tour. Beovich carefully noted in his diary his observations on the structures and systems in the various dioceses he passed through. In Rome there was the thrill of a private audience with Pius XII and time to visit people and places associated with his student days in the city. Then O'Collins hired a car, and drove his companions through Italy, Spain, Portugal and France, the journey planned around pilgrimages to Fatima, Lourdes and Lisieux. Beovich wrote in his diary that Lourdes had grown and shops had multiplied since his first visit in 1923, but the atmosphere of faith and piety remained the same.[156] After a few days in Germany where they saw the passion play at Oberammegau, the bishops progressed to Ireland where Beovich dutifully visited family and friends of his Irish-born priests and religious sisters as well as the Marian shrine at Knock. A tour of historic sites in England provoked reflection on the turmoil of the Reformation, the old medieval cathedrals seeming like 'dead museums'. After nine months away, Beovich arrived home at the end of October to an enthusiastic greeting from a 'huge crowd' at a liturgical reception in St Francis Xavier Cathedral. Perhaps there is some truth in the old adage that 'absence makes the heart grow fonder'. While the addresses of welcome verged on the obsequious, they seem to have been offered with genuine warmth.[157]

Five years later Beovich was off again, this time with Jim O'Collins and Pat Lyons.[158] They went first to Rome for their *ad limina* visit, and then represented the Australian hierarchy at the

International Eucharistic Congress in Rio de Janeiro. They arrived in Buenos Aires just after the suppression of a revolt against the government, during which a number of churches were desecrated and burnt. It was, for Beovich, a grim reminder of the reality of religious persecution. Returning to Europe, the trio travelled through France, England, Scotland, Ireland and Germany, the journey culminating in a memorable pilgrimage through the Holy Land with Cardinal Agagianian. After another exuberant welcome in the cathedral on Sunday 6 November, the editorial of the *Southern Cross* stressed that the archbishop had not been on holiday for six months, he had been representing his people, few of whom could hope to travel overseas themselves:

> Every Catholic would hold it a privilege to walk physically on the ground where Our Lord walked, to see the scenes that He saw, to visit the places sanctified by His presence. Unable to do that, it is deeply satisfying to know that our father-in-God has done it on our behalf. At Nazareth and Bethlehem, at Tabor and Jerusalem, the Successor of the Apostles who is our spiritual chief walked where the Lord had walked with the Apostles.[159]

In 1960 Beovich was only away for eleven weeks, from late April to early July. Most of his time was spent in Rome engaged in matters of diocesan business, such as the suppression of the Institute of St John the Baptist. The highlight was a private audience with the new pope. Whereas the austere and otherworldly Pius XII had looked on Beovich with 'piercing eyes' in 1950 and asked 'Are your priests spiritual men of interior life?', the 'affable and kindly' John XXIII seemed particularly interested in hearing about the harmonious relationship between church and state in Adelaide.[160]

The Divorce Bill

Although the cordial relationship between the Catholic Church and the civic authorities in Adelaide owed much to Beovich's diplomacy, it was part of a wider trend in the 1950s. It was generally accepted that a healthy society was undergirded by 'Christian beliefs' or 'Christian moral standards'.[161] The churches were the chief guardians of morality and church leaders were usually listened to with respect when they spoke out on moral issues. They were rarely criticised in the press. However, subtle but unmistakable shifts in social attitudes were taking place, as Beovich discovered to his cost in the late 1950s.

Throughout the western world, divorce rates rose steadily in the twentieth century, and as divorce became more common and financially accessible, there was pressure for reform of the law. This was manifest in Australia in 1957 when a private member's bill in the commonwealth parliament attempted to introduce national legislation to replace the differing and inconsistent state laws.[162] Beovich responded in his annual lecture at the Newman Institute by reiterating Catholic teaching. Marriage, he declared, was an indissoluble sacrament, one which only the Church could regulate. The state itself would lose by usurping the Church's authority 'because the harmony and stability of family relations upon which the well-being of the state is ultimately based will be unsettled and impaired by the facilities which are offered for divorce'. Beovich acknowledged the difficult position of Catholic judges, but he strongly recommended that they avoid divorce cases, and he exhorted Catholic lawyers not to participate at all unless they were assured by their bishop that a marriage was invalid according to Church law.[163] To help prevent marriages breaking down, he encouraged engaged and married couples to attend 'Pre-Cana' and 'Cana Conferences'. These originated in the United States as a Catholic marriage guidance movement. In one-day conferences, couples were given advice, usually from a medical doctor and an experienced lay person as well as a priest. The first Cana Conference was held in Adelaide in 1949. By the early 1960s, eight trained marriage guidance counsellors based at the Catholic Welfare Bureau were involved in the work.[164]

The attempt to reform divorce law in 1957 failed, but in 1958 the Menzies federal government took up the challenge and the quest for uniform legislation was led by the attorney-general, Sir Garfield Barwick. A controversial feature of his bill was the introduction of a new ground for divorce: if a marriage had completely broken down (the parties having been separated for five years, with no reasonable likelihood of resuming cohabitation), they could be divorced without one party having to prove that the other had committed a matrimonial offence such as adultery. A concerned

Beovich suggested to Leo Travers, president of the South Australian Law Society, that he call a meeting of Catholic lawyers at Aquinas College. On 8 October 1958 Beovich duly addressed a large gathering. He repeated much of his Newman Institute lecture and reiterated that lawyers could approach Church Office for help in difficult cases. 'I came away feeling very tired, but glad that the meeting had been held and hopeful that much good would come of it,' he wrote in his diary that night.

Beovich was less pleased at the annual meeting of the Australian hierarchy the following January when he was asked to prepare a special pastoral letter to be issued by all the bishops.[165] He reluctantly agreed, and used his Newman lecture as the basis for the draft which he sent to his episcopal colleagues in April. The majority responded positively, but the shrewd James Carroll warned against too negative a statement. He wanted greater emphasis on successful marriage and less extensive prohibitions on lawyers acting in divorce cases, as many considerations had to be taken into account in matters of conscience. He also thought it appropriate to express more sympathy for judges.[166] The final version did acknowledge that if Catholic judges were to decline all divorce cases, they could jeopardise their careers and compromise the public good. They could, therefore, be forgiven for 'material cooperation in something morally wrong' (granting exemption from the legal recognition of marriage even though they were aware that it could lead to a remarriage) provided there was no 'formal cooperation' (intention to 'sunder an indissoluble bond'). This subtle distinction did not apply to lawyers, who were told they could only 'act safely' in divorce cases with approval from the Church.

After the pastoral letter was finalised and sent to the press, Beovich received, via Justin Simonds, to whom it had been wrongly directly, James Duhig's response. Duhig, who had just become the first Australian Catholic bishop to receive a knighthood, disapproved:

> I have given the matter some thought, and, to be candid, I think it would be a mistake to go into details about the position and duties of Catholic judges sitting in divorce cases. Personally I would prefer to say that the Catholic judge dealing with divorce cases is administering the

> law of the country and not the teaching of the Church and that his decision does not in any way compromise either the Church or himself... I do not think it is necessary for us to give the whys and the wherefore of the Church's teaching ... Only the most ignorant Catholics can be unaware of the indissolubility of marriage.[167]

As Simonds wrote to Beovich when forwarding the letter, it was a pity that Sir James had not conveyed his comments when he received the draft copy.[168] At the other end of the spectrum, several bishops over-enthusiastically stressed the sinful nature of support for the divorce bill. Beovich deprecated such a 'bull in a china shop' approach, reflecting in his diary that Church leaders should confine themselves to explaining Christian principles, and then leave the laity to follow their well-informed consciences.[169]

As it happened, there was little public debate on divorce in the late 1950s and early 1960s. A few Anglican bishops joined the Catholic hierarchy in deploring the bill, as did prominent Methodist minister Alan Walker, but Barwick's bill had a relatively smooth passage through parliament in November 1959.[170] To Beovich's consternation, the majority of Catholic parliamentarians supported 'the anti-Christian legislation' and an opinion poll indicated that 51 per cent of Catholics were also in favour of it.[171] Attitudes to divorce were changing and there was nothing more that Beovich could do about it.

A Flourishing Diocese?

With the passing of the Matrimonial Causes Act 1959, the 1950s ended on a sour note for Matthew Beovich. There are other signs that the decade was less than a golden age. In the church and school building boom, quantity came at the expense of quality. Few of the new buildings had architectural merit. Many were hurriedly constructed using volunteer labour and cheap building materials such as asbestos, its carcinogenic properties not then known. Despite much heroic effort to maintain the separate Catholic education system, there was also a sinister side to the overcrowded classrooms, constant funding crises, and limited teacher training. The psychological toll on students and teachers cannot be explored here but there are hints of it in the sources.[172]

For Beovich, the decade was also marred by his long-running battle to suppress the Institute of St John the Baptist, the Movement debacle, and growing health problems.

Yet despite these caveats, the overwhelming impression one gets of the archdiocese of Adelaide in the 1950s is that it was 'a flourishing diocese' ruled by a wise and conscientious archbishop. The diocesan structures functioned well, and allowed parish priests a fair degree of latitude while ensuring they remained accountable to the archbishop. The initiatives Beovich had taken in the 1940s bore fruit: the Catholic Welfare Bureau and the Catholic Education Office, St Francis Xavier Seminary, Aquinas College and the Newman Institute. Talented young South Australian-born priests like James Gleeson, Edward Mulvilhill and Robert Wilkinson were given leadership opportunities, as were laymen like Edward Farrell and William Byrne of the Newman Institute and the leaders of the vibrant lay apostolate movements. No diocese in Australia could have done more to welcome migrants, foster ecumenism or establish a harmonious relationship with civic authorities. By the end of the decade the processions in honour of the Blessed Sacrament and Mary were attracting crowds of up to 20,000 people,[173] a ringing endorsement of the style of piety encouraged by the archbishop.

If ever there was a time 'when it all came together' (or seemed to do so) it was during the celebrations to commemorate the twenty-fifth anniversary of Beovich's consecration as archbishop of Adelaide. A special fifty-two page issue of the *Southern Cross* was published to mark the occasion, complete with a souvenir print of the archbishop.[174] Frank Walsh, the new Labor premier – the first Catholic to hold that position – praised Beovich's 'outstanding work' as a spiritual leader; Tom Playford, as leader of the opposition, acknowledged Beovich's courtesy and cooperation during his many years as premier. Archbishop Beovich, said Playford, was 'a man of complete sincerity, high culture and learning; he has been an inspiration to all who have been privileged to come into contact with him'. Similar tributes were paid by the heads of other Christian churches.[175] From Pope Paul VI, Beovich received the honour of being named as an assistant at the pontifical throne, a title dating from the eleventh century.[176]

While much was made of Beovich's personal contribution to the flourishing of Catholicism in South Australia, the jubilee was, in accordance with his wishes, really a celebration of the achievements of the diocese as a whole: a quarter of a century of expansion and progress. Author and diplomat Paul McGuire captured this in the toast he delivered at the layman's dinner to honour the archbishop. After gently chiding Beovich for excessive personal humility, he observed, 'You must surely feel at times a glow of satisfaction through your being. This is an occasion when we and all your laity can glow a little with you'.[177] Yet in the souvenir portrait the archbishop was not glowing. Standing in front of a crucifix, he looked tired and old. The jubilee dinner had to be postponed from its original date in April to July because Beovich was ill with his 'old abdominal complaint' and had to spend several weeks in Calvary Hospital. At the age of sixty-nine he was not resting on the achievements of the past but governing a diocese in the throes of dramatic change. The 1950s were over and the 1960s had begun.

EIGHT
'A School for Bishops' The Second Vatican Council

I started my formal schooling over 60 years ago and I'm still learning.

Matthew Beovich, 1965

A violent storm swept through Rome during the night of 10 October 1962. By morning the thunder and lightening had gone, but the bishops who had gathered for the opening of the Second Vatican Council awoke to grey skies and drizzling rain. Thankfully, the sun burst through the clouds as they walked into St Peter's Basilica, almost 2500 men in all, row upon row of white mitres and copes. From 1962 to 1965 most bishops would spend about three months a year in Rome, attending the first world-wide council in the Catholic Church since 1870. There would be more storms, but also profound developments in the Catholic Church's self-understanding, liturgy, theology and relations with other religious traditions.[1]

The impact of the Council on the Church in Australia was as dramatic as anywhere else, yet for more than three decades Australian historians paid little attention to it.[2] What was written was hardly flattering to the Australian bishops. Patrick O'Farrell sets the tone with his depiction of the hierarchy as 'frequently uncomprehending and even resistant to the spirit of change'.[3] Ian Breward followed suit in his survey of Australian religious history:

> Most Australian bishops were bemused observers of a process which shattered their convictions about the uniformity of the Roman Catholic Church ... Australian contributions to Council debates were few. The pragmatism and traditionalism of the Australian Church stood nakedly exposed.[4]

The best that Roger Thompson says is: 'The Australian Catholic episcopacy did not resist completely the changes.'[5]

In his 2001 doctoral thesis Jeffrey Murphy challenges the prevailing consensus. He argues that, while the Australian bishops did not play a spectacular role at the Council, they generally participated conscientiously and with considerable openness to reform.[6] Yet their reactions naturally varied, and Murphy discerns three main tendencies: support for significant reforms, resistance to change, and ambivalence. Matthew Beovich is one of the bishops whom Murphy finds too enigmatic to classify, but he suspects that while the archbishop of Adelaide eventually accepted the decisions of the Council, his heart was not really in it.[7]

Suggestions for the Agenda

Beovich certainly did not rush to respond in June 1959 when the pope's secretary of state, Domenico Tardini, asked the world's 2594 Catholic bishops to suggest possible subjects for discussion at the Council. Beovich only replied to Tardini, who had been one of his teachers at the Urban College of Propaganda Fide, on 20 April 1960, a month after receiving a reminder notice and seven months after Tardini's initial deadline had expired. His tardiness may indicate lack of interest: it is much more likely that, like his auxiliary bishop James Gleeson, he was content to leave the Council agenda 'to the experts' in Rome.[8]

In the end, almost 2000 'vota' were sent to Rome. A recent international study of the responses finds that the majority tended to be cautious, conformist, and concerned with discipline rather than doctrine.[9] A similar verdict was reached in 1988 with regard to the Australian bishops' suggestions – William Ryder ends his analysis with the comment: 'Pope John's call for renewal found here a small response on which to build.'[10] Undeterred, Murphy went over the Australian submissions again. He concludes that eleven out of twenty-nine respondents were clearly in favour of some reforms, such as Launcelot Goody of Bunbury who thought that the 'overriding theme' of the Council could be the goal of promoting Christian unity. Another eleven did not contribute any suggestions, including James Gleeson, who offered instead his prayers for the Council; and James O'Collins of Ballarat, who observed that the Church was in such a healthy state in his diocese that 'nothing came to mind'. Seven other bishops sent responses which Murphy puts in the too-hard basket, among them Matthew Beovich.[11]

Beovich's brief response contained four suggestions.[12] The first was that the Council could consider 'various means of promoting more and more the interior spiritual life both of priests from the diocesan clergy and of men and women from secular institutes'. He was the only bishop in Australia who explicitly asked for spirituality to be put on the agenda. This reflected his own priorities, and perhaps also the influence of Pope Pius XII, who had stressed the need for priests to cultivate their interior life in Beovich's first audience with him in 1950.

Beovich was one of only two Australian bishops to call for discussion on ecclesiology (the theology of the Church). He thought this could be based on papal statements on the concept of the Church as 'the mystical body of Christ', one of Pius XII's favourite expressions. The Council's reflections on the nature of the Church eventually resulted in its most important document, *Lumen gentium*, the Dogmatic Constitution on the Church. Beovich also requested clarification of the doctrine, so troublesome in an increasingly ecumenical and secular age, that 'outside the Church there is no salvation'. Murphy is not sure whether the implications of this are positive or not.[13] Given Beovich's efforts to improve relations between Catholics and the wider community in South Australia, endorsed by Pope John XXIII when they met in 1960, it surely reflects his interest in ecumenism. The Council would strongly affirm this, and present a much more optimistic view of salvation, most notably in *Lumen gentium, Unitatis redintegratio*, the Decree on Ecumenism, and *Nostra aetate*, the Declaration on the Relationship of the Church to Non-Christian Religions.

Beovich was also interested in the relationship between the Church and the world, which became the focus of *Gaudium et spes*, the Council's Pastoral Constitution on the Church in the Modern

World. He called for a 'more polished version' of the social teaching of the Church, with particular emphasis on the relationship between the Church and the civil state. He was doubtless thinking of the Movement debacle, but he also called for discussion on 'the dangers of unbridled nationalism', perhaps a legacy of the time he spent as a student in Mussolini's Italy. Only one other bishop in Australia raised the issue of church–state relations, although it was a concern of almost a quarter of the bishops who sent in suggestions from the United States.[14]

Lastly, Beovich, along with six other Australian bishops, recommended that the Council might consider how to reduce and simplify the penalties in canon law. This was done in the revised Code of Canon Law which was promulgated in 1983.

While far from radically innovative, Beovich's suggestions indicate that he was not out of touch with the issues which would arise at the Council. On the other hand, he did not realise how long it would take to clarify the Council's teaching – in that respect he was clearly unprepared for what happened. In June 1960 he heard that Pope John had appointed preparatory commissions to develop schemata or draft documents for the Council. He commented in his diary:

> I will hazard a guess that the different commissions will get to work rapidly, and from time to time will send statements to the bishops throughout the world for comments, views, etc., so that when the time comes for the meeting of the Council itself there will not be occasion for any prolonged discussion.

He later wrote in the margin: 'Wrong!'[15]

Seven schemata were dispatched to the bishops in July 1962. Beovich mentioned in his diary on 5 September that he was reading them, but the diary also reveals a kaleidoscope of activities in the final four weeks before he left Australia: two interstate trips, a stream of engagements and a constant battle to clear his desk of paperwork. A lecture on the latest developments in biblical scholarship by a visiting academic at the seminary was an interruption which Beovich 'offered up as a voluntary penance for the coming Council'.[16] The transition from pastoral administration to participation in the Council was not an easy one.

The First Session (1962)

On 24 September Beovich flew to Rome. In 1962 that meant an exhausting journey of over twenty-seven hours with six stops on the way. Waiting for him at the airport in Rome was Paul Jatulis, chaplain to the Lithuanian community in Adelaide from 1949 to 1957. Jatulis drove him to the Lithuanian College, not far from the Basilica of St John Lateran. The accommodation was simple but adequate, and Beovich ended up staying there for all four sessions of the Council. He was joined by Justin Simonds, still coadjutor archbishop of Melbourne, Patrick Lyons of Sale, and James O'Collins of Ballarat, the bishops with whom he spent his annual holiday each February at the presbytery at Koroit.

Thanks to some cunning strategising, reminiscent of Beovich's student days in Rome, the Koroit contingent ended up close to the main altar and the pope at the opening ceremony on 11 October 1962.[17] In his address, Pope John XXIII famously challenged the 'prophets of doom' who saw only problems in the modern world, and called on the Council fathers to express the ancient deposit of faith in a more positive and appropriate way. Commentators had no trouble identifying one of the chief targets of the pope's message: Cardinal Alfredo Ottaviani, the seventy-two-year-old secretary of the Holy Office and head of the preparatory theological commission. Loris Capovilla, the pope's secretary, later revealed that John told him that he could not resist glancing at Ottaviani every now and then to see how he was coping.[18] Yet, while the pope's address was very significant, it is worth remembering that it was in Latin, at the end of a five-and-a-half-hour 'Baroque endurance test'.[19] This must have lessened its impact at the time. Some advocates of liturgical reform went away disheartened by the 'triumphalistic pomp' of the opening ceremony,[20] but Beovich wrote in his diary that it was 'a wonderful and inspiring experience'.

The first working session of the Council, or general congregation, took place on Saturday, 13 October, in the hall which had been created in the central nave of St Peter's Basilica. It lasted less than fifty minutes. It came to a premature end when four cardinals appealed for more time for the Council fathers to consider their options before they voted on members for the commissions which would revise the Council documents. This has been interpreted as the first indication that the Council would not simply rubber stamp the decisions of the curia, the Vatican bureaucracy.[21] As Beovich never liked being rushed into a decision, he was pleased with the outcome. In the excited lobbying which followed, he was nominated by the Australian hierarchy for a place on the liturgy commission, but when the vote was finally taken on 16 October he was not elected.

The liturgy text was one of the most progressive and pastoral of the prepared drafts. It opened the door to greater use of the vernacular at the discretion of national episcopal conferences. It was the first to be debated, and the battle lines were soon drawn. The most notable opponents of change (sometimes labeled 'curial zealots' or 'intransigent traditionalists') were Cardinals Ottaviani, Ruffini and Dante. As young priests, all three had been on the faculty of the Urban College of Propaganda Fide, Beovich's beloved *alma mater*, during his time as a student in Rome. They were strongly supported by Cardinals Godfrey of Westminster and McIntyre of Los Angeles.

In his diary on 23 October Beovich wrote: 'I agree wholeheartedly with the opinions expressed by Cardinals Ottaviani, Ruffini, McIntyre and Godfrey of the Latin school.' On 30 October he reflected: 'So far it has appeared that the Germans, Dutch and French (to some extent) want drastic changes in the liturgy; likewise a number of younger bishops. The Irish, English, Scots and most of the USA and ourselves, along with the Roman curia, are conservative in these matters.' The next day he grumbled: 'Listening to the experiences and opinions voiced by some youthful bishops, one wonders if they think the Holy Spirit was absent from some previous periods of the Church's history, but is helping them now.' A meeting of the Australian hierarchy on 3 November revealed that some of the younger Australians had been infected by reformist zeal. By then Beovich was also beginning to rethink his position. According to Cardinal Heenan, many bishops who were opposed to the vernacular liturgy changed their minds when they heard bishops from communist countries explain how impossible it was to teach the faith except during the liturgy.[22] In his diary Beovich did not identify any particular speech as a turning point, but on 5 November he confided: 'I would think, at this stage ... there is what one could call a left wing and a right wing; in which case there would be wisdom in following a via media.' When the schema was finally put to a vote on 14 November, he voted in favour of it, as did the overwhelming number (97 per cent) of bishops.[23]

The excitement of attending the Council soon diminished as it proved to be a gruelling experience. There were 328 speeches during the debate on the liturgy; 88 fathers spoke on the first chapter alone.[24] Those who criticise the Australian bishops for not speaking more fail to take into account the sheer number of speeches and the amount of tedious repetition. Beovich thought his Australian colleagues exercised commendable restraint![25] Another problem was that Latin, under fire as the language of the liturgy, proved to be less than satisfactory as the language of the Council. Cardinal Cushing of Boston is said to have frankly admitted, 'I can't understand a word these guys say,' and to have packed up and gone home. Other bishops were observed reading newspapers or writing letters during the debates.[26] Beovich was more conscientious, but he struggled to follow Latin spoken with different accents, and sympathised with those who could not understand what was being said: 'This morning Cardinal Cushing left for Boston. I would think that anyone who cannot follow the Latin speeches must find the position very frustrating.'[27] Beovich also noted the irony of Cardinal McIntyre delivering a speech in very poor Latin in favour of Latin as the language of the Mass.[28]

General congregations were only held during the mornings. Afternoons and evenings were usually free and some bishops, like Guilford Young of Hobart, dashed around attending lectures given by the 'periti', theological advisers like Karl Rahner and Yves Congar. There is no evidence that Beovich ever did so. Even if he had been interested in new currents in theology (and he clearly was not at this time), he had to rise at 5 am so that he could spend half an hour in prayer (from 5.30 to 6.00) and then celebrate Mass before having breakfast and travelling to St Peter's by 9 am.[29] He was 'always tired after a morning's session',[30] and ready to return to his lodging to rest, go for a walk, or do something pleasant to unwind, like visit the zoo. Dinners at the Australian embassy and other social functions also took up time and energy. Even the appropriately named Young acknowledged that he found his stay in Rome exhausting, and he was twenty years younger than Beovich.[31] Beovich was among the 40 per cent of bishops who had been born in the previous century.[32] He was sixty-six in 1962, but he had been a bishop for twenty-two years which meant, when almost two thousand bishops were seated according to seniority in office, he was allocated seat number 26. In fact, regardless of age, a number of bishops became ill during their time in Rome; some, it was said, as a result of the tension engendered by the debates.[33] Within the first fortnight of the Council, four bishops actually died, one as he was entering the Council hall. Beovich had his ongoing battle with diverticulitis, and developed a bad cold in November, perhaps helped by the dismal wet weather. In December another cold turned into pneumonia. To add to this catalogue of woes, the first session of the Council took place against the backdrop of the Cuban missile crisis when it seemed the world was on the brink of war between the two superpowers, the United States and the Soviet Union.

On 14 November 1962 Cardinal Ottaviani rose to his feet to launch the schema on revelation. He knew it was in for a rough ride. The schema had already been savagely criticised and alternative ones were circulating.[34] On 17 November Beovich summarised objections to the draft: it was too scholastic and rigid, it lacked pastoral spirit and mature theological development, it disregarded the problem of salvation prior to revelation, it did not encourage theological reflection or biblical exegesis, and it was incomprehensible to non-Catholics. The best that defenders of the schema could say was that it had been prepared by some of the 'great minds of the Church' – in other words, an appeal to loyalty. Beovich responded accordingly: 'For my part I am Roman and in Rome I found a fount of inspiration, learning and piety. Consequently, I shall support the schema.' Amidst intense lobbying, the Council fathers voted on 19 November whether to retain the schema or toss it into the conciliar dustbin. On that morning Beovich had the honour of celebrating Mass at the beginning of the general congregation, in front of 2197 other bishops. It was the Mass of the Holy Spirit, and Beovich initially attributed the result of the voting to divine intervention: opponents of the schema failed to get the two-thirds majority which they required. Yet 61 per cent of the bishops indicated their dissatisfaction with the document. The pope intervened and sent it to be redrafted by a mixed commission made up of members from the doctrinal commission and the Secretariat for Christian Unity. Beovich welcomed this decision which, he realised, rescued the Council from a difficult position.[35]

Although he did not attend the general congregations, Pope John followed the debates on television and engaged in some subtle and not-so-subtle morale building.[36] In an audience on 11 November he enthusiastically explained to the Australian bishops how he had been inspired to call the Council. Two days later Beovich went to the coffee bar which had been established in the sacristy at St Peter's. There, he reflected the following week, 'one may have a cup of coffee, stretch one's legs and meet acquaintances from many lands. One also may occasionally pick up an item of interest, but often one hears news that is gossip at second or third hand, so hardly reliable'. On 13 November, while in search of a cup of coffee, he bumped into the retired English archbishop of Bombay, Thomas Roberts SJ.[37] Adrian Hastings wryly comments that 'in even the best administered autocracies mistakes occur occasionally and Archbishop Roberts was one of them. No one so honest, so independent ... so ingenuously frank should ever have been selected by pre-conciliar Rome as an archbishop – even of Bombay'.[38] Discussing the recent audience, Roberts told Beovich he was surprised the pope had spoken to the Australian bishops in Italian. Beovich replied that as most of them had been students in Rome, the language was not a problem. Roberts blurted out that 'he feared Roman students as an arm or upholder of the Curia'. A bemused Beovich wrote in his diary: 'What a strange Jesuit!' He was clearly shocked by the hostility toward the Vatican bureaucracy which surfaced at the first session. It was totally foreign to him.[39]

On 25 November Beovich attended a reunion at his old college. The pope celebrated Mass in the Propaganda chapel and Beovich afterwards wrote down his comments about the Council: 'We had been feeling our way because none of us had conciliar experience, now we were advancing more surely. The world must be impressed by the liberty of speech and differences of viewpoints among the bishops on those matters outside the deposit of faith.' Impressed? In his address at the close of the first session on 8 December, John XIII continued this theme. The 'sharply divergent views' which had arisen illustrated 'the holy liberty that the children of God enjoy in the Church' (Archbishop Roberts took this a bit further and said that the children of God could slide down the banisters in the house of the Lord).[40] However, the pope's positive assessment of the Council was overshadowed by the obvious fact that he was gravely ill. Before the closing ceremony, Beovich bumped into Cardinal Giobbe, Prefect of the Congregation of Rites and his much respected former rector at Propaganda. Giobbe told him he feared that the Modernist heresy had returned to haunt the Church.[41]

On 13 December 1962 Beovich arrived back in Adelaide, still suffering from pneumonia and 'very tired, miserable and grubby' after the long flight.[42] Next day he went to the seminary where the diocesan clergy were on retreat. 'We still have the Mass in Latin,' he is said to have assured the gathering, whereupon all the priests applauded.[43] Two days later Beovich tried to adopt Pope John's positive tone in an address in the cathedral:

> What had been accomplished in the eight weeks of the Vatican Council? A very large body moves slowly in the beginning. The Council is a huge body. Of necessity it had to begin slowly; then it proceeded to make sure and steady progress. Bishops of all colours and from all parts of the world gradually got to know one another, to hear one another's views, to learn of the problems in settled countries, in missionary fields, and behind the Iron Curtain.[44]

James Gleeson was not fooled by this reassurance; he knew that Beovich was 'a bit concerned'. However, Gleeson insisted that Beovich's return from the next session was very different. He came back 'on top of the world', really 'enthralled' with the Council.[45] So what had changed?

The Second Session (1963)

A significant difference between the first and second sessions was that in 1963 Beovich travelled by ship. This gave him a badly needed three-week interlude between Adelaide and Rome: time to rest and study the conciliar documents in the company of some of his episcopal friends. In 1963 his travelling companions were Justin Simonds, Norman Gilroy and Patrick O'Donnell of Brisbane. On the return journey there were three weeks to recover from the Council before reaching Adelaide.

In 1963 there was also a new pope whom Beovich deeply respected and trusted. Whereas John XXIII had talked with 'charismatic vagueness' of a new Pentecost,[46] Paul VI unfurled a clear plan for the Council. In his opening address on 19 September 1963 he explained that he wanted the Council fathers to come to a deeper understanding of the nature of the Church, promote its inner renewal, encourage Christian unity, and engage in dialogue with the modern world. Three weeks later Beovich reflected in his diary:

> One can now take stock of the second session. A year ago we assembled for the Council uncertain of its atmosphere and direction. Those of us who had been Roman students, certainly myself, would look for a lead from the Pope and the Holy See. Most of us would incline to the conservative side and would not welcome what we called innovations. What impressed us at the first session was to hear the problems of bishops in many countries and the exchange of ideas; what many of us did not relish, myself included, was the enthusiastic activity of a number of *periti* [theological experts] who looked for groups of bishops to expound their ideas, sometimes very novel.
>
> Now at this second session, the atmosphere has cleared, for me at any rate. It is certain that a vigorous and comparatively youthful pope is following closely the mind of Pope John ...
>
> Consequently, one can discern among the bishops a greater air of assuredness, and a desire to be in the van of progress, myself included.
>
> One notices that the *periti* are now not much in evidence for propaganda work, though their legitimate task of helping the commissions is praiseworthy. In the many fine speeches delivered by the bishops on the schema before us on the church, there is no evidence of national

> blocks or of that or this side of the Alps. We feel that the debate is stimulating and not boring. We are helped by the initiative of the USA bishops who are producing, day by day, a digest in English of the various speeches ...
>
> In addition, the commissions have done and are doing excellent work. There is still maximum freedom of debate. One feels that after a certain amount of uncertainty at the first session we are now safely launched.[47]

On 28 October 1963, to commemorate the anniversary of Pope John's election, Pope Paul celebrated Mass in the Council hall. Cardinal Suenens preached a tribute to John and to Paul who, he stressed, was continuing John's work. He exhorted the Council fathers to have courage. As Pope John had said: 'Fear comes only through lack of faith.' When Suenens left the pulpit, he was warmly embraced by Paul VI. Not much is made of this in the recent volume on the second session in the *History of Vatican II* series, but it had a profound impact on Beovich.[48] It confirmed that he had correctly discerned the wishes of Popes John and Paul. He resolved: 'I shall follow them and uphold them as best I can. As between the extreme schools, one is a little left of centre.'[49]

In *The Roman Mould of the Australian Catholic Church*, John Molony defines *Romanità* as 'unswerving loyalty to the office, and affection for the person of the Pope, acceptance of Rome and what it stands for as the centre and heart of Christendom, subservience to the Roman curia ... [and] a willing readiness to form and foster a local institutional Church according to Roman ideas'.[50] Murphy argues that the Australian bishops learnt a different kind of *Romanità* at Vatican II: loyalty to the pope did not necessarily entail subservience to the curia.[51] Beovich is an example of a bishop who made this adjustment at the Council.

One of the most important debates of the second session concerned the schema on the Church, and the emergence of what some would see as 'the guiding idea' of the Council: the concept of *communio*.[52] This is sometimes translated 'communion' or 'fellowship', although in fact it is a Latin translation of the Greek *koinonia* which originally meant 'participation'. A fluid theological term, it can be used to describe the nature of the Church as a sacrament (meaning a sign and instrument) of fellowship with God. It can also refer to participation in the Holy Spirit, in the local Christian community, and above all in the Eucharist. It is closely allied to what came to be regarded, in hindsight, as another leitmotif of the Council: the notion of the Church as 'the People of God'. In 1963, the chapter on the hierarchy in the Constitution on the Church, with its emphasis on the Church as an institution, was demoted from first to third place, behind those on 'The Mystery of the Church' and 'The People of God'.

What Beovich made of these theological developments is not clear, but he enjoyed the discussion and did not record any opposition. A highlight of the second session for him was the debate on episcopal collegiality.[53] A number of issues were interwoven. One concerned the very nature of episcopacy. The special role of bishops to represent Christ as teacher, priest and shepherd was strongly affirmed. Supporters of collegiality saw this as the fullness of priesthood, conferred by consecration. In other words, bishops receive their authority directly from Christ. It is not merely delegated by the pope. Then, in communion with the pope and with each other, bishops form an episcopal college and share responsibility for the universal church.

This view was bitterly opposed by a minority at the Council, including Cardinal Ottaviani, who thought that it undermined the First Vatican Council's emphasis on papal primacy. No bishop could have been more devoted to the papacy than Matthew Beovich, but 'after careful thought and prayer' he voted in favour of collegiality on 30 October. The doctrine reflected the lived experience of the Council where the bishops were acting collegially. Beovich rejoiced in this. One day he arrived early and sat watching the participants gather: 'In the happy and relaxed atmosphere of the Council, I savored this morning the universality of the Church.'[54] The contact with other bishops probably had a greater impact on him than the new currents in theology.

A sense of collegiality was also evident in the meetings of the national episcopal conferences which took place regularly during the Council, and after the Council assumed considerable responsibility for implementing its decrees. There was some heated discussion over what legislative power the conferences should enjoy. In a written submission, James Carroll of Sydney maintained that while unity should be strongly encouraged, individual bishops should retain the freedom to withdraw from national decisions. Beovich added his name to Carroll's appeal. This has been interpreted as an indication that he did not really embrace collegiality but was still captive to a Vatican I mentality.[55] However, what surely lay behind the submission was not the First Vatican Council but the Movement controversy of the 1950s. Beovich and the Sydney bishops would probably not have been able to divorce their dioceses from Santamaria's Movement if the decision had depended on a vote at a national meeting of the hierarchy. In the end, the Council decided that national conferences could develop their own regulations, subject to the approval of the Holy See.

Beovich was disappointed at the second session when the Council fathers narrowly voted to place a chapter on Mary at the end of the Constitution on the Church rather than devote a separate document to her. Before the Council there had been talk of new dogmas, speculation that Mary might be proclaimed mediatrix of all graces or even co-redemptrix. That did not happen. Instead there was a balanced statement which highlighted Mary's pre-eminence among human creatures while stressing her subordination to her son. This helped stop the escalation in Marian piety which had been occurring since the mid-nineteenth century, but Cardinal Agagianian reassured Beovich that the statement 'could not be construed as any lessening of the dignity of Our Lady or any down-grading of her pre-eminent role in the Church'.[56]

Beovich was particularly interested in the schema on ecumenism, which was also discussed at the second session. Although some Council fathers maintained that Christian unity could only be achieved when Orthodox and Protestant 'schismatics' returned to the Catholic fold, others were keen to foster common Christian witness, cooperation in works of charity, and dialogue. Cardinal Bea, the dynamic eighty-two-year-old president of the Secretariat for Christian Unity, frankly acknowledged the difficulties raised by the ecumenical movement, but argued that ecumenical action, carefully guided and promoted by the bishops, would help the renewal of Christian life for all.[57] Beovich was very impressed by Bea and found his appeal 'both convincing and moving'.[58] He made up his mind during the debate that he would lift restrictions on Catholics attending non-Catholic weddings, including the ban on them serving as bridesmaids and groomsmen.[59]

When Beovich returned to Adelaide in February 1964 after the second session, another opportunity presented itself to put theory into practice. He arrived home while Geoffrey Fisher, retired archbishop of Canterbury, was visiting relatives in South Australia. Hearing there would be a liturgical reception to welcome Beovich, Fisher asked if he could attend the service and hear Beovich's report on the Council. Gleeson, who was organising the event, agreed, but somewhat reluctantly as he was concerned about protocol.[60] Lord Fisher had met Pope John in 1960, but the meeting had been strictly private, with no photographs or press releases allowed. It would be very different in Adelaide on 9 February 1964. As the liturgy drew to a close, Beovich unexpectedly darted over to Fisher, who was seated in the congregation, grabbed him, and arm-in-arm they walked out of St Francis Xavier Cathedral. It was ecumenism in action, Beovich-style.[61] A few days later at Ennis, Beovich hosted a 'pleasant tea party' for Lord and Lady Fisher and the Anglican archbishop of Adelaide, Dr Reed, and his wife.[62]

In his address in the cathedral on 9 February 1964 Beovich mentioned the Constitution on the Sacred Liturgy. The final vote had taken place in a public session presided over by the pope on 4 December 1963. Although it encouraged much greater active participation by the Christian community in the liturgy, the constitution did not require the wholesale introduction of the vernacular. It did not ban it either. It merely approved the vernacular 'especially' for the readings and prayers of the faithful. Beovich advised his audience that Latin remained the language of the Mass, but the vernacular could be introduced according to the judgement of the bishops. He promised to give effect to the new constitution as soon as possible.[63] 'My attitude has changed since last year,' he recorded in his diary, 'and this is due to the fact that the Pope is keen on reforms in the Liturgy ... If he is, so am I; he always has the help of the Holy Spirit.'[64] In keeping with the Council's spirit of episcopal collegiality, Beovich did not act unilaterally. He spoke strongly in favour of liturgical reform at 'a highly successful' meeting of the Australian bishops in March 1964.[65] After Rome approved the resolutions adopted at the meeting, the bishops met again in June to plan their gradual implementation throughout Australia from July 1964.[66]

The Third Session (1964)

The third session began on 14 September 1964 with one of the Council's liturgical reforms which symbolically displayed the doctrine of episcopal collegiality. Twenty-four bishops from nineteen countries stood around the enlarged main altar in St Peter's Basilica and celebrated together the opening Mass with Pope Paul VI. As he wrote in his diary, it was 'the day of days' for Matthew Beovich because he was one of the chosen ones. He did not know why 'the lowly had been lifted from the dunghill', but he rejoiced in the honour.

With fourteen texts on the agenda, the third session was even more strenuous than the first two. In his notebook Beovich again commended the Australian bishops for contributing written submissions rather than adding to the tedious number of speeches.[67] The document which provoked the most heated debate was the one which affirmed that freedom in religious matters is an inherent human right. A particularly contentious paragraph acknowledged that other religious groups had a right to promote their beliefs and practices. This raised the ire of Beovich's friend, Pat Lyons, a firm adherent of the 'error has no rights' school. In a written submission he objected to the paragraph and called for a much stronger affirmation that the Catholic Church was the one, true church. At the other end of the spectrum, Guilford Young of Hobart argued the Catholic Church could not claim religious freedom for itself without conceding it to other groups, and this view eventually won out.[68] Norman Gilroy, however, thought the paragraph in question should be quietly dropped. Beovich added his name to Gilroy's submission.[69] It was, typically, the *via media*.

Another bishop was also striving to steer a middle course – the bishop of Rome.[70] That was not Beovich's only resemblance to Paul VI. They were close in age and temperament; both being rather shy, sensitive men with a warmth and sense of humour which sometimes broke through their innate reserve. The tragedy of Paul VI is that while his *via media* may have saved the Church from schism, it did not make him popular. Die-hard traditionalists were offended by his support for collegiality and ecumenism, while those with more progressive inclinations were dismayed to see curial cardinals like Ottaviani bounce back from the humiliations of the first session as stridently conservative as ever. On 2 October 1964 *Time* magazine quoted an unnamed Australian bishop who said of the pope: 'Let's face it, he's weak.' Cardinal Gilroy called an emergency meeting of the Australian hierarchy. Everyone denied uttering such heresy, and a missive was speedily dispatched to assure Pope Paul that he had their loyalty and obedience.[71] Undercurrents, however, remained.

Paul exacerbated tensions by making a surprise appearance at a working session of the Council on 6 November. He praised the schema on the missions, which had been prepared largely by Roman clerics associated with the Congregation for the Propagation of the Faith, and expressed his hope that the bishops would approve it. Unfortunately, in the words of a bishop who actually had experience as a missionary, the schema consisted of 'thirteen lifeless platitudes culled from some worm-cankered textbook on Missiology'.[72] Beovich obediently voted in favour of retaining the document as a basis for discussion, but he knew that Paul had backed the wrong horse and was not surprised when it was sent back to be rewritten.[73] He had, probably before Paul's intervention, added his name to the submission of Xaverius Geeraerts of the Missionaries of Africa, which called for the Council to develop a more adequate theology of mission, grounded in the mission of the Son and the Holy Spirit, and therefore part of the very nature of the Church.[74]

Why did Paul seem to favour the traditionalists at the third session? Bernard Pawley, one of the Anglican observers at the Council, wrote to the archbishop of Canterbury that he thought Paul had put a bit of weight on the conservative side to keep the balance and stop the boat rocking too much. Shortly afterwards, Pawley had an audience with the pope. Paul asked what he had reported, and agreed with his response: 'As captain of the ship I have to keep her on a steady course ... It is better for me to go ahead slowly and carry everyone with me than to hurry along and cause dissension.'[75] They were sentiments which Beovich would have heartily endorsed. The image of the Church as a ship was one which also appealed to him. In his address to the 400 laymen who gathered in Adelaide in July 1965 for the dinner to celebrate the twenty-fifth anniversary of his episcopal consecration, he remarked:

> Many times in the course of each century – and the present is no exception – the Church ... finds herself in rough waters. In perilous seas the passengers and the crew are careful not to rock the boat; they look to the captain of the ship – the man in charge.

For Beovich, that meant Pope Paul. Rather than compare Paul unfavourably with Pius XII, as conservatives were wont to do, or John XXIII, as more liberal Catholics did, Beovich believed that Paul combined the best qualities of both men: 'the keen intelligence, discernment and sound judgment of Pius XII' and the 'heartfelt goodness, affability and pastoral zeal of John XXIII'.[76]

The Fourth Session (1965)

After a short stay in Calvary Hospital caused by another bout of diverticulitis, Beovich left with his friend Justin Simonds for the fourth and final session of the Council on 6 August 1965. When it opened on 14 September 1965 he was promoted to seat number 11. Simonds was in the seat in front. In November 1963 he had finally succeeded Mannix as archbishop of Melbourne but was by now almost blind. Beovich guided him to and from his seat and filled in his ballot papers. As Simonds was a member of the commission for studies and seminaries, Beovich also read the necessary paperwork to him in their free time.[77]

There was still tension over the declaration on religious liberty, but Paul VI intervened and ordered that it be put to the vote before he addressed the United Nations on 4 October. Almost 2000 fathers voted in favour, only 224 against. Beovich was 'very pleased' with the result.[78]

Beovich was also interested in the speeches on the document on the Church in the modern world which he thought would be 'one of the outstanding works of the Council'.[79] As Pope John had wanted, the overall tone of *Gaudium et spes* was positive rather than defensive. It affirmed that the Holy Spirit was not absent from modern developments, but offered some serious critiques which were not welcomed by all bishops. At almost the last minute an attempt to derail the schema was made by Archbishop Hannan of New Orleans.[80] Upset by the lack of acknowledgement of the deterrent value of nuclear weapons in the document's condemnation of nuclear warfare, Hannan called on the Council fathers to vote against the whole schema if the 'errors' in the chapter were not corrected. Nine other bishops signed his submission, including Australia's Guilford Young.[81] In an efficiently organised campaign, Hannan's appeal was translated into different languages and nuns rushed around Rome hand-delivering a copy to each bishop. Beovich was not impressed.[82] Neither was Cardinal Ottaviani, who proved that the issue transcended 'progressive' and 'conservative' divisions by giving one of the most passionate speeches against war ever uttered.[83] In the end the schema was passed, 2111 to 251.

During the first session a joke went around the Council after Ottaviani had been absent for a few days. It was said that he had hailed a taxi to take him to the Council, and when the driver asked where he wanted to go, he had inadvertently said 'Trent'.[84] Beovich did go to the beautiful northern Italian city in November 1965. The archbishop of Trent invited a number of bishops from around the world to a ceremony in his cathedral to underline the nexus between the great sixteenth-century Council held in his city and Vatican II. As the representative of the Australian hierarchy, Beovich enjoyed his visit to Trent, but his mind was on the future rather than the past. He liked the way the congregation recited the Gloria and the Credo in Italian at the concelebrated Mass, and joined in singing hymns at the offertory and communion. He resolved to copy the new liturgical style when he returned to Adelaide.[85]

On 8 December 1965 the Second Vatican Council drew to a triumphant close with a ceremony watched by a vast crowd in St Peter's Square. 'The great Council has now entered history,' Beovich wrote in his diary, 'and in the aftermath we of our time will also enter history if we speedily and effectively put the decrees of the Council into operation. May God grant it.'[86] He was no longer ambivalent or 'resistant to the spirit of change'. Pope John XXIII had, Beovich was wont to remark, 'unwittingly set up an adult education course for bishops when he initiated the Council',[87] and Beovich had been a willing participant in this 'school for bishops'. Even though he had never made a speech in the Council hall, he had doggedly attended all the general congregations in spite of the difficulties involved, conscientiously followed the debates, and enthusiastically taken part in the liturgies. Through his involvement in meetings of the Australian hierarchy, his interaction with other bishops during the breaks from formal proceedings, and his support for a number of written submissions, he had engaged constructively in the discussion process. He had wisely recognised that genuine collegiality often requires that compromises be made. In his careful and prayerful pursuit of the *via media*, and his eventual willingness to move 'a little left of centre', Matthew Beovich was very much a Vatican II bishop.

NINE
'Zeal and Prudence' The Turbulent 1960s

> But how to express the excitement of those times! The 1960s were heady enough, but as the Church responded in a most positive way to the universal stirrings of the times, we, in Adelaide, were infected, too. Our state and diocesan culture pre-disposed us to receive this excitement with enthusiasm. Many though did not capture this spirit but continued to yearn for the traditional. They were cautious of changes lest the 'one, true Church' take a backward step, possibly even destroy itself.
>
> David Shinnick, 'Youthful Yearnings', 2000

For Matthew Beovich there was no gentle coasting into old age in his third and last decade as archbishop of Adelaide. After the stress and excitement of attending the Second Vatican Council, he had to reform his diocese in accordance with its decrees. Some Catholics still speak of 'the implementation of Vatican II' as if a series of changes could have been introduced in an orderly way to reinvigorate the Church. That was Beovich's hope in February 1966 when he returned to Australia after the final session of the Council.[1] It almost happened. In November that year an article in a national weekly, the *Bulletin*, was subtitled 'Breathing New Life into Catholicism'. However, author Peter Gough concluded that, with the exception of Guilford Young of Hobart, renewal was occurring *in spite* of the bishops, and he accurately predicted 'a stormy season ahead'.[2]

In fact, the bishops would have experienced turbulence even if the Second Vatican Council had never taken place. The generation born after the Second World War grew up with a rising standard of living and greater access to higher education. In the 1960s – that is, the remembered sixties, from c.1964 to c.1972 – the air of optimism which this generated gave way to intense questioning of established values and institutions. Nothing was too sacred in the decade of the pill, the miniskirt, the civil rights movement, the 'demo', hippies and LSD.[3] Belief in God declined, or at least it became more socially acceptable to admit that one did not believe.[4] The majority of Australians were not prepared to go that far, but neither were they willing to go to church regularly.[5] For many people the ideal of self-fulfillment replaced the humility, sense of duty and obedience to rules which had undergirded much pre-Vatican II piety. By the end of the 1960s, religion was well on the way to becoming 'a marginalized, privatized activity, something to be done between consenting adults'.[6]

If, as Adrian Hastings asserts, 'it was good to be an English Catholic bishop in 1960',[7] it became manifestly more difficult as the decade progressed, in Australia as well as England. Yet surprisingly little attention has been paid to this time. As Daniel Mannix and James Duhig died before the Council finished, their biographers did not need to consider the post-conciliar period, and most diocesan histories also avoid it.[8] What has been published generally demonstrates the lack of sympathy noted in accounts of the bishops' participation at the Council. In an article in the national newspaper, the *Australian*, in 1968 – titled appropriately, 'The Catholic Revolution' – Ian Moffit and Graham Williams maintained that 'priests and laity alike feel that too many of our 36 bishops are reacting with resignation, not excitement; with caution, not courage'. Most subsequent writers have concurred with this judgement.[9]

Promoting the Council

In Adelaide, Matthew Beovich saw nothing wrong with a cautious approach. Arriving back from the final session of the Council, he tried to dampen any expectation of radical change as he promised to implement conciliar reforms with 'zeal and prudence'.[10] Picking up the language of the Council, that 'the Church is not something above us, but we are the Church, people, religious, priests, and bishops', Beovich called on all Catholics in the diocese to participate in the work of renewal. However, he saw this as taking place above all in the individual person, and he exhorted clergy and laity alike to strive for greater holiness of life.[11]

From January to May 1966 a series of 'talks' was held in St Francis Xavier Cathedral on Sunday evenings: 'The Bishop Explains the Council.' It was originally planned that James Gleeson would give thirteen of them and Beovich would be responsible for seven. Unexpected illness forced a change of plans: Beovich went to Calvary Hospital in April suffering from a severe bout of influenza. As a result, he presented only three of the evening sessions, which is perhaps why Adelaide Catholics tend to associate Vatican II with Gleeson. They were also more likely to encounter the energetic coadjutor archbishop at the innumerable confirmation ceremonies, speech nights, and such like, which provided the bishops with further opportunities to promote conciliar teaching.

The talks which Beovich gave included one on the Council's decree on priestly training and another on the decree on the lay apostolate. In the former Beovich acknowledged the importance of a Christ-centred spirituality and greater preparation for pastoral work.[12] In the latter he spoke of lay men and women promoting Christian faith in the secular world, and playing more active roles within the Church.[13] In both, the cultivation of personal holiness remained an underlying concern, and for Beovich that included the virtues of humility and obedience. He was more progressive in his address on the Council's declaration on the relation of the Church to non-Christian religions. He deplored, in particular, the injustice and persecution which Jewish people had suffered at the hands of Christians, and insisted that any discrimination or harassment on the grounds of race, colour or religion was foreign to true Christianity.[14] He clearly had no sympathy for the 'error has no rights' position of arch-conservatives like retired French bishop Marcel Lefebvre, who emerged in the late 1960s as one of the most vehement critics of Vatican II. Overall, when speaking of the Council, Beovich promoted a carefully constructed blend of reform and traditional piety.

The cathedral talks were published in the *Southern Cross*. In a new spirit of openness, the diocesan paper also gave a detailed report on the Australian bishops' meeting in April 1966.[15] Norman Gilroy was elected president of the Australian Episcopal Conference and Beovich vice-president, an indication of the respect in which he was held by other bishops. Back in the Adelaide archdiocese, the chief item of business at the clergy conferences in March and July was how to find 'practical ways' to promote understanding of the Council.[16] In September almost seventy priests attended a three-day seminar at the seminary to study *Lumen gentium*, the Dogmatic Constitution on the Church.[17] Another special training session for priests, this time focused on the lay apostolate, was held at the Young Christian Workers' (YCW) centre at Stirling in the Adelaide Hills.[18]

In June 1966 the annual 'Diocesan Life Campaign' in Adelaide focused on 'Community Spirit in the Parish'. The campaigns had been initiated in 1962 by Robert Wilkinson, editor of the *Southern Cross*. The first one comprised four parish-based lectures on Pope John XXIII's encyclical, *Mater et Magistra*. The following year a home group approach was adopted, incorporating the YCW 'See, Judge, Act' methodology.[19] Helped by kits published in the *Southern Cross*, in 1966 participants were encouraged to reflect on their experiences of parish life, 'judge' them in the light of readings from Scripture and Council documents, and plan ways of improving community spirit. It was estimated that 10,000 parishioners took part. Beovich encouraged priests and religious to join home groups with lay people, and he commissioned lay group leaders at a ceremony in the cathedral.[20]

In the 1960s the Newman Institute of Christian Studies, which Beovich had established in 1948 as the education arm of the Movement, continued its evolution. In 1967 it became known as the Christian Life Movement. Full-time lay employees Bill Byrne (until 1968), Brian Moylan and David Shinnick, along with part-time teachers and members of the Institute's council, embraced conciliar ideas, especially the decree on the lay apostolate. They were convinced that it was no longer sufficient for lay Catholic men and women to be involved in pious sodalities and charitable organisations: they needed to develop a sense of responsibility for spreading Christianity in the world, and they had to be 'formed' to carry out this mission.[21] Throughout 1966 the men from the Newman Institute helped members of lay groups in the diocese reflect on the lay apostolate decree. They were also involved in 1966 in the establishment of the Lay Apostolate Liaison Committee (LALC) which was designed to coordinate the work of the various organisations. This seems to have been the first such body in Australia. Its president, Bill Brewer, described it in 1970 as 'the envy of the eastern states'.[22] The Adelaide group maintained contact with other 'adult lay apostolate formative movements' interstate, and in 1967 Bill Byrne became the secretary of the new national Catholic Federation of Christian Family and Social Apostolate Organisations. Byrne was also one of three Adelaide delegates to the Third World Congress of the Lay Apostolate which was held in Rome in October 1967. The other two were Carmel Clancy, diocesan president of the YCW, and Peter Davis, vice-president of the Aquinas Association of Catholic Graduates of the University of Adelaide, which changed its name in 1967 to the Newman Association.[23] At the congress in Rome, Byrne was elected a vice-president of the executive committee.[24] The Adelaide enthusiasts also developed a strong social justice orientation and interest in overseas aid, becoming involved in the Freedom from Hunger Campaign, a new Lenten appeal known as 'Project Compassion', and Australian Catholic Relief. Byrne left Adelaide in 1968 to become the Sydney-based national director of Australian Catholic Relief. All this took place with Gleeson's active involvement and Beovich's strong support.[25]

It seemed to those involved in the lay apostolate movement in Adelaide that they were at the forefront of efforts to implement the Council's teaching in Australia.[26] It is impossible to test the validity of this perception without examining the situation in all the other Australian dioceses, but Adelaide was at least on a par with Hobart, and it was well ahead of Townsville and Sydney.[27] It gained a reputation as a progressive diocese. Given Byrne's prominent role at the congress in Rome, it could even be argued that Adelaide was in the vanguard of international developments. However, in 1967 there was a reality check for the lay reformers. To help Byrne, Clancy and Davis prepare for the congress, readers of the *Southern Cross* were asked to answer a questionnaire on how effectively the decrees of the Council had been publicised, understood and put into practice at parish level.[28] As there were 34 main questions, and typed responses were requested, it is not surprising that no more than fifty people took the trouble to reply. The report compiled from the submissions concluded that, in spite of the extensive efforts which had been made to promote conciliar teaching, including the 'clear, vigorous, dynamic lead from the bishops', most Catholics had a poor grasp of what the bishops were saying and found the Council documents too verbose and complex to read. The majority did not consider themselves lay apostles, were not involved in lay apostolate organisations, and evidently did not want to be. A particular problem, one of the first discussed at a LALC meeting, was the lack of interest shown by teenagers and young adults.[29] Most respondents were keen for further changes – specific suggestions included sermons in discussion form, priests in everyday clothes, and the consecration of whole loaves of bread at Mass – but they recognised that many older Catholics would have difficulty accepting them.[30]

The Adelaide responses were similar to those nation-wide.[31] For Rosemary Goldie, an Australian woman who became assistant secretary of the Roman curia's Council for the Laity, they shed light on the laity's 'un-preparedness' for Vatican II and, therefore, the subsequent years of 'post-conciliar confusion'.[32] Yet it is difficult to see what more could have been done in the short term to promote the Council's teachings. Beovich realised that time was needed for changes to percolate slowly through the Catholic community. He was invited to preach in St Mary's Cathedral in Sydney on 9 July 1967 at a special Mass to inaugurate the 'Year of Faith' which Pope Paul VI had proclaimed to commemorate the nineteen-hundredth anniversary of the martyrdom of St Peter. Beovich used the occasion to acknowledge that there was danger in moving too slowly to implement changes, but even more danger in moving too quickly. He urged Catholics to have confidence in the judgement of their bishops and, above all, the pope, the successor of St Peter.[33] An appeal to loyalty might have worked before the Council. Unfortunately, in 1967 it raised the increasingly troublesome issue of authority.

The Transformation of the Liturgy

Of all the changes which took place in the Catholic Church in the 1960s, the most dramatic and obvious was the change in the language of the Mass from Latin to the vernacular. This began in mid-1964 and culminated in the introduction of a new rite in 1969. Amidst a multitude of minor changes, as the old liturgy was simplified, the number of genuflections and signs of the cross were reduced, and so on, there were two developments of profound symbolic significance. First, altars were brought forward so that priests could stand behind them and face the congregation instead of having their backs to the people. They thus appeared more like leaders of community celebrations than mediators between earth and heaven. Second, tabernacles were shifted in many churches from their place of honour behind the main altar to the side of the sanctuary or to a separate chapel. This was to ensure that the intense focus on the Eucharistic Host which had dominated pre-conciliar piety did not overshadow the liturgy of the Eucharist and the renewed understanding of the presence of Christ in the community. Devotions which had encouraged Eucharistic adoration (and provided opportunities for people to pray in English), like Benediction of the Blessed Sacrament and the Forty Hours Prayer, faded from prominence. On the other hand, it became more common for people to receive communion at every Mass they attended.[34]

In the archdiocese of Adelaide, liturgical reform was one of the main agenda items at clergy conferences from 1964 onwards.[35] The theme of the Diocesan Life Campaign in July 1964 was 'The Parish Around the Altar'. Beovich commissioned 600 lay men and women to lead small discussion groups in parishes reflecting on the meaning of the Mass. An estimated 7500 Catholics took part.[36] In addition, a five-part series (*Here is the Mass*) was screened on Channel 7 on Sunday evenings.[37] After rehearsals on Sunday, 16 August, the revised liturgy was celebrated for the first time throughout the diocese on the following Sunday.[38]

In February 1967 the *Southern Cross* invited readers to send their suggestions on different versions of the English translation of the Mass to Archbishop Young, vice-president of the International Committee on English in the Liturgy.[39] 'Liturgy: Your Views

Sought' proclaimed another headline in November 1967 in an article promoting the 'Catholics in Worship Convention' which was held on 10 December.[40] Brian Jackson, the seminary's youthful liturgy lecturer, and David Shinnick organised this as part of the diocese's preparation for the National Liturgical Convention which was held in Melbourne in January 1968. Discussion group leaders at the Adelaide event called for 'greater freedom in liturgical experimentation',[41] and they got a dose of it in Melbourne at an unscheduled 'guitar Mass' which was described as 'one of the highlights of the convention'.[42]

With the 'new Mass' on the way, efforts in Adelaide to promote education and discussion escalated in 1969. Over 500 people participated in a three-day 'Life and Worship Congress' in April 1969, another Jackson/Shinnick production, and about 1800 flocked to the cathedral for the final Mass of the congress on 29 April.[43] Parish groups were organised to reflect on congress themes. Priests were required to attend rehearsals at the seminary,[44] and as a follow-up to the April Congress, a 'Life and Worship Day' was held in November, also with about 500 participants. Shinnick remembers this 'as a charismatic time. The people were full of enthusiasm and hope for the future'.[45] In an article in the *Southern Cross*, Jackson stressed that the Mass was meant to be a celebration: 'I mean celebration. You know, let's have a party. Let's get together. Everyone involved. It's a joyful occasion.'[46]

Not everyone, however, was so excited. Only a few letters critical of liturgical changes were published in the diocesan paper from 1964 to 1968 but, faced with the final demise of Latin, they became more numerous and strident in 1969. One correspondent wrote: 'For me the Mass has lost its dignity, meaning and holiness. Why were not the people who make up the Church asked if they wanted the Mass changed? The new Mass was just thrust on us. Let us get back to the correct way of saying Mass.'[47] Similar sentiments were expressed by the man who demanded that the Australian bishops get Pope Paul VI to 'give us back the Mass ... if it was good enough for umpteen popes for umpteen centuries it is good enough for me'.[48] Another maintained: 'It is rightful and just that the Masses should be said and sung in Latin. It is our heritage. To be denied this right is shameful. In most cases it is the fault of the bishops.'[49] A small group of lay dissidents in Adelaide would eventually support the archconservative Society of Pius X, but not until after Beovich's retirement.

What was Beovich's role in all this? Although Guilford Young was the Australian bishop most associated with liturgical reform, Beovich spoke strongly in favour of a broad use of English at the Australian bishops' meeting in March 1964, and he was very pleased with the outcome.[50] At Christmas 1964 he led by example and celebrated Mass for the first time facing the congregation in the cathedral.[51] The following April he wrote in his diary after the Easter ceremonies:

> We are all edified by the faith and devotion of the people throughout the diocese. From various reports, the Revised Sacred Liturgy from the General Council, including the use of English, has received whole-hearted acclaim from priests and people. They are sharing more fully in the Liturgy. *Deo gratias*.[52]

As someone who had a deep devotion to the presence of Christ in the Blessed Sacrament, Beovich initially resisted shifting the tabernacle from behind the altar to a less prominent place. A confrontation with Jackson entered diocesan folklore: 'Over my dead body' is the mildest version of the words the archbishop is said to have uttered. When Beovich subsequently learnt that Giacomo Lercaro, president of the Council on the Sacred Liturgy in Rome, favoured the change, he accepted it with good grace.[53] 'After that, I don't think I could say anything he disagreed with,' Jackson recalls.[54] However, Lercaro also emphasised the importance in the renewal of the liturgy of the 'harmonious and disciplined co-operation' of priests, bishops, national episcopal conferences and the papacy. Beovich firmly insisted that changes should not take place without his approval but be implemented uniformly throughout the diocese, in accordance with the directives of the Australian Episcopal Conference.[55]

Unlike Gleeson, Beovich did not take part personally in the Life And Worship Congress in April 1969. He was away at the bishops' conference in New South Wales, but he left a letter of support to be read out at the congress.[56] He was not so cooperative six months later when it was announced that the 'new Mass' would be celebrated in the diocese for the first time at the 'Life and Worship Day' to be held on 16 November at Prince Alfred College – a Methodist school.[57] The organisers' choice of venue, based on practical considerations, was a further provocation to those Catholics who thought their liturgy was becoming too Protestant, and they had also made the mistake of not consulting the archbishop. From his sickbed in Calvary Hospital, where he was being treated for an infected cyst on his back, Beovich demanded that the 'Life and Worship Day' be moved to a Catholic site.[58] It was duly held at St Michael's College, Henley Beach.[59]

This incident highlights the fact that while Beovich allowed leading Catholics in the diocese a great deal of latitude, he could intervene decisively when he thought it was necessary. He was the one ultimately in charge, and in late 1969 he applied the brakes. Although some Australian dioceses planned to introduce the new rite on the first Sunday in Advent, Beovich decided on a later date, the first Sunday in Lent (15 February 1970) to allow more preparation time. In response to a request from a group of priests, concerned about 'many puzzling features of the new rite', he gave permission for more seminars to be held at the seminary at the conclusion of the priests' annual retreat in December. He also agreed that prior to 15 February the new rite could be celebrated on weekdays, with appropriate explanation and discussion, in churches, halls and even in private homes (at the request of the Christian Life Movement he had given permission for home discussion groups to have an annual Mass the year before).[60] He sensibly suggested, however, that 'it may be preferable to have study sessions with "dry runs" of different parts of the Mass rather than actual celebrations to preserve the dignity of the Mass and to give more opportunities for questions and explanations'.[61] At the opening of a new church at Goodwood on 14 December 1969 Beovich tried to reassure those worried about the changes: it would not be a new Mass, just a new order of the Mass. The sacrifice of the Mass remained the same. Christ would offer himself as on the cross, but it would be easier for people to participate with more intelligence and fervour.[62] Overall, Beovich's approach seems to have worked. Whatever Catholics felt privately, they made little public fuss. The first letter published in the *Southern Cross* after 15 February 1970 concerned a parish football club.[63]

Ecumenism

After the changes to the liturgy, the other most noticeable outcome of the Vatican Council was the much greater involvement of the Catholic Church in the ecumenical movement. As with liturgical reform, the Australian bishops attempted to implement changes in a coordinated and orderly way. Gleeson helped draw up a statement of principles which was approved at the hierarchy's meeting in 1965. It was clearly a compromise document. Catholic participation in ecumenical work was commended and Catholics were given permission to attend non-Catholic weddings, even as bridesmaids and groomsmen. Nevertheless, they were still required to get approval from their bishop before attending ecumenical gatherings, and they were forbidden to take part in the celebration of the Eucharist in Protestant churches.[64] Beovich supported this *via media* and was pleased that his friend Justin Simonds was also sympathetic to it: 'Pat Lyons and Jim O'Collins are still thinking of pre-conciliar days.'[65]

Another bishop who struggled to adapt to the Catholic Church's greater openness to other denominations was Hugh Ryan of Townsville. He reportedly returned from the Council resolving to be 'charitable to that damn fool Shevill' (the local Anglican bishop).[66] As Beovich had always tried to be charitable, in the wake of the Council he merely continued his earlier efforts to develop good relations with the leaders of other Christian communities. In March 1964 he spoke about the Council at a meeting of the Protestant Ministers' Fraternal at Port Adelaide.[67] A week later he was at 'Bishopscourt', the residence of the Anglican bishop of Adelaide, for a meeting with representatives of various denominations to discuss hospital and prison chaplaincies.[68] In April he dined at St Mark's College on the eve of the Anglican university college's feast day, and in June he gave a talk on the Council to about 160 guests of the South Australian branch of the Australian Council of Churches.[69] Beovich was on his annual holiday at Koroit in February 1965 when he received news that Winston Churchill had died, but he arranged for his coadjutor archbishop to attend a service held in St Peter's Cathedral in Adelaide to mark the occasion. He was interested to read that Cardinal Heenan had attended the funeral in England, 'so Arch. Gleeson was not alone'.[70] A month later Beovich was able to meet Michael Ramsey, the 'quiet and friendly' archbishop of Canterbury, at a 'warm and pleasant' dinner at Government House.[71] 'Heads of Churches' meetings, which had previously taken place on an informal basis became more regular (at least twice a year). In October 1966 Beovich went to the Methodist Conference to welcome on behalf of the Heads of Churches the incoming president, and in June 1968 he attended the installation of a new president of the Congregational Union, 'a friendly function'.[72] After many meetings, in that year the leaders of the different denominations finalised plans for the religious centre at the new Flinders University.[73]

In 1967 Beovich gave his priests permission to join 'ministers' fraternals' with their counterparts from other denominations,[74] and in some places inter-church councils were also formed, involving lay people.[75] For many Catholic families ecumenism became a practical reality as the number of 'mixed marriages' surged. In 1960 about 30 per cent of marriages in Catholic churches in the archdiocese of Adelaide involved a non-Catholic bride or groom. By 1969 the figure was 52 per cent.[76] The fact that Shinnick and Jackson chose a Protestant college as the venue for a Catholic liturgy seminar without consulting Beovich is another indication of how far ecumenism had progressed in Adelaide by 1969. 'There was a real sense of enthusiasm and hope,' a priest who was involved in the inter-church council at Glenelg recalls.[77] A danger which Beovich correctly discerned was that some enthusiasts would minimise the differences which remained between the churches and think that 'unity was just around the corner'. No less than Lyons and O'Collins did he believe that 'real unity meant the return of our separated brethren to the Catholic Church under the pope', and he was under no illusions about the time this would take to be accomplished.[78] He appreciated the complexity and challenges of the ecumenical movement, telling the ministers' fraternal at Port Adelaide:

> Any unity achieved by bargaining or compromise, or by soft-peddling unresolved differences would be spurious. No genuine unity can arise out of forsaking conscientious convictions sincerely held. So to achieve Christian unity we must begin to know one another, and even before that, know ourselves. We cannot force one another to see the same truth, but we can love one another warmly, sincerely and un-patronisingly.[79]

In his diocese he gave a good example of how this could be done.

Ironically, for some Catholics getting 'to know ourselves' may have been an even greater challenge than getting to know other Christians, as traditional markers of Catholic identity were dissolving, such as the Latin Mass and abstinence from meat on Fridays, which was made optional by the Australian bishops in 1967.[80] In addition, Catholics were given greater opportunities to voice their opinions in a Church which had prided itself on its hierarchy, and extolled obedience as a virtue. Some looked with dismay at this 'Protestantising' of Catholicism, for others it was heady new wine, drunk with enthusiasm. Unhappily for the latter, it was poured into wine skins which, while enlarged and stretched, remained essentially the same.

A More Participative Church?

Fired with enthusiasm from their own experience of coming together to discuss reform of the Church, the bishops at the Second Vatican Council approved decrees which recommended the creation of consultative bodies in their dioceses. In 1964, in accordance with the Constitution on the Liturgy, Beovich established a Diocesan Commission for Sacred Liturgy, Music and Art. Although the constitution permitted lay people to be involved, Beovich initially appointed only priests to the commission. It was not until 1970 that membership was widened and meetings became more frequent. In the early years members wrestled with practical issues such as postures in the revised liturgy (when to kneel, sit and stand), what kind of hymns were acceptable, and where the tabernacle should be placed. Beovich chaired the meetings himself, and for those who disliked wasting time, he demonstrated a commendable ability to get to the heart of a matter as soon as possible.[81] The flip side of this was that those who wandered off the point were sometimes curtly brought to order, and left with their feelings bruised.[82] It was not uncommon for priests to have their comments dismissed with the classic Beovich phrase, 'That's very interesting, Father'. This was an indication that the archbishop was not pleased, and the only sensible course of action was to shut up. Alas, for the uninitiated, it seemed like encouragement to continue. Another warning sign was a sudden increase in smoke from the archbishop's pipe. Beovich always retained the right to make the final decision, so further discussion was futile once he had clearly made up his mind.

It was the same when the Senate of Priests met for the first time on 29 June 1967, in accordance with the Decree on the Pastoral Office of Bishops, although the appointment process was a little more democratic. In May 1967 diocesan priests were divided into five groups according to age and seniority: they then voted to elect two representatives from each group. Four representatives were nominated by the male religious orders working in the diocese. The six diocesan consultors were automatically included, as was the rector of the seminary and priests in charge of special works, such as the Catholic Education Office and the Catholic Family Welfare Bureau. Beovich began the first meeting by reminding members that the Senate was a consultative body, called to advise the archbishop, and he particularly wanted them to reflect on spiritual renewal in the diocese in the light of the Second Vatican Council.[83]

As it happened, over the next three years the Senate's most notable achievement was the development of a salary and superannuation scheme for priests, a major practical change. Whereas previously each parish priest had retained the income from his parish, henceforth it would go into a common fund and be distributed according to a fixed scale of salaries and allowances. Great discrepancies in parish incomes were thus overcome and provision was made for priests to retire at the age of seventy-five, or earlier if their health declined. To facilitate this, in 1969 the Senate approved a proposal from the Little Sisters of the Poor to build a number of flats for retired priests. Previously most priests had stayed in their parishes until they died, were appointed to light chaplaincy duties, or were so ill that they were admitted to Calvary Hospital. The remuneration scheme was sensible but potentially divisive as it meant priests from wealthier parishes would be deprived of much of the income they had hitherto enjoyed. In Sydney, Gilroy faced bitter opposition over a similar proposal. One priest, Patrick Ford, likened it to socialisation and totalitarianism.[84] After much discussion and feedback from priests in Adelaide, statutes were finally approved at a clergy conference on 18 June 1970 by 67 votes to 20. Unlike Gilroy, Beovich swiftly implemented the majority decision. He was relieved that the priests had been able 'to handle it themselves'.[85] Democracy could be useful at times.

The Senate of Priests also played a significant role in the establishment of a uniform system of administration and financing for parish schools. As government funding began to flow to Catholic schools during the 1960s, the Catholic Education Office became an important conduit. In 1968 Edward Mulvihill, director of Catholic Education, proposed that each school should be required to set up a school board, with representatives from parents, teachers, religious and clergy, as well as a trained accountant, and that the board should submit regular financial reports to the Catholic Education Office.[86] On 18 September the Senate recommended that the archbishop approve the plan, which he did.[87] It was a measure of its effectiveness that it was subsequently adopted by the more independent schools owned by the religious orders. However, like the clergy remuneration scheme, it eroded the authority of the parish priest. In the Sydney archdiocese, some rather heavy-handed centralisation in the financing and control of Catholic schools generated further 'discontent and resistance' from priests such as Ford.[88] The smaller Adelaide archdiocese does not seem to have experienced that problem.

On the whole, it seems that the Senate of Priests functioned well as an advisory body to the bishop on practical administrative matters, and it provided a structure through which Beovich could, with little trouble, consult a number of priests on matters which affected them. It is not so easy to detect positive outcomes from the first Diocesan Pastoral Council, which was also recommended by the Decree on the Pastoral Office of Bishops.[89] The Pastoral Council comprised the two archbishops, Beovich and Gleeson, five priests, two nuns, and twenty lay people appointed by Beovich after being nominated by the Lay Apostolate Liaison Committee.[90]

While the lay members did not formally represent specific groups, an attempt was made to ensure that the major organisations in the diocese had at least one of their leading members on the Council. Similarly, the priests and religious sisters whom Beovich appointed were carefully chosen so that they could bring to the Council their experience of different aspects of Church life, most notably with regard to education, welfare and the needs of migrant communities. When the Council met for the first time on 31 March 1968, Beovich explained that 'the specific work of the Pastoral Council is to improve the religious life of the whole diocese, to investigate matters concerning pastoral works, to discuss them, and to come to practical conclusions about them'. If the new councillors were not quite sure what this implied, neither was the archbishop. He frankly admitted: 'As the bishops were at the beginning of the General Council, so are we apprentices in this Pastoral Council, but we will gradually find our feet.'[91]

Three years later, as the term of the first councillors came to an end, retired diplomat and author Paul McGuire expressed concern that the Council had only addressed ad hoc matters and had not 'made available to the bishop a comprehensive view of the church in the area'.[92] McGuire, who had a strong interest in social analysis, may have been politely saying that he had found meetings boring. David Shinnick, another of the original members of the Council, observes:

> A common feeling after meetings of the Diocesan Pastoral Council was one of frustration, because we never seemed to be clear about the purpose of the Council, except in general terms. There was no doubt that a lot of personal formation and development of a broader diocesan perspective took place among members. But the council was only advisory and lacked participation in any real decision making. It was not directly responsible either for its own recommendations. These seemed to be two weaknesses which kept it in a confused state.[93]

The issue of school boards illustrates the Council's ineffectiveness. After much discussion, the Council agreed on 30 June 1968 that a trust would be preferable to a board as a way of administering school finances.[94] The next meeting on 15 September was largely devoted to examining a model trust deed which had been prepared by the education sub-committee. It was decided that the trust deed and accompanying guidelines should be adopted on a provisional basis, and that the Council would meet again before the end of the year to give formal approval.[95] On 4 October 1968, however, the front page of the *Southern Cross* reported that Beovich had announced that every parish school would have a school board within a month.

In August 1970 concern was expressed by one councillor at the 'widespread dissatisfaction with the new liturgy among a considerable portion of congregations'.[96] As a result of this comment, the state of the liturgy was the major agenda item at the next Council meeting in November. Some councillors spoke positively of the new liturgy evoking a greater sense of community, of more people receiving communion, and of a general improvement in people's awareness of the importance of the Mass. Others complained about the lack of availability of Masses in Latin, and of the need for a deeper spirit of reverence, more appropriate hymns, and better-trained readers. In the end no recommendations for improvements were made, as Gleeson (for Beovich was in Rome) stated that responsibility for this area belonged to the newly re-formed Liturgical Commission.[97]

There was much discussion in 1970 regarding how the next Diocesan Pastoral Council should be constituted: in particular, whether representatives could be elected from parish pastoral councils. As there were seventy-four parishes, it was suggested that it would be better to elect members on a regional basis, but it was not clear how this could be done. A further complication was that not all parishes had established pastoral councils, although promoting their establishment was David Shinnick's major task in 1970.[98] In the end it was agreed that the archbishop would appoint members as before. Beovich used the occasion to reiterate that 'the Parish Pastoral Council is a pastoral body. Its purpose is to make us better Christians and to work for the salvation of souls'. As examples of work which a parish pastoral council could undertake, he cited making converts and ecumenical contacts and helping senior parishioners who were unable to drive get to Mass.[99] In practice, the parish councils faced the same problems as the diocesan body. Lay members were unable to make any real decisions without the approval of their parish priest, and their enthusiasm was easily dashed when their ideas were not received sympathetically by their priest or fellow parishioners.[100]

'In simple words, the layman seeks an adult role in the life of the Church,' commented one journalist in 1966.[101] In a speech on the lay apostolate that year, Beovich reiterated the importance of humility and obedience.[102] The development of a more participative, less authoritarian Church was clearly a long and complicated process. It could never have been anything else. Shinnick reflects:

> These early experiments in consultation and advice-seeking were inevitably frustrating coming as they did into a predominantly hierarchic Church. The changes were too slow and superficial for some; for others too fast and radical. Others again tried to find a middle course. But what was probably most lacking in those times was an appreciation of some plurality within the Church.[103]

Beovich, in particular, had little experience dealing with dissent, especially dissent from papal teaching. He would undoubtedly have endorsed a comment made by Gilroy in April 1968:

> It is often said that devotion to the Vicar of Christ is at the heart of Catholicism. It is a saying dear to every true son and daughter of the Church. It speaks of love, of reverence, loyalty, generosity. But the real test of devotion to the Holy Father is a spirit of docility – a willing readiness to accept his teaching and decisions.[104]

That attitude of docile acceptance which Gilroy and Beovich valued so highly was about to be severely tested.

The Humanae Vitae Crisis

As elsewhere in the western world, the issue which triggered the most tension in Catholic circles in Adelaide in the 1960s was birth control.[105] A commission of experts was appointed by the pope to examine the issue in the wake of the development of the oral contraceptive pill. In April 1967 the report of a majority of members of this commission was leaked to the press, indicating that married couples might be permitted to make their own decisions on contraception, in the light of values promoted by the Church.[106] Six months later a mini-congress was held in Adelaide to provide opinions for the diocese's three delegates to take to the World Congress of the Lay Apostolate in Rome. A show of hands revealed overwhelming support for a motion that 'the Holy See be asked to liberalise the Church's teaching on birth control'. One participant complained that there had not been sufficient discussion on the issue, prompting reporter Nicholas Kerr to write in the *Southern Cross*: 'the person sitting next to me hissed: "How can you be a Catholic today and not have discussed it?"'[107] A resolution was duly passed in Rome which stated that

> there is a need for a clear stand by the teaching authorities of the Church which would focus on fundamental moral and spiritual values, while leaving the choice of scientific and technical means for achieving responsible parenthood to parents acting in accordance with their Christian faith and on the basis of medical and scientific consultation.[108]

'Pope Gives Firm "No" to the Pill,' proclaimed the front page of the *Advertiser* on 30 July 1968, two days before Beovich's official copy of the encyclical *Humanae Vitae* arrived from Rome.[109] In the following days the responses of the Australian bishops also became front-page news. The new archbishop of Melbourne, James Knox, said he received the encyclical 'with a lively sense of gratitude', while auxiliary bishop Thomas Muldoon stressed in Sydney that the pope intended to 'bind gravely the consciences of all': 'This is a declaration of divine law, not merely Church law.'[110] Beovich released a statement to the press, which he also sent to priests to be read in every parish church on Sunday, 4 August. He was impelled to support the pope, but he uttered no expressions of gratitude and, like Paul VI in the actual encyclical, he acknowledged the hardship it would cause Catholics:

> Christ's Vicar has spoken: the previous teaching of the Church continues as we have always known it. Aided by God's grace, with faith and humility we will obey the Holy Father.
>
> To be a Catholic is to accept a life of suffering as well as love. No one welcomes the unquestioned suffering that refusing contraception involves. But Catholics have simply a different standpoint from almost everyone on earth. For Catholics loyalty to their Church is not a fringe affair. It involves loyalty to God himself. This loyalty has occasioned even martyrdom in the past. It will be the occasion of equal heroism as

> a result of the present decision. For Catholics when the Pope speaks as the successor of Saint Peter, as Shepherd of the whole Church, he is the voice of Christ and we accept his teaching.[111]

With the *Advertiser* headlines on 31 July 1968 highlighting widespread opposition to the encyclical ('World in Protest At Pope's Ban'; 'Pill Ruling "Disaster"'), Beovich was relieved to report in his diary that the Senate of Priests 'to my happiness ... carried a motion without dissent, upholding and giving obedience to the Pope's teaching'.[112] On 1 August he telephoned Gilroy to suggest the whole Australian hierarchy send a telegram of support to the pope. The following day Gilroy called back to say a meeting of the central commission of the Australian Bishops' Conference would be held in Melbourne on Monday, 5 August. Beovich duly flew to Melbourne and helped draft a statement which was released to the press on 7 August.[113] This warned it would be 'a grave act of disobedience' for Catholics to refuse to accept the encyclical. However, the statement also acknowledged Paul VI had not put the full weight of his teaching authority behind *Humanae Vitae* – it was not technically an infallible definition of faith – and it concluded on what was clearly intended to be a humane and pastoral note: 'we pray that husbands and wives may find in bishops and priests Christ-like kindness and understanding in the difficulties of their vocation of marriage.'[114] An unidentified Catholic spokesman in Adelaide interpreted the statement in the most lenient way possible, telling a reporter from the *Advertiser* that the bishops had 'removed the matter from essential Catholic doctrine to the field of practical duty. This meant that there was not necessarily any question of excommunication from the Catholic faith involved in a Catholic's decision as to how he accepted the pope's decision'.[115]

With reports coming in of the pope's 'suffering and anguish',[116] Beovich still wanted to contact him. On 9 August he sent a telegram to Cardinal Cicognani, the secretary of state at the Vatican, on behalf of the bishops of his province and the Senate of Priests, expressing 'unreserved obedience' to the encyclical.[117] Guilford Young's refusal to send a similar cable from the Hobart diocese caused a bitter dispute among his priests. One of his supporters was so outraged by accusations Young was disloyal to the pope that he publicly attacked the 'zealots' for their lack of respect and loyalty to their archbishop.[118] Priests in Adelaide were also divided, with some strongly in favour of the encyclical and others dismayed at its publication. The former would have been pleased with Beovich's 'loyalty cable'. The latter were probably appeased by his moderate stance at the special seminar which was held at the seminary to study the encyclical on 30 August, attended by almost 200 South Australian priests. It is remembered that Beovich exhorted priests to be as pastoral and understanding as possible, especially in the confessional: 'the priest in the confessional is above all a pastor, a shepherd, and he must be gentle with the sheep.'[119] An article in the *Southern Cross* explained that Catholics would commit a sin if they disregarded their conscience, but if they mistakenly believed that a wrong action (such as using contraceptives) was right, they could still in good conscience receive the sacraments.[120] This became an important loophole for priests who found the teaching of *Humanae Vitae* difficult to accept.[121] No priest in the Adelaide archdiocese was disciplined or suspended for public dissent, as happened in some dioceses interstate and overseas, and there was no subsequent wave of resignations from active priestly ministry, as was the case in Victoria and New South Wales.[122]

Another pastoral response in Adelaide was the establishment of the Catholic Family Planning Centre to teach the ovulation or rhythm method of avoiding pregnancy, the only form of birth control which *Humanae Vitae* deemed licit. Peter Travers, Beovich's secretary at the time, recalls that the archbishop began planning the centre the day after the encyclical was published 'to make it possible for people to obey'.[123] It opened early in 1969, a joint venture involving the Catholic Family Welfare Bureau, the Guild of St Luke for Catholic Doctors, the Cana Conference of Adelaide (the marriage guidance movement), the Christian Life Movement and the Catholic Women's League.[124] In the immediate wake of the encyclical, the *Southern Cross* published two articles by 'A Catholic Doctor' which gave detailed and frank advice on how a woman could detect when it was 'safe' for sexual intercourse by using a thermometer and monitoring vaginal discharges.[125]

While Beovich was able to minimise disunity amongst his

clergy by carefully negotiating a *via media* through the different reactions to *Humanae Vitae*, he was not so successful at diffusing the anger of a group of educated lay Catholics. He never seems to have explained or defended the theology and complex ethical reasoning behind the encyclical, why 'natural' methods of birth control were acceptable when 'artificial' methods were sinful. He simply maintained that the pope had to be obeyed because he was the pope, not because he was right. That shifted the focus of the controversy to the issue of authority. On 13 August Peter Davis and Francois Mai held a meeting of the Newman Association of Catholic Graduates at the University of Adelaide Staff Club. About ninety people attended, and 'by a clear majority' passed a number of resolutions which expressed dismay at the encyclical, withheld assent from it, and called on Beovich to petition the pope for another council to consider both marriage and family life and the teaching authority of the Church. To Beovich's displeasure, a report of the meeting featured prominently in the *Advertiser* the next day.[126] When approached by a reporter, he refused to comment on the resolutions. He merely reaffirmed his call to Catholics to give their 'loyal obedience' to the pope.[127]

Thirty-nine-year-old Peter Davis emerged as one of the encyclical's most vocal critics. As a lecturer in clinical biology at the University of Adelaide, and father of six children, he could speak from professional and personal experience. As one of the Adelaide representatives at the World Congress of the Lay Apostolate, he was annoyed the pope had rejected the advice he had received from lay Catholics. In an interview with a reporter published in the evening *News* on 14 September 1968, Davis recounted that, in spite of Beovich's disapproval, the Newman Association was 'pushing ahead with a detailed examination of Pope Paul's encyclical'. A committee had been established comprising medical doctors, social workers, marriage guidance counsellors, scientists, biologists and demographers, but – because Beovich, when invited, refused to appoint any – no theologians. 'We feel sure he will reconsider his decision,' Davis said.[128] His confidence was misplaced. The next day a meeting of the Diocesan Pastoral Council took place, chaired as usual by the archbishop. Although it was the first meeting of the Council since the controversial encyclical was published, *Humanae*

Vitae was not on the agenda. At the end of the meeting a heated discussion took place between Beovich and Davis. Beovich rebuked Davis for publicising his views in the press, and insisted that if the Newman Association wanted official recognition as a Catholic organisation it would have to accept the pope's teaching. According to David Shinnick, no one else on the Council was willing to challenge the archbishop, who clearly did not want the matter discussed further.[129] Beovich concluded privately that Davis was 'emotionally disturbed' and offered to pray for him.[130] Davis subsequently withdrew from active involvement in the Church.

Catholics were able to air their views in the 'Letters to the Editor' section in the *Southern Cross*. On 9 August four correspondents passionately supported the pope and/or attacked opposition to the encyclical. On the other hand, a woman who signed herself 'One of Them' was not impressed by Beovich's call to married couples to endure heroic suffering in married life:

> I did not get married in order to suffer but because I loved my husband and wanted to bear his children. For health and finance reasons my family is now limited, but my conscience is easy ... Let us not turn away from the Church in which we believe. But let us show that we are grown up in this matter. We are not naughty children being chided by a loving father.[131]

'Catholic Mother' wrote:

> It is part of our lives to take the pope's authority for granted. But since the Vatican Council it has also become part of our lives to believe we have an obligation to form our own consciences. It is all very well to say that Pope Paul's statement will play a big part in forming our consciences in this matter. But the truth is that we read, pondered, prayed and sought advice about this matter years ago ... Now we are in a bewildering position. Our conscience says yes and our pope says no.[132]

'Has no one thought of consulting Mrs Average Catholic?' wrote 'Just a Woman' after seeing in a later issue of the *Southern Cross* a photograph of the phalanx of male priests at the *Humanae Vitae* seminar on 30 August 1968, and reading the articles on family planning by the Catholic doctor who was also obviously male. 'She is the one most vitally concerned with the whole question ... Mrs

Average Catholic rise up! You have nothing to lose but your thermometer.'[133]

On 20 August Beovich wrote in his diary: 'Reports coming in from parishes. There is no turmoil, but general obedience and loyalty to the Pope. The "mass media" give a wrong impression, inflating pockets of resistance both here and overseas.' He probably underestimated the level of quiet dissent. A survey published in the *Australian* in November 1970 indicated that only 29 per cent of Catholics responded positively when asked, 'Do you accept the Pope's viewpoint that women should not use the pill?' Over half, 58 per cent, said 'no'.[134] It seems likely that in Adelaide, as elsewhere, *Humane Vitae* was the turning point which caused some Catholics to drift away from the Church and many others to remain but on their own terms. As they stopped participating in the sacrament of penance, the issue gradually became less troubling for priests. The magnitude of the crisis can be gathered from Beovich's diary note on 21 August 1968. For all his abhorrence of war and communism, he was relieved that the Russian invasion of Czechoslovakia had swept *Humanae Vitae* off the front page of the daily newspapers.

The Difficult Years

In retrospect, it can be seen that the storm over *Humanae Vitae* did not erupt in a clear sky. Months before the encyclical was issued, readers of the *Southern Cross* would have noticed an increasing number of articles dealing with problems in the Church. They were alerted to tensions around the globe, such as the battle between the modernising Sisters of the Immaculate Heart of Mary in Los Angeles and the elderly, conservative Cardinal McIntyre ('Nuns in Nylons Defy Cardinal').[135] From 1968 to 1970 they could follow the rise and fall of the Dutch National Pastoral Council, the most radical experiment in democracy in the Catholic Church ('Dutch Pastoral Council Wants Married Clergy').[136] Swiss theologian Hans Kung's wish list featured in a March issue. Kung thought clergy and lay representatives should participate in the nomination of bishops and the Catholic Church should drop 'out of date and ridiculous' pomp and ceremony, clerical dress, feudal titles, and so on.[137] Closer to home, Peter Davis said much the same thing in an article in January 1968 which was headlined 'The Failures of the Lay Congress'. Reflecting on his experiences in Rome the previous October, Davis maintained that the Church as an institution was out of touch with the world. It was failing to recognise 'that today man's aspirations are to democratic structures and procedures'.[138] There must have been times when Beovich winced as he read his diocesan paper, but Robert Wilkinson, the editor throughout the 1960s, testifies that he was allowed complete freedom to print such views.[139] Not all bishops were so generous. In Auckland James Liston dismissed two successive editors of his diocesan paper in 1969 and replaced them with a more conservative man, provoking demonstrations and a 'pray in' in the cathedral.[140] The fact that Wilkinson's editorials were usually balanced and moderate doubtless helps explain why Beovich trusted his judgement.

Pope Paul VI did reduce much of the medieval pomp and ceremony in the Vatican, but his credibility as a reformer slumped after *Humanae Vitae*, at least among 'progressive' Catholics. Yet as the turbulence increased, Beovich saw even greater need than before for adhering to the pope. An incident on one of his holidays at Koroit provided him with an illustration for a speech in 1969, delivered with typical self-deprecating humour:

> Archbishop Beovich said that he had once been among five bishops who had snatched a holiday and gone fishing. It was on a stretch of coast known for its sudden storms. One had come up while they were out at sea and they had to negotiate a cleft in the rocks. 'A bishop always thinks he knows the answers,' he said. They had all started to give orders. But they quickly had the sense to leave it to the man at the tiller – and got safely ashore.[141]

For Beovich, the point of the story was clear: it was Paul VI who was at the tiller of the Church.

At Koroit Beovich sometimes preached in the parish church, and in 1967 he gave a series of meditations in Lent on the inevitability of suffering in a Christian's life. The following year, in the heat of the *Humanae Vitae* controversy, he would return to this theme. The Koroit sermons testify that it was a basic component of his piety:

> Our vocation as a Christian implies suffering. Faith means suffering because it means giving up my own will and not doing what I feel like doing – the selfish thing, the easy thing, the thing that will rebound to my profit and glory – but rather what God wants me to do. The supreme example is Christ, who could have escaped death by compromising but who did God's Will even though He knew that obedience would lead Him to the cross ... Our Lord never said that the life of a Christian would be easy. Rather he told us that we would be expected to take up our cross daily and follow Him. Our Lord knew loneliness and discouragement and frustration too.

In contrast, society's new cultural style emphasised self-fulfilment, and priests were not immune to it. By the time Beovich retired in 1971 there was a large generation gap between himself and most of his priests. Only 20 of the 99 diocesan priests of 1971 had been among the 64 priests Beovich had found in Adelaide in 1940. In 1971 almost half (48) were younger than 40 years of age, and 16 had been born after 1940. Overall, the average age of priests was the same as in 1940 (44 years old), but 65 per cent of the priests of 1971 had been born in South Australia and only 21 per cent in Ireland, an almost exact reversal of the percentages for 1940.[142]

In 1969 a subcommittee of the Senate of Priests in Adelaide was formed to examine the difficulties and obstacles which confronted priests. In an interim report to the Senate, members of the committee (who were all under forty), spoke freely about the frustrations they detected arising from:

- Lack of appropriate training to help people experiencing personal problems;
- 'A mountain of paperwork' ('Was I ordained to be a clerk?');
- The inability of assistant priests to offer any real leadership in parishes, especially when parish priests refused to consult them on matters of parish policy;
- The lack of sympathy and understanding between priests of different ages;
- The lack of a positive approach to celibacy;
- Because of celibacy, the lack of someone 'to rely on emotionally';
- Difficulties in finding time to pray because of the pressure of parish work.

When Beovich read through the list, he must have been struck in particular by the comment:

> There is a sense of isolation resulting from barriers to genuine dialogue between the priests and their bishop. It is felt that a bishop must not only intend to be a father to his priests, he must appear to be a father. Too often the present conditions of life do not create an atmosphere in which a priest can approach his bishop easily and speak freely to him.[143]

A copy of the interim report and a request for feedback was sent to all the other diocesan priests and the 115 religious order priests who were working in the diocese. An article in the *Southern Cross* recounted that 24 submitted written replies, and from their responses emerged 'the need for more frequent and more personal contact between priests and bishops'.[144] When the report was discussed by the Senate of Priests, Beovich said 'he really desired that lines of communication be improved'.[145] He attempted to do that in a circular letter to priests in which he stressed that they were free to apply for any vacant parish and talk to him about possible future assignments. In the past he had sometimes consulted priests before shifting them, but most first heard about their transfer when they received a concisely worded letter of appointment to their new parish – it could consist of no more than one sentence.[146] When an assistant priest admitted that he was finding it very difficult to live with his parish priest, Beovich was sympathetic but brisk in the way he handled the matter. He arranged an immediate transfer to another parish, giving the stunned curate just three days to move.

After the proposal was discussed by the Senate of Priests, Beovich approved the formation of regional groups as a way of promoting friendship and support among priests, and it was decided that in future the elected members of the Senate would be representatives from the regions.[147] Some priests also began meeting informally to study together recent theological works,[148] and three went at the expense of the diocese to the meeting of priests in Sydney which led to the formation of the National Council of Priests.[149] Nothing else seems to have been done to address the problems which the subcommittee had identified, and one of its members left active priestly ministry in 1972. 'I must say that through 1967–1971, the period of my most intense personal upheaval, it would not have occurred to me to consult Archbishop Beovich,' he reflected three decades later. 'He was a remote figure and I was a sacerdotal minnow.'[150]

The Statistical Yearbook of the Church, published annually by the Vatican Secretariat of State, reveals that the number of men leaving the priesthood rose steadily from 640 in 1964 to a peak of 3690 in 1973, and then gradually subsided to just over 1000 a year in the mid-1980s.[151] In an article in the *Bulletin* in 1969, Michael Parer, a former priest, attributed the increasing number of departures to a 'crisis of identity'. Whereas once the priest had been better educated than most of his parishioners, and able to provide respected leadership, this was no longer automatically the case. To make matters worse, bishops did not understand 'the issues that torment many of their young priests'.[152] A large survey commissioned by the United States Bishops' Conference in the early 1970s concluded the major reason why most men left the priesthood was loneliness, followed by frustration over ecclesiastical superiors' lack of communication and cooperation.[153] Priests in the Adelaide archdiocese were clearly subject to those problems too. By the end of 1969 four had left. By 1988 the figure had risen to nineteen.[154] Most of them were men whom Beovich had ordained.

'He was grief stricken when any of his priests decided to leave the priestly ministry,' Gleeson recalled.[155] Beovich also thought he knew the main reasons why they left, and his judgement demonstrates the lack of empathy of which Parer complained. In his report to Rome in 1969, he claimed that each of the four 'defections' in Adelaide had been due 'to lapses in the spiritual life and the influence of women'.[156] He had no sympathy for eminent English theologian Charles Davis, who announced his decision to leave the Church as well as the priesthood in 1966 – although he said Mass for him. Davis's sudden departure received extensive press coverage around the world, with Davis, one of the theological advisers at Vatican II, openly discussing how he had come to doubt Church teaching. 'There is a woman in the case,' was Beovich's cynical diary comment. 'As the old parish priest is reputed to have asked when a brother priest said he was having doubts about the doctrine of the Blessed Eucharist, "What is her name?"'[157] In conversion with the Sister Provincial at Calvary Hospital in 1969, Beovich remarked 'that priestly and religious defections, always in evidence from apostolic days but more apparent now through press publicity, come through lack of prayer and sound interior life. When this protection is missing, then pride, vanity, and/or sensuality take charge. There are few exceptions'.[158] He was horrified to discover in March 1970 that one of his priests was involved in a long-term relationship with a woman: 'I told him to break the friendship, to improve and foster his spiritual life, and to see me each month. This he promised to do.'[159] A few days after this interview, tired and dispirited over the affair, Beovich asked Gleeson to take his place at the Easter Vigil.[160]

Beovich's lack of sympathy was exacerbated by his own exalted understanding of the priesthood. 'We priests consider God's greatest gift to us was when He called us to be His ministers,' he proclaimed in 1970 at the silver jubilee of Gleeson's ordination,[161] and for him that was undoubtedly the case. He told Alan Commins, rector of St Francis Xavier Seminary from 1964 to 1975, that once he had decided to become a priest, he had never had the slightest doubt about his vocation. At the time Commins found this difficult to believe, but looking back he thought it was probably true: 'He was that sort of man. He had made up his mind and that was it.'[162] Commitment, loyalty and obedience to ecclesiastical superiors were deeply ingrained in Beovich's psyche.

On the whole, however, departures from the priesthood were not a significant problem in the Adelaide archdiocese until after Beovich retired in 1971. While he had to deal with only four 'defections' in the 1960s, his episcopal colleagues in New South Wales and Victoria lost many times that number in 1968 and early 1969. Parer calculated that 'at least' sixty-five men had left, sixty of them from Victoria and New South Wales.[163] Even allowing for the much larger number of priests interstate, Adelaide seems to have escaped lightly. Part of the explanation for this must lie in the way Beovich encouraged the implementation of conciliar reforms. Adelaide priests who were ordained in the late 1960s tend to remember this as an exciting time of conciliar renewal rather than a time of crisis and confusion.[164]

Moreover, despite the concern of the subcommittee in 1969 that young assistant priests could exercise little authority in parishes, nearly all of those ordained in the 1950s were either in charge of parishes by 1971 or engaged in special works. Even if he struggled to relate to them on a personal level, Beovich was good at discerning the abilities of his younger priests and giving them significant positions of responsibility. Wilkinson was only 26 years old when Beovich appointed him editor of the *Southern Cross*. Mulvilhill became director of Catholic Education at 29, and Terry Holland director of the Catholic Family Welfare Bureau at 33. Gleeson, Beovich's choice as auxiliary bishop, was only 36 when consecrated in 1957, and Alan Commins was 40 when appointed rector of St Francis Xavier Seminary. At the other end of the age scale, Beovich insisted that elderly priests who were no longer capable of active ministry should retire and make way for younger men. Only four of the 54 diocesan parish priests were over 70 years old in 1971. There were 27 under 50, and 14 of these were under 40. There was, therefore, no large 'proletariat' of discontented and disempowered young and middle-aged priests in Adelaide as there seems to have been in some other dioceses, most notably Sydney, where Gilroy did not enforce the request he made to elderly priests to resign and it was not uncommon for men to celebrate their silver jubilees of ordination still as lowly curates.[165]

Education Matters

Tension was also evident at St Patrick's College, Manly, in the Sydney archdiocese. Former students complained to a reporter from the *Sydney Morning Herald* in 1967 that the college 'suffocated creative and imaginative work and personal fulfillment'.[166] Not even Beovich's beloved alma mater, the Urban College of Propaganda Fide in Rome, escaped the unrest which swept tertiary institutions in the late 1960s. There were forty-three Australian students there in 1969, including two from Adelaide, and they led a revolt against excessive discipline. Beovich heard an account of the turmoil the following year when he was visited by the new rector. The students from Australia and New Zealand had formed an Australasian Society and complained about such matters as lack of communication and the fact that the elderly rector and some of the lecturers were not sufficiently 'stimulating' or 'up to date'. Imitating student 'demos' in secular universities, some even wanted to picket and carry slogans in protest, but the majority decided on a slightly less confrontational approach and sent a petition to Cardinal Agagianian. Beovich was dismayed to learn that even on retreats, traditionally a time of intense private prayer, they wanted 'no silence but much discussion'. It did not surprise him that most of them, including the Adelaide students, had decided against ordination.[167]

St Francis Xavier Seminary in Adelaide fared much better. With Beovich's somewhat lukewarm support, Rector Alan Commins embraced the teachings of the Second Vatican Council, reduced the number of rules and regulations, and encouraged seminarians to take greater responsibility for their personal lives.[168] A significant outcome was that ordination rates remained relatively high. Eighteen men were ordained for the archdiocese of Adelaide between 1965 and 1969, the same number as between 1955 and 1959. Only twenty seminarians commenced formation for the priesthood for the archdiocese between 1965 and 1969, well down on the fifty-two who started between 1955 and 1959 – but this can be attributed in part to the fact that junior classes were no longer offered. The seminarians began their studies at a more mature age and fewer withdrew before ordination.

In 1964, with eighty-one seminarians crowded into the seminary (it served the Western Australian dioceses and the Vincentians as well as South Australia), Beovich confidently began planning its expansion so that it could accommodate up to 140 men.[169] A new four-storey wing with seventy-two rooms was duly blessed and opened by the apostolic delegate at the seminary's silver jubilee celebrations in May 1967. Although it cost over $600,000, thanks to careful financial management and the generosity of donors, Beovich was able to announce at the opening ceremony that a debt of only $20,000 remained to be paid.[170] As Beovich had always taken particular interest in the seminary, the expansion was hailed as 'a great personal triumph' for him.[171] Ironically, 1967 was the year numbers reached a peak (eighty-eight seminarians) and from then on began to decline.[172]

Beovich rejoiced as the long battle to obtain government

funding for Catholic schools was gradually won in the 1960s. 'To think that I would live to see the day!' he exclaimed in his diary when it was announced that $24 million had been allocated to private schools in the Commonwealth budget in 1969.[173] He was also pleased that his director of education, Edward Mulvilhill, played an important role in both coordinating the Catholic system and building good relationships with government and other independent schools. It was the kind of cooperation which Beovich relished and had pioneered in Melbourne in the 1930s. In 1966 Mulvilhill was awarded a Winston Churchill Fellowship to study overseas, and in 1967 was named in the Queen's Birthday Honours list as a member of the Order of the British Empire.[174] He later served on important federal and state government committees charged with distributing aid to independent schools.

Gratifying though these developments were to Beovich, they came at a time when over half of the Catholic children in his archdiocese were enrolled in state schools, and questions were being asked about the effectiveness of the separate Catholic system.[175] In Melbourne in 1970, Archbishop Knox dismissed the director of the Catholic Education Office, Father Patrick Crudden, after he suggested that greater effort should be put into religious education in government schools. His comments were interpreted as implying that the Catholic system should be wound down.[176] At a meeting of the Diocesan Pastoral Council in Adelaide in 1968, Beovich 'sensed a current of doubt as to the value of Catholic schools on the part of a few, possibly Davis, Byrne, Shinnick'. Fortunately, he concluded, they were very much in a minority.[177]

On the other hand, unlike some bishops who still proclaimed that it was sinful for Catholic parents to send their children to a non-Catholic school,[178] Beovich accepted the inevitability of this development. He thought that one of his greatest achievements as a bishop was the 'right of entry' scheme which he had negotiated in 1940, which allowed each denomination to give religious instruction to its children in state schools.[179] As the number of Catholic children in state schools grew, he encouraged the 'motor missions' and training programs for lay catechists which made Catholic involvement in this field possible. In 1967 he approved the establishment of a new department in the Catholic Education Office for religious education in state schools. It was run by Father Barrymore Hynes, who was also the supervisor of the Confraternity for Christian Doctrine. By the end of 1968 there were 800 members of the confraternity, and Hynes was providing support to eleven motor missions as well as training to lay catechists.[180] In December 1970 Beovich presented certificates to 150 graduating catechists at a rally in the cathedral and praised their 'vital work'.[181] That month it was announced a new centre for the confraternity of Christian doctrine would open in Goodwood, with two additional full-time employees to train the many more catechists who would be needed for state schools in the 1970s.[182] However, the provision of religious instruction had become too great a burden for other denominations. The Methodist Church formally withdrew from the scheme in 1968, followed by the Anglican Church in 1972. The South Australian Methodist Conference asked that it be replaced by a non-denominational course on religious education. Under the Education Act of 1972, one was introduced – a study of religion in which the historic importance of Christianity in Australian culture was acknowledged, but the subject was treated in as neutral a way as possible.[183] Within a few years even that subject had all but disappeared, and so South Australian state schools became 'more secular than ever before'.[184]

By 1970 the quality of religion education within Catholic schools was also troubling Beovich. He did not like the trend away from the traditional question-and-answer catechism to a 'life-centred' approach in which students were encouraged to find God in their own experiences of life. When the Australian Episcopal Conference reviewed in August 1970 the draft of *Come Alive*, a new text for senior grades, Beovich spoke out against it:

> The life centered approach ... has some attractive aspects, but hardly any theology. Indeed in the hands of some teachers it could become a kind of humanism – the love of neighbour not based on the love of God – and become further ego centred ... there could well be on the part of the students a general fog of moral or doctrinal confusion.[185]

He was annoyed to discover in November that, in spite of his objections, the draft had gone to print.[186]

Moral Issues

The role of guardian of public morality, which church leaders in the modest religious revival of the 1950s had assumed quite comfortably, became increasingly difficult to sustain as the trend toward a more liberal, secular society gained momentum, and as divisions opened up within denominations. Under the charismatic Labor premier Don Dunstan (1967–1968 and 1970–1979), and the moderate Liberal and Country League leader Steele Hall (1968–1970), South Australia gained a reputation as the most progressive state in Australia.[187] Beovich supported some easing of restrictions, including legislation to extend the availability of sport and public entertainment on Sundays. Maintaining 'Sunday observance' was still important to some of the Protestant denominations, but as long as Christians were free to worship God on Sundays, Beovich could see no harm in them afterwards taking part in sport and recreation: 'Sunday for the Christian need not be funereal.'[188] He was pleased Dunstan had thought to consult the heads of churches about the matter, and believed Dunstan would be a good premier.[189]

Beovich also supported the 'yes' vote in the 1967 referendum to amend the Australian constitution to allow the Commonwealth Government to become more involved in Aboriginal affairs, previously the concern of state governments. The referendum did not, as is sometimes assumed, confer the vote, equal wages or citizenship on Indigenous Australians; these developments occurred separately. Nevertheless, there was great symbolic significance in the fact that 90 per cent of Australians voted in favour of amendments designed to improve the lot of Aboriginal people. 'Indeed, the referendum has come to act as a form of historical shorthand for a decade of change in the area of Aboriginal affairs,' writes a recent commentator.[190] Before the vote took place on 27 May 1967, Nicholas Kerr took a delegation of Aboriginal women to Archbishop's House to meet Beovich and be photographed with him for a front-page article in the *Southern Cross*.[191] Kerr admits that he was 'a bit nervous about the meeting', as were the women. Beovich's inherent kindness, often concealed beneath a brusque exterior, came to the fore as he welcomed his visitors. Neva Wilson, who was there with her mother and sister, 'all dressed up', remembers the archbishop as 'formal and polite, but we felt comfortable'.[192] Kerr, who had 'always seen Archbishop Beovich as a rather remote, austere person', was amazed at the relative lack of formality:

> He was totally informal and relaxed ... He made them feel at home. He took little Kathleen Agius, who was there with her mother, and sat her on his knee. He chatted to the women about their families. And he told them how the leaders of the Catholic Church, and all the other mainstream churches, were doing all they could to encourage Australians to vote 'yes' for Aboriginal rights ... He joked gently as they all posed for the photographer. The women were greatly encouraged. They quite enjoyed themselves.[193]

A less pleasant issue on which Beovich utterly refused to compromise was abortion. In December 1968 the attorney-general in the Hall government, Robin Millhouse, introduced a bill which was largely based on the British Abortion Act of 1967. This decriminalised induced abortion by medical practitioners when it was deemed necessary for the physical or mental health of a woman or any of her existing children, or when there was a substantial risk that a child would be born with serious abnormalities. It was the first time such legislation had been introduced in Australia, so for supporters and opponents there was much at stake. The Humanist Society in South Australia formed an Abortion Law Reform Association to lobby the government for liberalisation.[194] Catholics were at the forefront of a campaign to achieve the opposite result. Throughout 1969 David Shinnick, as secretary of the Christian Life Movement, devoted much time and effort to organising protest meetings in Catholic parishes, petitions to send to politicians, and so forth.[195] The response from the major Protestant denominations was muted. While the Anglican bishop of Adelaide personally opposed the bill, the Anglican Synod made no public statement, and the leadership of the Congregational Union, Presbyterian Church, Churches of Christ and Methodist Church supported the legislation, only objecting to induced abortion on socioeconomic grounds.[196]

Between December 1968 and February 1969 the bill was referred to a parliamentary select committee of inquiry which considered seven written submissions and heard from thirty-three witnesses. The strongest attack on the legislation came from Beovich, who insisted in a written submission:

> Every human being, even a child in the mother's womb, has a right to life directly from God and not from the parents or from any human society or authority ... Instead of liberalising abortion, steps should be taken to provide mothers in distress with the medical, social and psychiatric care they need. There should be a more humane understanding of unwed mothers and their children and we should provide them with real help. In general more adequate social and family policies should be planned and developed with greater generosity by legislators.[197]

Beovich did not address the committee in person. Instead he appointed three people to speak on behalf of the Catholic Church. Wisely he chose suitably qualified lay Catholics rather than priests: an obstetrician and gynaecologist (Karl Texler), a social worker (Margaret Gibson) and a barrister (David Haese). The committee's report noted that they did not take such an 'extreme position' as their archbishop. Texler acknowledged that 'I would be against any provision to ban abortion utterly from our society, even though I personally consider it wrong'. Haese said that he was not opposed to putting the common law on abortion into statutory form, and Gibson avoided answering the question: 'Do you think the position might ever arise where abortion was the only solution?'[198] In its report which was tabled in parliament on 18 February 1969, the committee recommended to the House of Assembly that the bill be passed.

After some minor amendments, the bill successfully passed through both the Legislative Council and House of Assembly on 4 December 1969. On 14 November 1969, Premier Hall, who had just voted in favour of the legislation in the House of Assembly, attended a speech night at St Michael's College, Henley Beach. He had to sit through a stinging speech in which Beovich attacked deliberate abortion as 'an unspeakable crime' which should be condemned in all circumstances.[199] At the opening of the new church at Goodwood the following month, Beovich lashed out again: 'Do not be surprised if, after their initial success, the same so-called "humanists" who couldn't care less about God, start suggesting as the next step that the killing off of the aged and unfit would be for the common good.'[200] Conceding the battle had been lost, he called on Catholics to observe 28 December, the Feast of the Holy Innocents, as a special day of prayer for children who died as a result of abortion.[201] This became an annual event, an opportunity to protest at the escalation in the number of abortions in the wake of the new legislation.[202]

While the vigorous campaign waged by Beovich and other members of the Catholic community clearly failed in its main aim, it may have had some impact. There is evidence in opinion polls that Catholic attitudes in Australia hardened between June 1968 and February 1969, and Catholics were much more likely to oppose liberalisation than Protestants, especially those Catholics who were regular church-goers.[203] However, the figures would not have given Beovich much comfort. In February 1969 a Gallop poll indicated that just over a third of Catholics (37.5 per cent) thought abortion should not be legal under any circumstances. This had risen from 23 per cent in June 1968, a gratifying trend, but it implies that almost two thirds of Catholics were prepared to condone abortion in some cases. This is consistent with a survey in the United States which indicated that 72 per cent of Catholics in 1974 believed abortion was acceptable if the unborn child was known to have serious physical or mental abnormalities.[204] As with birth control, this suggests by the 1970s Catholics were likely to make decisions on such matters according to their own consciences rather than official church teaching. Perhaps the most surprising aspect of the abortion debate in 1969 is that, while there were passionate responses from both ends of the spectrum, the issue did not seem to arouse widespread community interest.

The Vietnam War

A more controversial issue was the Vietnam War, largely due to the introduction of selective military conscription in November 1964. The opposition leader in the federal parliament was Beovich's friend from schooldays, Arthur Calwell. A veteran of the bitter anti-conscription campaigns of the First World War, he strongly opposed the National Service Act and could see little benefit in Australia 'blundering' into a civil war in South East Asia.[205] Yet despite the lack of bipartisan support, Prime Minister Menzies went ahead and in April 1965 announced the deployment of a battalion to South Vietnam.

The previous month twelve Anglican bishops had urged the government to work towards a peaceful settlement.[206] In contrast, the Australian Catholic bishops are alleged to have 'lapsed into almost total silence on Vietnam'.[207] Reasons for this are not hard to find. The Second World War had revealed Australia's vulnerability to attack from the north, and the Cold War had heightened fear of communism. With Vietnam split between a communist north and a pro-western south, it was clear where sympathies would lie. This was true of the community generally. The war was not initially unpopular. A Morgan Gallup Poll in July 1965 indicated that 59 per cent of Australians supported Australian involvement, more than double the 27 per cent who were opposed to it.[208]

In fact, not all the Catholic bishops were silent. The strong element of anti-communism within the Catholic Church in Australia, and the presence of a significant Catholic minority in Vietnam, encouraged a 'hawkish' response. Even Guilford Young, widely regarded as the leading 'moderate' in the Australian hierarchy, issued a statement in June 1965 in which he claimed there was 'a moral right to resist [the North Vietnamese] – indeed a duty'.[209] Arthur Fox, auxiliary bishop of Melbourne, proclaimed in August 1966: 'I have said before and I repeat it now that the Government of Australia is protecting our own country by sending troops to fight in Vietnam; this is a morally correct action.'[210] James O'Collins of Ballarat and Bernard Stewart of Sandhurst made similar comments.[211] When the Melbourne diocesan paper, the *Advocate*, protested against conscription, Fox issued a public statement which chided the editor and supported the government.[212]

Young, Fox, O'Collins and Stewart were all associated with the National Civic Council, which strongly supported the war, but Gilroy, no friend of Santamaria, also backed the war effort. In response to the announcement that conscripts would go to Vietnam, Gilroy declared that 'the Government must be presumed to have acted conscientiously in the fulfillment of this obligation [of safeguarding Australia]. The common good demands that the legislative enactments of a representative Government should be respected'.[213] The Catholic peace group which was formed in Sydney, like its counterpart in Melbourne, received little support from the local bishops and encountered some open hostility.[214]

In his diary Beovich used adjectives like 'ghastly' and 'atrocious' whenever he mentioned the war in Vietnam.[215] He was more circumspect in public and confined himself to praying for peace. In October 1966 he energetically promoted Pope Paul VI's encyclical *Christi Matri Rosarii* which pleaded for an immediate end to hostilities. Beovich encouraged Catholics to pray the rosary daily for the intention of peace, and he exhorted parishes and religious communities to organise special prayer vigils.[216] On 4 October 1966, the feast day of St Francis of Assisi, he presided at a special Mass for peace in the cathedral, and he made peace the theme of the annual Eucharistic procession at the Passionist Monastery at Glen Osmond on 9 October and the Marian procession at the seminary on 30 October. It was estimated that about 10,000 took part in the latter event, making it 'one of Adelaide's biggest and most orderly peace marches'.[217]

It was also in October 1966 that President Lyndon Johnson of the United States visited Australia, a public relations triumph for the Holt Coalition government. As the Australian Labor Party pledged to withdraw troops from Vietnam, the November 1966 election was fought largely on the war issue, and the Coalition's resounding victory was a vindication of its foreign policy. Although Beovich never publicly disclosed how he voted, his diary reveals that he was disturbed by the election result. He was also dismayed to learn that Cardinal Spellman of New York had visited troops in Vietnam at Christmas and prayed for victory:

> In fact Spellman is calling for a holy war. To the soldiers he said, 'You are fighting for God'. The Pope on the other hand sees the conflict as an impartial observer, and in the spirit of the Second Vatican Council, he feels that a negotiated peace rather than military victory by either side is the way to end the war. The Pope is right (as Pope Benedict was right in 1917), but nationalism blinds people. It seems to have blinded the majority of Australians.[218]

When the Australian Bishops' Conference met in April 1967 the bishops issued a statement which liberally quoted from the pope's encyclical of the previous year and called on citizens to review the moral issues raised by the war. [219] As it did not give much guidance on how this could be done, some opponents of the war were disappointed. Nevertheless, the statement was sufficiently different from the rhetoric of the hawkish bishops for Max Charlesworth to speculate in an article in the *Age* on the role the archbishop of Adelaide may have had in its production, as 'it is rumored, [he] has grave reservations both about conscription and the Vietnam War'.[220] Neither the minutes of the meeting nor Beovich's diary shed any light on this, but it is probable that he was involved as he was still vice-president of the episcopal conference and a member of its executive body.

No one should have been left in any doubt about Beovich's opposition to the war after the Marian procession later that year. In his address to the gathering, he proclaimed: 'Will men never learn that nothing is solved in war, everything may gradually be solved in peace.' This does not mean, however, that he supported the groups which sprang up to protest against the war. Formed in 1967, and dominated by academics from the University of Adelaide and Flinders University, the South Australian Campaign for Peace in Vietnam (CPV) was 'possibly the most moderate and cautious of all the peace and anti-Vietnam war groups which made up the Australian peace movement'.[221] Yet at the Marian procession, Beovich responded to a rhetorical question with a typical emphasis on personal piety: 'In these dire circumstances, what can ordinary people do? We must escalate our prayers to God and our penance for peace.' Taking a swipe at strident elements in the anti-war movement, he added: 'It is better than most anti-war rallies and demonstrations which are often anything but the mark of a peace-loving people.'[222]

Opposition to the war gradually grew. By 1969 Morgan polls indicated that 40 per cent of Australians wanted the troops withdrawn. The following year it was about 50 per cent.[223] Catholic opinions were almost identical to national responses.[224] At their annual meeting in April 1969, the Australian bishops made a modest (albeit ultimately unsuccessful) contribution to the conscription debate by issuing a statement which called on the government to develop an alternative to military service for conscientious objectors.[225] The bishops also formed the National Commission on Justice and Peace. Under the chairmanship of James Gleeson, this began to offer more outspoken critique of government policies, including the extension of the war into Cambodia in 1970.[226]

In November 1969 the state-based CPV joined the national Vietnam Moratorium Campaign (VMC). The first campaign culminated on 8–9 May 1970 when rallies were held around Australia. About 50,000 people marched in Melbourne and 20,000 in Sydney on Friday, 8 May. In Adelaide about 1000 protesters, mainly university students, were harassed by a group of intoxicated soldiers on the evening of 8 May, but the major rally in Adelaide the following day passed peacefully. It attracted about 5000 demonstrators, including an ecumenical group known as Christians for Peace. Only a small number of anti-moratorium protesters chanted 'Here come the Commies'.[227]

The Catholics who marched in Melbourne and Sydney on 8 May 1970 did so in spite of their bishops' disapproval. In Melbourne, Knox issued a statement which attacked the campaign, saying 'it could well become a threat to public order', while a spokesman for Gilroy in Sydney described it as 'hardly worthy of Christian participation'. Both press statements also implied that it would be wrong to abandon the South Vietnamese.[228] Gilroy would not even countenance a prayer vigil linked to the moratorium because he believed the campaign to be 'of communistic inspiration'.[229]

The annual Marian procession in Adelaide was scheduled to take place on 3 May 1970. Marshals wanted Beovich to make a similar statement to Knox and Gilroy to prevent the procession becoming associated with the moratorium. Beovich refused on the grounds that it would only inflame the situation further.[230] When visited by supporters of the VMC, he insisted that no 'partisan or political activity' should take place at the Marian procession, but he offered to hold a special Mass for peace in the cathedral on the day of the rally on 9 May.[231] With the 'letters to the editor' section of the *Southern Cross* indicating that Catholics were bitterly divided over Vietnam and the moratorium campaign, often along generational lines, this was an appropriate compromise. The Mass did not completely resolve the tension – university students handing out moratorium leaflets after the procession on 3 May were abused by some of the participants – but it stopped it escalating. Interstate, the Vietnam War coalesced with the papal encyclical on birth control as the trigger which drove many men from the priesthood.[232] Beovich's benign response ensured that the archdiocese of Adelaide fared much better. No priest left over the issue. One woman wrote to the *Southern Cross*: 'I was proud to be associated with the Christians for Peace group in the moratorium march. It was a heartwarming experience to be present at the Mass in the cathedral beforehand with about 200 eager and happy young people.'[233]

Towards Retirement

By mid-1970 the most important phase of the revolution inaugurated by the Second Vatican Council was over. Catholics in the archdiocese of Adelaide were becoming accustomed to the new way of celebrating the Eucharist. Some were still grieving for the Latin Mass, but most had accepted the changes and more received holy communion each week. The members of the first Senate of Priests and Diocesan Pastoral Council were nearing the end of their terms. While these experiments in the development of consultative structures had not been entirely successful, they had led to some positive outcomes, such as the salary and superannuation scheme for priests and the growth in 'a broader diocesan perspective' among lay people.[234] The controversy over *Humanae Vitae* had died down, and as Australian troops were gradually withdrawn from Vietnam in the early 1970s, tension eased on that front too.

Returning from the final session of the Second Vatican Council in February 1966, Beovich had promised to implement its reforms 'with zeal and prudence' and that is exactly what he did in the remainder of his time as archbishop. Unfaltering in his commitment to the Council, he gave strong support to James Gleeson and a talented group of priests and lay people who found new and creative ways to promote conciliar teaching. Occasionally Beovich applied the brakes when he feared that the reform process was going too fast. He was aware that not all Catholics could keep up with the pace of change, or approach it with the same degree of enthusiasm. He realised that there was a need for further education.

A story in David Shinnick's memoirs highlights this. It also demonstrates Beovich's brisk approach to administration and his ability to delegate while retaining ultimate control over diocesan policy. Shinnick remembers that he went to see Beovich in 1970. He had submitted a report to the archbishop which proposed that he, Shinnick, take responsibility for a number of tasks in the diocese, such as furthering the development of parish pastoral councils. He was accompanied by James Gleeson:

> After the preliminaries were dealt with, Archbishop Beovich went straight to the point. 'This is an excellent report, David. You must all have put a lot of time and thought into it. Now, Archbishop Gleeson, I think we'll leave it aside for now. The big need for the future is adult religious education, don't you think?' I was aghast. Where did this come from? 'Now, David, give it some thought, keep in touch with Archbishop Gleeson, and see what you can do about it.' End of conversation.[235]

While Shinnick was startled by the sudden change in direction, he 'appreciated Archbishop Beovich's shrewdness in discerning the needs of the diocese, especially in relation to the future'. Building on the work which had already been done in the Newman Institute and the Christian Life Movement, Shinnick set about developing the Catholic Adult Education Centre. It was announced in the *Southern Cross* on 29 January 1971 that this would offer a range of topics and small group discussions on liturgy, theology, scripture and social justice matters. It was one of Beovich's last initiatives before he retired on 1 May 1971.

In as far as it is possible to make comparisons, the archdiocese of Adelaide seems to have emerged from the turbulent 1960s in a better state than most other Australian Catholic dioceses. The fact that it was a relatively small diocese helped. With half a million more Catholics, and over four times as many diocesan priests, Norman Gilroy in Sydney had had a much harder task than Beovich. However, in his more compact administration, Beovich demonstrated great wisdom in the way he utilised the abilities of his younger priests, persuaded older ones to retire, encouraged the formation of regional groups of priests, and allowed the rector to relax the regime at the seminary before discontent reached a crisis point. In his response to *Humanae Vitae*, Beovich was more sensitive to the pain the encyclical could cause Catholics than some of his episcopal colleagues interstate, and his reaction to the Vietnam War was much less simplistic and divisive. He continued to cultivate in the 1960s good relations with the leaders of other Christian churches and the state's civic leaders. The Vatican Council did not revolutionise his thinking in this respect but confirmed the course on which he had been set since his arrival in Adelaide in 1940.

In 1970 Beovich could be proud of the fact that the number of Catholics in South Australia had risen steadily in the 1960s. The growth was not as rapid as in the heady days of the 1950s, but as migrants continued to arrive from southern Europe, and refugees from South-East Asia, the Catholic Church fared much better than most Protestant denominations, which either remained static or experienced a decline in membership.[236] In the 1971 census, 20 per cent of South Australians – one in five – identified themselves as Catholic or Roman Catholic, a figure which was modest in comparison with the national average of 27 per cent, but well up on the 12 per cent of 1933.

There was a shadow side to Beovich's episcopal ministry in this period. It had been present since 1940 but became more noticeable in his latter years as he aged and became less visible to the Catholic community. An essentially shy man, he could appear aloof and remote. As the generation gap between himself and most of his priests widened, he was not able to be a father to them in any genuine sense of the word, and he could not be a friend. He willingly established the consultative structures recommended by the Vatican Council, but found it difficult to listen patiently to different viewpoints, and almost impossible to comprehend dissent from Church teaching, especially papal teaching. It was a characteristic of his that once he had made up his mind, he would commit himself fully to a course of action or way of thinking. That trait, admirable as it was at times, had the negative consequence of making him unable to empathise with those who were not so strong-willed, who came to doubt their vocation or question Church teaching, or found the hierarchical nature of the Church stifling and self-abnegation unfulfilling. In that respect, Beovich was out of step with the spirit of the times.

Keeping his eyes firmly on the pope as he sailed through turbulent seas, Beovich made it safely to shore on 1 May 1971 when he handed the government of the diocese to his loyal deputy, James Gleeson. It was a good time to retire. He had steered the diocese through the most dramatic period of change in the Catholic Church since the sixteenth century, and morale amongst the clergy and laity was still quite high. Fifty-year-old Gleeson abounded with energy and enthusiasm. Having worked closely with Beovich for twenty-five years, he was well-equipped to continue the initiatives which Beovich had begun as well as face the challenges of the 1970s. Leaving them to Gleeson's biographer, the final chapter will consider the last phase of Beovich's life, when he took up the new role of emeritus archbishop.

TEN
'THE GOLDEN YEARS' EMERITUS ARCHBISHOP

I am trying to do the will of God. If He calls me tonight, that's OK.

Matthew Beovich, 1980

An Adelaide diocesan priest recalls his housekeeper answering the telephone one day, about 1970: 'It's the archbishop,' said the voice at the other end. 'Which one?' she asked, not knowing whether she was talking to Matthew Beovich or James Gleeson. 'The real one!' was the terse reply from Beovich.[1] As coadjutor archbishop, Gleeson had right of succession, but only as much authority as Beovich was willing to delegate. While the older bishop appreciated having 'a faithful and energetic assistant',[2] he kept a firm hold on the reins of power in the 1960s. He was somewhat taken aback when the issue of a retirement age for bishops was mooted at the Second Vatican Council.[3] It was an ingrained tradition that bishops were the 'fathers' of their dioceses, and that it was a job for life. Most died in office, only very few resigning due to ill health. The issue of mandatory retirement was not resolved at the Council, but in 1966 Pope Paul VI ruled that bishops should tender their resignations at the age of seventy-five.

Once the pope had issued instructions on retirement, there was no doubt that Beovich would loyally comply, but as he entered his seventy-fifth year in 1970 he was genuinely relieved to do so. 'More than thirty years as archbishop have taken their toll, and the constantly increasing work in a rapidly growing diocese requires a more active mind and body,' he wrote to the pope on 29 June 1970. 'Thanks be to God they exist in my coadjutor archbishop James Gleeson.'[4] In November he was told that his retirement had been approved, and that he could hand over the government of the diocese to Gleeson the following May. He was very pleased to learn that the pope had decided to change the status of retired bishops.[5] Instead of being assigned to a titular diocese, usually an extinct one in the Middle East or North Africa, they could bear the official title of former bishop or emeritus bishop of the diocese they had served. Beovich was one of the first Catholic bishops to whom this new rule applied.

Before his resignation took effect, Beovich made one final *ad limina* visit to his beloved Rome. Accompanied by Vincent Tiggeman, who had been his secretary from 1955 to 1965, he left Adelaide on 19 September 1970. After a long sea journey, travelling via the Panama Canal, he reached Rome on 25 October. Apart from finalising his retirement, there was little business to transact and Beovich had 'a very happy time' wandering through the places which had meant so much to him in his student years, including the old Urban College in the Piazza di Spagna, the village of Castelgandolfo where he had spent summer holidays, and the basilica of St John Lateran where he had been ordained.[6] He visited his fellow student and teacher, Cardinal Agagianian, and his old rector, Cardinal Giobbe: 'We had a happy conversation and parted for the last time in this world.'[7] His audience with the pope was on 12 November 1970. Although Paul VI spoke with animation, Beovich detected 'glimpses of fatigue'.[8] The bishop of Rome was only one year younger than he, but would not consider retirement himself.

Beovich originally intended to return to Adelaide by sea in February 1971. These plans were changed when it was announced in May 1970 that Paul VI would make the first papal visit to Australia later that year. Beovich booked an airline ticket, and flying straight from Rome, reached Sydney on 26 November, four days ahead of the pope. On 30 November Paul VI arrived at Mascot Airport in Sydney and was welcomed by Prime Minister John Gorton, Governor-General Paul Hasluck, a beaming

Cardinal Gilroy, and various other dignitaries.[9] Despite all the turbulence of the previous years, the pope's three-day visit was a great success. Cheering crowds greeted him wherever he went and the media coverage was overwhelming positive. A survey in the *Australian* indicated that even if they did not accept his teaching on birth control, the majority of Catholics and a significant minority of other Christians admired him.[10] A highlight of the visit was Paul VI's participation in an ecumenical prayer service in the Sydney Town Hall. Although it was marred by the refusal of the Anglican bishop of Sydney to attend, it showed how much relations between the Christian denominations had improved since the Vatican Council. At Gilroy's request, Beovich greeted official guests on the steps of the town hall and introduced them to the pope. 'A glorious day,' Beovich wrote in his diary on 1 December. Gilroy described the pope's visit as the 'greatest event that occurred in the whole of my episcopate'.[11]

Back in Adelaide, Beovich began a final round of official engagements. The Chrism Mass on 6 April 1971, when the clergy of the diocese gathered in the cathedral for the blessing of the holy oils, provided an opportunity for Beovich to address all his priests:

> I am indeed grateful for your loyal and generous cooperation over the years ... My final words to you are the words of Pope Pius XI: 'We must be outstanding for the holiness of our lives. Holiness is the most important quality of the Catholic priest; without it, all his other gifts count for little; with it he can do marvellous work even though he has little else.'[12]

At a farewell Mass at the seminary on 23 April, Beovich repeated a statement which Paul VI had issued to seminarians in Rome the previous March, warning about the danger of being influenced by 'strange thoughts that have become a fashion'. More positively, he encouraged the young men to 'try to have an inner life. Listen to the Spirit. Have faith. Try to pray to the Lord'. After he had typed this out, Beovich took up a pen and added, 'Not mechanically but heart to heart'.[13] Throughout his life the sincerity and warmth of his personal faith had softened what could otherwise have been a rigid dogmatism.

In a relatively simple ceremony in St Francis Xavier Cathedral on Saturday, 1 May 1971, Beovich led Gleeson to the *cathedra*, the episcopal chair, and declared to the congregation: 'Here is your archbishop.' 'The whole function went without a hitch,' he reported in his diary. Official guests included most of the bishops from around Australia, the premier of South Australia, the lord mayor of Adelaide, a representative of the governor, and the heads of other churches. A 'great crowd' flocked to the seminary the following day for the Marian procession. Due to heavy rain, the actual procession was cancelled, but the crowd prayed the rosary and, to Beovich's delight, he was presented with the first installment of money for a bursary to educate a priest at the seminary. An appeal conducted in parishes throughout the diocese had raised more than $10,000, an appropriate retirement gift for someone whose personal needs were few but who had immense regard for the Catholic priesthood. On Monday, 3 May 1971, the priests of the diocese gathered at Alden Manor, Glenelg, for a dinner to mark both Beovich's retirement and Gleeson's installation. A fortnight earlier the lord mayor had hosted a luncheon in Beovich's honour at the town hall.

Once the formalities in Adelaide were over, Beovich travelled to Ballarat to be with his old friend Jim O'Collins, as O'Collins handed over his diocese to Ronald Mulkearns on 21 May. The following month Norman Gilroy also retired, and Beovich went to Sydney for the installation of his successor, James Freeman, on 20 August.

Retirement

In retirement Beovich continued to live at Ennis at Medindie. He retained the long, narrow, book-lined study on the western side of the old mansion, along with his small suite of rooms upstairs in the old servants' quarters. Three Franciscan Sisters of the Heart of Jesus from Malta lived in the convent in the grounds behind the house. They were responsible for pastoral work in the Maltese Catholic community in Adelaide as well as cooking and cleaning at Ennis. James Gleeson chose to remain at Archbishop's House, West Terrace, but he arranged for a young priest to live at Ennis, usually the diocesan vocations director. The pretext for this was that there were more spare bedrooms at Medindie than West

Terrace. In reality, it was to ensure there would be at least one other person in the house at night as Beovich aged and became increasingly frail.[14] He accepted his increasing weakness philosophically. 'At my age you either go in the head or in the legs, and I've gone in the legs,' was his frequent retort to questions about his health.[15] Sometimes in later years he added, 'I'm afraid I can't say the same about Bishop O'Collins'.[16] O'Collins continued to play golf until an advanced age, but his mind began to wander toward the end of his life.

Beovich's legs might not have worked as well as they once did, but he was determined to keep his brain active. In 1972 he embarked on a disciplined reading regime: a study of commentaries on the documents of the Second Vatican Council, interspersed with P. G. Wodehouse novels for relaxation.[17] Roy Richardson, the vocations director who lived at Ennis in the mid-1970s, remembers Beovich dividing the day into periods, with set times for reading theology, general history and books about sport.[18] Carlton was his favourite team in the Victorian Football League, and he keenly supported the South Australian side in Sheffield Shield cricket matches, and the Australian team in international test matches. Sometimes he watched cricket or football on television, but as he admitted himself, he was not a good loser and tended to turn the set off if his team was not playing well.[19]

Initially Beovich's health was good. A newspaper reporter who interviewed him on his seventy-fifth birthday in 1971, just before his retirement, was impressed by 'this slight, sprightly man who bubbles with good cheer'.[20] On 3 March 1973, however, while he was getting dressed in his bathroom, Beovich fell heavily, breaking two ribs and hurting his back.[21] A few months later, on 8 July 1973, he felt a bit 'uncomfortable' in the morning. He said Mass in his private chapel at Ennis as usual and tried to relax. On the midday news he heard that his old school friend, Arthur Calwell, had died.[22] The following day, as he was preparing a condolence telegram to send to Calwell's widow, Elizabeth, he experienced a second, more severe coronary attack, and was taken by ambulance to Calvary Hospital.[23] For a few days he was seriously ill, but after being cared for by the Little Company of Mary, he returned to Ennis five weeks later 'in great spirits and thrilled to be home'.[24] He was equally pleased in October when John Rice, his doctor for many years, condoned three pipes a day.[25] After a slow recovery, there were no more major health crises until his final illness.

Retirement did not mean an end to pastoral work. Beovich was a familiar figure at Calvary Hospital as he regularly visited patients, often on Sunday afternoons. Looking back at the end of 1972, he calculated that he had attended 61 functions in that year and given 25 prepared talks. He tried wherever possible to be present at requiem Masses for priests, religious and lay people he had known, and, more happily, jubilee celebrations commemorating significant milestones in priesthood and religious life.[26] In his diary in 1967, Beovich confided that with increasing age he felt 'a bit of nervous tension before certain important appointments when I'm expected to speak, but this does not apply to liturgical functions or sermons'.[27] The sermon notes and transcripts which survive from his later years indicate that he usually gave short, simple exhortations on the great importance of the priesthood and religious life, the reality of Christ's presence in the Eucharist, and the certainty of life beyond death.

Maintaining contact with episcopal friends interstate, Beovich travelled to Bendigo in January 1972 for the twenty-fifth anniversary of Bernard Stewart's consecration as bishop of Sandhurst, and to Ballarat in December that year for the fiftieth anniversary of James O'Collins's ordination to the priesthood. Beovich's own golden jubilee was also approaching – he and O'Collins had been ordained in the same ceremony in Rome on 23 December 1922. He did not mention that in his homily at the thanksgiving Mass in the cathedral in Ballarat on 12 December. He kept the focus on O'Collins and, above all, on the 'tremendous gift' of the priesthood: 'It is God who calls a person to be priest – to minister to His people and build up the Body of Christ ... How great is God's love, by which both Himself and His Passion and Death are ever really present to us in the Mass and in the Tabernacle.'[28]

Beovich returned to Adelaide on 13 December, O'Collins accompanying him on the overnight train. On Friday evening, 15 December 1972, there was a special Mass in St Francis Xavier Cathedral, preceded by another dinner for clergy at Alden Manor,

Glenelg. At Beovich's insistence this was a joint celebration, commemorating not only his own anniversary of ordination, but also the golden jubilee of one of the diocesan priests.[29] The actual anniversary on 23 December passed like many other days. Beovich attended the requiem Mass for the father of a diocesan priest, and celebrated the Eucharist for the Sisters of St Joseph in their chapel at Kensington.[30] Three days later he concelebrated a Mass at Glenelg to mark the fiftieth wedding anniversary of long-time diocesan employee Darcy Woodards and his wife.[31]

Occasionally, in Gleeson's absence, Beovich celebrated the sacrament of confirmation, handed out prizes at school speech nights, and presided at the annual dedication of infants to Mary in the Cathedral in May. After Philip Kennedy was consecrated as auxiliary bishop of Adelaide on 17 March 1973, there was less need for Beovich to deputise for Gleeson, and he was able to recede further into the background. He continued to attend special services in the cathedral, such as ordinations and the Easter liturgies, but he would sit discreetly at the side of the sanctuary and take no formal part in the ceremonies.

When he retired, Beovich resolved that he would not interfere in diocesan administration. There were times when this required a considerable exercise of will-power. He reported in his diary on 2 June 1973 that he had managed to remain silent when Gleeson had visited him and enthusiastically described a plan to erect a multi-storey building alongside the cathedral. Although a good investment, the office tower would have completely overshadowed the cathedral. As it happened, the plan fell through and lawn and trees now grow on the site.

Beovich also detached himself from the national bishops' meetings. 'I look from afar at the Bishops' Conference, sorry for the bishops in their problems but very, very glad to be away from them,' Gilroy wrote to Beovich in September 1973. In his reply, Beovich agreed that 'problems are not becoming fewer at the Bishops' Conference. From time to time as matters arise or don't arise, I have to say to myself, "Shut up and make no comment". So far, thank God, I have succeeded'.[32]

Nicholas Kerr interviewed Beovich 'well after he retired' for an article in the *Southern Cross*, probably the one which was published on 10 April 1980 to commemorate the fortieth anniversary of his consecration as archbishop of Adelaide. 'I asked him if he had any thoughts on developments in the teaching of catechetics which he'd like to share,' Kerr recalls. 'He said, "Mr Kerr, I have some very strong thoughts on this subject. But it wouldn't do you, me, or anyone else any good if I told you what they were. Next question".'[33]

Thomas Horgan remembered Beovich saying that one of the things he enjoyed most about retirement was the absence of protocol.[34] To illustrate this, Gleeson recounted that the day after Beovich retired, 2 May 1971, the telephone rang in the Brighton presbytery. When William Collins, the parish priest, answered it, he heard: 'Hello, Bill, it's Matt here.' Collins thought someone was playing a joke on him. It sounded like Matthew Beovich's voice, but as archbishop of Adelaide Beovich had never called priests by their first names.[35] In retirement he began to do so, at least in private conversation with senior priests like Collins, who had arrived in Adelaide from Ireland in 1936, and Horgan, the first priest whom Beovich ordained in 1941. For bishops of Beovich's generation, retirement brought some relief from what Gilroy once described as the 'necessary isolation' of their office.[36] 'Only after he retired did priests begin to experience the personal warmth which as a bishop he had rigorously controlled,' remarks John Maguire of Hugh Ryan, bishop of Townsville from 1938 to 1967.[37] Some Adelaide priests had a similar experience. It is a sad indictment of the style of leadership favoured by the majority of bishops of the pre-Vatican II era – but there was greater formality in society as a whole in their time, of course.

The only member of his staff whom Beovich had always called by his Christian name was Keith Koen, his chauffer from 1940.[38] From 1 May 1971 Koen officially worked for Gleeson, but continued to drive Beovich when needed (unlike Beovich, Gleeson could drive himself). When Koen retired in 1978, Gleeson allowed him to keep his last diocesan car, and once a week he took Beovich for an outing.[39] A favourite route was along the sea front, sometimes with a visit to the presbytery at Brighton or Glenelg. Beovich also occasionally joined the priests living at Archbishop's House, West Terrace, for their midday meal. Robert Aitken, then administrator of the cathedral parish, testifies that these lunches were inclined to be more leisurely than they had been during Beovich's days in charge, as he seemed to enjoy the opportunity to talk.[40]

Like many shy and introverted people, Beovich may have been torn between a desire for friendship and a need for solitude. A few priests like Tom Horgan called in to see him at Ennis, but Beovich had been so successful at keeping some distance between himself and his priests that most were loath to intrude on his privacy.[41] The house become a venue for meetings in the diocese, and Gleeson hosted dinner parties there, but on those occasions Beovich usually retreated to his private quarters, as he did after each evening meal with the resident vocations director.[42] Bill Byrne recalls being invited by Gleeson to a meal at Ennis in the 1970s, along with his wife and four children. The youngest child wandered out of the dining room, and another was sent to fetch him back. This was repeated until all the children had disappeared. The adults then went in search and found the children clustered around the elderly archbishop. They had innocently strayed into his private domain and been warmly welcomed.[43] A Polish cardinal who travelled to Australia in February 1973 for the International Eucharistic Congress in Melbourne would no doubt also have received a sincere welcome when he stopped in Adelaide to visit the Polish Catholic community. Beovich, however, was on holiday in Ballarat at the time, and left Gleeson and diocesan priest Leon Czechowicz to entertain Karol Wojtyla. After Wojtyla was elected Pope John Paul II in 1978, Beovich went back to his 1973 diary and noted when the future pope had stayed at Ennis.

Beovich made Ennis available for meetings, functions and hospitality to visiting clerics because, in spite of his love of solitude, he regarded the house as diocesan property rather than his private home. In December 1970, when Jim O'Collins was contemplating his own retirement, he wrote to ask his friend what arrangements he had made. Beovich replied that he would continue to live in his quarters at Ennis, and that he planned to receive an income of about $1000 a year from an investment of $20,000.[44] He later noted on a copy of the letter that he had relinquished the income from the diocese at the end of 1972, 'and the principal remained where it belonged in the Diocesan Works Fund'. From 1 October 1973 he received the old age pension of $46 a fortnight, and from 1 July 1976 he paid $1000 annually from the pension towards his board at Ennis: 'Should end up penniless or centless. Deo Gratias.' As a 'gentle man not fond of money', he clearly met the criteria for a bishop outlined in the *Didache* in the early second century. He was not completely destitute at his death, however. According to the terms of his will, his estate, amounting to just over $4000, went to his successor, James Gleeson. In a codicil added to the will in 1964, he left £500 to Keith Koen, but this was cancelled in 1977 when he presented Koen with $1000 as 'a modest token of gratitude and appreciation for your years of loyal and faithful service'.[45] There were no other bequests.

Remembering Friends

Those who live a long life can expect to experience some grief as family members and friends predecease them. By the time Beovich retired, three of his closest episcopal colleagues had died. Alf Gummer of Geraldton had been in poor health, but news of his death on 5 April 1962 still came as 'a great shock'.[46] In June 1967 Pat Lyons spent a few days at Ennis. Beovich was concerned as his friend looked unwell, but Lyons refused to discuss the reason. Beovich subsequently realised that it had been a farewell visit.[47] Lyons died from cancer on 13 August 1967. Three months later, on 3 November 1967, Beovich lost another close friend, Justin Simonds. This time the sad news was not a shock. Suffering from a series of strokes, Simonds had spent the final year of his life at the Mercy Hospital in Melbourne. Throughout 1966 and 1967 Beovich travelled to Melbourne as often as he could to spend time at his friend's bedside. In a typical gesture, he recorded the worsening state of Simonds's health at each visit on the back of a travel itinerary.[48]

Beovich delivered the sermons at the requiem Masses for Gummer and Simonds, and spoke at the Months' Mind for Lyons. His tributes to his friends highlight what he valued in episcopal ministry. In Geralton for Gummer's funeral service, he took as his text Psalm 1, 'Blessed is the man ... whose delight is the law of the Lord'. In words which could equally have been applied to himself, he praised Alf Gummer as a kind and encouraging leader, a firm and tenacious defender of the faith, and a prudent administrator.[49] In the cathedral in Sale on 4 October 1967, Beovich admitted that Pat Lyons's reticence 'could sometimes baffle his friends and irritate others'.[50] Nevertheless, he presented Lyons's austere approach to ministry as thoroughly normal:

> The priest or bishop has few who mourn a personal loss. His life is given to the Church in almost an impersonal way. The bishop is the father of his diocese. He labours and toils, and lives and dies, and the grave closes over him. For a few days the hearts of all are filled with solemn grief; they gather around the lifeless body, and their prayers mingle with the tears of relatives and close friends. Then there is left only a name and a memory – and these quickly fade. This is a wholesome thought both for the proud and the humble. But, of course, death is not the end.

The chilling phrase, 'His life is given to the Church in almost an impersonal way', captured not only the reserve so characteristic of Patrick Lyons but Beovich's own commitment to self-denial. Fostered, no doubt, by their formation in Rome and the spirituality of the time, it also reflects the austerity and zeal of the Tridentine ideal of episcopal ministry which cast a long shadow over modern Catholicism.

Preaching in St Patrick's Cathedral in Melbourne on 7 November 1967, Beovich presented Justin Simonds as an outstanding priest: 'a man of prayer and interior life, strong in the faith, obedient to authority, and zealous in the care of souls.'[51] He acknowledged the obvious fact that Daniel Mannix's longevity had deprived Simonds of the opportunity to rule the archdiocese of Melbourne until 1963, by which time his own health had begun to decline. It was delicately done, with no direct criticism of Mannix:

> He came to assist the venerable Archbishop Mannix who had not asked for a helper, yet gave his new assistant a cordial welcome. He treated him exactly as he himself had been treated when he was a coadjutor. This meant that Archbishop Simonds had the fullness of the priesthood but little of its responsibility; that is, he did not share in the government of the archdiocese. Humanly speaking there was something tragic in this, and I do not think it would bear repetition in these days following the Second General Council of the Vatican.

Beovich praised the role Simonds had played in the wider Church: 'speaking of his learning and knowledge, I would venture the opinion that he held first place among the bishops of Australia, and many of his contributions at their general meetings were of great value for the welfare and progress of the Church.' Episcopal collegiality was something which Beovich had valued from his earliest days as a bishop and had not just absorbed at the Second Vatican Council.

Beovich also retained an intense regard for the pope. When asked to submit a tribute to Norman Gilroy, who died in Sydney on 21 October 1977, Gilroy's similar loyalty sprang to his mind: 'He esteemed the Holy Father. Indeed to St Peter's successor and to the Holy See he was always and utterly obedient.' A further indication of Gilroy's holiness, for Beovich, was his exalted understanding of the priesthood: 'He cherished the gift of his priesthood. In the years when he was a cardinal he inscribed these words in the visitors' book of his alma mater: "The priesthood is the greatest honour that one can receive in this world."' Overall, Beovich concluded:

> I consider that his life was holy beyond the ordinary. It had an affinity, perhaps, with the child-like way of St Teresa of Lisieux; a simple but not an easy way in which by cooperating with divine grace, he consistently did the Will of God in faith, hope, love and humility.[52]

Again, Beovich could have been writing about himself.

Requiem, 1981

In due course, it was Beovich's turn to receive such accolades. He became steadily weaker in 1981 but continued to live at Ennis and was able to say Mass daily in the chapel there. A blood clot developed in his leg and on 16 October he was taken to Calvary Hospital. Nurses reported hearing him mutter, 'Lord, take me'.[53] He died on 24 October 1981.

Twenty-two bishops from around Australia gathered in Adelaide for the requiem Mass on Thursday, 29 October 1981. The principal celebrant was Cardinal Sir James Freeman, archbishop of Sydney and president of the Australian Episcopal Conference. The most notable absentee was, ironically, the archbishop of Adelaide. Before Beovich died, James Gleeson had flown to Rome for meetings and a holiday in Europe. Both men had realised it was possible that Beovich would not live to see Gleeson's return. With more concern for the workaholic Gleeson's health than his own, Beovich insisted that he go, and not cut short his badly needed holiday in the advent of his death. It was agreed that auxiliary bishop Philip Kennedy would be responsible for the funeral arrangements.[54]

In a press release issued on 24 October 1981, Kennedy declared: 'I mourn the death of a simple and gracious man, a wise and humble leader whose only ambition was to spend himself and be spent in the service of Christ.' It was appropriate that the requiem Mass was a simple, hope-filled and Christ-centred liturgy.[55] In a cathedral decked with red and white flowers, readings from Scripture proclaimed life beyond death (Wisdom 3:1–9, 1 John 3:1–2, and John 6:51–59). The Eucharistic overtone of the gospel passage was a reminder of the centrality of the sacrament in Beovich's life. The honour of carrying to the altar the bread and wine for the Eucharist went to Vera Beovich, Keith Koen, the three Franciscan sisters from Ennis and a sister of the Little Company of Mary who had known Beovich for many years and nursed him during his final illness.

Assembled dignitaries included the governor, premier and leader of the opposition, a testimony to the good relations Beovich had cultivated with civic leaders. His participation in the ecumenical movement was reflected in the number of heads of Christian denominations who attended the service. Anglican and Greek Orthodox bishops were there, along with senior representatives from the Lutheran, Uniting and Presbyterian churches, the Churches of Christ and the Salvation Army.

An estimated 1500 to 2000 people crowded into the cathedral for the ceremony, many getting no further than the narthex or foyer. Six of the leading laymen of the diocese were the pallbearers. Catholic school children joined more than two hundred priests and seminarians in forming a guard of honour as the cortege left the cathedral and made its way to the cemetery at West Terrace. When it reached its destination, Beovich's body was buried in a simple grave alongside the remains of his predecessors, Robert Spence and Andrew Killian.

In a moving homily at the requiem Mass, Kennedy highlighted Beovich's commitment to good citizenship, concern for migrants, support for ecumenism and, above all, his quest for holiness, 'a holiness which expressed itself in love of God and neighbour. It was a goal he pursued with fierce consistency'. These themes predominate in the other tributes which were paid after his death.[56] The governor of South Australia, Sir Keith Seaman, commented that 'Archbishop Beovich was a warm, approachable and caring man who touched the life of the community at many points. The whole state has been enriched by this saintly and sensitive leader, and he will be greatly missed'.[57] The former Anglican bishop of Adelaide, T. T. Reed, remembered 'a great Christian leader for whom I had a warm regard ... His practical wisdom, courteous manner, and clear and concise statements were of great service to the Heads of Churches at their meetings'.[58] Representatives of Catholic migrant communities recalled the late archbishop with particular gratitude:

> We trust you see this farewell note from your heavenly abode and understand our feelings behind the written words. 'Your Grace' is a nice title and there are many other nice titles in this worldly life, but we believe that 'true friend' is the nicest and greatest of all these ... And you were our true friend when we arrived here thirty years ago. Your memory lives in our souls and we know we will meet again.[59]

Keith Koen told a reporter from the *Advertiser* that his former boss had been 'a kind, gentle man' with a great sense of humour.[60] At the Office for the Dead, held in the cathedral the evening before the requiem Mass, Tom Horgan recalled Beovich's 'often salty' wit and gave some examples of his kindness: 'the parish Mass supplied at short notice; weekly visits to the sick ...; the firm, warm hand that said what words could not say to one bereaved; the patient and delicate reaction to a priest given to sharing a yarn or two: "I feel you've told me this before, Father, but tell me again anyway".'[61] In a condolence card to Philip Kennedy, a nurse at Calvary Hospital remembered how Beovich had tried not to disturb the nursing staff when visiting patients in the hospital on Sunday afternoons because 'he never wanted to be a bother to anyone'.[62]

An aspect of Beovich's life which was not mentioned at the requiem Mass was his involvement in the political controversies of the 1950s. After the service, John Bannon, then leader of the opposition in the South Australian House of Assembly, expressed in a letter to Philip Kennedy:

> the special significance that the late Archbishop Beovich has for the Australian Labor Party in this state. He is remembered very warmly indeed by very many people in our Party, particularly for the crucial role he played in the 1950s when sectarian divisions were beginning to emerge. Not only the Labor Party, but, I believe, the political and social life of this state, has benefited greatly from the fact that there was no split within our Party, nor any real bitterness of a type that occurred, for instance, in Victoria. It was before my time in politics, but whenever the subject is raised the key role played by the late Archbishop is always referred to.[63]

It is the nature of panegyrics that they usually focus on the positive features of a person's life, but in 1981 there were clearly many people who remembered Matthew Beovich with affection and mourned his passing. Tributes to his warmth and friendliness are difficult to reconcile with the words 'remote', 'aloof' and 'austere' which, two decades after his death, feature commonly in people's reminiscences. However, Philip Kennedy acknowledged Beovich's innate reserve in his homily on 29 October 1981, telling the congregation at the requiem Mass how much Beovich relished the many hours he spent in prayer 'with the one intimate friend of his life, the Risen Christ'. Later Kennedy added, 'In this self-effacing and shy man we divined depths of piety which remained in the privacy of his heart and mind'.

At the Office for the Dead, Tom Horgan described Beovich as 'a man of friendly dignity'. Dignity was, for Beovich, a very important quality for a priest and a bishop, and he was clearly able to maintain it without succumbing to pomposity. Not all bishops were so successful at that. Doug Warren, bishop of the New South Wales rural diocese of Wilcannia-Forbes, encountered Beovich at gatherings of the hierarchy. Writing to apologise to Kennedy for his inability to attend the requiem Mass, he dryly remarked: 'I had a rather sneaking regard for Matty's holy cynicism & open approach to the unstuffing of shirts – he did it so well.'[64] It is an intriguing insight into Beovich's contribution to the Australian Episcopal Conference which does not feature in any formal minutes.

It was not Beovich's 'holy cynicism' which struck Bill Byrne but his 'natural optimism' and faith and trust in people, manifest in the support he gave the lay Catholics of his diocese who worked in the Newman Institute and later the Christian Life Movement.[65] Cynicism and optimism are another seemingly incompatible combination of attributes, but in Beovich both stemmed from his conviction that God was in control of human history. In this light, achievements and concerns appeared less significant to him than they might otherwise have done. Apparent success or failure in any transitory human endeavour was ultimately irrelevant so long as one was getting closer to God. That attitude helped him accept change in the wake of the Second Vatican Council, and then adjust to retirement after so many years in charge of the archdiocese of Adelaide.

In his homily on 29 October 1981, Philip Kennedy said that Beovich thought of his retirement as 'golden years'. The phrase is a cliché, but it does seem that, apart from the health scare in 1973 and his final illness, the elderly Beovich enjoyed a relaxed lifestyle away from the cares of diocesan administration. With characteristic dignity and restraint, he let his successor take over the government of the diocese while he slipped quietly into the background. He thus remained faithful to the ancient tradition that a bishop should be a unifying figure in his diocese. Comfortable with solitude, Beovich spent much time praying and reading, yet in an unobtrusive way he continued to undertake pastoral work. His main weakness as archbishop of Adelaide had been a tendency toward brusqueness in his dealings with people, a common failing amongst the bishops of his generation who tended to accept an autocratic style of leadership as normal. Retirement released Beovich from that straitjacket, enabling him to become an exemplary emeritus archbishop.

Notes

Prologue

1 Letter to Elizabeth Beovich, 4 September 1921, Adelaide Catholic Archdiocesan Archives (hereafter ACAA). The article, an account of Archbishop Daniel Mannix's visit to Rome in April 1921, was published in the *Tribune* on 16 June 1921, p. 4.

2 For this approach to biography see Barbara Tuchman, 'Biography as a Prism of History' in *Practicing History*, Macmillan, London, 1982, pp. 80–90; Laura Kalman, 'The Power of Biography', *Law & Social Inquiry*, vol. 23, no. 2, 1998, pp. 479–530; Wilfrid Prest, 'Lawyers Lives and Lies' in *Living History*, eds Susan Magarey and Kerrie Round, Australian Humanities Press, Adelaide, 2005, pp. 39–56.

3 Patrick O'Farrell, *The Catholic Church and Community*, rev. 3rd ed., University of New South Wales Press, Sydney, 1992; Edmund Campion, *Australian Catholics*, Viking, Melbourne, 1987; Naomi Turner, *Catholics in Australia*, 2 vols, Collins Dove, Melbourne, 1992.

4 Prest, 'Lawyer's Lives', p. 41.

5 Edmund Campion, 'On the Park Bench', La Trobe University Essay, *Australian Book Review*, no. 212, July 1999.

6 Katharine Massam, *Sacred Threads: Catholic Spirituality in Australia, 1922–1962*, University of New South Wales Press, Sydney, 1996.

7 O'Farrell, *Catholic Church and Community*, pp. x–xi.

8 *The Ministry of Oversight: The Office of Bishop and President in the Church*, Australian Lutheran-Roman Catholic Dialogue, Adelaide, 2007.

9 See Acts 20:17 and Acts 20:28. An overview of the development of ministry can be found in Kenan Osborne, *Priesthood*, Paulist Press, New York, 1988, and Joseph Martos, *Doors to the Sacred*, rev. ed., Liguori/Triumph, Liguori, MO, 2001, pp. 400–460.

10 See Titus 1:7–9 and Timothy 3:1–7.

11 *Didache* 15. A recent translation can be found in Bart Ehrman, ed., *The Apostolic Fathers*, Loeb Classical Library, Harvard University Press, Cambridge, Mass, 2003, pp. 417–433.

12 See Ehrman, *Apostolic Fathers*, pp. 218–353.

13 H. A. Drake, *Constantine and the Bishops*, John Hopkins University Press, Baltimore, 2000, p. 103.

14 For this development, see Peter Brown, *The Rise of Western Christendom*, 2nd ed., Blackwell Publishing, Malden, MA and Oxford, 2003, pp. 157 ff.

15 Gregory I, *Pastoral Care*, ed. Henry Davis, Ancient Christian Writers 11, Newman Press, New York, 1950, p. 21. See also Brown, *Rise of Western Christendom*, pp. 207–215; Claudia

Rapp, *Holy Bishops in Late Antiquity*, University of California Press, Berkeley, 2005, pp. 53–55.

16 See, for example, Christopher Haigh, *English Reformations*, Clarendon Press, Oxford, 1993, pp. 8–11.

17 The decrees of the Council can be found in Norman P. Tanner, ed., *Decrees of the Ecumenical Councils*, vol. 2, Sheed & Ward, London, 1990.

18 See John C. Olin, *Catholic Reform from Cardinal Ximenes to the Council of Trent*, Fordham University Press, New York, 1990; R. Po-Chia Hsia, *The World of Catholic Renewal, 1540–1770*, 2nd ed., Cambridge University Press, Cambridge, 2005; and Michael Mullet, *The Catholic Reformation*, Routledge, London & New York, 1999.

19 For these developments, see Robert Aubert, ed., *The Church in a Secularised Society* (*The Christian Centuries*, vol. 5), Paulist Press, New York, 1978, pp. 56–69; Nicholas Atkin and Frank Tallett, *Priests, Prelates & People*, Oxford University Press, New York, 2003, p. 130 ff; Eamon Duffy, *Faith of Our Fathers*, Continuum, London & New York, 2004, pp. 68–87. For England, see J. Derek Holmes, *More Roman than Rome*, Burns & Oates, London, 1978; and Adrian Hastings, *A History of English Christianity, 1920–1990*, SCM, London, 1991. For the United States, see Gerard P. Fogarty, ed., *Patterns of Episcopal Leadership*, the Bicentennial History of the Catholic Church in America, Macmillan, New York, 1989. Part III, the period 1910–1960, is titled 'Romanization and Modernization', pp. 167–249.

20 John N. Molony, *The Roman Mould of the Australian Catholic Church*, Melbourne University Press, Melbourne, 1969, p. 1.

21 O'Farrell, *Catholic Church and Community*, pp. 217–218.

22 B. A. Santamaria, *Daniel Mannix: The Quality of Leadership*, Melbourne University Press, Melbourne, 1984, p. 148.

23 B. A. Santamaria, *Santamaria: A Memoir*, Oxford University Press, Melbourne, 1997, p. 17.

24 In the former category, see Walter Ebsworth, *Archbishop Mannix*, H. H. Stephenson, Melbourne, 1977. For the latter, James Griffin, 'Mannix, Daniel', *Australian Dictionary of Biography* [hereafter *ADB*], vol. 10, eds Bede Nairn and Geoffrey Serle, Melbourne University Press, Melbourne, 1986, pp. 398–404. For Santamaria's response to Griffin, see 'Mannix: Putting the Record Straight', *Quadrant*, vol. 35, March 1991, pp. 51–56. Griffin's counter-attack, 'Revision or Reality? Daniel Mannix in *ADB 10*', is in Richard Davis et al., *Irish-Australian Studies*, Sydney, 1996, pp. 133–145. See also Griffin's 'A Towering Intellectual?' in Paul Ormonde, ed., *Santamaria: The Politics of Fear*, Spectrum, Melbourne, 2000, pp. 35–39.

25 B. A. Santamaria, *Daniel Mannix*; Michael Gilchrist, *Daniel Mannix: Wit and Wisdom*, 2nd ed., Freedom Publishing, Melbourne, 2004. See also Santamaria, *Archbishop Mannix: His Contribution to the Art of Public Leadership in Australia*, Melbourne University Press, Melbourne, 1978; and Gilchrist, 'Leadership with a Light Reign: The Un-Clericalist Episcopacy of Archbishop Mannix', *Australasian Catholic Record* [hereafter *ACR*], vol. 57, no. 3, 1980, pp. 385–401.

26 T. P. Boland, *James Duhig*, University of Queensland Press, Brisbane, 1986.

27 T. P. Boland, *The Ascent of Mount Tabor: Writing the Life of Archbishop Duhig*, Aquinas Memorial Lecture, Aquinas Library, Brisbane, 1986, p. 14.

28 Griffin, 'Mannix, Daniel', *ADB* 10, p. 400.

29 For a review of Australian episcopal biographies, see T. P. Boland, 'Thirty Years On: The O'Farrell Era', *ACR*, vol. 75, no. 2, 1998, p. 147. The most notable addition since then is Philip Ayres, *Prince of the Church: Patrick Francis Moran, 1830–1911*, Miegunyah Press, Melbourne, 2007.

30 John Luttrell, 'Norman Thomas Cardinal Gilroy as Archbishop of Sydney', PhD thesis, University of Sydney, 1997, p. 57. Before his appointment to Sydney, Gilroy was bishop of Port Augusta from 1934 to 1937. See John Luttrell, 'Bishop Gilroy and the Diocese of Port Augusta', *ACR*, vol. 80, no. 2, 2003, pp. 189–200. Thomas Boland is responsible for the entry on Gilroy in the *ADB*, vol. 14, ed. John Ritchie, Melbourne University Press, Melbourne, 1996, pp. 275–279.

31 Luttrell, 'Norman Thomas Cardinal Gilroy', p. 299.

32 James O'Toole, 'The Role of Bishops in American Catholic History: Myth and Reality in the Case of Cardinal William O'Connell', *Catholic Historical Review*, vol. 77, no. 4, 1991, pp. 595–615; idem. 'The Name that Stood for Rome: William O'Connell and the Modern Episcopal Style', in *Patterns of Episcopal Leadership*, ed. Fogarty, pp. 167–249.
33 O'Toole, 'The Role of Bishops in American Catholic History', p. 596.
34 William McCarthy, *James Patrick O'Collins: A Bishop's Story*, Spectrum, Melbourne, 1996.
35 Patrick O'Farrell, review of *James Duhig* by T. Boland in *ACR*, vol. 64, no. 2, 1987, p. 215.
36 Boland, *Duhig*, p. 65.
37 Gilchrist, *Daniel Mannix*, Dove, Melbourne, 1982, p. iv.
38 Massam, *Sacred Threads*, p. 3.

CHAPTER ONE 'A Real Australian'

1 Robert Wilkinson, interview by author, 11 June 2002.
2 The basic details of his life can be found in a letter from Matthew Beovich to a Croatian relative, Dragan Beović, in reply to a request for information, 23 May 1981, ACAA. Further information was kindly supplied by Ilija Sutalo, author of *Croatian Pioneers in Australia*, Wakefield Press, Adelaide, 2004. Mate also appears in Croatian official documents as Matteo Beović and Mattheus Beović, the spelling varying according to the language: Croatian, Italian or Latin. In Australia, he became known as Mat, Charles Mat or Matthew Beovich. To avoid confusion with his son, I will use the Croatian form of Matthew.
3 Sutalo, *Croatian Pioneers in Australia*, p. 17 ff; idem. 'Early Croatian Settlement in Victoria' in *The Australian People*, ed. James Jupp, Cambridge University Press, Cambridge, 2001, pp. 239–240.
4 For Melbourne in this period, see Geoffrey Blainey, *Our Side of the Country*, Methuen Haynes, Sydney, 1984; Andrew Brown-May, *Melbourne Street Life*, Australian Scholarly Publishing, Melbourne, 1998; Graeme Davidson, *The Rise and Fall of Marvellous Melbourne*, Melbourne University Press, Melbourne, 1978; James Grant & Geoffrey Serle, *The Melbourne Scene 1803–1956*, Hale & Iremonger, Sydney, 1978; Ann Larson, *Growing Up in Melbourne*, Australian Family Formation Project Monograph 12, Australian National University, Canberra, 1994.
5 Daniel Donegan to Beovich, 23 December 1969, ACAA.
6 Matthew John Beovich, letter to the author, 30 January 2000.
7 *Advocate*, 6 July 1933, p. 14; death certificate.
8 I am indebted to their great-grandson, Brendon Walker, for supplying copies of their marriage and death certificates, list of children and assorted family photographs.
9 *Southern Cross*, 5 May 1967, p. 1.
10 ibid., 10 April 1980, p. 2.
11 Sutalo, 'Early Croatian Settlement in Victoria', in *The Australian People*, pp. 239–240.
12 Larson, *Growing Up in Melbourne*, p. 168.
13 ibid., p. 26.
14 Letter to Elizabeth, 1 April 1923.
15 *Tribune*, 25 October 1923, p. 4.
16 *Southern Cross*, 10 April 1980, p. 2.
17 Rev. James Curtain, referring to his grandmother and father, in conversation with the author, 8 February 2003.
18 *Advocate*, 30 June 1949.
19 'John O'Brien' [P. J. Hartigan], *Around the Boree Log and Other Verses*, Sydney, 1921.
20 Patrick O'Farrell, *The Irish in Australia*, rev. ed., New South Wales University Press, Sydney, 1993, p. 149; idem, *The Catholic Church and Community*, 3rd rev. ed., New South Wales University Press, Sydney, 1992, p. 369.
21 Norman Gilroy, interview by Hazel de Berg, 19 January 1972. Tape 567, Oral History Section, National Library of Australia.
22 Letter to Elizabeth, 1 April 1923.
23 Matthew John Beovich, letter to the author, 30 January 2000.
24 Joan Taylor, letter to the author, 17 February 2000. I am very grateful to Joan Taylor and Jack Beovich for their willingness to share their father's story with me. Jack had some

contact with his uncle when he was at St Patrick's College, Ballarat, in the 1940s. En route from Adelaide to Melbourne, or vice versa, Archbishop Beovich would call in to see his nephew, but contact was lost after Jack left school.

25 The obituary with details of Vera's life was supplied by Sr Philomena Kalmund from the Sisters of St Joseph Congregational Archives, Mount Street, North Sydney.

26 Richard Broome, *Coburg*, Lothian Publishing Company, Melbourne, 1987, pp. 174–175.

27 As Matthew Beovich was the executor of his father's will, papers relating to the estate are in the ACAA. According to the terms of the will, Matthew, Frank and Vera each received a share of the proceeds of the sale of the property, with Matthew allocated an additional £600.

28 R. Henderson, *Ninety Years in the Master's Service*, Andrew Elliot, Edinburgh, 1911, p. 222, cited in Hans Mol, *The Faith of Australians*, Allen & Unwin, Sydney, 1985, p. 165.

29 Mol, *Faith of Australians*, p. 168

30 For the history of the school, see Ronald Stewart, *The Spirit of North*, St. Joseph's College, Melbourne, 2000. For education in a Christian Brothers' school in the early twentieth century, see also Chris McConville, *St Kevin's College 1918–1993*, Melbourne University Press, Melbourne, 1993; and Katharine Massam, *On High Ground: Images of One Hundred Years at Aquinas College, Western Australia*, University of Western Australia Press, Perth, 1998.

31 Larson, *Growing Up in Melbourne*, pp. 85–86, 89.

32 Matthew Beovich, 'Sixty Years Ago', *Spectra* (fortnightly publication of the student body of St Joseph's College, North Melbourne), 16 April 1969, p. 2.

33 *Advocate*, 5 December 1908, p. 22. The year before he received first prize for the fourth grade. *Advocate*, 4 January 1908, p. 16.

34 *Advocate*, 30 December 1911, p. 29.

35 A. A. Calwell, *Be Just and Fear Not*, Lloyd O'Neil, Melbourne, 1972, pp. 27–28.

36 Beovich to Michael Gilchrist, 16 November 1976, ACAA.

37 *Southern Cross*, 10 April 1980, p. 2.

38 ibid., 10 April 1980, p. 1.

39 K. T. Livingstone, *The Emergence of an Australian Catholic Priesthood 1835–1915*, Catholic Theological Faculty, Sydney, 1977, pp. 222–229; K. J.Walsh, *Yesterday's Seminary: A History of St Patrick's, Manly*, Allen & Unwin, Sydney, 1998, p. 105.

40 Beovich, 'Sixty Years Ago', p. 2; *Advocate*, 24 January 1914, p. 80.

41 *Tribune*, 16 August 1917, p. 6.

42 Colm Kiernan, *Calwell*, Thomas Nelson, Melbourne, 1978, p. 17.

43 It is the custom of the Christian Brothers to publish detailed necrologies. For Geoghegan, see LBL, 'Brother Matthew Ambrose Geoghegan', *Christian Brothers Educational Record*, 1942, pp. 349–359.

44 From a draft article Calwell wrote for *Spectra* in 1973, cited in Mary Elizabeth Calwell, 'Early Religious Influences on Arthur A. Calwell', qualifying essay to enter Master of Theology degree, Melbourne College of Divinity, undated, p. 13. For Calwell, see also Mary Elizabeth Calwell, 'Arthur Calwell and His Times', *Australasian Catholic Record* [hereafter *ACR*], vol. 65, no. 3, 1988, pp. 279–291.

45 Beovich, 'Sixty Years Ago', p. 2.

46 I. S. Mullen, 'Br Jeremiah Berchmanns McSweeny', *Christian Brothers Educational Record*, 1956, p. 164.

47 ibid., p. 164.

48 Handwritten notes in the ACAA written after McSweeny's death in 1952, probably a draft of comments Beovich sent to I. S. Mullen when he was preparing the necrology for the *Christian Brothers Educational Record*.

49 Barry M. Coldrey, *'A Most Unenviable Reputation': The Christian Brothers and School Discipline Over Two Centuries*, Tamanariak Publishing, Melbourne, 1991.

50 Beovich's notes on McSweeny, ACAA.

51 Draft *Spectra* article, M. E. Calwell, p. 13.

52 Beovich's notes on McSweeny, ACAA.

53 Mullen, 'Br Jeremiah Berchmanns McSweeny', pp. 152–181.

54 McConville, *St Kevin's College*, pp. 47, 64–65.

55 For a discussion of 'masculine' and 'feminine' spiritual styles, see Katharine Massam, *Sacred Threads*, University of New South Wales Press, Sydney, 1996, pp. 25 ff.

56 Beovich's handwritten notes for the Golden Jubilee of the Past Pupils' Association (1963) are in the ACAA.

57 From Beovich's sermon in 1928 at the celebrations to mark the Silver Jubilee of St Joseph's College, cited in *St Joseph's College, North Melbourne, Jubilee Review*, 1928, p. 29.

58 *Tribune*, 15 June 1916, p. 7.

59 *Advocate*, 12 May 1917, p. 19.

60 Clara Staffa Geoghegan, 'Archbishop Thomas Joseph Carr and the Catholic Laity, Melbourne, 1887–1917', part 1, *ACR*, vol. 68, no. 2, 1991, p. 160.

61 The notebook is now in the ACAA. Matt won second prize in an elocution competition in 1917. *Advocate*, 31 March 1917, p. 29.

62 Three were by the popular Victorian writer Felicia Hemans and one by Lord Byron. James Clarence Mangan, an Irish Romantic poet of the early nineteenth century, was another favoured poet, while Irish-America provided the eminently respectable 'drawing-room ballads' of Thomas Moore (see O'Farrell, *The Irish in Australia*, p. 178). A more distinctively Australian flavour can be found in the three poems by Adam Lindsay Gordon and Maurice O'Reilly's 'Little Convent School'.

63 It should not be confused with the Society for Business and Professional Men which began in New South Wales in 1919, members becoming known as Knights of the Southern Cross.

64 Thomas Boland, *Thomas Carr*, University of Queensland Press, Brisbane, 1997, p. 278.

65 Beovich recalled his involvement in the knighthood in a speech (undated) to the Knights of the Southern Cross (the businessmen's society). The notes for the speech are in the ACAA.

66 For the ACF in Melbourne see Clara Staffa Geoghegan, 'Archbishop Thomas Carr and the Catholic Laity, Melbourne, 1887–1917', part 2, *ACR*, vol. 68, no. 3, 1991, pp. 322–330. See also Michael Hogan, *The Sectarian Strand*, Penguin, Melbourne, 1987, pp. 182–184.

67 *Advocate*, 15 May 1915, p. 17.

68 It is now in the ACAA.

69 *Advocate*, 22 April 1916, p. 15.

70 ibid., 25 August 1917, p. 13.

71 *Southern Cross*, 31 July 1970, p. 1.

72 *Advocate*, 1 August 1929, p. 20.

73 *Southern Cross*, 10 April 1980, p. 2.

74 What follows is based primarily on Thomas Boland's biography of Thomas Carr and article, 'Carr and Moran: A Comparison in Episcopal Styles', *Journal of the Australian Catholic Historical Society*, vol. 16, 1994–1995, pp. 25–37.

75 Ian Breward, *History of the Australian Churches*, Allen & Unwin, Sydney, 1993, pp. 92–98; Robert D. Linder, *The Long Tragedy: Australian Evangelical Christians and the Great War, 1914–1918*, Openbook, Adelaide, 2000, p. 25. Linder claims, on the basis of 1911 census figures, that as much as 40–45 per cent of the Australian population may be classified as 'evangelical' in the early twentieth century.

76 Brendan Hayes, 'Archbishop Carr: The Beginnings as Teacher and Controversialist' in *Irish-Australian Studies: Papers Delivered at the Sixth Irish-Australian Conference, July 1990*, ed. Philip Bull, Chris McConville & Noel McLachlan, La Trobe University Press, Melbourne, 1991, pp. 80–90.

77 Boland, *Thomas Carr*, p. 282.

78 ibid., p. 283; O'Farrell, *The Irish in Australia*, pp. 183, 246.

79 Geoghegan, 'Archbishop Thomas Carr', part 1, p. 156.

80 Boland, 'Carr and Moran', p. 33,

81 Boland, *Thomas Carr*, p. 187.

82 ibid., pp. 189, 349–350.

83 Maksimilijan Jezernik, 'Il Pontificio Collegio Urbano de Propaganda Fide', *Sacrae Congregationis de Propaganda Fide, Memoria Rerum* (Rom/Freiburg/Wien: Herder, 1975), p. 121. It is not clear how many places Melbourne was entitled to, but according to the college journal, four students in 1920 were from the Melbourne archdiocese. *Alma Mater*, 1921, pp. 150–151.

84 It seems to have been quite a common practice. One of Mannix's successors, George Pell, had an aunt whose second name was 'Mannix', and a portrait of Mannix hung above the fireplace in his grandparents' home. See George Pell, review of *Daniel Mannix* by Michael Gilchrist in *ACR*, vol. 60, no. 2, 1983, p. 212. Patrick O'Farrell recounts that his parents, who lived in New Zealand, had a photograph of Mannix in their sitting room. See his *Vanished Kingdoms*, New South Wales University Press, Sydney, 1990. p. 244.

85 In his controversial entry on Mannix in the *Australian Dictionary of Biography*, vol. 10, p. 402, James Griffin concludes that, while Mannix was quick-witted, he was intellectually shallow. He qualified for his doctorate in divinity, but his doctorate in laws was honorary and he only ever published one substantial article.

86 In addition to the Mannix biographies, see Michael McKernan, *Australian Churches at War*, Catholic Theological Faculty and Australian War Memorial, Sydney and Canberra, 1980, pp. 172–173; idem. 'Catholics, Conscription and Archbishop Mannix', *Australian Historical Studies*, vol. 17, no. 68, 1977, pp. 299–314; Jeff Kildea, 'Australian Catholics and Conscription', *Journal of Religious History*, vol. 26, no. 3, 2002, pp. 298–313.

87 *Tribune*, 1 February 1917; *Advocate*, 3 February 1917.

88 Octavius Lake in the *Australian Christian Commonwealth*, 7 December 1917, p. 2. See also Linder, *The Long Tragedy*, p.89. Linder points out that while most evangelical clergyman supported conscription, rank and file members were divided, a split which clearly transcended denominational and class boundaries.

89 See Glen Withers, 'The 1916–1917 Conscription Referenda: A Cliometric Reappraisal', *Historical Studies*, vol. 20, 1982, p. 45.

90 Naomi Turner, *Catholics in Australia*, Collins Dove, Melbourne, 1992, vol. 1, pp. 301–302; Patrick O'Farrell, *Catholic Church and Community*, pp. 330–301.

91 'He demonstrated that Catholics could assert themselves, need not cower before the "classes" and that Catholicism need not be a badge of shame but an inheritance to be proudly flaunted and asserted. Mannix articulated the hopes of the Catholic working class at a time of political isolation, frustration and polarisation brought about by the War; while his efforts often increased those pressures, he gave Catholics a surer sense of identity and they loved him for it.' McKernan, 'Catholics, Conscription and Archbishop Mannix', *Australian Historial Studies*, vol. 17, no. 68, 1977, p. 309. See also B. A. Santamaria, *Daniel Mannix*, Melbourne University Press, Melbourne, 1984, p. 83.

92 McKernan, *Australian Churches at War*, pp. 122–123.

93 Boland, *Thomas Carr*, p. 377.

94 As Niall Brennan comments, 'Nothing that Dr Mannix said was untrue, or even unreasonable. He stood for the truth – as he saw it, anyway – courageously and constantly, but he was aggressive and offensive; not often, certainly, but too often for a man in his position. His trouble was that he never quite realised his position. All the people who said that Dr Mannix was a cunning politician were wrong, and when he put his episcopal foot in it, as he did over and over again, it was because he was not a politician at all.' *Dr Mannix*, Rigby, Adelaide, 1964, pp. 171–172.

95 *Advocate*, 12 May 1917, p. 19.

96 *Advocate*, 11 August 1917, p. 27.

97 ibid., 25 August 1917, p. 13.

Chapter Two 'The Centre of Christianity'

1 The history of the college is recounted in Nicola Kowalsky, *Pontificio Collegio Urbano de Propaganda Fide*, Rome, 1956, and Maksimiljan Jezernick, 'Il Collegio Urbano' in *Sacrae Congregationis de Propaganda Fide Memoria Rerum*, ed. J. Metzler, Herder, Rome, 1972, vol. 1, pp. 465–482; vol. 2, pp. 283–298; vol. 3, p. 121. See also Edward Iserloh, Joseph Glazik and Hubert Jedin, eds, *Reformation and Counter Reformation* (*History of the Church*, vol. 5), Crossroad, New York, 1980, pp. 610–614; Stephen Neill, *A History of Christian Missions*, 2nd ed., Penguin, London, 1986, pp. 152–155.

2 Edmund Campion, review of *The Popes in the Twentieth Century* by Carlo Falconi, London, 1968, in the *Sydney Morning Herald*, 30 March 1968, cited by John Molony, *The Roman Mould of the Australian Catholic Church*, Melbourne University Press, Melbourne, 1969, p. 3.

Molony himself studied at the Urban College of Propaganda Fide in the mid twentieth century. For his own account of his experiences, see *Luther's Pine*, Pandanus Books, Canberra, 2004.

3 Matthew Beovich's Diary [hereafter Diary], 16 August 1917.
4 Diary, 13 August 1917.
5 From 21 August to 9 September 1917.
6 Matthew Beovich to Elizabeth Beovich [hereafter Letter to Elizabeth], 2 September 1917.
7 Diary, 30 August 1917.
8 Diary, 28 August 1917; 3 September 1917.
9 Letter to Elizabeth, 9 September 1918.
10 Diary, 20 September 1917.
11 Diary, 27 September 1917.
12 Diary, 1 and 3 October, 1917.
13 Diary, 13 October 1917.
14 Diary, 31 October, 2 November, 7 November.
15 Diary, 28 October 1917; 1 November 1917; 11 November 1917.
16 Letter to Elizabeth, 6 December 1917.
17 Diary, 3 December 1917.
18 Urban College and the Pontifical Urban University are now located at via Urbano VIII on the Janiculum Hill alongside the Vatican.
19 Maksimiljan Jezernik, 'il Collegio Urbano' in *Sacrie Congregationis de Propaganda Fide Memoria Rerum*, Herder, Rome, 1972, vol. 3, p. 121. There is a list of students in the college journal, *Alma Mater*, vol. 3, 1921, pp. 150–152.
20 Letter to Elizabeth, 16 December 1917; 'Propaganda and Manly', *Manly*, vol. 1, October 1921, p. 42.
21 Letter to Elizabeth, 7 November 1920.
22 Diary, 4 February 1918.
23 Diary, 25 June 1918.
24 Diary, 23 June 1919; 1 July 1919.
25 Letter to Elizabeth, 10 October 1918.
26 Joseph White, *The Diocesan Seminary in the United States*, Notre Dame University Press, Notre Dame, Indiana, 1989, p. 269.
27 Diary, 25 June 1920.
28 Diary, 27 June 1922, 20 June 1923.
29 For an introduction to the Modernist controversy see Roger Aubert, *The Church in a Secularised Society*, The Christian Centuries, vol. 5, Darton, Longman & Todd, London, 1975, pp. 188–203; Owen Chadwick, *A History of the Popes, 1830–1914*, Oxford University Press, Oxford, 1998, pp. 346–359. For its impact in Rome: John Pollard, *The Unknown Pope: Benedict XV and the Pursuit of Peace*, Geoffrey Chapman, London, 1999.
30 T. P. Boland, *James Duhig*, University of Queensland Press, Brisbane, 1986, p. 51.
31 Diary, 19 November 1918.
32 Diary, 12 November 1919.
33 Diary, 8 April 1922.
34 Diary, 16 June 1919.
35 For other personal accounts of the process, see John Heenan, *Not the Whole Truth*, Hodder & Stoughton, London, 1971, pp. 60–61; and Anthony Kenny, *A Path From Rome*, Sidgwick & Jackson, London, 1985, p. 46.
36 Letter to Elizabeth, 9 July 1919.
37 Diary, 28 November 1918.
38 Diary, 8 November 1919.
39 Letter to Elizabeth, 13 November 1919.
40 Boland, *Duhig*, p. 52.
41 Diary, 6 November 1920.
42 Diary, 24 January 1921.
43 Diary, 7 March 1921.
44 Letter to Elizabeth, 9 March 1921.

45 Diary, 7 March 1921. Lists of results in the college archives confirm the figures in Beovich's diary and supplement those which are missing.
46 Diary, 2 March 1923.
47 Diary, 20 June 1923.
48 'De Confessione Auriculari, Praesertim, Prioribus Ecclesiae Saeculis', D.D. Dissertation, Urban College of Propaganda Fide, 1923. Beovich did not keep a copy. The original is in the library of Urban University. In Latin, it is only 57 pages long (approximately 12,500 words). However, to fulfill the requirements of the degree, Beovich also had to complete course work and pass the dreaded oral exam.
49 Aubert, *Church in a Secularised Society*, pp. 173, 179; Hubert Jedin and John Dolan, eds, *The Church in the Industrial Age* (*History of the Church*, vol. 10), Crossroad, New York, 1981, p. 312.
50 'De Confessione Auriculari', p. 57.
51 Diary, 4 December 1917, 24 December 1917.
52 Peter Hebblethwaite, *John XXIII*, Geoffrey Chapman, London, 1984, p. 275.
53 For a comparison between Protestant and Catholic theological education, from an ecumenical Protestant perspective, see W. Wagoner, *The Seminary: Protestant and Catholic*, Sheed & Ward, New York, 1966.
54 The postcard, dated 23 April 1918, is in the ACAA.
55 'Rules of Propaganda College', the booklet, in English, was handed to Beovich on 3 December 1917. It is now in the ACAA.
56 Diary, 14 October 1918.
57 Diary, 30 December 1917.
58 'Rules of Propaganda College'.
59 See, for example, Aubert, *Church in a Secularised Society*, p. 130; and *The Church in an Industrial Age*, Roger Aubert et al, eds (*History of the Church*, vol. 9), Burns & Oates, London, 1981, p. 415; Joseph Martos, *Doors to the Sacred*, rev. ed., Liguori/Triumph, Liguori, Missouri, 2001, pp. 437–445; Kenan Osborne, *Priesthood*, Paulist Press, New York, 1988, pp. 280–292; Bernard Cooke, *Ministry to Word and Sacraments*, Fortress Press, Philadelphia, 1976, p.152; Thomas O'Meara, *Theology of Ministry*, Paulist Press, New York, 1983, p. 125.
60 Diary, 6 and 9 December 1920; 1 and 11 February 1921; 12 March 1921; 20 May 1918; 20 June 1921.
61 Diary, 1 April 1918; 1 February 1919; 14 September 1919; 30 October 1919; 18 June 1920; 14 November 1921.
62 Diary, 8 and 10 October 1918.
63 Dermot Keogh, 'Mannix, De Valera and Irish Nationalism', *Australasian Catholic Record* [hereafter *ACR*], vol. 65, no. 2, 1988, p. 161. However, the disgraced seminarian did go on to become a bishop.
64 Diary, 30 November 1918; 1 February 1920; 19 January 1921; 21 October 1921; 6 January 1922; 18 April 1922; 8 August 1962; 6 November 1970.
65 Diary, 16 December 1920.
66 Diary, 20 March 1921.
67 Diary, 8 February 1922.
68 'Rules of Propaganda College', pp. 5–6.
69 Diary, 8 May 1920.
70 Letter to Elizabeth, 9 March 1921.
71 Diary, 3 April 1918.
72 Letter to Elizabeth, 16 January 1919.
73 Diary, 23 and 24 December 1920,
74 Diary, 31 December 1919. The quotation is from Tennyson's 'In Memoriam': 'Ring out the old, ring in the new ...'
75 Diary, 25 December 1918.
76 For O'Collins's time in Rome, see William McCarthy, *James Patrick O'Collins*, Spectrum Publications, Melbourne, 1996, pp. 21–29. For Gilroy, see John Luttrell, 'Norman Thomas Cardinal Gilroy as Archbishop of Sydney', Ph.D. thesis, University of Sydney, 1997, pp. 21–24.

77 Norman Gilroy, interview by Hazel de Berg, 19 January 1972. Tape 567, Oral History Section, National Library of Australia.
78 Beovich described it in a letter to Elizabeth, 8 August 1918.
79 Diary, 29 August 1918.
80 Letter to Elizabeth, 10 October 1918.
81 McCarthy, *James Patrick O'Collins*, pp. 36–37.
82 Diary, 14 October 1919.
83 Diary, 30 September 1921.
84 Letter to Elizabeth, 21 August 1919.
85 Pollard, *The Unknown Pope*, p. 204.
86 The Society features in many diary entries between July 1919 and September 1922.
87 The notebook is now in the ACAA.
88 Diary, 24 July 1922.
89 The notes are amongst his private papers in the ACAA.
90 See, for example, *Southern Cross*, 21 October 1949, p. 1; 30 October 1953, p. 7.
91 Diary, 21 July 1918.
92 Diary, 8 August 1922.
93 Diary, 25 December 1917; 31 January 1918; 21 and 25 February 1918; 7, 8, 10, 14 October 1918.
94 Diary, 18 November 1918; 13 January 1919. In an Apostolic Exhortation in 1915, Benedict pleaded: 'Abandon the mutual threat of destruction. Remember, Nations do not die; humiliated and oppressed, they bear the weight of the yoke imposed upon them, preparing themselves for their comeback and transmitting from one generation to the next a sad legacy of hatred and vendetta.' Pollard, *The Unknown Pope*, p. 117.
95 Diary, 9 May 1919.
96 Diary, 3 January 1919.
97 Diary, 16 August 1918.
98 Diary, 3 January 1919; 23 May 1920.
99 Diary, 18 November 1918.
100 In addition to the Mannix biographies, which all highlight the incident, see Keogh, 'Mannix', pp. 159–173.
101 *Advocate*, 9 November 1918, p. 23; Letter to Elizabeth, 7 March 1919.
102 Diary, 4 April 1921.
103 *Tribune*, 16 June 1921, p. 4.
104 From a transcript of the speech, written by fellow student Frank Kissane, which is tucked into the third volume of Beovich's diary.
105 For the Manly Union, see K. J. Walsh, *Yesterday's Seminary*, Allen & Unwin, Sydney, 1998, pp. 170–176; Patrick O'Farrell, *The Catholic Church and Community*, p. 358 ff.; and Edmund Campion, *Australian Catholics*, Aurora Books, Melbourne, 1987, pp. 73–75.
106 Patrick O'Farrell, *The Irish in Australia*, rev. ed., University of New South Wales Press, Sydney, 1993, p. 293.
107 Patrick & Deirdre O'Farrell, *Documents in Australian Catholic History*, Geoffrey Chapman, London, 1969, vol. 2, pp. 192–193.
108 O'Farrell, *Documents*, vol. 2, p. 199.
109 Gilroy, De Berg interview; Luttrell, 'Norman Thomas Cardinal Gilroy', p. 20; Thomas Boland, 'Gilroy, Sir Norman Thomas', *Australian Dictionary of Biography*, vol. 14, ed. John Ritchie, Melbourne University Press, Melbourne, 1996, p. 276.
110 Diary, 20 May 1921.
111 Diary, 27 May 1921.
112 Diary, 8 June 1921. He did not keep a copy or summarise its contents in his diary.
113 Diary, 8 June 1921. The establishment of seminaries in mission countries, and the consequent development of native priests and bishops, was a particular concern of Benedict XV. It was the chief thrust of the apostolic letter *Maximun Illud* ('On the Propagation of the Catholic Faith throughout the World') in 1919. In *The Unknown Pope*, p. 203, Pollard describes this as a 'radical' policy designed to prepare the way for the post-colonial future of the Church in Africa, Asia and Oceania.

114 Diary, 1 July 1921. In November 1917 a Rome-based friend of Michael Kelly, archbishop of Sydney, wrote to warn Kelly that Bartholomew Cattaneo, Cerretti's successor, would not favour the Irish bishops because 'he has swallowed some ideas given him by some bouncing Australian students at Propaganda'. See Walsh, *Yesterday's Seminary*, p. 174. The letter was sent before Beovich reached Rome but he mentioned in his diary that the Australian students had an enjoyable meeting with Cattaneo on 25 March 1923.
115 Robert Wilkinson, interview by author, 11 June 2002.
116 Boland, *Duhig*, p. 46.
117 Pollard, *The Unknown Pope*, p. 213.
118 Letter to Elizabeth, 23 December 1917.
119 Diary, 11 February 1918.
120 Kenny, *Path From Rome*, p. 43.
121 ibid., p. 67.
122 Diary, 16 May 1920.
123 Kenny, *Path From Rome*, p. 60.
124 Gilroy, De Berg interview, 1972.
125 Diary, 5 February 1922.
126 Gilroy, De Berg interview, 1972.
127 Aubert, *Church in a Secularised Society*, pp. 545–546.
128 Diary, 29 June 1923.
129 Letter to Elizabeth, 23 March 1920.
130 Apostolic Letter *Officiorum Omnium*, 1 August 1922 in *The Catholic Priesthood*, ed. Pierre Veuillot, Dwyer, Sydney, 1957, p. 151.
131 See Bernard Cooke, *Ministry to Word and Sacraments*, pp. 610–611.
132 McCarthy, *James Patrick O'Collins*, p. 27.
133 Diary, 17 March 1923.
134 Diary, 7 July 1923.
135 Diary, 16–20 July 1923.
136 Diary, 19 July 1923.
137 Diary, 23–24 July 1923.
138 Aubert, *Church in a Secularised Society*, p. 546.
139 Diary, 24 December 1922.
140 Diary, 26–27 July 1923.
141 Diary, 20 June 1923. 'By the Grace of God, helped by Our Lady, St Anthony and the Little Flower [Thérèse], I obtained the D.D.'
142 *Story of a Soul*, translated by John Clarke, 3rd ed., ICS Publications, Washington, DC, 1996.
143 Diary, 2 August 1923.
144 Diary, 23 August 1923.
145 Diary, 19 August 1923.
146 Diary, 11 August 1923.
147 Diary, 4 July 1923.
148 Diary, 6 and 10 July 1923.
149 Diary, 11 August 1923.
150 Diary, 20 August 1923.
151 Archbishop James Gleeson, who did not travel outside Australia until the 1960s, acknowledged in an interview with the author on 24 July 1997 that he only really came to appreciate the universality of the Catholic Church when he joined bishops from around the world at the Second Vatican Council. He realised then that Matthew Beovich had acquired his broader understanding of Catholicism during his student days in Rome.
152 Letter to Elizabeth, 23 June 1923.
153 McCarthy, *James Patrick O'Collins*, p. 28.

Chapter Three 'Propagating the Faith'

1 Matthew Beovich to Elizabeth Beovich, 21 August 1923, 3 October 1923, ACAA.
2 A special social was held at North Brunwick (*Advocate*, 11 October 1923, p. 23; 18 October 1923, p. 20). Beovich was also invited to an assembly at his old school, St Joseph's College,

North Melbourne (*Advocate*, 25 October 1923, p. 27; *Tribune*, 25 October 1923, p. 4) and a dinner was organised in his honour by the Past Pupils' Association (*Advocate*, 1 November 1923, p. 17).

3 D. F. Bourke, *History of the Catholic Church in Victoria*, Catholic Bishops of Victoria, Melbourne, 1988, p. 251. St Margaret Mary's Church, North Brunswick, was built in 1920.

4 *Advocate*, 11 October, 1923, p. 9.

5 According to census data, the number of Catholics in the Melbourne metropolitan area rose from 159,936 in 1921 to 186,945 in 1933, but the total population of Melbourne increased from 783,503 (20.4 per cent Catholic) to 991,934 (18.8 per cent Catholic). Bourke, *History of the Catholic Church in Victoria*, p. 251.

6 Hans Mol, *Faith of Australians*, Allen & Unwin, Sydney, 1985, p. 53. See also Naomi Turner, *Catholics in Australia*, Collins Dove, Melbourne, 1992, vol. 1, p. 323; vol. 2, pp. 11–14; Patrick O'Farrell, *Catholic Church and Community*, 3rd rev. ed., New South Wales University Press, Sydney, 1992, pp. 371–372.

7 *Advocate*, 24 January 1924, p. 10.

8 Beovich to Cardinal Van Rossum, 6 January 1927, ACAA.

9 Edmund Campion, *Australian Catholics*, Aurora Books, Melbourne, 1987, pp. 141–142.

10 Turner, *Catholics in Australia*, vol. 1, p. 248.

11 ibid., vol. 1, p. 234.

12 Beovich to Van Rossum, 24 April 1930, ACAA.

13 Reports courtesy of the Presentation Sisters Archives, Brighton, Victoria.

14 J. T. McMahon, 'The Leakage Problem', *Australasian Catholic Record* [hereafter *ACR*], vol. 14, no. 4, 1937, p. 208.

15 Beovich to Van Rossum, 24 April 1930.

16 Colette Egan, SGS, courtesy of the Good Samaritan Archivists, February 2000.

17 Letter to the author from Sister Camilla and Good Samaritan Archivists, Sydney, February 2000; Winefride Murphy PBVM, 1 March 2000; Patricia Gifford, in conversation with the author, 2004.

18 See, for example, Turner, *Catholics in Australia*, vol. 1, p. 248; and Gerard Rummery, 'The Development of the Concept of Religious Education in Catholic Schools 1872–1972', *Journal of Religious History*, vol. 9, 1977, pp. 302–317.

19 M. B. Hanrahan, 'The Teaching of the Catechism', *ACR*, vol. 1, no. 2, 1924, pp. 21–25; no. 3, 1924, pp. 21–27; no. 4, 1924, pp. 31–36; *ACR*, vol. 2, no. 1, 1925, pp. 35–40; no. 2, 1925, pp. 119–126; no. 3, 1925, pp. 225–232; no. 4, 1925, pp. 326–333. Arthur O'Brien, 'The Practical Aim of Religious Teaching', *ACR*, vol. 3, no. 2, 1926, pp. 125–128; *ACR*, vol. 6, no. 2, 1929, pp. 125–132. O'Brien was a priest of the Bathurst diocese. Hanrahan was master of method at the Christian Brothers Training College in Sydney from 1914 to 1930, provincial of the Christian Brothers in Australia from 1930 to 1943, and then master of method again from 1943 until his death in 1953. See Graham English, 'An Independent Mind in Motion: M. B. Hanrahan and Catholic Religious Education in the 1920s in Australia', *ACR*, vol. 82, no. 3, 2005, pp. 281–289.

20 Circular to 'The Teacher in Charge', 11 March 1929, and leaflets in the archives of the Catholic Education Office, Melbourne [hereafter, CEO, Melb.].

21 He explained the process in a circular to 'The Teacher in Charge', 22 January 1927, CEO, Melb.

22 Circular to 'The Teacher in Charge', 11 March 1929, CEO, Melb.

23 Both the 1925 and the 1929 syllabus are in the CEO, Melb.

24 Circular, 11 March 1929; *Advocate*, 2 January 1931.

25 Technically most were religious congregations not orders, and female members were sisters not nuns, but in practice the finer distinctions of ecclesiastical law were often ignored and the term 'order' was commonly applied to congregations, and 'nun' to sisters.

26 Beovich to Michael Gilchrist, 13 December 1976, ACAA.

27 Beovich, 'Catholic Education in Victoria: A Brief Historical Survey', *Advocate*, 6 December 1934, p. 60.

28 J. T. McMahon, 'The Irish Renaissance in Christian Doctrine', *ACR*, vol. 6, no. 3, 1929, p. 230.

29 See, for example, *The Annual Report on Catholic Education in the Archdiocese of Melbourne for the Year Ending 31 December 1933*, CEO, Melb.
30 A point emphasised by Richard Selleck, 'An Overview' in *Catholic Education in Victoria*, Catholic Education Office, Melbourne, 1986, p. 104. See also Thomas O'Donoghue *Upholding the Faith: The Process of Education in Catholic Schools in Australia, 1922–1965*, Peter Lang, New York, 2001, pp. 11, 29 ff.
31 Cited by Robert McPhee, 'Daniel Mannix: A Study of Aspects of Catholic Educational Policy in Victoria, 1913–1945', M.Ed. thesis, Melbourne University, 1980, p. 125.
32 Beovich's notes on his interview with Brother Reidy, 8 November 1927, CEO, Melb.
33 Loretta (Sister Marina) Brennan, 'The Beginning and End of the Catechism Era in the Melbourne Church', B.Th. Essay, Catholic Theological College, Clayton, undated but probably 1980, p. 13. Brennan interviewed Beovich on 21 September 1980. A copy of her essay is in the ACAA.
34 Anne O'Brien, *Blazing a Trail: Catholic Education in Victoria 1963–1980*, David Lovell Publishing, Melbourne, 1999, p. 8. In the foreword to *Blazing a Trail* Hedley Beare depicts the Catholic Education Office in Melbourne arising from virtually nothing in 1963, the year of Mannix's death. In Frank Rogan's *Short History of Catholic Education: Archdiocese of Melbourne, 1839–1980*, Catholic Education Office, Melbourne, 2000, the period 1919–1939 is covered in less than two pages, almost half the book being devoted to 1960–1980. Ronald Fogarty gives Beovich some credit for the development of the Catholic education system in his magisterial *Catholic Education in Australia, 1806–1950*, vol. 2, Melbourne University Press, Melbourne, 1959, p. 440.
35 Daniel Conquest, letter to the author, 21 August 1997.
36 B. A. Santamaria, *Daniel Mannix*, Melbourne University Press, Melbourne, 1984, p. 148. See also Michael Gilchrist, *Daniel Mannix: Wit and Wisdom*, 2nd ed., Freedom Publishing, Melbourne, 2004, p. 179; Walter Epsworth, *Archbishop Mannix*, H. H. Stephenson, Melbourne, 1977, p. 355.
37 Santamaria, *Mannix*, pp. 148–149.
38 ibid., p. 153. See also Gilchrist, *Daniel Mannix*, p. 142.
39 Conquest, 21 August 1997.
40 He was the college's first male student. See *Mercy Teachers' College*, Institute of Catholic Education, Melbourne, 1984, p. 41.
41 Thomas Boland, *Thomas Carr*, University of Queensland Press, Brisbane, 1997, p. 179.
42 Alan Barcan, *A History of Education in Australia*, Oxford University Press, Melbourne, 1980, p. 267.
43 W. A. Greening, 'The Mannix Thesis in Catholic Secondary Education in Victoria', *Melbourne Studies in Education 1961–1962*, p. 292.
44 *Advocate*, 4 September 1930, p. 16.
45 'The Cost of Education: State Board of Investigation: Valuable Evidence by Dr Beovich', *Tribune*, 25 June 1931, p. 5.
46 For St Colman's and Brother Bowler, see R. S. Steward's article on Bowler in *The Christian Brothers Educational Record*, 1972, pp. 174–198.
47 Conquest, 21 August 1997.
48 Monica Margaret McKenzie, 'Catholic Religious Women Educators as Agents of Social Change', MA Thesis, Monash University, 1994, pp. 102, 115.
49 Helen Malone, quoted in McKenzie, 'Catholic Religious Women Educators', p. 108.
50 June Nicholls, note to the author, 9 February 2000, courtesy of the Good Samaritan Archivists, Glebe Point, Sydney.
51 Alice Gleeson PBVM, letter to the author, 28 February 2000.
52 Some correspondences is in the Christian Brothers' archives at Parkville, Victoria.
53 McKenzie, 'Catholic Religious Women Educators', p. 100; Mary Kavanagh in *Catholic Education in Victoria*, p. 32.
54 A. B. Hanley, 'Catholic Technical Schools of Australia', *Catholic Education Congress 1936*, p. 309.
55 John Kelly, interview by Michael Gilchrist, 11 October 1976. See Gilchrist, 'The Role of Dr Mannix in Victorian Catholic Education, 1913–1923, and its Determinants', M.Ed.

Thesis, University of Melbourne, 1978, appendix 19. Gilchrist helpfully attached transcripts of his interviews as appendices.

56 A. B. Hanly, 'Catholic Technical Schools', *Australian Catholic Education Congress: Adelaide, Australia, November 8–15, 1936*, Advocate Press, Melbourne, 1937, p. 310; Minutes of meetings of 'The Archbishop's Committee on Technical Education' (in Beovich's handwriting) are in the CEO, Melb.

57 *Advocate*, 22 April 1937, p. 7; *Tribune*, 22 April 1937, p. 2.

58 McKenzie, 'Catholic Religious Women Educators', p. 110.

59 'Cost of Education in Victoria: Evidence Given by the Rev. M. Beovich Before the Board of Enquiry Appointed by the State Government in 1931', p. 5, CEO Melb.

60 Bourke, *History of the Catholic Church in Victoria*, p. 263.

61 Beovich, 'Catholic Education in Australia' in K. S. Cunningham, G. A. McIntyre and W. C. Radford, *Review of Education in Australia*, Melbourne University Press, Melbourne, 1938, p. 105.

62 Fogarty, *Catholic Education in Australia*, vol. 2, pp. 451–452.

63 Correspondence in the Christian Brothers' archives was kindly supplied by Br Kelty, Treacy Centre, Parkville, Victoria.

64 Helen Praetz, *Building a School System*, Melbourne University Press, Melbourne, 1980, p. 42. In a letter to his superior-general in Rome, dated 24 October 1932, Hanrahan mentioned that he had been told by some of the senior consulters in Melbourne that some Brothers were criticising 'some new arrangements of the archbishop regarding education' and were refusing to use the test paper Beovich had supplied for the Christian Doctrine examination. He had 'had a chat' to Beovich and Mannix and was relieved to report that 'from neither did I get anything that indicated strained relations between them and ourselves'. Letter courtesy of Br Obbens, St Mary's Province Administration, Balmain, NSW.

65 Praetz, *Building a School System*, p. 24.

66 'Regulations for Schools of the Diocese of Melbourne', Catholic Education Office, 1937 (Christian Brothers' Archives, Parkville).

67 Conquest, 21 August 1997.

68 Fogarty, *Catholic Education in Australia*, vol. 2, p. 423.

69 Patrick Crudden, director of the Catholic Education Office in Melbourne from 1968 to 1970, told Gilchrist that Mannix 'simply cut off the good work that had been done in public relations in the education field by Carr'. See Gilchrist, 'The Role of Dr Mannix', Appendix 24.

70 John Roberts, Registrar, and J. A. Seitz, President of the Council of Public Education, to Beovich, 14 December 1939, ACAA.

71 'Minutes of Meeting of the Archbishop's Committee on Primary Education', 6 June 1929, CEO, Melb.

72 'Cost of Education in Victoria', p. 7; Annual Report, 1933, p. 4; Barcan, *History of Education in Australia*, p. 279. The merit certificate survived in Victoria until 1947.

73 Beovich, 'Catholic Education in Australia', p. 105; Barcan, *History of Education in Australia*, pp. 274, 284.

74 *Annual Report*, 1933, p. 4.

75 ibid. Much of the work on the *Children's World* was initially done by Ellen (Mother Patrick) Callinan IBVM. By 1937 almost 200,000 copies were being sold annually.

76 *Annual Report*, 1933, p. 7.

77 Beovich to F. Hassett of the Catholic Tax Payers' Association, July 1937, CEO Melb.

78 Beovich to Ellen [Mother Patrick] Callanan, 20 February 1931, CEO Melb. For Callanan, see Rosemary Williams, 'Callanan, Ellen', *ADB*, vol. 13, ed. John Ritchie, Melbourne University Press, Melbourne, 1993, pp. 339–340.

79 Ellen [Mother Patrick] Callanan, *And Forbid Them Not! A Series of Lessons on Christian Doctrine for Little Children*, Advocate Press, Melbourne, 1933, pp. 10–11.

80 Praetz, *Building a School System*, p. 18.

81 *Archdiocese of Melbourne: Syllabus of Religious Instruction in Primary and Secondary Grades*, Advocate Press, Melbourne, 1934.

82 M. Sheehan, 'Some Remarks on the Catechism Problem', *ACR*, vol. 14, no. 3, 1937, p. 182.

83 The notes are in the CEO, Melb.
84 Among its admirers were M. B. Hanrahan, M. M. De Sales, M. M. Frances Frewin and M. M. Angela, from the Christian Brothers and the Good Samaritan, Loreto and Dominican Sisters respectively. *Australian Catholic Education Congress, Adelaide, 1936*, Advocate Press, Melbourne, 1937, pp. 101, 425, 434, 438.
85 ibid., p. 104.
86 ibid., pp. 317–322. Beovich delivered the paper again at the Mass for teachers in St Patrick's Cathedral at the beginning of the following school year. It was printed in the *Advocate* (4 February 1937, p. 10) and the *Tribune* (4 February 1937, p. 1).
87 According to McPhee, Beovich and Mannix wrote the agenda for the meeting. 'Daniel Mannix: A Study of Aspects of Catholic Education Policy in Victoria', p. 149.
88 *Southern Cross*, 30 April 1971, p. 5.
89 Beovich to Br Trevor Dean CFC in reply to a request for information on the development of the catechism, dated 1960, ACAA.
90 Sheehan, 'Some Remarks on the Catechism Problem' *ACR*, vol. 14, no. 4, 1937, p. 183.
91 ibid., pp. 185–188.
92 Beovich to Dean, 1960.
93 Beovich told McPhee that he worked on the draft with Mannix for 'many months' from 2 pm to 4 pm, 'Daniel Mannix: A Study of Aspects of Catholic Education Policy in Victoria', p. 150. Loretta Brennan, who interviewed Beovich for her essay on the catechism in 1980, narrows the time Beovich and Mannix spent working together on the draft to two months, 'every day for two hours after lunch'. 'The Beginning and End of the Catechism Era', p. 22.
94 There is a copy of the draft in the ACAA.
95 The following correspondence regarding the catechism is in the CEO, Melb.
96 Joseph Dwyer to Beovich, 11 October 1937.
97 Terrence McGuire to Mannix, 10 January 1938.
98 Romuald Hayes to Mannix, 15 January 1938.
99 Kelly to Mannix, 27 January 1938.
100 Beovich to Trevor Dean, 1960.
101 Edward Gleeson to Mannix, 10 May 1938.
102 Simonds to Beovich, 31 May 1938.
103 Gilroy to Beovich, 29 June 1938.
104 Leslie Rumble, very ruefully, to Beovich on 2 February 1939.
105 Campion, *Australian Catholics*, p. 146; idem, *A Place in the City*, Penguin, Melbourne, 1994, p. 123.
106 Campion, *A Place in the City*, p. 123.
107 Selleck, 'An Overview', pp. 101–103.
108 Adrian Hastings, *A History of English Christianity 1920–1990*, 3rd ed., SCM, London, 1991, pp. 279–278.
109 Beovich, *Companion to the Catechism*, 2nd ed., Advocate Press, Melbourne, 1939, p. 60. It was not possible to locate a copy of the first edition.
110 Santamaria, *Mannix*, p. 177.
111 Herbert Jedin, Konrad Repgen and John Dolan, *History of the Church*, vol. 10, Crossroad, New York, 1981, p. 308.
112 Massam, *Sacred Threads*, University of New South Wales Press, Sydney, 1996, p. 195.
113 *Advocate*, 30 April 1925, p. 20.
114 ibid., 25 May 1925, p. 20.
115 ibid., 10 September 1925, p. 9.
116 ibid., 3 December 1925, p. 14.
117 ibid. 27 November 1926, p. 8; *Tribune*, 24 November 1927, p. 1; *Advocate*, 24 November 1927, p. 24; 8 November 1928, p. 16.
118 Agatha Le Breton, *Father Tom*, ACTS 501. See also Edmund Campion, *Great Australian Catholics*, David Lovell Publishing, Melbourne, 1997, pp. 74–76; idem. *Australian Catholics*, pp. 131–133.
119 Michael Joseph Watson, *The Virgin Mother: What Catholics Do Not Believe*, ACTS 518, 1927.
120 Anon., *God's Voice in the Soul: A Convert's Story*, ACTS 585, 1931.

121 Albert Power, *Do Catholics Think For Themselves?*, ACTS 619, 1932.
122 Henry Johnston, *The Church Built on a Rock*, ACTS 561, 1929.
123 *Advocate*, 28 April, 1927, pp. 18–19; 24 November 1927, p. 24; 8 November 1928, p. 16.
124 ibid., 28 November 1929, p. 20.
125 Mol, *Faith of Australians*, p. 172.
126 *Advocate*, 23 November 1933, p. 10; 27 November 1930, p. 18; 3 December 1931, p. 12; 27 October 1932, p. 12.
127 Daniel A. Lord, *God and the Depression*, ACTS 633, 1933.
128 J. B. Roper, *Capitalism and Communism: Judged by Catholic Principles*, ACTS 618, 1932.
129 'A Teacher', *The Child in School and at Home*, ACTS 625, 1932.
130 Clara Staffa Geoghegan, 'Archbishop Thomas Carr and the Catholic Laity, Melbourne, 1887–1917', *ACR*, vol. 68, no. 3, 1991, p. 320.
131 T. A. Murphy, 'The Circulation of Catholic Literature in Australia', *ACR*, vol. 7, no. 2, April 1930, p. 124.
132 *Advocate*, 17 November 1927, p. 21.
133 ibid., 8 November 1929, p. 16.
134 James Gleeson in conversation with the author.
135 *Advocate*, 28 November 1929, p. 22.
136 ibid., 25 November 1926, p. 8.
137 ibid., 24 November 1927, p. 24.
138 ibid., 8 November 1928, pp. 16–17.
139 ibid., 28 November 1929, p. 14.
140 ibid., 28 November 1929, p. 22.
141 *Australian Catholic Truth Society: Its First Quarter of a Century*, ACTS 576, p. 10.
142 *Advocate*, 23 November 1933, p. 10.
143 ibid., 25 February 1932, p. 10; 3 March, p. 10; 24 March, 1932, p. 13; 7 April 1932, pp. 16, 17.
144 ibid., 14 April 1932, p. 12; 17 November 1932, p. 17; 18 May 1933, p. 17.
145 It is not clear for how long. By the time he was elected archbishop of Adelaide, Denys Jackson had the role of 'Onlooker'. *Advocate*, 21 December 1939, p. 3.
146 ibid., 21 December 1939, p. 3; *Tribune*, 21 December 1939, p. 1.
147 Beovich to Van Rossum, 4 April 1930.
148 See 'Benedict XV and Pius XI: Some Outstanding Incidents', lecture delivered at the Australian Catholic Federation Summer School, *Tribune*, 12 February 1925, p. 1; *Advocate*, 12 February, p. 15; 'Rome and Lourdes' at St Mary's Young Men's Club, Sale, ibid., 25 June 1925, p. 11; 'Pagan and Christian Rome' at St Margaret Mary's, North Brunswick, ibid., 25 November 1926, p. 20; 'Rome' at St Mary's Hall, Geelong, ibid., 27 October 1927, p. 26; 'What the Popes have Done for Civilisation', lecture published in full in the *Advocate* 9 August 1928, pp. 6–7; 'Pope Pius XI, World's Greatest Christian', ibid., 13 May, 1937, p. 10; *Tribune*, 13 May, 1937, p. 2.
149 Conquest, 21 August 1997, and interview, 19 February 1998.
150 ibid.
151 James O'Toole, 'The Name that Stood For Rome: William O'Connell and the Modern Episcopal Style' in *Patterns of Episcopal Leadership*, ed. Gerard P. Fogarty, the Bicentennial History of the Catholic Church in America, Macmillan, New York & London, 1989, p. 181.
152 Winefride Murphy PBVM to author, 1 March 2000.
153 Mol, *Faith of Australians*, p. 119.
154 Beovich, 'Catholic Education and Catechetics in Australia'. Report compiled at the request of the Australian bishops for the Conference on Education and Catechetics held in Rome in 1950.
155 Diary, 15 December 1939. He commenced keeping a diary again on 12 December 1939 after he heard that he had become archbishop-elect of Adelaide.

Chapter Four 'Calling God Back to the Council Chambers'

1 Matthew Beovich's diary [hereafter Diary].
2 For the history of Catholicism in South Australia in the nineteenth and early twentieth centuries, see Margaret Press's twin volumes: *From Our Broken Toil: South Australian*

Catholics, 1336–1906 and *Colour and Shadow: South Australian Catholics 1906–1962*, Catholic Archdiocese of Adelaide, 1986 and 1991. See also David Hilliard, 'The City of Churches' in *William Shakespeare's Adelaide, 1860–1930*, ed. Brian Dickey, Association of Professional Historians, Adelaide, 1992, pp. 61–86; idem, 'The Catholic Church and Community in Adelaide' in *Making Space*, ed. Fay Gale, St Aloysius College, Adelaide, 2000, pp. 1–20.

3 Press, *From Our Broken Toil*, p. 133.

4 Australia wide, their percentages were: Methodist 13.3; Baptist 2.4; Congregational 1.9 and Churches of Christ 0.64. See Hilliard, 'City of Churches', pp. 62, 82; idem, 'Religion' in *South Australian Historical Statistics*, Wray Vamplew et al., eds, Historical Monograph, vol. 3, History Project Inc., Sydney, 1984, pp. 137–143.

5 The Lutheran national average was 2.0 per cent. Hilliard, 'City of Churches', p. 82.

6 Hilliard, 'City of Churches', pp. 62–63.

7 For the history of the cathedral, see Brian Andrews, *The Cathedral Church of St Francis Xavier*, Catholic Church Endowment Society, Adelaide, 1996.

8 David Hilliard, *Catholics in Kingswood*, Kingswood Catholic Parish Pastoral Council, Adelaide, 1994; Joan Brewer, *A History of the Catholic Parish of St Peters, 1934–1984*, St Peter's Parish, Adelaide, 1984; John Chambers et al, *The Rays of the Crucifix*, Dulwich-Burnside Catholic Parish, Adelaide, 1994.

9 Richard Healy CFC, *The Christian Brothers of Wakefield Street, 1878–1978*, Christian Brothers' College, Adelaide, 1978; John Bourke CFC, *The Rostrevor Story, 1923–1983*, John Bourke, Adelaide, 1991; Peter Donovan & Bernard O'Neil, *In the Marist Tradition: Sacred Heart College, Adelaide, 1897–1997*, Sacred Heart College, Adelaide, 1997.

10 Gale, ed., *Making Space*; Helen Northey, *Living the Truth: The Dominican Sisters in South Australia, 1868–1958*, Holy Cross Congregation of Dominican Sisters, Adelaide, 1999; Stephanie Burley & Katherine Teague, *Chapel, Cloister & Classroom: Reflections on the Dominican Sisters at North Adelaide*, Lutheran Publishing House, Adelaide, 1993.

11 For prominent lay Catholics, see Margaret Press, *Colour and Shadow*, passim. See also J. F. Corkery, 'Alderman, Sir Harry Graham', *Australian Dictionary of Biography* [hereafter *ADB*], vol. 13, ed. John Ritchie, Melbourne University Press, Melbourne, 1993, p. 22; John Playford, 'Cameron, Archie Galbraith', *ADB*, vol. 13, pp. 346–348; Katharine Massam, 'McGuire, Dominic Mary Paul', *ADB*, vol. 15, ed. John Ritchie, Melbourne University Press, Melbourne, 2000, pp. 222–225; idem. 'Dominic Paul McGuire', *Wakefield Companion to South Australian History*, Wakefield Press, Adelaide, 2001, p. 343; Peter A. Howell, 'John and Mary Fennescey', *ADB* supplementary volume, ed. Christopher Cunneen, Melbourne University Press, Melbourne, 2005, pp. 126–127.

12 *Census of the Commonwealth of Australia, 30 June 1947*, vol. 1, pp. 334–345.

13 See David Hilliard, 'Religion in Playford's South Australia' in *Playford's South Australia: Essays on the History of South Australia, 1933–1968*, eds Bernard O'Neil, Judith Raftery and Kerrie Round, Association of Professional Historians, Adelaide, 1996, pp. 253–274.

14 Peter Howell, 'Playford, Politics and Parliament' in *Playford's South Australia*, p. 47.

15 Stewart Cockburn, *Playford*, Axiom, Adelaide, 1991, p. 220.

16 Patrick O'Farrell, *The Catholic Church and Community*, 3rd rev. ed. New South Wales University Press, Sydney, 1992, p. 318.

17 *Advertiser*, 9 May 1913. See Press, *Colour and Shadow*, p. 60; M. French, 'O'Reily, John', *ADB*, vol. 11, ed. Geoffrey Serle, Melbourne University Press, Melbourne, 1988, pp. 96–97; Ruth Schumann, 'The Catholic Priesthood in South Australia, 1844–1915', *Journal of Religious History*, vol. 16, no. 2, 1990, p. 77.

18 Press, *Colour and Shadow*, p. 155; Ruth Schumann, 'Spence, Robert William', *ADB*, vol. 12, ed. John Ritchie, Melbourne University Press, Melbourne, 1990, pp. 30–31.

19 Press, *Colour and Shadow*, pp. 158–60; R. J. Egar, 'Killian, Andrew', *ADB*, vol. 9, ed. Bede Nairn and Geoffrey Serle, Melbourne University Press, Melbourne, 1983, pp. 591–592.

20 Hilliard, 'The Catholic Church and Community in Adelaide' in *Making Space*, ed. Fay Gale, St Aloysius College, Adelaide, 2000, p. 6.

21 See *Australian Catholic Education Congress*, Advocate Press, Melbourne, 1937.

22 *Southern Cross*, 12 April 1940, supp. p. v.

23 *Australasian Catholic Directory 1940*, Pellegrini, Sydney, 1940, p. 283.

24 The statistics for Melbourne are more impressive: 105 parishes, 251 churches, 181 diocesan priests, 187 priests in religious orders, 181 brothers, 1594 religious sisters, 201 schools with 41,160 students, and 26 charitable institutions of various kinds. See *Australasian Catholic Directory 1940*, p. 245.

25 'Record of Diocesan Clergy'. In 1940, after Beovich took over as archbishop of Adelaide, his secretary compiled a list of the diocesan priests in an exercise book. A record was made of their place of birth, date of birth, and date of ordination. Beovich often noted in his own handwriting when priests were appointed to parishes or other positions.

26 Diary, 14 March 1940. It is now in the ACAA.

27 Diary, 15 December 1939.

28 See Thomas Boland, *James Duhig*, University of Queensland Press, 1986, pp. 287–289; John Luttrell, 'Norman Thomas Cardinal Gilroy as Archbishop of Sydney', PhD thesis, University of Sydney, 1997, pp. 84–92.

29 B. A. Santamaria, *Daniel Mannix*, Melbourne University Press, Melbourne, 1984, pp. 181–189; and Michael Gilchrist, *Daniel Mannix*, 2nd ed., Freedom Publishing, Melbourne, 2004, pp. 153–155, 178–80. However, as John Luttrell points out, the circumstances surrounding Sheehan's resignation are still obscure. See 'Norman Thomas Cardinal Gilroy as Archbishop of Sydney', p. 86; idem, 'Bishop Gilroy and the Diocese of Port Augusta', *ACR*, vol. 80, no. 2, April 2003, p. 198.

30 When Panico first visited Melbourne in 1936 he struggled in a speech to find the word 'sunshine'. Mannix, behind him, murmured 'moonshine' and Panico picked up the cue, to the delight of the audience. See Gilchrist, *Mannix*, pp. 154–155.

31 Diary, 13 December 1940.

32 Diary, January 1940.

33 These included a concert arranged by the Christian Brothers in the Cathedral Hall (*Advocate*, 14 March 1940, p. 2) and a gathering of representatives of school children in the archdiocese of Melbourne, at which Beovich was presented with the gold pectoral cross which can be seen in most photographs of him taken from then on (*Advocate*, 4 April 1940, p. 7).

34 Daniel Conquest, interview by the author, 19 February 1998; *Southern Cross*, 5 April 1940, p. 1.

35 *Advocate*, 3 July 1930, p. 20.

36 William McCarthy, *James Patrick O'Collins*, Spectrum Publications, Melbourne, 1996, pp. 39–40.

37 For Beovich's consecration, see the *Southern Cross*, 12 April 1940. Most of that edition is devoted to the arrival of the new archbishop in South Australia. His consecration was also reported in the *Advertiser* (8 April 1940, p. 7), *Tribune* (11 April 1940, p. 1) and *Advocate* (11 April 1940, p. 3).

38 For a description of the ceremony, see *Southern Cross*, 5 April 1940, pp. 13, 17. See also P. Phelan, 'The Ceremony of Consecration of a Bishop', *Australian Catholic Truth Society Record*, 22 May 1954. Beovich, wearing his mitre, is among a group of bishops pictured on the front cover.

39 *Southern Cross*, 12 April 1940, p. 11.

40 *Advertiser*, 8 April 1940, p. 7.

41 Note to Good Samaritan Archivists from Sister Camilla Gall, passed on to the author, 15 February 2000.

42 *Advocate*, 4 April 1940, p. 7.

43 Interview, 19 February 1998.

44 Made of white wool, from lambs blessed in the basilica of St Agnes in Rome on her feast day, the pallia are blessed on the feast day of Sts Peter and Paul and rest in an urn over the tomb of St Peter. Originally worn only by the pope himself, the custom of distributing pallia to archbishops dates back to at least the sixth century.

45 *Southern Cross*, 12 April 1940, supplement, iv.

46 ibid., 12 April 1940, p. 7.

47 ibid., 19 December 1941, p. 9; 26 November 1943, p. 3.

48 ibid., 12 April 1940, supp., p. viii.

49 ibid., p. viii. Beovich made a similar comment to an *Advertiser* journalist in an interview on Sunday evening: 'As well as archbishop, I have become a citizen of South Australia, and I trust I shall play my part as a good citizen in the civic welfare of this state.' *Advertiser*, 8 April 1940, p. 7.
50 *Southern Cross*, 19 April 1940, p. 9.
51 The Australian National Secretariat of Catholic Action had been established in Melbourne in 1937, and the Young Christian Workers' Movement (YCW) and the National Catholic Rural Movement soon afterward. See Bruce Duncan, *Crusade or Conspiracy?: Catholics and the Anti-Communist Struggle in Australia*, University of New South Wales Press, Sydney, 2001, pp. 22–23, 39.
52 *Southern Cross*, 14 April 1940, p. vi.
53 ibid, 12 April 1940, supplement, p. iv.
54 *Southern Cross*, 12 April, supplement vi.
55 He would remain vicar-general until his death in 1951. See *Southern Cross*, 3 March 1950, p. 11 and 15 June 1951, p. 7.
56 Darcy Woodards, 'Archbishop Beovich'. At Beovich's request, Woodards wrote an account of his work for the diocese in 1973. He died the following year. A typescript is in the ACAA.
57 In recognition of his many years of devoted service to the archdiocese, Beovich arranged for Woodards to receive the Cross of St Leo from Pius XII in 1946, and a papal knighthood from Pope John XXIII in 1960.
58 *Southern Cross*, 19 April 1940, p. 9; 10 May, p. 13; 31 May, p. 7.
59 ibid., 19 April, p. 7; 26 April, p. 9.
60 ibid., 26 April, p. 4; 31 May, p. 15.
61 ibid., 17 May, p. 9.
62 ibid., 24 May, pp. 9, 17.
63 ibid., 17 May, p. 15; 7 June, p. 7.
64 ibid., 17 May, p. 14.
65 ibid., 3 May, p. 11.
66 The report in the *Southern Cross* on 10 May, p. 11, did not mention the number. There were 222 babies in 1947 – a record year. *Southern Cross*, 30 May 1947, p. 7.
67 ibid., 17 May, p. 9.
68 ibid., 3 May, p. 4; 7 June, p. 9.
69 ibid., 3 May, p. 17; 7 June, p. 11.
70 ibid., 31 May, p. 11.
71 See Gavin Brown, 'Mass Performance: A Study of Eucharistic Ritual in Australian Catholic Culture, 1900–1962', Ph.D. thesis, University of Melbourne, 2003.
72 Diary, 23 May 1940. Notes of the meeting with the apostolic delegate and the bishop of Port Augusta on 10 April 1940 are in the ACAA.
73 Diary, 30 May 1940.
74 Diary, 18 April and 16 May 1940.
75 Diary, 30 April and 23 May 1940.
76 Diary, 10 May 1940.
77 *Southern Cross*, 17 December 1943, p. 6.
78 Diary, 19 July and 23 July 1940.
79 B. Condon, 'All at Work in the Lord's Garden: The 1940 Act and Beyond' in *Dissent in Paradise: Religious Education Controversies in South Australia*, P. C. Almond and P. G. Woolcock, Murray Park College of Advanced Education, Adelaide, 1975, p. 21 ff.
80 See, for example, his speech at the annual concert at Sacred Heart College, *Southern Cross*, 6 September 1940, p. 9.
81 ibid., p. 7.
82 John Bourke CFC, interview by the author, 10 February 2004; Healy, *Christian Brothers of Wakefield Street*, p. 162.
83 *Southern Cross*, 12 April 1940, supp. viii.
84 ibid., p. vi. Much of what follows can also be found in Josephine Laffin, '"Calling God Back to the Council Chambers': An Archbishop's Response to World War Two', *Journal of the Historical Society of South Australia*, no. 35, 2007, pp. 82–97.

85 ibid., 31 May 1940, p. 11.
86 Diary, 19 July 1940. For Hannan, see Margaret Press, *Colour and Shadow*, p. 50.
87 For a report of the event, see *Southern Cross*, 2 August 1940, p. 9. Beovich's address is in the ACAA.
88 *Southern Cross*, 10 January 1941, p. 9; 6 June 1941, p. 9. See also 31 October 1941, p. 7, 9. For similar statements in the United States, see Kathleen Riley, *Fulton J. Sheen*, Alba House, New York, 2004, pp. 117 ff.
89 Quoted in Stuart Macintyre, *The Oxford History of Australia*, vol. 4: *The Succeeding Age, 1901–1942*, Oxford University Press, Melbourne, 1993, pp. 328–329.
90 *Southern Cross*, 30 January 1942, p. 9.
91 CUSA involved the Catholic Soldiers' Guild, the War Work Auxiliary of the Guild of Social Studies, and the Australia Club. See *Southern Cross*, 15 May 1942, p. 9; 29 May 1942, p. 7; 12 June 1942, p. 12.
92 ibid., 24 July 1942, p. 9.
93 Boland, *Duhig*, p. 313; Geoffrey Bolton, *The Oxford History of Australia*, vol. 5: *The Middle Way, 1942–1995*, 2nd ed., Oxford University Press, Melbourne, 1996, p. 17.
94 *Southern Cross*, 21 August 1942, p. 9.
95 ibid., 30 October 1942, p. 7; Ruth Schumann, '"Charity, Work, Loyalty": A History of the Catholic Women's League in South Australia: 1914–1979', BA Hons thesis, Flinders University, 1979, p. 63.
96 *Southern Cross*, 9 April 1943, p. 7.
97 Circular from Beovich to priests of the archdiocese of Adelaide, 22 July 1943.
98 Bolton, *The Middle Way*, p. 30.
99 *Pattern for Peace: Statement on Reconstruction Presented to the Federal Government on Behalf of the Catholic Community*, National Secretariat of Catholic Action, Melbourne, 1943. See also B. A. Santamaria, *Santamaria: A Memoir*, Oxford University Press, Melbourne, 1997, p. 81; Bruce Duncan, *Crusade or Conspiracy: Catholics and the Anti-Communist Struggle in Australia*, University of New South Wales Press, Sydney, 2001, pp. 54–56.
100 Transcript in ACAA. See also *Southern Cross*, 14 May 1943, p. 7; 21 May 1943, p. 7.
101 *Advertiser*, 11 May 1933, p. 3.
102 Diary, 12 September 1943. The transcript is in the ACAA. It was the first of a series of three talks. The moderator of the Presbyterian Church of Australia and the Anglican bishop of Newcastle were the other speakers.
103 Arnold D. Hunt, *This Side of Heaven: A History of Methodism in South Australia*, Lutheran Publishing House, Adelaide, 1985, pp. 356–357.
104 *Southern Cross*, 21 August 1942, p. 9.
105 ibid., 8 August 1948, p. 7.
106 Gerald Henderson, *Mr Santamaria and the Bishops*, Studies in the Christian Movement 7, St Patrick's College, Sydney, 1982, pp. 46–47.
107 Diary, 3 January 1942.
108 Diary, 11 and 12 May 1942.
109 Boland, *Duhig*, p. 302.
110 Diary, 3 January 1942, margin note.
111 Diary, 25 July 1943.
112 See Boland, *Duhig*, p. 307. Gilroy sent a draft of his cable to Churchill and Roosevelt to all bishops before the final version was sent. In addition to Duhig, the archbishop of Hobart and the bishop of Rockhampton dissented. Four other bishops did not reply.
113 Circular to Priests, 24 March 1944.
114 Boland, *Duhig*, pp. 307–308.
115 Circular to Priests, 24 March 1944.
116 *Southern Cross*, 14 April 1944, p. 1.
117 *Advertiser*, 10 April, 1944, p. 6.
118 Diary, 9 April 1944.
119 Woodards, 'Archbishop Beovich', 1973, typescript in ACAA.
120 *Advertiser*, 8 April, p. 6.
121 Beovich to Panico, 7 December 1944.

122 'Visit to Italian Prisoners of War in South Australia', a report prepared by Beovich for the apostolic delegate, 6 June 1944.
123 'Informal Meeting of Members of the Hierarchy Assembled in Adelaide on the Occasion of the Centenary of the Church in SA'.
124 Letter from Modotti to Beovich, undated.
125 Anthony Cappello, 'Rome or Ireland?: The Religious Control of the Italian Community', *Journal of the Australian Catholic Historical Society*, vol. 23, 2002, pp. 59–72.
126 Diary, 8 November 1944.
127 Boland, *Duhig*, p. 211.
128 ibid., p. 305.
129 He wrote in his diary on 25 April 1944, after another meeting of the hierarchy: 'The Delegate adds to his stature as a priest and a diplomat. I am sorry Dr Mannix did not make the journey.'
130 Panico to Beovich, 14 August 1945; Beovich to Panico, 23 August 1945.
131 Diary, 15 April 1040; James Gleeson, 'The Church in Adelaide during My Years as a Priest and Bishop', *ACR*, vol. 65, no. 3, 1988, p. 292.
132 Diary, 5 November 1942; 22 June 1943; 11 November 1943. Robin was the Anglican bishop of Adelaide from 1941 to 1956. See David Hilliard, *Godliness and Good Order: A History of the Anglican Church in South Australia*, Wakefield Press, Adelaide, 1986, p. 115.
133 See Adrian Hastings, *A History of English Christianity, 1920–1990*, SCM Press, London, 1991, pp. 392–395.
134 Letter from Gilroy to Beovich, 11 June 1943, and Beovich's reply of 15 June. Attached is a clipping from a Sydney paper with the statement, including the additions. In the following sentence, Beovich's contribution appears in italics: 'All who profess the Christian Faith, *without compromising their own doctrines*, possess, nevertheless, in the virtue of Love and Charity common ground on which to rally *for the recognition and defence of Christian influence in national and international affairs*.'
135 For the text of the statement, see *Southern Cross*, 19 November 1943, p. 7; for a report on the gathering in the Town Hall, see *Southern Cross*, 10 December, 1943, p. 7; Gleeson, 'The Church in Adelaide During My Years as a Priest and Bishop', p, 292.
136 See Katharine Massam and John H. Smith, 'Images of God: Civil Religion and Australia at War, 1939–1945', *Australian Religion Studies Review*, vol. 11, no. 2, 1998, pp. 57–71.
137 Circular to Priests, 5 May 1945.
138 Gleeson, 'The Church in Adelaide During My Years as a Priest and Bishop', p. 293.
139 'Mankind must clear its heart of bitterness and hatred, for the essence of the Christian life was love of God and of neighbour. And our neighbour was all mankind. Hatred could only beget war, not peace.' *Advertiser*, 17 August 1945, p. 7.
140 *Southern Cross*, 14 September 1945, p. 3.
141 Boland, *Duhig*, pp. 315–316.
142 Gilchrist, *Mannix*, p. 186.
143 Bolton, *The Middle Way*, p. 19.
144 Boland referring to Gilroy, but Beovich was more outspoken in his condemnation of the Allied bombing raids. Boland, 'Gilroy', *ADB*, vol. 14, p. 277.
145 *Southern Cross*, 2 April 1965, p. 2.

Chapter Five 'A Benevolent Father'

1 The original document is in the ACAA. An English translation can be found in the *Southern Cross*, 12 April 1940, supplement vi.
2 Edward Mulvihill, 'My Recollections of Archbishop Matthew Beovich', typescript given to author, 19 June 2002; also Brian Jackson, interview by author, 15 January 2004.
3 Notes for Christmas sermon, 25 December 1949 (there is a box with Beovich's surviving sermon notes in the ACAA).
4 Transcript of radio broadcast, 17 March 1946.
5 Notes for Easter Sunday sermon, 1948.
6 Notes for Feast of Christ the King, 27 October 1946.
7 *Southern Cross*, 17 December 1943, p. 9.

8 See B. A. Santamaria, *Daniel Mannix*, Melbourne University Press, Melbourne, 1984, p. 148; John Luttrell, 'Norman Thomas Cardinal Gilroy as Archbishop of Sydney', PhD Thesis, University of Sydney, 1997, pp. 67–71.
9 Matthew Beovich's Diary [hereafter Diary], 14 July 1940.
10 'Procedures at Canonical Visitation', undated but in the 'Circulars to Priests' folder for 1940, ACAA.
11 Although Beovich made several attempts to learn to drive a car, he never persevered. Keith Koen, interview by author, 9 April 1998; William Kelly, interview by author, 21 January 1998.
12 Keith Koen, 9 April 1998.
13 Imelda Kempsen, telephone conversation with the author, 12 September 2003.
14 Thomas Horgan, interview by author, 23 September 1997; William Kelly, 21 January 1998.
15 See, for example, *Southern Cross*, 15 November, 1940, p. 7; 22 November 1940, p. 7.
16 Morrison to Beovich, 1 October 1942.
17 Statistics supplied by Morrison in his visitation booklet, 25–27 September 1942.
18 *Southern Cross*, 2 October 1942, p. 9.
19 ibid., 6 November 1942, p. 5.
20 Diary, 22 May 1941.
21 Darcy Woodards, 'Archbishop Beovich', 1973, typescript in ACAA, p. 11.
22 Diary, 22 July 1942.
23 Circular to Priests, 15 May 1943.
24 For a list see Margaret Press, *Colour and Shadow*, Catholic Archdiocese of Adelaide, 1991, p. 229. 'Years of Consolidation' is the title of the chapter which covers this period in Edmund Campion, *Australian Catholics*, Aurora Books, Melbourne, 1987.
25 *Southern Cross*, 20 September 1940, p. 9.
26 Sister M. Margaret to Beovich, 10 May 1948.
27 Diary, 2 November 1917.
28 Kelly, 21 January 1998.
29 *Southern Cross*, 2 April 1965, p. 23.
30 Mulvihill, 'My Recollections'.
31 Horgan, 23 September 1997.
32 Mulvihill, 'My Recollections'.
33 W. T. Southerwood, *The Wisdom of Guilford Young*, Stella Maris Books, Hobart, 1989, p. 711.
34 James Gleeson, 'The Church in Adelaide During my Years as a Priest and Bishop', *Australasian Catholic Record* [hereafter *ACR*], vol. 65, no. 3, 1988, p. 297.
35 James Gleeson, interview by author, 8 October 1997. See Stewart Cockburn, *Playford: Benevolent Despot*, Axiom, Adelaide, 1991.
36 For an account of this from a bishop's perspective, see John C. Heenan, *A Crown of Thorns: An Autobiography, 1951–1963*, Hodder & Staughton, London, 1974, p. 26.
37 Interviews by author: Leonard Faulkner (27 August 2002), Thomas Horgan (23 September 1997) and Vincent Tiggeman (16 May 2002).
38 Faulkner, 27 August 2002.
39 Horgan, 23 September 1997.
40 The two curates were Peter Ward and Neil Kelly. Ward remembered the incident in his tribute to Kelly after Kelly's death. *Southern Cross*, November 2002, p. 23.
41 Peter Travers, interview by author, 28 November 2002.
42 Beovich to Morrison, 12 June 1945; Morrison to Beovich, 21 June 1945.
43 Kelly, 21 January 1998.
44 Before Leonard Faulkner went to study in Rome in 1946, Beovich asked if he drank alcohol. 'I said: 'No, Your Grace, I am a member of the Total Abstinence Society.' And he said: 'Not any more, you are not! You will drink what is put on the table in Rome. It is an important aspect of the diet.' Interview, 27 August 2002.
45 Horgan, 23 September 1997.
46 Mulvihill, 'My Recollections'.
47 *Southern Cross*, 2 April 1965, p. 23.
48 ibid.

49 Woodards, 'Archbishop Beovich', p. 3.
50 Horgan, 23 September 1997.
51 Travers, 28 November 2002.
52 In 1950 the statistics were: 9 Jesuits, 5 Carmelites, 7 Dominicans, 8 Sacred Heart Fathers, 7 Passionists, 3 Salesians and 2 Franciscans, 20 Christian Brothers and 29 Marist Brothers, 201 Sisters of St Joseph, 107 Dominican Sisters, 125 Sisters of Mercy, 45 Dominican Sisters, 5 Sisters of the Good Samaritan, 26 Loreto Sisters, 8 Sisters of Our Lady of the Sacred Heart, 18 Little Sisters of the Poor, 16 Carmelite Nuns, 10 Sisters of the Good Shepherd, and 42 Nursing Sisters of the Little Company of Mary.
53 *Southern Cross*, 2 April 1965, p. 24.
54 ibid.
55 Helen Northey, *Living the Truth*, Holy Cross Congregation of Dominican Sisters, Adelaide, 1999, pp. 147, 224–225.
56 Documents relating to the amalgamation are in the ACAA. Peter Travers recalls being told by Monsignor Bayard, parish priest of Naracoorte at the time, that Beovich had bullied the sisters into agreeing to the amalgamation. Interview, 28 November 2002. See also Anne McLay, *Women on the Move*, Sisters of Mercy, Adelaide, 1996, pp. 238–246.
57 A brief history of the South Australian province of the Sisters of St Joseph of the Sacred Heart can be found at www.sosj.org.au/about/south_australia/history.html.
58 Robert Wilkinson, interview by author, 11 June 2002.
59 For a brief history of the Institute, see Press, *Colour and Shadow*, pp. 38–39; Pauline Payne, *Thebarton Old and New*, Thebarton City Council, Adelaide, 1996, p. 120; and Peter Donovan, *Between the City and the Sea: A History of West Torrens from Settlement in 1836 to the Present Day*, Wakefield Press, Adelaide, 1986, pp. 92–93, 159–160. There are also two unpublished essays in the ACAA: Tim Costelloe, 'A Study of the History of the Institute of the Brothers of St John the Baptist', BTh essay, undated but presented to the ACAA in 1986; and Anthony Moester, 'The Salesians of Don Bosco at Brooklyn Park, 1943–1998', 1998. All treat the brothers quite gently. Anthony Michael Keenan takes a slightly more critical stance in 'The Boys' Reformatory at Brooklyn Park: A History 1898–1941', M.Ed. thesis, University of Adelaide, 1988.
60 *Southern Cross*, 19 April 1940, p. 7.
61 Correspondence from two brothers to Beovich, dated 8 June 1940 and 17 June 1940, is in the ACAA. Beovich also wrote an account of his dealings with the brothers of St John the Baptist to send to Rome in 1948. [Hereafter it will be referred to as Beovich, 1948.]
62 'Report of Very Rev. P. McCabe MSC on Brothers of St John the Baptist', 30 March 1941.
63 Diary, 14 August 1942; Beovich, 1948.
64 The indults of secularisation are dated 21 and 25 August 1942 respectively.
65 Beovich to John Panico, 18 December 1942. Panico granted permission for the transfers and ruled that the institute should not be permitted to receive any new members. Panico to Beovich, 24 December 1942.
66 Panico to Beovich, 8 January 1948.
67 Ted Cooper, *Grateful Heirs: The Story of the Salesian Presence in Australia, 1927–1967*, Salesians of Don Bosco, Melbourne, 1999, p. 206.
68 Paul Marella to Beovich, 7 September 1951.
69 Beovich to Marella, 18 September 1951.
70 Statistics for the number of inmates at each institution are in the *Australasian Catholic Directory*, Pellegrini, Sydney, 1940, p. 283.
71 *Southern Cross*, 6 December 1940, p. 11; ibid., 16 May 1941, p. 9.
72 Beovich's own copy of the *Catholic Directory* for 1942 with the most recent figures added in his handwriting.
73 *Southern Cross*, 10 October 1941.
74 James Gleeson, 'History of the Diocesan Charities Appeal', draft prepared in 1987, ACAA.
75 Woodards, 'Archbishop Beovich', p. 6; Diary, 8 June 1941; 31 August 1941; circular to priests, 16 October 1941; *Southern Cross*, 5 September 1941; 22 January 1943; Gleeson, 'History of the Diocesan Charities Appeal', p. 1.
76 Gleeson, 'History of the Diocesan Charities Appeal', p. 2.

77 The historical background to the development of the Catholic Welfare Bureau is summarised by Peter D. Travers in 'Planning in a Church Welfare Agency', Master of Social Administration thesis, Flinders University, 1979, pp. 2–3.
78 *Southern Cross*, 12 December 1941, p. 13.
79 Travers, 'Planning in a Church Welfare Agency', p. 3. See also Brian Dickey, *Rations, Residence, Resources: A History of Social Welfare in South Australia Since 1836*, Wakefield Press, Adelaide, 1986, p. 248.
80 Travers, 'Planning in a Church Welfare Agency', pp. 3–4.
81 ibid., p. 4.
82 ibid., p. 25.
83 Extract from the Brooklyn Park Salesian House Chronicle, cited by Anthony Moester in his unpublished essay in the ACAA, 'The Salesians of Don Bosco at Brooklyn Park'.
84 Diary, 31 July 1946; *Southern Cross*, 2 August 1946, p. 7; 9 August 1946, p. 7.
85 Commonwealth of Australia, *Official Committee Hansard: Senate Community Affairs References Committee, 16 March 2001*, CA 308.
86 McLay, *Women on the Move*, p. 204.
87 ibid., p. 206.
88 Diary, 20 July 1941; *Southern Cross*, 25 July 1941, p. 9.
89 Northey, *Living the Truth*, p. 259.
90 William David Waterford, 'The Content and Extent of Catholic Boys' Secondary Schooling in the Archdiocese of Adelaide 1930–1950: A Study of Social and Ecclesial Factors', M.Ed. thesis, Flinders University, 1994, pp. 63–66.
91 *Southern Cross*, 30 January 1942, p. 9.
92 ibid., 29 January 1943, p. 7.
93 A talk given to the Dominican Sisters at Cabra Convent, 29 December 1945.
94 Gleeson, 'The Church in Adelaide During My Years as a Priest and Bishop', p. 294.
95 Gleeson, 8 October 1997.
96 For a more detailed history of the seminary, see Margaret Press, *St Francis Xavier Seminary*, St Francis Xavier Seminary, Adelaide, 1992.
97 Notes of the initial meeting on 10 April are in the ACAA.
98 Diary, 23 May 1940.
99 The Beovich-Prendiville correspondence is in the ACAA. Press claims that Prendiville did not like Johnston and so was not sorry to lose him. Press, *St Francis Xavier Seminary*, p. 9.
100 ibid., p. 15.
101 The other two were Louis Travers and Patrick Molloy, in addition to Johnston, James Bourke and Thomas Horgan.
102 Press, *St Francis Xavier Seminary*, p. 111.
103 ibid., p. 112.
104 Diary, 1 December 1956.
105 Some were recalled by Alan Commins CM (rector 1964–1975), interview by author, 20 January 1998.
106 David Shinnick, 'Memoirs', vol. 1, 'Youthful Yearnings and Beyond, 1930–1970', typescript in ACAA, pp. 77, 101.
107 For the history of Aquinas College, see Michael Head, *Fire on the Hill*, Aquinas College, Adelaide, 2002, pp. 5–22.
108 Hannan to Beovich, 10 April 1940.
109 Diary, 7 June 1940.
110 Diary, 26 November 1941; Minutes of the meeting, in Beovich's handwriting, ACAA; Head, *Fire on the Hill*, p. 23.
111 Mignon Hannan, interview by Michael Head, 15 June 1999, *Fire on the Hill*, p. 23.
112 Diary, 24 January 1947.
113 Head, *Fire on the Hill*, p. 29.
114 Diary, 28 August 1948; Head, *Fire on the Hill*, pp. 31–32.
115 Woodards, 'Archbishop Beovich', p. 5.
116 Diary, 22 December 1948.

117 Bruce Duncan, *Crusade or Conspiracy?*, University of New South Wales Press, Sydney, 2001, p. 132.
118 See Katharine Massam's account in *Making Space*, ed. Fay Gale, St Aloysius College, Adelaide, 2000, pp. 106–109.
119 See Massam, *Sacred Threads*, University of New South Wales Press, Sydney, 1996, pp. 234, 236.
120 Beovich attempted to reassure those disappointed by the change that 'the name only is changed; the work will be the same, but by the change of name you will more perfectly fulfill the wishes of the Holy Father'. *Southern Cross*, 28 March 1947, p. 10.
121 Bernard Moriarty, *Fifty Years of Therry, 1943–1993*, Therry Dramatic Society, Adelaide, 1993, p. 1.
122 Edith Egan, one of the original members of the society, telephone conversation with the author, 16 December 2005.
123 For women's involvement in the Church, see Anne O'Brien, *God's Willing Workers: Women and Religion in Australia*, University of New South Wales Press, Sydney, 2005; Sally Kennedy, *Faith and Feminism*, Studies in the Christian Movement 9, St Patrick's College, Sydney, 1985.
124 Luttrell, 'Norman Thomas Cardinal Gilroy', pp. 132–136.
125 Patricia Pieterek, telephone conversation with the author, 17 July 2003.
126 *Southern Cross*, 23 August 1940, p. 9.
127 ibid., 18 October 1940, p. 9.
128 ibid., 20 September 1940, p. 7.
129 Beovich's correspondence in 1946 with Father K. O'Hannan, chaplain of the guild, is in the ACAA.
130 *Southern Cross*, 23 August 1940, p. 9.
131 ibid., 2 April 1965, p. 35. 'There is so much good in people,' Beovich told Ruth Schumann in an interview on 14 August 1979. "'Charity, Work, Loyalty": A History of the Catholic Women's League in South Australia', B.A. Hons thesis, Flinders University, 1979, p. 59.
132 Remembered by many people, including Patrick Kelly. *Southern Cross*, 2 April 1965, p. 35.
133 Woodards, 'Archbishop Beovich', p. 10.
134 *Southern Cross*, 2 April 1965, p. 35.
135 Faulkner, 27 August 2003.
136 Interviews with Gleeson, Faulkner, Horgan, Commins and Travers.
137 Woodards, 'Archbishop Beovich', pp. 1–2.
138 Faulkner, 27 August 2002.
139 See the special issue of the *Southern Cross*, 2 April 1965.
140 Mulvihill, 19 June 2002.
141 Diary, 4 September 1942.
142 Diary, 15 May 1943.
143 Diary, 27 May 1943; 13 September 1943. Vincent Tiggeman recalls Beovich telling him that he changed his mind 'because he didn't think his successors would thank him for refusing to accept such a wonderful gift'. Note to the author, September 2005.
144 His official coat of arms also highlighted his Irish ancestry, with three crests from the Kenny armorial device. See *Southern Cross*, 5 April 1940, p. 1.
145 *Advertiser*, 16 March 2004, p. 9.
146 Diary, 21 and 23 January 1958; *Southern Cross*, 8 June 1945, p. 7; 3 August 1945, p. 3 (50th anniversary of ordination); 13 May, 1955, p. 7 (83rd birthday); 31 January 1958, p. 1 (death). See also David Hilliard, *Catholics in Kingswood*, Kingswood Catholic Parish Pastoral Council, 1994, pp. 28–29.
147 Horgan, 23 September 1997.
148 ibid.
149 James Gleeson, 8 October 1997; Keith Koen, 9 April 1998. Until 2003, when it was dispersed, Beovich's large collection of books was still in the study at Ennis. Almost a hundred boxes were taken away.
150 Adrian Hastings, *History of English Christianity, 1920–1990*, 3rd ed., SCM, London, 1991, pp. 483–484.

151 Koen, 9 April 1998.
152 Daniel Conquest, interview by author, 19 February 1998.
153 According to the 2001 census, the post code area of Koroit had the seventh highest percentage of Catholics in the nation (51.4 per cent). See Robert Dixon, *The Catholic Community in Australia*, Openbook, Adelaide, 2005, p. 63.
154 J. J. Russell, *Journey in Faith: Koroit Catholic Parish, 1886–1986*, Timothy J. Auld, Koroit, Victoria, 1986, pp. 8, 10.
155 ibid., p. 10.
156 Koen, 9 April 1998.
157 Letter to the author, 21 August 1997.
158 Laurie Bayliss, interview by John Luttrell, 'Norman Thomas Cardinal Gilroy', p. 291.
159 Robert Rice, interview by author, 16 November 2004.
160 Norman Gilroy, quoted by Edmund Campion, *Great Australian Catholics*, Viking, Melbourne, 1987, p. 68.
161 'Relatio: Facta ab Archiepiscopo Adelaidensi de Diocesi Adelaidensi in Australia Meridionali Anno 1950', p. 4, ACAA.

Chapter Six 'A Dangerous Experiment'

1 The most comprehensive recent work is Bruce Duncan, *Crusade or Conspiracy?: Catholics and the Anti-Communist Struggle in Australia*, University of New South Wales Press, Sydney, 2001. See also Ross Fitzgerald, *The Pope's Battalions: Santamaria, Catholicism and the Labor Split*, University of Queensland Press, Brisbane, 2003; Gerard Henderson, *Mr Santamaria and the Bishops*, St Patrick's College, Manly, Sydney, 1982; Paul Ormonde, *The Movement*, Thomas Nelson, Melbourne, 1972; and Robert Murray, *The Split*, Cheshire, Melbourne, 1970. For Santamaria's own account, see his autobiography, *Against the Tide*, Oxford University Press, Melbourne, 1981, and the revised edition, *Santamaria: A Memoir*, Oxford University Press, Melbourne, 1997. Collections of conference papers can be found in Brian Costar, Peter Love & Paul Strangio, eds, *The Great Labor Schism*, Scribe Publications, Melbourne, 2005; and *50 Years of the Santamaria Movement*, Eureka Street Papers no. 1, Jesuit Publications, Melbourne, 1992.
2 Patrick O'Farrell, *Vanished Kingdoms*, New South Wales University Press, Sydney, 1990, pp. 277–279; Santamaria, *Santamaria: A Memoir*, pp. 177–178.
3 Duncan, *Crusade or Conspiracy?*, pp. 389–393. See also Henderson, *Mr Santamaria and the Bishops*, pp. 164–166.
4 Santamaria, *Santamaria: A Memoir*, p. 4.
5 ibid., p. 8.
6 Edmund Campion, 'Irish Religion in Australia', *Australasian Catholic Record*, vol. 55, no. 1, 1978, p. 11.
7 See Katharine Massam, *Sacred Threads*, University of New South Wales Press, Sydney, 1996, p. 195.
8 See Henderson, *Mr Santamaria and the Bishops*, pp. 156–158.
9 *Southern Cross*, 3 September 1943, p. 7.
10 There is some confusion as to when the Movement actually began. Santamaria himself gave a number of dates ranging from 1937 to 1945. See Henderson, 'B. A. Santamaria, Santamarianism and the Cult of Personality', *50 Years of the Santamaria Movement*, p. 46.
11 Santamaria to Beovich, 22 July 1944.
12 See, for example, B. A. Santamaria, *The Price of Freedom*, Melbourne, 1964, p. 58; idem, *Daniel Mannix*, Melbourne University Press, Melbourne, 1984, p. 232; and *Santamaria: A Memoir*, p. 76.
13 The memorandum was quoted in 'The Social Studies Movement, Sydney, Australia, October 1956', p. 6. This was the submission prepared for the pope and Vatican officials by the bishops who had become opposed to the Movement in 1956. Beovich's copy is in the ACAA. For the 1945 meeting, see also Duncan, *Crusade or Conspiracy?*, p. 73 ff.
14 Santamaria, *Santamaria: A Memoir*, p. 74.
15 See Fitzgerald, *The Pope's Battalions*, pp. 71–72.

16 See John Warhurst, '"The Communist Bogey": Communism as an Election Issue in Australian Federal Politics, 1949–1964', PhD thesis, Flinders University, 1977, pp. 38–42.
17 See Massam, *Sacred Threads*, p. 92; and Thomas Kselman and Steven Avella, 'Marian Piety and the Cold War in the United States', *Catholic Historical Review*, vol. 72, 1986, pp. 403–424.
18 John Maguire, *Prologue: A History of the Catholic Church as Seen From Townsville, 1863–1983*, Church Archivists' Society, Toowoomba, 1990, p. 153.
19 From Santamaria's memorandum to the bishops in 1945, quoted in Duncan, *Crusade or Conspiracy?*, p. 81.
20 Santamaria, *Santamaria: A Memoir*, p. 137.
21 See Ormonde, *The Movement*, pp. 20–22; and Edmund Campion, 'A Question of Loyalties', *50 Years of the Santamaria Movement*, pp. 10–12.
22 Campion, 'A Question of Loyalties', p. 10,
23 Ormonde, *The Movement*, p. 162.
24 'The Twelve Months Plan', undated and unsigned document in Beovich's papers, probably circa 1945.
25 For a South Australian man's reminiscences of his involvement in the Movement as the 'census officer' responsible for collecting details of trade union membership, see David Shinnick, 'Memoirs', vol. 1, 'Youthful Yearnings and Beyond', typescript in the ACAA, p. 142.
26 Henderson, *Mr Santamaria and the Bishops*, p. 172; Fitzgerald, *The Pope's Battalions*, p. 95; and Warhurst, 'Communist Bogey', p. 41.
27 See, for example, Murray, *The Split*, p. 18; and Henderson, *Mr Santamaria and the Bishops*, p. 102.
28 Fitzgerald, *The Pope's Battalions*, p. 289. See also Ross McMullin, *The Light on the Hill: The Australian Labor Party 1891–1991*, Oxford University Press, Melbourne, 1991, p. 269.
29 Malcolm Saunders, 'The Labor Party and the Industrial Groups in South Australia 1946–1955: Precluding the Split', *Journal of the Historical Society of South Australia*, vol. 33, 2005, p. 74.
30 ibid., pp. 77–79.
31 See P. Duffy, 'Catholic Judgments on the Origins and Growth of the Australian Labor Party Dispute, 1954–1961', MA thesis, University of Melbourne, 1967. Warhurst cites these figures in 'Communist Bogey', p. 78.
32 Like many internal Movement documents in Beovich's papers in the ACAA, this one is unsigned and has no date. It was probably written by Farrell for Beovich in 1957.
33 Saunders, 'The Labor Party and the Industrial Groups', pp. 73 ff. See also Malcolm Saunders and Neil Lloyd, 'Remembering the Past and Hoping for the Future: why there was no Labor split in South Australia in 1954–1956', *The Great Labor Schism*, pp. 76–94.
34 Santamaria, *Santamaria: A Memoir*, p. 86.
35 Saunders and Lloyd, 'Remembering the Past', p. 84.
36 *Southern Cross*, 16 April 1948, p. 7.
37 ibid., 8 November 1957, p. 4.
38 In *The Movement* (p. 17), Paul Ormonde quoted from the letter without naming the bishop. He referred to the author as 'a country priest'. He gave the full text in 'The Movement: Politics By Remote Control', in *Santamaria: The Politics of Fear*, Paul Ormonde, ed., Spectrum Publications, Melbourne, 2000, p. 182.
39 Duncan, *Crusade or Conspiracy?*, pp. 125, 170; Fitzgerald, p. 77. See also David Strong, 'Lalor, Harold', *The Australian Dictionary of Jesuit Biography*, Halstead Press, Sydney, 1999, p. 188.
40 See, for example, a report of Beovich's address to the Legacy Club of South Australia. *Southern Cross*, 15 August 1947, p. 7.
41 *Southern Cross*, 28 May 1948, p. 1. For Fulton Sheen, see Kathleen Riley, *Fulton J. Sheen*, Alba House, New York, 2004, especially chapter 5.
42 *Southern Cross*, 22 September 1944, p. 11; 11 May 1951, p. 7.
43 Patrick Morgan, ed., *B. A. Santamaria: Your Most Obedient Servant, Selected Letters: 1938–1996*, Miegunyah Press, Melbourne, 2007.

44 Minutes of the meetings of the episcopal committee are in the ACAA. A note from Santamaria attached to the 24 October 1946 minutes mentions the difficulties which had arisen over the previous two years between ANSCA and the Catholic Action bodies. See also Duncan, *Crusade or Conspiracy?*, pp. 99–101.
45 Minutes of meeting, 7–8 April 1948; also Matthew Beovich's Diary, 8 April 1948.
46 Minutes of meeting, 15 March 1949.
47 See Duncan, *Crusade or Conspiracy?*, pp. 130–132.
48 ibid., pp. 98–99.
49 Diary, 24 December 1945.
50 Niall Brennan, *Dr Mannix*, Rigby, Adelaide, 1964, p. 316.
51 See Arthur Calwell, *Be Just and Fear Not*, Rigby, Adelaide, 1978, p. 128.
52 *Tribune*, 30 May 1946; Michael Gilchrist, *Daniel Mannix*, 2nd ed., Freedom Publishing, Melbourne, 2004, p. 189.
53 Diary, 18–20 May, 1946; *Southern Cross*, 24 May 1946, p. 1.
54 *L'Osservatore Romano*, 2 September 1944; *Acta Apostolicae Sedis*, vol. 36, 1944, pp. 252–254; Jan Olav Smit, *Pope Pius XII*, Burns & Oates, London, 1949, pp. 268; Michael Chinigo, ed., *The Teaching of Pope Pius XII*, Methuen, London, 1958, pp. 335–336.
55 A copy of the letter and the draft statement are in the ACAA. See also Duncan, *Crusade or Conspiracy?*, pp. 112–121.
56 Thomas Boland, *James Duhig*, University of Queensland Press, Brisbane, 1986, p. 327.
57 Chifley to Gilroy, 4 October 1948, ACAA.
58 Clyde Cameron, *The Confessions of Clyde Cameron, 1913–1990*, ABC Enterprises, Sydney, 1990, p. 91.
59 See Warhurst, 'The Communist Bogey', p. 126.
60 *Advertiser*, 12 October 1948.
61 Boland, *Duhig*, pp. 149–152.
62 Cameron, *Confessions*, p. 81. See also Jenny Stock, 'The Role of Religion in the 1951 Referendum to Ban the Communist Party: the South Australian Example', *Australian Religion Studies Review*, vol. 11, 1998, pp. 49–51.
63 Diary, 9 November 1949.
64 Stewart Cockburn, *Playford*, Axiom, Adelaide, 1991, p. 223.
65 Shinnick, 'Youthful Yearnings', p. 143,
66 Morgan, *Your Most Obedient Servant*, pp. 558–559.
67 Personal statement (undated) from Santamaria to members of the Episcopal Committee on Catholic Action, including quotations from a letter from Mannix to Santamaria dated 13 December 1948.
68 Quoted in Henderson, *Mr Santamaria and the Bishops*, p. 160.
69 See Henderson, *Mr Santamaria and the Bishops*, chapter 6.
70 Santamaria, *Santamaria: A Memoir*, p. 44
71 Minutes of meeting, 3 April 1951.
72 Morgan, *Your Most Obedient Servant*, p. 75. See also Phillip Dreery, 'Santamaria, the Movement and the Split: A Re-examination', *Journal of the Australian Catholic Historical Society*, vol. 22, 2001, p. 53. In 1953 Santamaria claimed that there were 14 members of the Movement in the Cain government.
73 Diary, 18 December 1952.
74 Extracts were included as an appendix to 'The Social Studies Movement'. For the story behind the *Bombay Examiner* article, see Duncan, *Crusade or Conspiracy?*, pp. 188–194, 263–266.
75 The document is now in David Shinnick's papers in the ACAA.
76 The typescript of the lecture on 29 July 1953 is in the ACAA.
77 Minutes, 17 November 1953.
78 The typescript for the lecture is in the ACAA.
79 Beovich to Arthur Fox, April 1954. For the dispute over the 1954 statement, see Henderson, *Mr Santamaria and the Bishops*, pp. 85–91.
80 Minutes, 28–29 April 1954.
81 Minutes, 23 September 1954.

82 For example, Brian McKinlay repeatedly refers to Santamaria's Movement as 'the Catholic Action Movement' in his *A Centenary of Struggle: The ALP*, Collins Dove, Melbourne, 1988.
83 O'Collins to Beovich, 17 September 1954; 'Financial Statement Presented by Bishop of Ballarat, 1954–1955'.
84 Cameron, *Confessions*, pp. 103–104.
85 ibid., p. 104.
86 Santamaria, *Santamaria: A Memoir*, p. 167.
87 Cameron, *Confessions*, p. 104.
88 *Advertiser*, 12 August 1954, p. 1. See also *Advertiser*, 9 August 1954, p. 3; and *Southern Cross*, 13 August 1954, p. 7.
89 For recent summaries, see Peter Love, 'The Great Labor Split of 1955: An Overview' in *The Great Labor Schism*, pp. 1–20; and Fitzgerald, *The Pope's Battalions*, pp. 108–148. Contrary to a widespread belief that Evatt was mentally ill, Phillip Dreery argues that he 'acted rationally in response to a generally perceived threat', 'Santamaria, The Movement and the Split: A Re-examination', pp. 47–58.
90 Diary, 8 October 1956.
91 Diary, 23 December 1954.
92 See Duncan, *Crusade or Conspiracy?*, pp. 206 ff.
93 Diary, 23 December 1954.
94 For example, John Hepworth, 'The Movement Revisited: A South Australian Perspective', BA Hons thesis, University of Adelaide, 1982, p. 102.
95 *Southern Cross*, 20 March 1955, p. 7.
96 Beovich, interview by John Warhurst, 26 June 1974, cited in Warhurst, 'The Communist Bogey', p. 318.
97 Duncan, *Crusade or Conspiracy?*, p. 258.
98 Minutes, 20–21 April, 1955.
99 'The Social Studies Movement', pp. 17–18.
100 Farrell to Santamaria, 17 April 1956.
101 ibid.
102 See Geraldine Little, 'The Democratic Labor Party in South Australia', BA Hons thesis, University of Adelaide, 1968, p. 17 ff. Little interviewed Beovich in 1968.
103 He outlined what he told Farrell and Gleeson 'a few days ago' in his diary on 12 November 1955. He subsequently elaborated on his reasons in a speech to the bishops' conference in January 1956 (notes in the ACAA) and in his report to the apostolic delegate on the Movement crisis dated 9 October 1956.
104 His address to the Knights of the Southern Cross on 21 December 1955 is in the ACAA.
105 Diary, 12 November 1955.
106 *Southern Cross*, 18 November 1955, p. 7.
107 Janet McCalman, *Struggletown: Public and Private Life in Richmond, 1900–1965*, Melbourne University Press, Melbourne, 1984, p. 237.
108 Calwell, *Be Just*, p. 171. See also Niall Brennan, *The Politics of Catholics*, Hill Publishing, Melbourne, 1972, pp. 28 ff.
109 Boland, *Duhig*, p. 359. See also Maguire, *Prologue*, pp. 161, 218–219.
110 Beovich to Elizabeth Calwell, 12 November 1973.
111 Diary, 25 November 1955.
112 Cameron, *Confessions*, p. 91.
113 See John Warhurst, 'The Australian Labor Party (Anti-Communist) in South Australia, November–December, 1955: "Molotov" Labor Versus "Coffee Shop Labor"', *Labor History*, vol. 32, 1977, pp. 73–74.
114 Saunders and Lloyd, 'Remembering the Past', p. 89; P. L. Reynolds, *The Democratic Labor Party*, Jacaranda, Brisbane, 1974, p. 54; Dean Jaensch, 'Democratic Labor Party' in *The Wakefield Companion to South Australian History*, Wakefield Press, Adelaide, 2001, pp. 146–147; Little, 'The Democratic Labor Party', passim.
115 Saunders and Lloyd, 'Remembering the Past', p. 88.
116 ibid., p. 88.
117 *Southern Cross*, 30 September 1955, pp. 1, 3; 7 October 1955, pp. 3, 7.

118 Minutes, 17 November 1955.
119 Daniel Mannix, 'Statement for the Bishops Regarding the Social Studies Movement, 21 December 1955'.
120 His notes are in the ACAA.
121 Diary, 27 January 1956.
122 Minutes, 24–27 January 1956; Beovich to Carboni, 9 October 1956.
123 Diary, 24 March 1956.
124 Reply of members of the national executive to members of the episcopal committee on the Catholic Social Studies Movement, 24 March 1956.
125 Diary, 28 June 1956.
126 Diary, 5 July 1956.
127 For Carboni's support for Santamaria, see Duncan, *Crusade or Conspiracy?*, pp. 220, 250, 267–268, 288, 298, 301, 303, 359.
128 National officers and full-time officials of the Social Studies Movement to Beovich, 18 July 1956. All bishops received the letter.
129 Diary, 20 July 1956. Also Ted Farrell to 'Melbourne', 22 August 1956, based on a draft in Beovich's handwriting.
130 Santamaria to Beovich, 5 September 1956. Yet in a letter to James McAuley, c. 1 September 1955, Santamaria assured McAuley that Catholics could still join the reconstructed national movement, even if a diocese retained its own movement. See Duncan, *Crusade or Conspiracy?*, p. 301.
131 Santamaria, *Santamaria: A Memoir*, p. 167.
132 The correspondence is in the ACAA, along with a response from Farrell to Beovich, dated 24 October 1956, denying that there was 'a vacuum'.
133 John Kane, *Exploding the Myths*, Angus & Robertson, Sydney, 1989, p. 151.
134 O'Farrell, *Vanished Kingdoms*, p. 278.
135 Circular letter to the bishops, 2 August 1956.
136 Naughton and Nash to Carboni, 4 September 1957.
137 Carboni to Beovich, 7 September 1957.
138 'Summary' prepared 11 September 1957 to be sent with a letter from Beovich to Carboni, 30 September 1957.
139 Margret Mills, *Woman, Why Are You Weeping?*, Newsweekly Books, Melbourne, 1997, p. 35. See also Josephine Sheehan, 'Australian Catholics and the 1955 Split: A Micro-Study of Personal Experiences and Reminiscences', BA Hons thesis, Flinders University, 1988, p. 74.
140 Letter to author from R.W.S., 11 September 2005.
141 Cameron, *Confessions*, p. 104.
142 Diary, 29 September 1956; 17 October 1956.
143 Gilroy, Beovich, Duhig (Brisbane), O'Brien (Canberra-Goulburn), Simonds (coadjutor, Melbourne), O'Donnell (coadjutor, Brisbane), Norton (Bathurst), Farrelly (Lismore), Fox (Wilcannia-Forbes), McCabe (Wollongong), Cahill (Cairns), Toohey (Maitland), O'Loughlin (Darwin), Lyons and Carroll (Sydney auxiliary bishops).
144 Diary, 2 October 1956; Minutes, 2 October 1956. For an account of Bishop Ryan of Townsville's refusal to take part, see Maguire, *Prologue*, p. 162.
145 'The Social Studies Movement', p. 24.
146 ibid.
147 Carboni to Beovich, 4 October 1956; Beovich's response, 9 October, 1956. Beovich was directed to send six copies, one each for the pope, the Holy Office and the Congregation of Propaganda Fide, two for the Vatican secretariat of state and one for the archives of the delegation.
148 For the Democratic Party, formed in 1919, see Patrick O'Farrell, *The Catholic Church and Community*, 3rd ed., University of New South Wales Press, Sydney, 1992, pp. 346–348.
149 A copy of Carboni's address, delivered on 22 January 1957 at St Patrick's College, Manly, is in the ACAA.
150 Robert Wilkinson, interview by author, 11 June 2002.

151 Fumasoni-Biondi to Gilroy, 27 May 1957 and 25 July 1957. The latter was sent in error to Mannix, so there was some delay before Gilroy and Beovich saw it. See Duncan, *Crusade or Conspiracy?*, chapter 23.
152 Henderson, *Mr Santamaria and the Bishops*, p. 129.
153 Beovich to Gilroy, 3 September 1957.
154 Diary, 6 September 1957.
155 Carroll to Gleeson, 9 September 1957.
156 The envelope is now with Beovich's papers in the ACAA.
157 Minutes of meeting, 28–30 January, 1958; Diary, 30 January 1958.
158 Diary, 12 March 1958. A circular to priests summarising matters discussed at the conference on 12 March, dated 26 March 1958, is in the ACAA.
159 Diary, 25 March 1958.
160 David Shinnick, *Journey into Justice*, David Shinnick, Adelaide, 1982, p. 21. See also Shinnick, 'Youthful Yearnings', pp. 144–145.
161 Carroll to Gleeson, 5 October 1957.
162 A copy of a letter from Mannix to Gilroy, 19 August 1957, is in the ACAA, along with the response Mannix received from Rome, 3 November 1957.
163 Carroll to Gleeson, 2 December 1957; and Gleeson's reply, 9 December 1957.
164 Santamaria, *Santamaria: A Memoir*, p. 184.
165 The letter from Simonds to Beovich, dated 29 March 1958, is in the ACAA. For Simonds's perspective, see the chapter 'Turbulent Times' in Max Vodola, *Simonds*, Catholic Education Office, Melbourne, 1997, pp. 69–83.
166 See Henderson, *Mr Santamaria and the Bishops*, p. 138.
167 For the election, see Duncan, *Crusade or Conspiracy?*, pp. 353–358.
168 *Sydney Morning Herald*, 2 December 1958.
169 Diary, 15 March 1959.
170 Diary, 24 April 1962.
171 Thomas McCabe to Beovich, 8 September 1958. See also Henderson, *Mr Santamaria and the Bishops*, p. 131.
172 A point made in a report on a NCC meeting in Melbourne in April 1958, in Farrell's papers in the ACAA. It seems to have been prepared by Farrell for Beovich. See also 'Effects in South Australia of Work of Supporters of Mr. B.A. Santamaria (1955–1957)' and 'Survey: Division among Catholics – Work Hampered', another undated document in the ACAA.
173 Diary, 15 March 1959.
174 'Lacordaire', 'In the Tinsel World: Cardinal Gilroy's Temporal Dilemmas', *Nation*, 24 October 1959, p. 13. See also Duncan, *Crusade or Conspiracy?*, pp. 363–364.
175 Carroll to Beovich, 31 July 1959.
176 Diary, 31 August 1959.
177 Diary, 15 September 1959; 25 August 1961; 6 December 1956.
178 See Duncan, *Crusade or Conspiracy?*, pp. 373–374.
179 Toohey to Beovich, 27 June 1960.
180 Diary, 29 June 1960.
181 B.A. Santamaria, 'Religion and Politics: An Approach', *Twentieth Century*, 24, no. 4, 1960, pp. 352–369.
182 Diary, 4 September 1960. A copy of his talk is in the ACAA.
183 Diary, 29 July 1961; 5 August 1961; 19 August 1961; 25 August 1961. A copy of the address is also in the ACAA.
184 James Gleeson, interview by author, 8 October 1997.
185 William McCarthy, *James Patrick O'Collins*, Spectrum, Melbourne, 1996, p. 83.
186 Daniel Conquest to the author, 21 August 1997.

Chapter Seven 'A Flourishing Diocese'

1 Matthew Beovich's Diary [hereafter Diary], 31 May 1960.
2 'Relatio by the Archbishop for the Archdiocese of Adelaide in South Australia – 1960' (Beovich's report on the state of his diocese to the Holy See).

3 See especially David Hilliard, 'Popular Religion in Australia in the 1950s: A Study of Adelaide and Brisbane', *Journal of Religious History*, vol. 15, 1988, pp. 219–235; idem, 'God in the Suburbs: the Religious Culture of Australian Cities in the 1950s', *Australian Historical Studies*, vol. 24, 1991, pp. 399–419; idem, 'Church, Family and Sexuality in 1950s Australia', *Australian Historical Studies*, vol. 28, no. 109, 1997, pp. 133–146.

4 David J. O'Brien, 'When it all came together: Bishop John J. Wright and the diocese of Worcester, 1950–1959', *Catholic Historical Review*, vol. 85, no. 2, 1999, pp. 175–194.

5 Adrian Hastings, *A History of English Christianity, 1920–1990*, 3rd ed., SCM, London, 1991, p. 561.

6 See James Jupp, *Immigration*, Australian Retrospectives, Sydney University Press, 1991.

7 See Graeme Hugo, 'Playford's People: Population Change in South Australia' in *Playford's South Australia*, eds Bernard O'Neil, Judith Raftery and Kerrie Round, Association of Professional Historians, Inc., Adelaide, 1996, pp. 29–46. See also Eric Richards, 'The Peopling of South Australia' in *The Flinders History of South Australia: Social History*, ed. Eric Richards, Wakefield Press, Adelaide, 1986, pp. 134–139.

8 *Census of the Commonwealth of Australia, 30 June 1961*, vol. IV: *South Australia*, Commonwealth Bureau of Statistics, Canberra, 1963, pp. 26, 42–49.

9 'Relatio 1960', p. 1.

10 Naomi Turner, *Catholics in Australia*, Collins Dove, Melbourne, 1992, vol. 2, pp. 187 ff.; Patrick O'Farrell, *Catholic Church and Community*, University of New South Wales Press, Sydney, 1992, pp. 404–405; Frank Lewins, *The Myth of the Universal Church: Catholic Migrants in Australia*, Australian National University, Canberra, 1978; Adrian Pittarello, *'Soup Without Salt': The Australian Catholic Church and the Italian Migrant*, Centre for Migration Studies, Sydney, 1980; idem, 'Migrants and the Catholic Church in Australia', *Australasian Catholic Record* [hereafter *ACR*], vol. 65, no. 2, 1988, pp. 141–158; idem, 'Australian Immigration and the Church', *ACR*, vol. 70, no. 3, 1993, pp. 305–313; Pino Bosi, *On God's Command: Italian Missionaries in Australia*, CIRC, Sydney, 1989; Anthony Pagononi, *Valiant Struggles and Benign Neglect: Italians, Church and Religious Societies in Diaspora: The Australian Experience from 1950 to 2000*, Centre for Migration Studies, New York, 2003.

11 Frank Mecham, *The Church and the Migrants: 1946–1987*, St Joan of Arc Press, Sydney, 1991, p. 149; Monica Tolcvay, 'Community and Church: Italian Migrants and the Catholic Church in Australia, 1900–1975, with special reference to South Australia', PhD Thesis, Flinders University, 2005, p. 362.

12 *Southern Cross*, 20 March 1953, p. 5. See also Mecham, *The Church and the Migrants*, pp. 148–149.

13 *Southern Cross*, 10 February 1950, p. 1.

14 ibid., 5 January, 1951, p. 15.

15 James Gleeson, 'The Church in Adelaide During My Years as a Priest and Bishop', *ACR*, vol. 65, no. 3, 1988, p. 295.

16 *Southern Cross*, 15 December 1950, p. 9.

17 'Relatio 1960', p. 4.

18 Correspondence in the ACAA includes Jatulis to Beovich, 16 March 1948; Beovich to Cyril Chambers (minister for the Army), 1 December 1948; Arthur Calwell (minister for immigration) to Chambers, 9 December 1949; Chambers to Beovich, 10 December 1949.

19 Mecham, *The Church and the Migrant*, p. 149.

20 Robert Egar, interview by author, 15 December 2004. See also *Southern Cross*, 15 October 1954, p. 3; 18 April 1958, p. 1.

21 *Southern Cross*, 26 September 1958, p. 1; Diary, 28 August 1960.

22 Vincent Tiggeman to the author, February 2006.

23 Kaczmar to Beovich, 15 August 1949; Beovich to Kaczmar, 30 August 1949; 10 September 1949.

24 Bohdan Lapka, 'Overview of Ukrainian Catholic Churches in Adelaide' in *Concise History of the Ukrainian Catholic Church in South Australia*, Nasha Meta, Adelaide, 2001, pp. 167–175. See also Paul Babie, 'Australia's Ukrainian Catholics, Canon Law, and the Eparchial Statutes', *ACR*, vol. 81, no. 1, 2004, pp. 32–48, p. 167.

25 Diary, 20 April 1952; *Southern Cross*, 24 April 1952, p. 7.
26 Circulars to Priests, 25 September 1951; 14 May 1958.
27 Email from Theodosius Andr to Paul Babie, 8 October 2004, passed on to the author.
28 Minutes of the annual meeting of the hierarchy, 9–10 April 1953.
29 Diary, 9 January 1960; 20 November 1960; typescript of speech at opening of Lithuanian Catholic Centre, 20 November 1960.
30 For a short history of the Capuchins in Adelaide, see *Fifty Years: History of the Capuchins in Adelaide, 1953–2003*, St Francis of Assisi Parish, Adelaide, 2003.
31 Tolcvay, 'Community and Church', pp. 350, 352.
32 Fr Claude OFM Cap. to minister general in Rome, 14 June 1965, translated into English and cited in a letter from John Cooper OFM Cap. to V. Thomas, 22 August 2001, ACAA.
33 Notes in Beovich's handwriting, dated 8 November 1955 and 10 November 1955. See also Tolcvay, 'Community and Church', pp. 338–346.
34 Diary, 23 August 1960; Gleeson to George Crennan, national director of Federal Catholic Immigration Committee, 3 April 1961.
35 Diary, 3 March 1956.
36 *Southern Cross*, 15 December 1950, p. 9.
37 Antonio Paganoni and Desmond O'Connor, *Se La Processione Va Bene ... Religiosità Popolare Italiana Nel Sud Australia*, Centro Studi Emigrazione, Rome, 1999, pp. 118–119.
38 Pittarello, *'Soup Without Salt'*, p. 86. See also Stefano Girola, 'Saints in the Suitcase: Italian Popular Catholicism in Australia', *ACR*, vol. 80, no. 2, 2003, pp. 164–174.
39 Diary, 5 March 1962; *Southern Cross*, 9 March 1962.
40 *Southern Cross*, 27 June 1952, p. 7.
41 Diary, 16 November 1952; *Southern Cross*, 21 November 1952, p. 7.
42 *Southern Cross*, 20 July 1956.
43 ibid., 27 March 1953, p. 3.
44 Diary, 10 April 1955; 16 April 1955; *Southern Cross*, 14 April 1955.
45 *Southern Cross*, 14 January 1955, p. 14; Diary, 17 April 1955; *Southern Cross*, 22 April 1955, p. 7.
46 ibid., 20 July 1956, p. 3.
47 See Katharine Massam, *Sacred Threads*, University of New South Wales Press, Sydney, 1996, p. 79.
48 *Southern Cross*, 26 August 1949; A copy of Beovich's address is in the ACAA.
49 ibid., 23 August 1957, p. 3. See also Hilliard, 'Popular Religion in Australia in the 1950s', p. 223.
50 Address at the inaugural Marian procession.
51 *Southern Cross*, 10 November 1950, p. 1.
52 ibid., 10 November 1950, p. 1.
53 Hilliard, 'God in the Suburbs', pp. 415–416.
54 A booklet with photographs, speeches and the texts of homilies was printed to commemorate the occasion: *Mother of God and Mother of Men: Record of the Marian Congress held in Adelaide, SA, October 24–28th, 1951.*
55 *Mother of God and Mother of Men*, pp. 21–22.
56 ibid., p. 84. See also the *Advertiser*, 25 October, 1951, p. 3; 26 October 1951, p. 3; 27 October 1951, p. 3; 29 October 1951, p. 3.
57 Diary, 24 October 1951.
58 'Relatio of the Archbishop of Adelaide, 1955', p. 6.
59 *Southern Cross*, 4 December 1953, p. 1.
60 ibid., 30 October 1953, p. 6.
61 Beovich, 'Catholic Education and Catechetics in Australia'. Report compiled at the request of the Australian Bishops for the Conference on Education and Catechetics held in Rome in 1950.
62 'Relatio of the Archbishop of Adelaide, 1955', p. 8.
63 Diary, 1 April 1952.
64 Clarie Bell, *The Parish of Woodville/Findon*, Mater Dei Presbytery, Adelaide, 1987, p. 19.

65 Anne McLay, *Women on the Move*, Sisters of Mercy, Adelaide, 1996, p. 183. See also *Southern Cross*, 20 January 1951, p. 10.
66 'Relatio of the Archbishop of Adelaide, 1955', p. 3.
67 Sisters of Our Lady of the Sacred Heart (1947); De la Salle Brothers (1954); Daughters of Our Lady Help of Christians (1954); Good Samaritan Sisters (1954); Sisters of the Resurrection (1956); and Brigidine Sisters (1962).
68 'Report on the Archdiocese of Adelaide in South Australia, 1969'. This 'relatio' included an appendix with statistics from previous decades.
69 Notes of his address are in the ACAA.
70 *Southern Cross*, 6 September 1957, p. 7.
71 Diary, 26 April 1954.
72 James Gleeson, interview by the author, 8 October 1997.
73 *Southern Cross*, 31 October 1958.
74 Diary, 17 July 1952; 23 April 1953; Beovich to Mother Mary Leone, RSJ, 25 September 1953.
75 Minutes of the meeting, 9–10 April 1953.
76 *Southern Cross*, Friday 29 March 1957, p. 7.
77 ibid., 31 October 1958, p. 3.
78 ibid., 13 February 1959, pp. 1, 3.
79 ibid., 4 September 1959, p. 7.
80 *Catholic Catechism 1* was published in 1962 and *Catholic Catechism II* in 1963, followed by the *My Way to God* series of books in 1964. John Kelly, the director of Catholic Education in Melbourne, was largely responsible, assisted by James Gleeson as secretary of the bishops' committee for education. See Gleeson, 'The Church in Adelaide During My Years as a Priest and Bishop', p. 298.
81 *Southern Cross*, 18 January, 1963, p. 3.
82 Diary, 1 November 1960.
83 Diary, 30 April 1961.
84 *Southern Cross*, 9 May 1957, p. 3.
85 Diary, 2 August 1961; 9 August 1961.
86 *Southern Cross*, 23 March 1962, p. 2; 27 April 1962, p. 1.
87 Diary, 11 July 1962. For the incident at Goulburn, see Joshua Puls, 'The Goulburn Lockout', *ACR*, vol. 81, no. 2, 2004, pp. 169–183.
88 Edmund Campion, *Australian Catholics*, p. 173.
89 *Southern Cross*, 2 August 1963, p. 16.
90 Thomas Ormonde, quoted by Paul Ormonde in *Santamaria and the Politics of Fear*, Spectrum Publications, Melbourne, 2000, p. 180.
91 Circular to priests, 22 December 1950.
92 Diary, 7 January 1954.
93 See Thomas Boland, *James Duhig*, University of Queensland Press, Brisbane, 1986, pp. 192–193.
94 Diary, 27 July 1952; *Southern Cross*, 8 August 1952, p. 11.
95 For the Wells Way, see Hilliard, 'Popular Religion in Australia in the 1950s', p. 230; Ian Breward, *History of the Australian Churches*, Allen & Unwin, Sydney, 1993, p. 136.
96 Gleeson, 'The Church in Adelaide', p. 300.
97 See, for example, the correspondence in the ACAA concerning the Capuchins and the ownership of property in the Newton parish.
98 Diary, 1 April 1956.
99 Gavin Brown, 'Mass Performance: A Study of Eucharistic Ritual in Australian Catholic Culture, 1900–1962', Ph.D. thesis, University of Melbourne, 2003, p. 198.
100 Diary, 10 October 1959. The first Catholic programme, 'Catholic Vision' screened on NWS 9 on Sunday 11 October 1959. In 1960 it ran regularly from 5.30 to 6 pm. 'Catholic Life' was on Sunday nights on ADS 7 from 10.40 to 11.10 pm.
101 *Southern Cross*, 12 February 1960, p. 5.
102 See Kevin Hilferty, 'The Making of a Diocesan Editor, or the Education of Young Kevin', *ACR*, vol. 65, no. 3 & 4, 1988, pp. 303–314, 448–454.
103 Robert Wilkinson, interview by author, 11 June 2002.

104 Diary, 20 September 1957.
105 Margaret Lam to Beovich, 17 October 1954; Beovich to Lam, 20 October 1954.
106 Letter to the author, 18 September 2000.
107 *Southern Cross*, 15 May 1959, p. 3; 2 April 1965, p. 39.
108 John Brewer, interview by author, 15 July 2003; Diary, 1 October 1958; 25 October 1958.
109 Peter Donovan, *Towards the New Jerusalem*, Blackwood Parish Council, Adelaide, 1986, p. 41.
110 Diary, 15 June 1957.
111 Diary, 31 December 1958; 5 January 1959; 16 January 1959; 19 January 1959. See also *Southern Cross*, 16 January 1959, p. 3; 23 January 1959, pp. 1, 7.
112 Diary, 16 January 1959.
113 Diary, 21 March 1962.
114 Diary, 15 March 1962. See also *Southern Cross*, 13 October, 1961.
115 Diary, 31 December 1954.
116 Diary, 29 September 1956; 17 October 1956.
117 Diary, 20 January 1957; *Advertiser*, 7 January 1957.
118 Diary, 6 December 1956.
119 *Southern Cross*, 29 March 1957, p. 1.
120 A list of responsibilities for the two bishops was drawn up in 1961 and is now in the ACAA.
121 Keith Koen, interview by author, 9 April 1998.
122 Gleeson to Beovich, 2 December 1965.
123 Diary, 15 March 1956; Vincent Tiggeman, interview by author, 16 May 2002; and Peter Travers, interview by author, 28 November 2002.
124 Alan Commins, interview by author, 20 January 1998; and Brian Jackson, interview by author, 15 January 2004.
125 Calvary nurse Patricia Hearnshaw to Philip Kennedy, 1981.
126 Boland, *Duhig*, pp. 342–343.
127 Diary, 1 July 1956; 7 September 1958.
128 Diary, 3 April 1960; 10 April 1960.
129 Notes for his address to the graduation ceremony on 12 December 1951 are in the ACAA.
130 Homily, undated, for a feast of St Joseph the Worker.
131 Addresses to the St Vincent de Paul Society, 19 July 1961; 19 July 1962.
132 Homily at blessing of St John Vianney Church, Burnside, 17 June 1962.
133 Massam, *Sacred Threads*, p. 149.
134 *Southern Cross*, 1 May 1959, p. 1. The expert was Michael Scott, a Jesuit priest and rector of Aquinas College who was awarded a Carnegie travel grant in 1957 to study developments in religious art and architecture in North America and Europe. See Michael Head, *Fire on the Hill*, Aquinas College, 2000, p. 68.
135 *Southern Cross*, 1 May 1959, p. 1.
136 Diary, 24 March 1966.
137 Diary, 19 March 1962.
138 *Southern Cross*, 17 October 1958, p. 7.
139 Stewart Cockburn, *Playford*, Axiom, Adelaide, 1991, p. 223.
140 Hilliard, 'Religion in Playford's South Australia' in *Playford's South Australia*, p. 255.
141 Diary, 19 November 1957.
142 Diary, 18 October 1958; *Southern Cross*, 24 October 1958, p. 1.
143 Diary, 24 October 1958.
144 Diary, 24 March 1964; 8 May 1964; 23 June 1964.
145 Diary, 12 August 1954.
146 Head, *Fire on the Hill*, p. 50.
147 ibid., pp. 177–182.
148 Diary, 18 March 1958.
149 'Relatio, 1960', p. 7.
150 *Southern Cross*, 15 May 1959, special supplement, p. 5.
151 ibid., 29 May 1959, p. 3.
152 ibid., 25 September 1959, p. 3.

153 Diary, 28 July 1954.
154 Diary, 28 October 1957.
155 See also William McCarthy, *James Patrick O'Collins*, Spectrum Publications, Melbourne, 1996, pp. 85–88.
156 Diary, 3 July 1950.
157 *Southern Cross*, 3 November 1950, pp. 1, 7.
158 See McCarthy, *James Patrick O'Collins*, pp. 89–91.
159 *Southern Cross*, 11 November 1955, pp. 1, 6.
160 Diary, 11 May 1950; *Southern Cross*, 17 October 1958, p. 7; Diary, 25 June 1960; *Southern Cross*, 22 July 1960, p. 1.
161 See Hilliard, 'God in the Suburbs', p. 410.
162 Malcolm Broun, 'Historical Introduction' in *Australian Divorce Law and Practice*, Paul Toose, Ray Watson and David Benjafield, Law Book Company, Sydney, 1968, pp. xciii–cvi; Ken Elford, 'Marriage and Divorce' in *Flinders History of South Australia: Social History*, ed. Eric Richards, pp. 312–332.
163 *Southern Cross*, 9 August 1957, pp. 6–7; *Advertiser*, 6 August 1957, p. 3.
164 *Southern Cross*, 2 April 1965, pp. 12, 32, 43; Hilliard, 'Church, Family and Sexuality in Australia in the 1950s', pp. 139–140.
165 Diary, 28 January 1959.
166 Carroll to Beovich, 25 April 1959.
167 Duhig to Simonds, 30 June 1959.
168 Simonds to Beovich, 3 July 1959.
169 Diary, 28 August 1960.
170 Elford, 'Marriage and Divorce', p. 326; *Advertiser*, 20 November, 1959, pp. 1, 12; 28 November 1959, pp. 1, 13.
171 Diary, 16 July 1959; 29 November 1959.
172 See, for example, Anne McLay, *Women on the Move*, pp. 218–221.
173 *Southern Cross*, 25 September, p. 3; 30 October 1959, p. 1.
174 ibid., 2 April 1965.
175 ibid., p. 2.
176 ibid., p. 1.
177 ibid., 16 July 1965, p. 2.

Chapter Eight 'A School for Bishops'

1 An early version of this chapter was published as 'The Archbishop of Adelaide at Vatican II' in *Australasian Catholic Record* [hereafter *ACR*], vol. 80, no. 3, 2003, pp. 319–333.
2 'Vatican II and After' is the shortest chapter in Patrick O'Farrell's *Catholic Church and Community*, 3rd rev. ed, New South Wales University Press, Sydney, 1992. Edmund Campion focuses on the changes in Australian Catholicism in the 1960s rather than the Council itself in *Australian Catholics*, Aurora Books, Melbourne, 1987. Naomi Turner makes only a few scattered references to the Council in *Catholics in Australia*, Collins Dove, Melbourne, 1992.
3 O'Farrell, *Catholic Church and Community*, p. 410.
4 Ian Breward, *History of the Australian Churches*, Allen & Unwin, Sydney, 1993, p. 163.
5 Roger Thompson, *Religion in Australia*, 2nd ed., Oxford University Press, Melbourne, 2002, p. 129.
6 Jeffrey Murphy, 'The Australian Hierarchy and Vatican II: 1959–1965', Ph.D. thesis, Griffith University, 2001. Chapters have been published as a series of articles in the *Australasian Catholic Record*, vols. 78–80, 2001–2003.
7 Murphy, 'The Australian Hierarchy and Vatican II', pp. 236–237.
8 James Gleeson, interview by Stephen Watkins, 1 February 1999, for the ABC Radio National *Encounter* programme 'The Conciliar Experience: A Reflection on Vatican II' broadcast on 18 March, 1999.
9 See Etienne Fouilloux, 'The Antepreparatory Phase' in *History of Vatican II*, vol. 1, gen. ed. Giuseppe Alberigo, Orbis, Maryknoll, 1997, pp. 107–108. [Hereafter the series will be cited as *HVII*.]

10 William Ryder, 'The Australian Bishops' Proposals for Vatican II', *ACR*, vol. 65, no. 1, 1988, p. 76.
11 Murphy, 'The Australian Hierarchy and Vatican II', p. 102. See also Appendix 1, pp. 327–401, for English translations of the responses and the final synthesis.
12 Beovich to Tardini, 20 April 1960.
13 Murphy, 'The Australian Hierarchy and Vatican II', p. 97.
14 J.A. Komonchak, 'U.S. Bishops' Suggestions for Vatican II', *Cristianesimo nella storia*, Instituto per le Scienze Religiose, vol. 15, 1994, p. 344.
15 Mathew Beovich's Diary [hereafter Diary], 5 June 1960.
16 Diary, 22 August 1962.
17 See William McCarthy, *James Patrick O'Collins*, Spectrum Publications, Melbourne, 1996, p. 123.
18 *HVII*, vol. 2, p. 18.
19 Peter Hebblethwaite, *John XXIII*, Geoffrey Chapman, London, 1984, pp. 430–432.
20 *HVII*, vol. 2, p. 12.
21 ibid., vol. 2, pp. 26 ff.
22 John Heenan, *A Crown of Thorns*, Hodder & Staughton, London, 1974, pp. 368–369.
23 *HVII*, vol. 2, 148–149.
24 ibid., vol. 2, 110–111.
25 Diary, 26 October 1962; 6 November 1962.
26 John Moorman, *Vatican Observed*, Darton, Longman & Todd, London, 1967, pp. 20–21.
27 Diary, 30 October 1962.
28 Notebook, 5 November 1962 (Beovich made notes in this during Council debates).
29 Diary, 21 October 1962 (an account of his daily routine).
30 Diary, 7 November 1962.
31 W.T. Southerwood, *The Wisdom of Guilford Young*, Stella Maris Books, Hobart, 1989, pp. 195, 204.
32 *HVII*, vol. 2, 172.
33 Alberic Stacpoole, *Vatican II By Those Who Were There*, Geoffrey Chapman, London, 1986, p. 3.
34 See *HVII*, vol. 2, pp. 233 ff.
35 Diary, 21 November 1962.
36 Hebblethwaite, *John XXIII*, p. 450.
37 Diary, 13 November 1962.
38 Adrian Hastings, *History of English Christianity, 1920–1990*, SCM, London, 1991, p. 565.
39 As it was also to Cardinal Heenan, see *Crown of Thorns*, p. 343.
40 Hebblethwaite, *John XXIII*, pp. 464–465.
41 Diary, 8 December 1962.
42 Diary, 13 December 1962.
43 Robert Egar, interview by author, 15 December 2004; Robert Aitken, interview by author, 1 November 2004.
44 A typescript of his address is in the ACAA. See also *Southern Cross*, 21 December 1962, p. 1.
45 James Gleeson, interview by author, 8 October 1997.
46 Hebblethwaite, *John XXIII*, p. 335.
47 Diary, 13 October 1963.
48 *HVII*, vol. 3, p. 9. See also Xavier Rynne, *Vatican Council II*, Orbis, Maryknoll, 1999, p. 213.
49 Diary, 28 October 1963.
50 John Molony, *The Roman Mould of the Australian Catholic Church*, Melbourne University Press, Melbourne, 1969, p. 168.
51 Murphy, 'The Australian Hierarchy and Vatican II', pp. 174 ff.
52 See Walter Kasper, *Theology and Church*, SCM, London, 1989, p. 149.
53 For a summary of the Council's teaching on bishops, see Hermann Pottmeyer, 'Episcopacy' in *The Gift of the Church*, ed. Peter Phan, Liturgical Press, Collegeville, Minnesota, 2000, pp. 337–353.
54 Notebook, 16 October 1963.

55 Robert Rice, 'Some Reflections on the Contributions of Matthew Beovich and James Gleeson to the Second Vatican Council', *ACR*, vol. 78, no. 1, 2001, p. 51.
56 Diary, 29 October 1963.
57 *HVII*, vol. 3, p. 273.
58 Notebook, 70th General Congregation.
59 Notebook, 22 November, 1963; Diary, 26 November 1963.
60 Alfred Stirling, *A Distant View of the Vatican*, Hawthorn Press, 1975, p. 178. Stirling, the Australian ambassador to Rome during the Council, recounts that he was told this by Gleeson.
61 See *Advertiser*, 10 February 1964.
62 Diary, 11 February 1964.
63 *Southern Cross*, 14 February 1964, p. 8. A copy of the address is in his diary.
64 Diary, 18 November 1963.
65 Diary, 5 March 1964.
66 Diary, 10 June 1964.
67 Notebook, 1 October 1964; 21 October 1964.
68 Murphy, 'The Australian Hierarchy and Vatican II', pp. 217–223; *HVII*, vol. 4, p. 126.
69 Rice, 'Some Reflections', pp. 53–54.
70 For Paul VI, see Peter Hebblethwaite, *Paul VI*, HarperCollins, London, 1993.
71 Diary, 30 September 1964.
72 Donal Lamont, '*Ad Gentes*: A Missionary Bishop Remembers', in Stacpoole, *Vatican II By Those Who Were There*, p. 276.
73 The vote for redrafting was passed 1601 to 311. Diary, 9 November 1964.
74 Rice, 'Some Reflections', p. 55; *HVII*, vol. 4, p. 340.
75 Hebblethwaite, *Paul VI*, pp. 404–406.
76 *Southern Cross*, 19 July 1965, p. 19. He made a similar comment in his diary on 18 November 1965.
77 Diary, 27 September 1965.
78 Diary, 16 and 21 September 1965.
79 Diary, 17 November 1965.
80 Ralph Wiltgen, *The Rhine Flows into the Tiber*, Augustine Publishing Co., Chawleigh, Devon, 1966, pp. 278–281.
81 Murphy, 'The Australian Hierarchy and Vatican II', p. 312.
82 Diary, 4 December 1965.
83 Moorman, *Vatican Observed*, p. 169; Rynne, *Vatican Council II*, pp. 504–505.
84 Moorman, *Vatican Observed*, p. 45.
85 Diary, 24 November 1965.
86 Diary, 8 December 1965.
87 James Gleeson, 'The Church in Adelaide during my Years as a Priest and Bishop', *ACR*, vol. 65, no. 3, 1988, p. 300.

Chapter Nine 'Zeal and Prudence'

1 *Southern Cross*, 11 February 1966, pp. 1–3.
2 *Bulletin*, 12 November 1966, pp. 31, 33, 35.
3 For Australia, the literature on the 1960s includes Donald Horne, *Time of Hope: Australia 1966–72*, Angus & Robertson, Sydney & Melbourne, 1980; and Helen Townsend, *The Baby Boomers*, Simon & Schuster, Sydney, 1988. For the impact on religion, see especially David Hilliard, 'The Religious Crisis of the 1960s: The Experience of the Australian Churches', *Journal of Religious History*, vol. 21, 1997, pp. 209–227; Adrian Hastings, *History of English Christianity*, 3rd ed., SCM, London, 1991, chapter 37; Sydney Ahlstrom, *A Religious History of the American People*, Yale University Press, New Haven, 1972, chapter 63; Ronald Flowers, *Religion in Strange Times*, Mercer University Press, 1984; Wade Clark Roof, *A Generation of Seekers*, Harper San Francisco, New York, 1993; and Robert Ellwood, *The Sixties Spiritual Awakening*, Rutgers University Press, New Brunswick, New Jersey, 1994.
4 A Gallop poll in 1970 indicated that 87 per cent of Australians claimed to believe in God, down from 95 per cent in 1949 (see Hans Mol, *The Faith of Australians*, Allen & Unwin,

1985, p. 130). Census figures for South Australia show that whereas only 0.33 per cent claimed to have 'no religion' in 1961, there were 8.17 per cent in that category in 1971. See David Hilliard, 'Religion' in *South Australian Historical Statistics*, Vamplew Wray et al, Historical Statistics Monograph 3, History Project Inc., Sydney, 1984, p. 140.

5 According to Morgan Gallop polls, in 1970 25 per cent of Australian respondents had attended church in the week the survey was conducted, down from 30 per cent in 1960. The Catholic Church fared better than the other major denominations but still experienced a decline in the weekly attendance of its adherents from 75 per cent in 1954 to 51 per cent in 1970. See Mol, *Faith of Australians*, p. 56.

6 Neil Omerod, *Introducing Contemporary Theologies*, E. J. Dwyer, Sydney, 1990, p. 11.

7 Hastings, *History of English Christianity*, p. 561.

8 An important exception is John P. Maguire, *Prologue: A History of the Catholic Church as seen from Townsville, 1863–1983*, Church Archivists' Society, Toowomba, 1990. See also W.T. Southerwood, *The Wisdom of Guilford Young*, Stella Maris Books, Hobart, 1989.

9 Patrick O'Farrell, *The Catholic Church and Community*, 3rd ed., University of New South Wales Press, Sydney, 1992, p. 410; Ian Breward, *History of the Australian Churches*, Allen & Unwin, Sydney, 1993, pp. 162–167; Roger Thompson, *Religion in Australia*, 2nd ed., Oxford University Press, Melbourne, 2002, p. 129; and Paul Collins, *Mixed Blessings*, Penguin, Melbourne, 1986, pp. 188–189. For outside Australia, see Peter Hebblethwaite, *The Runaway Church*, Collins, Glasgow, 1978; Adrian Hastings, ed., *Modern Catholicism*, SPCK & Oxford University Press, London & New York, 1991; and Andrew Greeley, *The Catholic Revolution*, University of California Press, Berkeley, 2004.

10 *Southern Cross*, 4 February 1966, p. 1.

11 ibid., 11 February 1966, pp. 1–3.

12 ibid., 11 March 1966, p. 4.

13 ibid., 22 April 1966, p, 4.

14 ibid., 25 March 1966, p. 6.

15 ibid., 29 April 1966, pp. 1, 2–3, 12.

16 Matthew Beovich's Diary [hereafter Diary], 9 March 1966; 6 July 1966.

17 Diary, 6 September 1966; *Southern Cross*, 9 September 1966, p. 1.

18 *Southern Cross*, 9 December 1966, p. 1.

19 David Shinnick, *Jouney into Justice*, David Shinnick, Adelaide, 1982, p. 22.

20 *Southern Cross*, 20 May 1966, p. 3; 3 June 1966, p. 1.

21 ibid., 24 February 1966, p. 3.

22 ibid., 3 April 1970, p. 4.

23 ibid., 27 January 1967, p. 1.

24 ibid., 27 October 1967, p. 1.

25 Bill Byrne, interview by author, 13 December 2004.

26 David Shinnick, interview by author, 21 November 2002; Denis Edwards, interview by author, 10 December 2004; Byrne, 13 December 2004.

27 See Maguire, *Prologue*, p. 235 (Townsville); Southerwood, *Wisdom of Guilford Young*, chapter 7 (Hobart); Naomi Turner, *Catholics in Australia*, vol. 2, Collins Dove, Melbourne, 1992, pp. 294–298 (Sydney).

28 *Southern Cross*, 17 March 1967, p. 2.

29 ibid., 22 April 1966, p. 1.

30 ibid., 21 April 1967, p. 1.

31 Reported in the *Southern Cross*, 6 October 1967, p. 2; 13 October 1967, p. 2; 20 October 1967, p. 2.

32 Rosemary Goldie, *From a Roman Window*, HarperCollins Religious, Melbourne, 1998, p. 93.

33 *Southern Cross*, 14 July 1967, pp. 1–2.

34 Senate of Priests, Minutes, 29 June 1967. See also Greeley, *Catholic Revolution*, p. 38.

35 Diary 30 June 1964; Circular to priests, 22 June 1964.

36 *Southern Cross*, 3 July 1964, p. 1; 21 August 1964, p. 1.

37 ibid., 10 July 1964, p. 1.

38 ibid.,14 August 1964, p. 1.

39 ibid., 24 February 1967; 21 April 1967, p. 13.

40 ibid., 10 November 1967.
41 ibid., 15 December 1967, p. 1.
42 ibid., 9 February 1968, p. 5.
43 ibid., 24 April 1969, p. 1; Shinnick, 'Youthful Yearnings', unpublished memoirs, ACAA, pp. 291–292.
44 See *Southern Cross*, 3 October 1969, pp. 8–9, for explanatory notes and photographs of Brian Jackson in the seminary chapel demonstrating to priests how the Mass should be celebrated.
45 Shinnick, *Journey into Justice*, p. 28.
46 *Southern Cross*, 7 November 1969, p. 6.
47 ibid., 30 May 1969, p. 13.
48 ibid., 23 May 1969, p. 13.
49 ibid., 24 October 1969, p. 13.
50 Diary, 5 March 1964.
51 *Southern Cross*, 12 March 1965, p. 1.
52 Diary, 18 April 1965.
53 The letter which Lercaro sent Gilroy, dated 30 June 1965, was copied and distributed to the Australian bishops. Beovich in turn circulated it to his priests on 30 July 1965.
54 Brian Jackson, interview by author, 15 January 2004.
55 Circular to priests, 19 February 1964; Notes for clergy conference, 10 March 1965; *Southern Cross*, 12 March 1965, p. 1; Liturgical Commission, Minutes, 29 March 1967.
56 *Southern Cross*, 24 April 1969, pp. 1, 12.
57 ibid., 3 October 1967, p. 1.
58 Diary, 4 October 1969; Brian Jackson, 15 January 2004.
59 *Southern Cross*, 21 November 1969, p. 2.
60 See Shinnick, *Journey into Justice*, p. 22.
61 Circular to priests, 13 November 1969; *Southern Cross*, 21 November 1969, p. 2.
62 *Southern Cross*, 19 December 1969, pp. 1, 4; The notes of the sermon are in his diary.
63 ibid., 27 February 1970, p. 11. A 1974 study in the USA indicated that four out of five Catholics approved of the new vernacular liturgy. See Greeley, *Catholic Revolution*, p. 37.
64 *Southern Cross*, 30 April 1965, p. 3.
65 Diary, 24 April 1965.
66 The remark was addressed to Father Tom Boland who repeated it in an interview with Jeffrey Murphy. See 'The Australian Hierarchy at Vatican II', Ph.D. Thesis, Griffith University, 2001, p. 155.
67 Diary, 16 March 1964.
68 Diary, 24 March 1964.
69 Diary, 24 April 1964; 17 June 1964; text of address in the ACAA.
70 Diary, 3 February and 15 February 1965.
71 Diary, 27 March 1965.
72 Diary, 14 October 1966; 6 June 1968.
73 Diary, 8 November 1968.
74 'Summary of Matters Discussed at the Clergy Conference, 10 May 1967'.
75 See *Southern Cross*, 24 February 1967, p. 3.
76 Peter Murnane, 'Inter-Faith Marriage and the Catholic Church in Australia', BA Hons thesis, Flinders University, 1970, p. 19.
77 Robert Rice, interview by author, 16 November 2004.
78 Diary, 16 March 1964.
79 The text of the address delivered on 16 March 1964 is in the ACAA.
80 *Southern Cross*, 14 April 1967, p. 1.
81 Thomas Horgan, interview by author, 23 September 1997.
82 Alan Commins, interview by author, 20 January 1998.
83 Senate of Priests, Minutes, 29 June 1967.
84 Patrick Ford, 'Subsidiarity and Sacradotal Sustentation', *ACR*, vol. 47, no. 4, 1970, pp. 290–305; John Luttrell, 'Norman Thomas Cardinal Gilroy as Archbishop of Sydney', Ph.D. thesis, University of Sydney, 1997, pp. 231–236.
85 Diary, 18 June 1970.

86 Edward Mulvilhill, 'My Recollections of Archbishop Matthew Beovich', 19 June 2002; letter to the author, 23 September 2004.
87 Senate of Priests, Minutes, 18 September, 1968; Circular to priests, 29 September 1968.
88 Luttrell, 'Norman Thomas Cardinal Gilroy', pp. 213–214. See also Kelvin Canavan, 'The Development of the Sydney Catholic Education Office', *ACR*, vol. 75, no. 4, 1988, pp. 441–447.
89 'It is much to be desired that in every diocese there should be established its own pastoral council. The diocesan bishop himself should preside over it; and specially selected clergy, religious and laity should play their part in it. The function of this council will be to examine those matters affecting pastoral activities, to assess them and to put forward practical conclusions concerning them.' Norman P. Tanner, ed., *Decrees of the Ecumenical Councils*, vol. II: *Trent to Vatican II*, Sheed & Ward, London, 1990, p. 932.
90 A list of members and their photographs can be found in the *Southern Cross*, 15 December 1967, p. 1.
91 Diocesan Pastoral Council (DPC) Minutes, 31 March 1969.
92 DPC Minutes, 9 August 1970.
93 Shinnick, *Journey into Justice*, p. 28.
94 DPC Minutes, 30 June 1968.
95 DPC Minutes, 15 September 1968.
96 DPC Minutes, 9 August 1970.
97 DPC Minutes, 15 November 1970.
98 See *Southern Cross*, 13 March 1970, p. 1; 20 March 1970, p. 3.
99 DPC Minutes, 9 August, 1970.
100 See, for example, Peter Donovan, *Towards The New Jerusalem*, Blackwood Parish Council, Adelaide, 1986, pp. 50–55.
101 Peter Gough, 'A Year after Vatican II: Breathing New Life into Catholicism', *Bulletin*, 12 November 1966, p. 33.
102 *Southern Cross*, 22 April 1966, p. 2.
103 Shinnick, *Journey into Justice*, p. 29.
104 Extract from *L'Osservatore Romano*, 4 April 1968 (English language edition), in Patrick O'Farrell, *Documents in Australian Catholic History*, Geoffrey Chapman, London, 1969, p. 366.
105 See Hebblethwaite, *Runaway Church*, pp. 209 ff.; and Leo Pyle, ed., *The Pope and the Pill*, Darton, Longman & Todd, London, 1968.
106 The story broke in the *National Catholic Reporter* in the USA on 19 April and the English *Tablet* on 22 April. It was on the front page of the *Southern Cross* on 28 April.
107 *Southern Cross*, 29 September 1967, p. 1.
108 ibid., 27 October 1967, 1; *3rd World Congress for the Lay Apostolate: Report of the South Australian Delegates*, LALC, Adelaide, 1968, p. 8.
109 Diary, 30 July; 1 August 1968.
110 *Advertiser*, 30 July 1968, p. 1.
111 Circular to priests, 1 August 1968; *Australian*, 31 July 1968, p. 1; *Advertiser*, 31 July 1968, p. 3.
112 Diary, 31 July 1968. According to Robert Egar (interview by author, 15 December 2004), one of the members of the Senate, it was not unanimous as two priests abstained from voting.
113 Diary, 5 August 1968. Present at the meeting were Cardinal Gilroy, Archbishops Beovich, Knox and Young, and Bishops Cahill and Toohey.
114 *Southern Cross*, 9 August 1968, p. 1.
115 *Advertiser*, 7 August 1968, p. 1.
116 ibid., 1 August 1968, p. 1; *Southern Cross*, 16 August 1968, p. 1.
117 Diary, 9 August 1968; *Southern Cross*, 16 August 1968, p. 1.
118 Southerwood, *Wisdom of Guilford Young*, pp. 419, 422–423.
119 Robert Aitken, interview by author, 1 November 2004; also Leon Czechowicz, interview by author, 5 February 2004.
120 *Southern Cross*, 6 September 1968, p. 4.
121 A survey of American priests in 1972 indicated that the number who would deny absolution to Catholics who used contraception had fallen from 26 per cent (before *Humanae Vitae* was

issued) to 13 per cent in 1972. The number prepared to accept the responsibility of Catholics to form their own moral judgement had risen from 31 to 44 per cent. See Greeley, *Catholic Revolution*, p. 36.

122 In the *Bulletin*, 17 May 1969, p. 28, former priest Michael Parer estimated that at least 65 priests had left in the previous eighteen months, 60 of them from Victoria and New South Wales.

123 Peter Travers, interview by author, 28 November 2002.

124 *Southern Cross*, 14 February 1969, p. 3.

125 ibid., 30 August 1968, p. 4; 6 September 1968, p. 4.

126 Diary, 13 and 14 August; *Advertiser*, 14 August 1968, p. 3.

127 *Advertiser*, 15 August 1968, p. 3.

128 *News*, 14 September 1968, p. 2.

129 DPC Minutes, 15 September 1968; David Shinnick, telephone conversation with the author, 3 December 2004.

130 Diary, 15 September 1968.

131 *Southern Cross*, 9 August, p. 6.

132 ibid., 9 August, p. 6.

133 ibid., 13 September 1968, p. 6.

134 *Australian*, 23 November 1970, p. 11. Whereas a survey in the United States in 1966 indicated that 56 per cent of Catholic respondents thought that contraception was always wrong, in 1974 the figure was just 16 per cent. See Andrew Greeley, *Catholic Revolution*, University of California Press, Berkeley, California, 2004, p. 39.

135 *Southern Cross*, 12 January, 1968, p. 15.

136 ibid., 19 January 1968, p. 12.

137 ibid., 29 March 1968, p. 5.

138 ibid., 19 January 1968, p. 4.

139 Robert Wilkinson, interview, 11 June 2002, and telephone conversation, 4 December 2004.

140 Nicholas Reid, *James Michael Liston*, Victoria University Press, Wellington, 2006, pp. 288–292. See also Kevin Hilferty, 'The Making of a Diocesan Editor, or The Education Of Young Kevin', *ACR*, vol. 75, nos. 3 & 4, 1988, pp. 303–314, 448–454; Val Noone, *Disturbing the War: Melbourne Catholics and Vietnam*, Spectrum, Melbourne, 1993, p. 202.

141 *Southern Cross*, 11 July 1969, p. 3.

142 These statistics have been compiled largely from 'Record of Diocesan Clergy', an exercise book in which Beovich and his secretary recorded details of all priests from 1940 to 1968.

143 'Interim Report of the Sub-Committee on the Life and Ministry of Priests', 4 July 1969.

144 *Southern Cross*, 21 November 1967, p. 7.

145 Senate of priests, Minutes, 12 November 1969.

146 Circular to priests, 23 October 1969. Robert Rice first heard of a new appointment when he received the following letter, dated 7 December 1956: 'Dear Father Rice, You are hereby appointed as Assistant Priest to Rev. Father Collins in the parish of Brighton as from the 24th December. With every kind wish, I am, Yours sincerely in J.C., + Matthew Beovich.'

147 Senate of priests, Minutes, 12 November 1969; 10 June 1970.

148 Denis Edwards, interview by author, 10 December 2004.

149 Robert Egar, interview by author, 15 December 2004. The Adelaide representatives were Egar, Wilkinson and Peter McIntyre. For the formation of the National Council of Priests, see Edmund Campion, *Rockchoppers*, Penguin Books, Melbourne, 1982, p. 195 ff.

150 Anthony Lowes, email to the author, 19 November 2004.

151 See also Michael Gaine, 'The State of the Priesthood' in *Modern Catholicism*, ed. Adrian Hastings, pp. 246–255.

152 Michael Parer, 'Priests Who Leave', *Bulletin*, 17 May 1969, p. 30; 24 May 1969, p. 37. See also Parer's autobiography, *Dreamer by Day: A Priest Returns to Life*, Angus and Robertson, Sydney, 1972.

153 Gaine, 'The State of the Priesthood', p. 249.

154 James Gleeson, 'The Church in Adelaide During My Years as a Priest and Bishop', *ACR*, vol. 65, no. 3, 1988, p. 301.

155 ibid., p. 301.

156 'Report on the Archdiocese of Adelaide in South Australia, 1969', p. 4.
157 Diary, 23 December 1966. See also Charles Davis, *A Question of Conscience*, Hodder and Stoughton, London, 1967.
158 Diary, 27 July 1969.
159 ibid., 22 March 1970.
160 ibid., 27 March 1970.
161 *Southern Cross*, 31 July 1970, p. 1.
162 Alan Commins CM, interview by author, 20 January 1998.
163 See his article, 'Priests Who Leave', *Bulletin*.
164 Roy Richardson, interview by author, 9 December 2004; Denis Edwards, interview by author, 10 December 2004. Both were ordained in 1966.
165 Richardson, 9 December 2004; Egar, 15 December 2004; Luttrell, 'Norman Thomas Cardinal Gilroy', pp. 259–271.
166 Edmund Campion, *Australian Catholics*, Aurora Books, Melbourne, 1987, p. 226. See also K. J. Walsh's *Yesterday's Seminary*, Allen and Unwin, Sydney, 1998, chapter 10.
167 Diary, 10 July 1970.
168 Commins, 20 January 1998.
169 Diary, 18 March 1964; 10 April 1964; 25 May 1964; 26 May 1964; 12 June 1964; 16 July 1964; 8 March 1965; 6 June 1965.
170 ibid., 14 May 1967.
171 *Southern Cross*, 19 May 1967, p. 2.
172 Protestant churches also faced a decline in recruitment. See Hilliard, 'Religious Crisis', p. 222.
173 Diary, 13 August 1969.
174 *Southern Cross*, 16 June 1967, p. 1.
175 In his 1969 report to Rome, Beovich acknowledged that there were 22,628 Catholic children in Catholic schools (a slight rise from 20,931 in 1959) and 28,673 Catholic children in state schools (up from 11,749 in 1959).
176 For Crudden, see Campion, *Rockchoppers*, pp. 176–178; and *Australian Catholics*, p. 222.
177 Diary, 30 June 1968.
178 In Auckland, James Liston tried to enforce a ban on Catholic children to state schools. See Reid, *James Michael Liston*, p. 279.
179 Diary, 1 November 1960. See also B. Condon, 'All at Work in the Lord's Garden: The 1940 Act and Beyond' in *Dissent in Paradise: Religious Education Controversies in South Australia*, eds P. C. Almond and P. G. Woolcock, Murray Park College of Advanced Education, Adelaide, 1975, p. 21 ff.
180 *Southern Cross*, 10 January 1969, p. 5.
181 ibid., 18 December 1970, p. 3.
182 ibid.
183 Arnold Hunt, *This Side of Heaven: A History of Methodism in South Australia*, Lutheran Publishing House, Adelaide, 1985, pp. 390–391.
184 David Hilliard, *Godliness and Good Order: A History of the Anglican Church in South Australia*, Wakefield Press, Adelaide, 1986, p. 153.
185 Notes inserted in his Diary, 20 August 1970; Australian Episcopal Conference, Minutes, 17–21 August 1970.
186 Diary, 28 November 1970.
187 See Horne, *Time of Hope*, p. 163; Andrew Parkin and Allan Patience, eds, *The Dunstan Decade*, Longman Cheshire, Melbourne, 1981.
188 *Southern Cross*, 13 October 1967; *Advertiser*, 6 October 1967, p. 1; 7 October 1967, p. 3.
189 Diary, 18 February 1968.
190 John Gardiner-Garden, 'The Origin of Commonwealth Involvement in Indigenous Affairs and the 1967 Referendum', Background Paper 11, 1996–1997, Parliament of Australia, Parliamentary Library, http://www.aph.gov.au/library/pubs/BP/1996-97/97bp11.htm, accessed 24 January 2008.
191 See *Southern Cross*, 5 May 1967, p. 1.

192 Neva Wilson (then Grzybowicz), interview by Mandy Paul, email to the author, 23 May 2007.
193 Nicholas Kerr, email to the author, 30 January 2008.
194 Jill Blewett, 'The Abortion Law Reform Association of South Australia 1968–1973' in *The Other Half: Women in Australian Society*, ed. Jan Mercer, Penguin, Harmondsworth, Middlesex, 1975, pp. 377–394.
195 Many articles in the *Southern Cross* were devoted to the issue. See in particular, 16 January 1969, p. 1.
196 Thérèse Nicholas, 'Abortion Law Reform in South Australia', BA Hons thesis, Flinders University, 1970, pp. 85–86; Hunt, *This Side of Heaven*, p. 398.
197 'Report of the Select Committee, 18 February 1969' cited in John Fleming and Daniel Overduin, *Wake Up Lucky County! A Reflection on Social Issues During the Last Decade*, rev. ed., Lutheran Publishing House, Adelaide, 1982, p. 37.
198 ibid., p. 38.
199 *Southern Cross*, 21 November 1969, p. 1; *Advertiser*, 15 November 1969.
200 *Southern Cross*, 19 December 1969, p. 1.
201 Circular to priests, 18 December 1970.
202 *Sunday Mail*, 26 December 1970, p. 1. For statistics, see Fleming and Overduin, *Wake Up Lucky County!*, pp. 54–62.
203 See P. R. Wilson & D. Chappell, 'Australian Attitudes Towards Abortion, Prostitution and Homosexuality', *Australian Quarterly*, vol. 40, no. 2, 1968, p. 10.
204 Greeley, *Catholic Revolution*, p. 39
205 Colm Kiernan, *Calwell*, Thomas Nelson, Melbourne, 1978, p. 246.
206 David Hilliard, 'Pluralism and New Alignments in Society and Church 1967 to the Present' in *Anglicanism in Australia*, gen. ed. Bruce Kaye, Melbourne University Press, Melbourne, 2002, p. 128.
207 Henry Albinski, *Politics and Foreign Policy in Australia*, Duke University Press, Durham, North Carolina, 1970, p. 128.
208 Geoffrey Bolton, *Oxford History of Australia*, vol. 5, 2nd ed., Oxford University Press, Melbourne, 1996, p. 167.
209 Southerwood, *Wisdom of Guilford Young*, p. 303.
210 *Advocate*, 4 August 1966, p. 7.
211 ibid., 17 June 1965, p. 3; 23 June 1966, p. 7.
212 ibid., 17 March 1966; 24 March 1966, p. 1.
213 Luttrell, 'Norman Thomas Cardinal Gilroy', pp. 252–259.
214 For accounts written by former priests who were involved in the peace movement, see Val Noone, *Disturbing the War*, Spectrum, Melbourne, 1993; and C. F. Bowers, 'The Catholic Church in Sydney & the Vietnam Conflict', *Australian Left Review*, vol. 71, 1979, pp. 30–37. For the peace movement in general, see Malcolm Saunders, 'Opposition to the Vietnam War in South Australia, 1965–1973', *Journal of the Historical Society of South Australia*, vol. 10, 1982, pp. 61–71; idem, 'The Vietnam Moratorium Movement in Australia: 1969–1973', PhD thesis, Flinders University, 1977.
215 Diary, 3 October 1966; 1 April 1968; 7 December 1968.
216 Circular to priests and religious, 27 September 1966; *Southern Cross*, 30 September 1966, p. 1.
217 *Southern Cross*, 4 November 1966, p. 3.
218 Diary, 29 December 1966.
219 The statement was printed in the *Southern Cross*, 14 April 1967, p. 1. See also Noone, *Disturbing the War*, pp. 134–135.
220 *Age*, 14 April 1967, p. 5.
221 Saunders, 'Opposition to the Vietnam War', p. 63.
222 *Southern Cross*, 3 November 1967; text of address in ACAA.
223 Horne, *Time of Hope*, p. 59.
224 Albinski, *Politics and Foreign Policy in Australia*, p. 133.
225 *Southern Cross*, 2 May 1969, pp. 1, 12.
226 ibid., 8 May 1970, p. 1.
227 *Advertiser*, 9 May 1970, p. 3; *Sydney Morning Herald*, 9 May 1970, p. 1.

228 Saunders, 'Vietnam Moratorium Movement', pp. 89–92; Noone, *Disturbing the War*, p. 248; *Age*, 20 April 1970, p. 1; *Sydney Morning Herald*, 2 May 1970, p. 6.
229 Gilroy to Michael Horsburgh, 28 April 1970, cited by Luttrell, 'Norman Thomas Cardinal Gilroy', p. 258.
230 Diary, 1 May 1970.
231 ibid., 30 April 1970.
232 See Ian Moffitt and Graham Williams, 'The Angry Young Men of the Church', *Australian*, 19 September 1967, p. 9. In an unpublished manuscript cited by Saunders ('Vietnam Moratorium Movement', p. 96), Williams wrote that 'an estimated fifty priests and other clergy resigned or were forced out of the church because of their peace activities'. See also Noone, *Disturbing the War*, pp. 272–273; Hilliard, 'The Religious Crisis of the 1960s', p. 225.
233 *Southern Cross*, 22 May 1970, p. 13.
234 Shinnick, *Journey into Justice*, p. 28.
235 Shinnick, 'Youthful Yearnings', pp. 337–338.
236 See Hilliard, 'Religion' in *South Australian Historical Statistics*, Vamplew Wray et al, Historical Statistics Monograph, vol. 3, History Project Inc., Sydney, 1984, pp. 137–145.

Chapter Ten 'The Golden Years'

1 Vincent Tiggeman, interview by author, 16 May 2002.
2 Beovich to Pope Paul VI, 29 June 1970.
3 Matthew Beovich's Diary [hereafter Diary], 12 November 1963.
4 A copy of the letter is attached to the report on the archdiocese which he submitted in July 1970.
5 Diary, 12 November 1970.
6 ibid., 23 November 1970.
7 ibid., 18 November 1970
8 ibid., 12 November 1970.
9 For an account of the papal tour, see *Visit of Pope Paul VI to the Far East, Australia and the Pacific*, Libreria Editrice Vaticana, Vatican, 1971. A photographic record can be found in Michael Parer, *Four Papal Days*, Alella Books, Sydney, 1970.
10 *Australian*, 24 November 1970, p. 1.
11 Gilroy, interview by Hazel De Berg, 19 January 1972. National Library of Australia, Oral History Section, tape 567.
12 *Southern Cross*, 16 April 1971, p. 1; Diary notes.
13 The typescript is in the ACAA.
14 John Chambers, interview by author, 10 December 2004; Roy Richardson, interview by author, 9 December 2004. Chambers lived at Ennis from 1971 to 1974; Richardson from 1975 to 1978.
15 First related to author in a letter from Daniel Conquest, 21 August 1997, and subsequently recalled by many people in conversation.
16 Richardson, 9 December 2004.
17 Diary, 13 March 1972.
18 Richardson, 9 December 2004.
19 Beovich, interview by Garth Rawlins, *Sunday Mail*, 30 March 1980, p. 24; Thomas Horgan, interview by author, 23 September 1997; Chambers, 10 December 2004.
20 Mike Quirk, 'Retiring Archbishop is Footy Fan', *News*, 1 April 1971, p. 49.
21 Diary, 3 March 1973; 8 March 1973.
22 ibid., 8 July 1973.
23 ibid., 9 July 1973 (presumably written some time afterward); Beovich to Elizabeth Calwell, 19 October 1973.
24 Gleeson to Vera Beovich, 16 August 1973
25 Diary, 15 October 1973.
26 ibid., 31 December 1972.
27 ibid., 31 December 1967.
28 The typescript for his sermon is in the ACAA.

29 The priest was Charles Thompson. Born in Melbourne in 1897, he had been ordained in 1922 after studying at St Patrick's College, Manly. He was the administrator of the cathedral parish when Beovich arrived in Adelaide in 1940. *Southern Cross*, 24 May 1974, p. 2.
30 Diary, 23 December 1972.
31 ibid., 26 December 1972.
32 Gilroy to Beovich, 11 September 1973; Beovich to Gilroy, 18 September 1973.
33 Nicholas Kerr to author, 30 January 2008.
34 Horgan, 23 September 1997.
35 James Gleeson, 8 October 1997.
36 Norman Gilroy, quoted by Edmund Campion, *Great Australian Catholics*, Viking, Melbourne, 1987, p. 68.
37 John Maguire, *Prologue: The Catholic Church as Seen From Townsville, 1863–1983*, Church Archivists' Society, Toowomba 1990, p. 128.
38 Keith Koen, interview by author, 9 April 1998.
39 *Advertiser*, 30 October 1981 ('Traveling Partners Part'); Pauline Smitheram (Keith Koen's daughter) in conversation with author.
40 Robert Aitken, 1 November 2004.
41 Robert Egar, 15 December 2004.
42 Richardson, 9 December 2004; Chambers, 10 December 2004.
43 Bill Byrne, 13 December 2004.
44 O'Collins's letter to Beovich, and a copy of Beovich's reply, dated 24 December 1970, are in the ACAA.
45 Beovich to Koen, 24 October 1977.
46 Diary, 5 April 1962.
47 ibid., 23 June 1967.
48 It is now in the Melbourne Diocesan Historical Commission. See Max Vodola, *Simonds*, Catholic Education Office, Melbourne, 1997, p. 95.
49 The typescript of the sermon is in the ACAA.
50 Typescript in ACAA.
51 ibid.
52 Beovich to Bishop Dougherty, 24 July 1979, in reply to an invitation in the minutes of the Australian Episcopal Conference for those who knew Gilroy to submit reports concerning his holiness of life.
53 Philip Kennedy, homily at Beovich's requiem Mass, 29 October 1981. A copy is in the ACAA. It was published in the *Southern Cross*, 5 November 1981, pp. 28–29.
54 *Southern Cross*, 29 October 1981; James Gleeson, interview by author, 24 July 1997.
55 The booklet for the service is in the ACAA. See also *News*, 29 October 1981, p. 9; *Advertiser*, 30 October 1981; *Southern Cross*, 5 November 1981, pp. 1–2, 8–9.
56 See *Sunday Mail*, 25 October 1981, p. 6; *Advertiser*, 26 October 1981, p. 7; *Southern Cross*, 29 October 1981, pp. 3, 5–6.
57 *Sunday Mail*, 25 October 1981, p. 60.
58 *Southern Cross*, 29 October 1981, p. 5.
59 Note attached to a condolence letter from J. Herendi, on behalf of the Hungarian Catholic community, to Kennedy on 28 October 1981. There is a folder of condolence cards and letters in the ACAA.
60 *Advertiser*, 30 October 1981.
61 *Southern Cross*, 5 November 1981, p. 9.
62 Pat Hearnshaw to Kennedy, undated.
63 John Bannon to Kennedy, 2 November 1981.
64 Doug Warren to Kennedy, 19 November 1981.
65 Bill Byrne, 'Archbishop Beovich', *National Outlook*, February 1982, p. 22.

Bibliography

Archives

Much of the research for this book was done in the Adelaide Catholic Archdiocesan Archives (ACAA). As the ACAA was in the process of being reorganised and catalogued at the time of writing, the archivist asked that no box numbers be given. Within the wider collection, there are a number of boxes containing material specifically related to Matthew Beovich. In these can be found his diaries, sermon notes, documents on the Movement, and some correspondence. However, most of his correspondence is filed elsewhere, in folders relating to particular parishes, religious orders, etcetera.

For Beovich's time in Melbourne I was able to locate some information in the Melbourne Diocesan Historical Commission; the Catholic Education Office Archives, East Melbourne; Christian Brothers' Archives, Parkville, Victoria; Good Samaritan Sisters' Archives, Glebe Point, NSW; Presentation Sisters' Archives, Brighton, Victoria; and the archives of the Sisters of St Joseph, Sydney. I consulted the archives of the Pontifical Urban University in Rome for Beovich's doctoral thesis and academic records.

Newspapers and Periodicals

The archdiocese of Adelaide's weekly paper, the *Southern Cross*, was an invaluable source. The Melbourne Catholic papers (the *Advocate* and the *Tribune*) also provided fascinating insights into the Church in the early twentieth century. The Catholic journals, *Alma Mater*, *Australasian Catholic Record*, *Christian Brothers' Educational Record* and *Manly* supplied further information. Beovich kept clippings in his diary of many articles in the South Australian secular newspapers: the *Advertiser*, *News* and *Sunday Mail*. These papers, along with the interstate *Age* and *Sydney Morning Herald* and national *Bulletin* and *Australian* were also consulted for the Catholic hierarchy's reaction to important events such as the Vietnam War and the *Humanae Vitae* controversy.

Interviews

Many people shared their memories of Matthew Beovich with me in informal conversations. Taped interviews were conducted with:

Rev. Monsignor Robert Aitken (ordained in 1952), 1 November 2004
Bro. John Bourke CFC, 10 February 2004
Mr John and Mrs Joan Brewer, 17 July 2003
Mr William Byrne, 13 December 2004

Rev. John Chambers (ordained in 1961), 10 December 2004
Rev. Alan Commins CM (rector of St Francis Xavier Seminary, 1964–1975), 20 January 1998
Rev. Daniel Conquest (priest of the archdiocese of Melbourne), 19 February 1998
Rev. Leon Czechowicz (ordained in 1967), 5 February 2004
Rev. Dr. Denis Edwards (ordained in 1966), 10 December 2004
Rev. Monsignor Robert Egar (ordained in 1957), 15 December 2004
Most Rev. Leonard Faulkner (ordained in 1950), 27 August 2002
Most Rev. James Gleeson (ordained in 1945), 24 July 1997 and 8 October 1997
Rev. Monsignor Thomas Horgan (ordained in 1941), 23 September 1997
Rev. Dr Brian Jackson CM, 15 January 2004
Rev. William Kelly (ordained in 1942), 21 January 1998
Mr. Keith Koen (Beovich's chauffer from 1940 to 1971), 4 April 1998
Rev. Monsignor Robert Rice (ordained in 1956), 16 November 2004
Mr Roy Richardson (former priest of the archdiocese of Adelaide, ordained in 1966), 9 December 2004.
Mr David Shinnick, 21 November 2002
Rev. Monsignor Vincent Tiggeman (ordained in 1951, Beovich's secretary from 1955 to 1965), 16 May 2002
Assoc. Prof. Peter Travers (former priest of the archdiocese of Adelaide, ordained in 1959, Beovich's secretary from 1965 to 1971), 28 November 2002
Rev. Robert Wilkinson (ordained in 1955), 11 June, 2002

Personal Histories

In 1973 long-term diocesan employee Darcy Woodards presented to Matthew Beovich a typescript of his reminiscences. Titled simply, 'Archbishop Beovich', it is in the ACAA. Three volumes of David Shinnick's unpublished memoirs are also in the diocesan archives. The first volume, 'Youthful Yearnings and Beyond', covers the period 1930 to 1970 and includes Shinnick's memories of life as a seminarian in the 1940s, involvement in the Movement in the 1950s, and work for the archdiocese of Adelaide in the 1960s. Edward Mulvilhill responded to my request for an interview by writing on 19 June 2002, 'My Recollections of Archbishop Matthew Beovich'.

Published Primary Sources

For Beovich's time in Melbourne, published primary sources include the paper he delivered to the Catholic Education Congress in 1936, 'Religious Education: Its Place in the Catholic School', *Australian Catholic Education Congress*, Adelaide, Australia, 8–15 November, 1936, Advocate Press, Melbourne, 1937. Beovich also contributed an article, 'Catholic Education in Australia', to K. S. Cunningham, G. A. McIntyre and W. C. Radford, eds, *Review of Education in Australia*, Melbourne University Press, Melbourne, 1938. It was not possible to locate a copy of the first edition of his *Companion to the Catechism*, but Archbishop Gleeson gave me a copy of the second edition, published by the Catholic Education Office, Melbourne, in 1939.

Other relevant catechetical material from this period includes:

Callanan, Ellen (Mother Patrick), *And Forbid Them Not!: A Series of Lessons on Christian Doctrine for Little Children*, Advocate Press, Melbourne, 1933
Catechism of Christian Doctrine Adapted for Australia by the 2nd and 3rd Plenary Councils, Sydney, 1939
Catechism for General Use in Australia issued with Episcopal Authority on the Occasion of the 4th Plenary Council, 1937, Australian Catholic Truth Society, Melbourne, 1938
Primer Catechism for Use in Junior Grades, Advocate Press, Melbourne, 1939

Theses and Unpublished Essays

Brennan, Loretta, 'The Beginning and End of the Catechism Era in the Melbourne Church', BTh essay, Melbourne College of Divinity, 1980
Brown, Gavin, 'Mass Performance: A Study of Eucharistic Ritual in Australian Catholic Culture, 1900–1962', PhD thesis, University of Melbourne, 2003

Calwell, Elizabeth, 'Arthur A. Calwell: The Early Years, 1929–1945', MTh thesis, Melbourne College of Divinity, 1998
Costelloe, Timothy, 'A Study of the History of the Institute of St John the Baptist', BTh essay, Melbourne College of Divinity, c. 1986
Gilchrist, Michael, 'The Role of Dr Mannix in Victorian Catholic Education, 1913–1923, and its Determinants', MEd thesis, University of Melbourne, 1978
Hepworth, John, 'The Movement Revisited: A South Australian Perspective', BA Hons thesis, University of Adelaide, 1982
Kavanagh, Mary, 'The Educational Work of the Presentation Sisters in Victoria, 1873–1960', MEd thesis, University of Melbourne, 1965
Keenan, A. M., 'The Boys Reformatory at Brooklyn Park: A History 1898–1941', MEd thesis, University of Adelaide, 1988
Little, Geraldine, 'The Democratic Labor Party in South Australia', BA Hons thesis, University of Adelaide, 1968
Luttrell, John J., 'Norman Thomas Cardinal Gilroy as Archbishop of Sydney', PhD thesis, University of Sydney, 1997
McKenzie, Monica Margaret, 'Catholic Women Educators as Agents of Social Change', MA thesis, Monash University, 1994
McPhee, Robert, 'Daniel Mannix: A Study in Aspects of Catholic Education Policy in Victoria, 1913–1945', MEd thesis, Monash University, 1980
Murnane, Peter, 'Interfaith Marriage and the Catholic Church in Australia: Aspects of its Rate of Occurrence, its Causes, and the Changing Attitudes towards it', BA Hons thesis, Flinders University, 1970
Murphy, Jeffrey J., 'The Australian Hierarchy and Vatican II: 1959–1965', PhD thesis, Griffith University, 2001
Nicholas, Therese, 'Abortion Law Reform in South Australia', BA Hons thesis, Flinders University, 1970
Reid, Nicholas Evan, 'Churchman: A Study of James Michael Liston, Bishop of Auckland, 1920–1970', PhD thesis, University of Auckland, 2004
Saunders, Malcolm, 'The Campaign for Peace in Vietnam (SA) 1967–1972', BA Hons thesis, Flinders University, 1972
Saunders, Malcolm, 'The Vietnam Moratorium Movement in Australia, 1969–1973', PhD thesis, Flinders University, 1977
Schumann, Ruth, '"Charity, Work, Loyalty": A History of the Catholic Women's League in South Australia: 1914–1979', BA Hons thesis, Flinders University, 1979
Sheehan, Josephine, 'Australian Catholics and the 1955 Split: A Micro-study of Personal Experiences and Reminiscences', BA Hons thesis, Flinders University, 1988
Thomas, Vincent, 'The Role of the Laity in Catholic Education in South Australia from 1836 to 1986', PhD thesis, Flinders University, 1989
Travers, Peter D., 'Planning in a Church Welfare Agency', MSA thesis, Flinders University, 1972
Warhurst, John Lewis, 'The Communist Bogey: Communism as an Election Issue in Australian Federal Politics 1949–1964', PhD thesis, Flinders University, 1977
Waterford, William David, 'The Content and Extent of Catholic Boys Secondary Schooling in the Archdiocese of Adelaide 1930–1950: A Study of Social and Ecclesial Factors', MEd thesis, Flinders University, 1994

Publications Relating to the Archdiocese of Adelaide

Anderson, Elizabeth, *On Fertile Soil: A History of the Catholic Church in the Stirling District*, Catholic Parish of Stirling, Stirling, 1987
Andrews, Brian, *The Cathedral Church of St Francis Xavier*, Adelaide Catholic Church Endowment Society, Adelaide, 1996
Bell, Clarrie, *The Parish of Woodville/Findon: A History of a Catholic Community*, Mater Dei Presbytery, Adelaide, 1987
Brewer, Joan, *A History of the Catholic Parish of St Peter's, 1934–1984*, St Peter's Parish, Adelaide, 1984
Bourke, John, *The Rostrevor Story, 1923–1983*, John Bourke, Adelaide, 1991

Burley, Stephanie and Teague, Katherine, *Chapel, Cloister and Classroom: Reflections on the Dominican Sisters at North Adelaide*, St Dominic's Priory, Adelaide, 1993

Chambers, John, et. al., *The Rays of the Crucifix. Links in the Chain: A Brief History of the Catholic Church in the Dulwich-Burnside Parish, 1869–1994*, Dulwich-Burnside Catholic Parish, Adelaide, 1994

Donovan, Peter, *Towards the New Jerusalem: A History of the Catholic Community at Blackwood*, Blackwood Parish Council, Adelaide, 1986

Donovan, Peter and Bernard O'Neil, *In the Marist Tradition: Sacred Heart College, Adelaide, 1897–1997*, Sacred Heart College, Adelaide, 1997

Egar, Robert, 'Killian, Andrew', *Australian Dictionary of Biography*, vol. 9, ed. Bede Nairn and Geoffrey Serle, Melbourne University Press, Melbourne, 1983, pp. 591–592

Fifty Years of the Capuchins in Adelaide, 1953–2003: St Francis of Assisi Parish, Newton, Newton Catholic Parish, 2003

Foale, Marie, *Think of the Ravens: The Sisters of St Joseph in Social Welfare, South Australia, 1867–1980*, Sisters of St Joseph, Adelaide, 2001

Forbes, Ian L. D., *Calvary Hospital Adelaide: In Celebration of One Hundred Years of the Service of the Sisters of the Little Company of Mary at Calvary Hospital Adelaide, 1900–2000*, Calvary Hospital Inc., Adelaide, 2000

Gale, Fay, ed., *Making Space: Women and Education at St Aloysius College, Adelaide, 1880–2000*, St Aloysius College, Adelaide, 2000

Gleeson, James William, 'The Church in Adelaide during My Years as a Priest and Bishop', *Australasian Catholic Record*, vol. 65, no. 3, 1988, pp. 292–302

Harrison, Helen, *Laudate Dominum: Music at Adelaide's Catholic Cathedral, 1845–1995*, Helen Harrison, Adelaide, 1997

Hartshorne, Heather and Wilkinson, Josie, *The Carmelite Priests and Brothers in South Australia, 1881–1999*, Pennington Catholic Parish, Adelaide, 1999

Head, Michael, *Fire on the Hill: Aquinas College, 1950–2000*, Aquinas College, Adelaide, 2002

Healy, Richard, *The Christian Brothers of Wakefield Street, 1878–1978*, Christian Brothers College, Adelaide, 1978

Hilliard, David, *Catholics in Kingswood: The Catholic Church in the Mitcham District, 1869–1994*, Kingswood Catholic Parish Pastoral Council, Adelaide, 1994

Laffin, Josephine, 'The Archbishop of Adelaide at Vatican II', *Australasian Catholic Record*, vol. 80, no. 3, 2003, pp. 319–333

Laffin, Josephine, 'The Public Role of Bishops: Matthew Beovich, the ALP Split and the Vietnam War', *Australasian Catholic Record*, vol. 84, no. 2, 2007, pp. 131–144

Laffin, Josephine, '"Calling God Back to the Council Chambers": An Archbishop's Response to World War Two', *Journal of the South Australian Historical Society*, no. 35, 2007, pp. 82–92

Massam, Katharine, *Sacred Threads: Catholic Spirituality in Australia, 1922–1962*, University of New South Wales Press, Sydney, 1996

McCormack, Helen, *The History of St Mary of the Angels Catholic Church, Port Lincoln*, Port Lincoln Catholic Parish, Port Lincoln, 1986

McLay, Anne, *Women on the Move: Mercy's Triple Spiral. A History of the Adelaide Sisters of Mercy*, Sisters of Mercy, Adelaide, 1996

Mills, Margret, *Woman: Why Are You Weeping? Women in the Church in South Australia*, News Weekly Books, Melbourne, 1997

Mother of God and Mother of Men: Record of the Marian Congress held in Adelaide, South Australia, 24–28 October 1951, Catholic Archdiocese of Adelaide, Adelaide, 1952

Northey, Helen, *Living the Truth: The Dominican Sisters in South Australia, 1868–1958*, Holy Cross Congregation of Dominican Sisters, Adelaide, 1999

Press, Margaret, *From Our Broken Toil: South Australian Catholics, 1836–1906*, Catholic Archdiocese of Adelaide, Adelaide, 1986

Press, Margaret, *Colour and Shadow: South Australian Catholics, 1906–1962*, Catholic Archdiocese of Adelaide, Adelaide, 1991

Press, Margaret, *St Francis Xavier Seminary: The First Fifty Years, 1942–1952*, St Francis Xavier Seminary, Adelaide, 1992

Press, Margaret, '"Poor but Very Good": The South Australian Catholic Story', *Australasian Catholic Record*, vol. 68, no. 2, 1991, pp. 192–197
Rice, Robert, 'Some Reflections on the Contribution of Matthew Beovich and James Gleeson to the Second Vatican Council,' *Australasian Catholic Record*, vol. 78, no. 1, 2001, pp. 46–61
Schumann, Ruth, 'The Practice of Catholic Piety in Colonial South Australia', *Flinders Journal of History and Politics*, vol. 9, 1983, pp. 6–29
Schumann, Ruth, 'The Catholic Priesthood of South Australia, 1844–1915', *Journal of Religious History*, vol. 16, 1990, pp. 51–73
Schumann, Ruth, 'Spence, Robert William', *Australian Dictionary of Biography*, vol. 12, ed. John Ritchie, Melbourne University Press, Melbourne, 1990, pp. 30–31
Shinnick, David, *Journey into Justice*, David Shinnick, Adelaide, 1982
St. Ignatius, Norwood, 1869–1969, Norwood Catholic Parish, 1969
Wilkinson, Josie, *The Silver Anniversary of Our Lady of Mount Carmel Church, 1960–1985*, Pennington Catholic Parish, Adelaide, 1985

Other Books and Articles

Ahlstrom, Sydney, *A Religious History of the American People*, Yale University Press, London, 1972
Alberigo, Giuseppe, ed., *History of Vatican II*, 4 vols, Peeters, Leuven, 1995–2003
Atkin, Nicholas and Tallett, Frank, *Priests, Prelates and People: A History of European Catholicism since 1750*, Oxford University Press, New York, 2003
Aubert, Roger, *The Church in a Secularised Society*, vol. 5, The Christian Centuries, Darton, Longman & Todd, London, 1978
Aubert, Robert et al, eds, *The Church in the Industrial Age* (*History of the Church*, vol. 9, eds Jedin and Dolan) Burns & Oates, London, 1981
Barcan, Alan, *A History of Education in Australia*, Melbourne University Press, Melbourne, 1980
Blainey, Geoffrey, *A Short History of the 20th Century*, Viking, Melbourne, 2005
Boland, T. P., *James Duhig*, University of Queensland Press, Brisbane, 1986
Boland, T. P., 'The Ascent of Mount Tabor: Writing the Life of Archbishop Duhig', Aquinas Memorial Lecture, Aquinas Library, Brisbane, 1986
Boland, T. P., *Thomas Carr: Archbishop of Melbourne*, University of Queensland Press, Brisbane, 1997
Boland, T. P., 'Carr and Moran: A Comparison in Episcopal Styles', *Australian Catholic Historical Society Journal*, vol. 16, 1994–1995, pp. 25–37
Boland, T. P., 'Gilroy, Sir Norman Thomas', *Australian Dictionary of Biography*, vol. 14, ed. John Ritchie, Melbourne University Press, Melbourne, 1996, pp. 275–278
Boland, T. P., 'Thirty Years On: The O'Farrell Era', *Australasian Catholic Record*, vol. 75, no. 2, 1998, pp. 145–156
Bolton, Geoffrey, *The Oxford History of Australia*, vol. 5: *The Middle Way: 1942–1995*, 2nd ed., Oxford University Press, Melbourne, 1996
Bosi, Pino, *On God's Command: Italian Missionaries in Australia*, CIRC, Sydney, 1989
Bossy, John, *Christianity in the West*, 1400–1700, Oxford University Press, Oxford, 1985
Bourke, D. F., *The History of the Catholic Church in Western Australia, 1829–1979*, Catholic Archdiocese of Perth, Perth, 1979
Bourke, D. F., *A History of the Catholic Church in Victoria*, Catholic Bishops of Victoria, Melbourne, 1988
Brennan, Niall, *Dr Mannix*, Rigby Ltd., Adelaide, 1964
Breward, Ian, *Australia: 'The Most Godless Place under Heaven'? Melbourne College of Divinity Bicentennial Lectures*, Lutheran Publishing House, Adelaide, 1988
Breward, Ian, *A History of the Australian Churches*, Allen & Unwin, Sydney, 1993
Breward, Ian, *A History of the Churches in Australasia*, Oxford University Press, Oxford, 2001
Byrnes, Gregory, 'Archbishop Sheehan: A Biographical Sketch', *Journal of the Australian Catholic Historical Society*, 1992, pp. 24–35
Byrne, Neil, *Robert Dunne 1830–1917: Archbishop of Brisbane*, University of Queensland Press, Brisbane, 1991

Byrne, Neil, 'Writing Robert Dunne: Brisbane's First Catholic Archbishop' in *Irish-Australian Studies: Papers Delivered at the 7th Irish-Australian Conference*, ed. Rebecca Pelan, July 1993, Crossing Press, Sydney, 1994

Calwell, Arthur, *Be Just and Fear Not*, Rigby, Adelaide, 1978

Calwell, Mary Elizabeth, 'Arthur Calwell and his Times', *Australasian Catholic Record*, vol. 65, no. 3, 1988, pp. 279–291

Campion, Edmund, *Rockchoppers: Growing Up Catholic in Australia*, Penguin Books, Melbourne, 1982

Campion, Edmund, *Australian Catholics: The Contribution of Catholics to the Development of Australian Society*, Aurora Books, Melbourne, 1987

Campion, Edmund, *Great Australian Catholics*, Viking, Melbourne, 1987

Campion, Edmund, *A Place in the City: Living Around the Cathedral, From the Mysteries to the Wider World*, Penguin, Melbourne, 1994

Campion, Edmund, 'Irish Religion in Australia', *Australasian Catholic Record*, vol. 50, no. 1, 1978, pp. 4–16

Carey, Hilary, *Believing in Australia: A Cultural History of Religions*, Allen & Unwin, Sydney, 1996

Catholic Education in Victoria. Yesterday, Today and Tomorrow, Catholic Education Office of Victoria, Melbourne [1986]

Chadwick, Owen, *The Christian Church in the Cold War* (*Penguin History of the Church*, rev. ed.), Penguin, London, 1993

Cockburn, Stewart, *Playford: Benevolent Despot*, Axiom, Adelaide, 1991

Coldrey, Barry M., *'A Most Unenviable Reputation': The Christian Brothers and School Discipline Over Two Centuries*, Tamanariak Publishing, Melbourne, 1991

Cooke, Bernard, *Ministry to Word and Sacraments: History and Tradition*, Fortress Press, Philadelphia, 1976

Costar, Brian, Love, Peter and Strangio, Brian, eds, *The Great Labor Schism: A Retrospective*, Scribe Publications, Melbourne, 2005

Croke, Brian, 'Politics and Prelates: The Carroll Style', *Journal of the Australian Catholic Historical Society*, vol. 22, 2001, pp. 31–45

Davidson, Graeme, *The Rise and Fall of Marvellous Melbourne*, Melbourne University Press, Melbourne, 1978

Deery, Philip, 'Santamaria, the Movement and the Split: A Re-examination', *Journal of the Australian Catholic Historical Society*, vol. 22, 2001, pp. 47–58

Duffy, Eamon, *Faith of Our Fathers: Reflections on Catholic Tradition*, Continuum, London and New York, 2004

Duncan, Bruce, *Crusade or Conspiracy?: Catholics and the Anti-Communist Struggle in Australia*, University of New South Wales Press, Sydney, 2001

Dunn, Patrick J., *Priesthood: A Re-Examination of the Roman Catholic Theology of the Presbyterate*, Alba House, New York, 1990

Ebsworth, Walter, *Archbishop Mannix*, H. H. Stephenson, Melbourne, 1977

Ellwood, Robert, *The Sixties Spiritual Awakening: American Religion Moving from Modern to Postmodern*, Rutgers University Press, New Brunswick, NJ, 1994

Fifty Years of the Santamaria Movement: A Conference Held in the State Library of New South Wales, 2 May 1992, Eureka Street Papers, no. 1, Jesuit Publications, Melbourne, 1992

Fitzgerald, Ross, *The Pope's Battalions: Santamaria, Catholicism and the Labor Split*, University of Queensland Press, Brisbane, 2003

Fogarty, Gerald, ed., *Patterns of Episcopal Leadership, Bicentennial History of the Catholic Church in America Authorized by the National Conference of Catholic Bishops*, Macmillan, New York, 1989

Fogarty, Ronald, *Catholic Education in Australia, 1806–1950*, vol. 2: *Catholic Education Under the Religious Orders*, Melbourne University Press, Melbourne, 1959

Gilchrist, Michael, *Daniel Mannix: Wit and Wisdom*, 2nd ed., Freedom Publishing, Melbourne, 2004

Goldie, Rosemary, *From a Roman Window: Five Decades: The World, The Church and the Catholic Laity*, HarperCollins Religious, Melbourne, 1998

Greeley, Andrew, *The Catholic Revolution: New Wine, Old Wineskins, and the Second Vatican Council*, University of California Press, Berkeley, California, 2004
Greening, W. A., 'The Mannix Thesis in Catholic Secondary Education in Victoria', *Melbourne Studies in Education, 1961–1962*, Melbourne University Press, Melbourne, 1962
Haines, Gregory, 'Aspects of Australian Piety', *Australasian Catholic Record*, vol. 55, no. 3, 1978, pp. 231–243
Hastings, Adrian, *A History of English Christianity, 1920–1990*, 3rd ed., SCM, London, 1991
Hastings, Adrian, ed., *Modern Catholicism: Vatican II and After*, SPCK and Oxford University Press, London and New York, 1991
Hastings, Adrian, ed., *A World History of Christianity*, W. B. Eerdmans, Grand Rapids, Mich., 1999
Hebblethwaite, Peter, *The Runaway Church*, Collins, Glasgow, 1978
Hebblethwaite, Peter, *John XXIII: Pope of the Council*, Geoffrey Chapman, London, 1984
Hebblethwaite, Peter, *Paul VI: The First Modern Pope*, Harper Collins, London, 1993
Heenan, John C., *A Crown of Thorns: An Autobiography, 1951–1963*, Hodder and Staughton, London, 1974
Henderson, Gerard, *Mr Santamaria and the Bishops* (*Studies in the Christian Movement*, vol 7), St Patrick's College, Manly, 1982
Hilliard, David, *Godliness and Good Order: A History of the Anglican Church in South Australia*, Wakefield Press, Adelaide, 1986
Hilliard, David, 'Popular Religion in Australia in the 1950s: A Study of Adelaide and Brisbane', *Journal of Religious History*, vol. 15, 1988, pp. 219–235
Hilliard, David, 'God in the Suburbs: the Religious Culture of Australian Cities in the 1950s', *Australian Historical Studies*, vol. 24, 1991, pp. 399–419
Hilliard, David, 'Religion in Playford's South Australia' in *Playford's South Australia: Essays on the History of South Australia, 1933–1969*, eds Bernard O'Neil, Judith Raftery and Kerrie Round, Association of Professional Historians, Inc., Adelaide, 1996
Hilliard, David, 'Church, Family and Sexuality in Australia in the 1950s', *Australian Historical Studies*, vol. 109, 1997, pp. 133–156
Hilliard, David, 'The Religious Crisis of the 1960s: The Experience of the Australian Churches', *Journal of Religious History*, vol. 21, 1997, 209–227
Hogan, Michael, *The Sectarian Strand: Religion in Australian History*, Penguin, Melbourne, 1987
Horne, Donald, *Time of Hope: Australia 1966–1972*, Angus & Robertson, Melbourne, 1980
Hunt, Arnold D., *This Side of Heaven: A History of Methodism in South Australia*, Lutheran Publishing House, Adelaide, 1985
Iserton, Edward et al, eds, *Reformation and Counter Reformation* (*History of the Church*, vol. 5, eds Jedin and John Dolan), Crossroad, New York, 1980
Jaensch, D., ed., *The Flinders History of South Australia: Political History*, Wakefield Press, Adelaide, 1986
Jedin, Hubert et al, eds, *The Church in the Modern Age* (*History of the Church*, vol. 10, eds Jedin and Dolan), Burns & Oates, London, 1981
Johnston, Elizabeth, 'Eris O'Brien: Historian and Scholar', *Journal of the Australian Catholic Historical Society*, vol. 24, 2003, pp. 17–30
Jupp, James, ed., *The Australian People: An Encyclopedia of the Nation, Its People and their Origins*, rev. ed., Cambridge University Press, 2001
Kalman, Laura, 'The Power of Biography', *Law and Social Inquiry*, vol. 23, 1998, pp. 477–530
Kennedy, Sally, *Faith and Feminism: Catholic Women's Struggles for Self-Expression* (*Studies in the Christian Movement*, vol. 9), St Patrick's College, Manly, 1985
Kenny, Anthony, *A Path from Rome: An Autobiography*, Sidgwick & Jackson, London, 1985
Kiernan, Colm, *Calwell: A Personal and Political Biography*, Thomas Nelson, Melbourne, 1978
Kselman, Thomas and Avella, Steven, 'Marian Piety and the Cold War in the United States', *Catholic Historical Review*, vol. 72, 1986, pp. 403–424
Larson, Ann, *Growing Up in Melbourne: Family Life in the Late Nineteenth Century*, Australian Family Formation Project Monograph 12, Australian National University, Canberra, 1994
Lewins, Frank, *The Myth of the Universal Church: Catholic Migrants in Australia*, Australian National University, Canberra, 1978

Livingstone, Tess, *George Pell*, Duffy & Snellgrove, Sydney, 2002
Luttrell, John, 'Bishop Gilroy and the Diocese of Port Augusta', *Australasian Catholic Record*, vol. 80, no. 2, 2003, pp. 189–200
Macintyre, Stuart, *The Oxford History of Australia*, vol. 4, *The Succeeding Age: 1901–1942*, Oxford University Press, Melbourne, 1993
Magarey, Susan and Round, Kerrie, *Roma the First: A Biography of Dame Roma Mitchell*, Wakefield Press, Adelaide, 2007
Maguire, John P., *Prologue: A History of the Catholic Church as Seen From Townsville, 1863–1983*, Church Archivists Society, Toowomba, 1990
Martos, Joseph, *Doors to the Sacred: A Historical Introduction to the Sacraments in the Christian Church*, rev. ed., Liguori/Triumph, Liguori, Missouri, 2001
Massam, Katharine, 'The Blue Army and the Cold War: Anti-Communist Devotion to the Blessed Virgin in Australia', *Australian Historical Studies*, vol. 97, 1991, pp. 420–428
Massam, Katharine and Smith, John H., 'Images of God: Civil Religion and Australia at War 1939–1945', *Australian Religion Studies Review*, vol. 11, 1998, pp. 57–71
McCarthy, William J., *James Patrick O'Collins: A Bishop's Story*, Spectrum Publications, Melbourne, 1996
McKernan, Michael, 'Catholics, Conscription and Archbishop Mannix', *Australian Historical Studies*, vol. 17, no. 68, 1977
McLeod, Hugh, *Religion and the People of Western Europe, 1789–1970*, Oxford University Press, Oxford, 1981
McLeod, Hugh, 'Building the Catholic "Ghetto": Catholic Organisations, 1870–1914' in *Voluntary Religion, Studies in Church History*, vol. 23, eds W. J. Sheils and Diana Wood, Basil Blackwell, Oxford, 1986, pp. 411–444
McMullin, Ross, *The Light on the Hill: The Australian Labor Party, 1891–1991*, Oxford University Press, Melbourne, 1991
Meecham, Frank, *The Church and the Migrants, 1946–1987*, St Joan of Arc Press, Sydney, 1991
Mol, Hans, *The Faith of Australians*, Allen & Unwin, Sydney, 1985
Molony, John N., *The Roman Mould of the Australian Catholic Church*, Melbourne University Press, Melbourne, 1969
Molony, John N., *Luther's Pine: An Autobiography*, Pandanus Books, Canberra, 2004
Molony, John N., *Australia: Our Heritage*, Australian Scholarly Publishing, Melbourne, 2005
Moorman, John, *Vatican Observed: An Anglican Impression of Vatican II*, Darton, Longman & Todd, London, 1967
Murphy, Jeffrey, 'The Catholic Church in Queensland on the Eve of Vatican II', *Proceedings of Brisbane Catholic Historical Society*, vol. 7, 2000, pp. 1–30
Murphy, Jeffrey, 'Developing Perceptions about the Council and the Preparatory Phase: 1960–1962', *Australasian Catholic Record*, vol. 79, no. 1, 2002, pp. 75–86
Murphy, Jeffrey, 'Of Pilgrims and Progressives: Australian Bishops at Vatican II (The First Session: 1962)', *Australasian Catholic Record*, vol. 79, no. 2, 2002, pp. 189–213
Murphy, Jeffrey, 'Romanità Mark II: Australian Bishops at Vatican II (The Second Session: 1963)', *Australasian Catholic Record*, vol. 79, no. 3, 2002, pp. 341–363
Murphy, Jeffrey, 'On the Threshold of Modernity: Australian Bishops at Vatican II (The Third Session: 1964)', *Australasian Catholic Record*, vol. 79, no. 4, 2002, pp. 444–468
Murphy, Jeffrey, 'Sane, Advanced Conservatism: Australian Bishops at Vatican II (The Third Session Continues: 1964)', *Australasian Catholic Record*, vol. 80, no. 2, 2003, pp. 219–247
Murphy, Jeffrey, 'The Far Milieu Called Home: Australian Bishops at Vatican II (The Final Session: 1965)', *Australasian Catholic Record*, vol. 80, no. 3, 2003, pp. 343–369
Murray, Robert, *The Split: Australian Labor in the Fifties*, Cheshire, Melbourne, 1970
Noone, Val, *Disturbing the War: Melbourne Catholics and Vietnam*, Spectrum, Melbourne, 1993
O'Brien, Anne, *Blazing a Trail: Catholic Education in Victoria, 1963–1980*, David Lovell Publishing, Melbourne, 1999
O'Brien, David J., 'When it all came together: Bishop John J. Wright and the diocese of Worchester, 1950–1959', *Catholic Historical Review*, vol. 85, pp. 175–194
O'Farrell, Patrick, *Vanished Kingdoms: Irish in Australia and New Zealand – A Personal Excursion*, New South Wales University Press, Sydney, 1990

O'Farrell, Patrick, *The Catholic Church and Community: An Australian History*, 3rd rev. ed., New South Wales University Press, Sydney, 1992
O'Farrell, Patrick, *The Irish in Australia*, rev. ed., University of New South Wales Press, Sydney, 1993
O'Farrell, Patrick, 'Lay Spirituality and Historical Conditioning', *Australasian Catholic Record*, vol. 55, no. 1, 1978, pp. 36–42
O'Farrell, Patrick, 'Piety and Prayer as Historical Problems', *Australasian Catholic Record*, vol. 55, no. 3, 1978, pp. 221–230
O'Farrell, Patrick, 'Kelly, Michael', *Australian Dictionary of Biography*, vol. 9, ed. Bede Nairn and Geoffrey Serle, Melbourne University Press, Melbourne, 1983, pp. 556–558
O'Farrell, Patrick, 'The Writing of Australian Catholic History, 1980–1990', *Australasian Catholic Record*, vol. 73, no. 2, 1991, pp. 131–145
O'Neil, Bernard, Raftery, Judith and Round, Kerry, eds, *Playford's South Australia: Essays on the History of South Australia, 1933–1968*, Association of Professional Historians, Inc., Adelaide, 1996
Ormonde, Paul, *The Movement*, Thomas Nelson, Melbourne, 1972
Ormonde, Paul, ed., *Santamaria and the Politics of Fear*, Spectrum Publications, Melbourne, 2000
Osborne, Kenan B., *Priesthood: A History of the Ordained Ministry in the Roman Catholic Church*, Paulist Press, New York, 1988
O'Toole, James, 'The Role of Bishops in American Catholic History: Myth and Reality in the Case of Cardinal William O'Connell,' *Catholic Historical Review*, vol. 77, 1991, pp. 595–615
Pagononi, Anthony, *Valiant Struggles and Benign Neglect: Italians, Church and Religious Societies in Diaspora: The Australian Experience from 1950 to 2000*, Centre for Migration Studies, New York, 2003
Pittarello, Adrian, *'Soup Without Salt': The Australian Catholic Church and the Italian Migrant: A Comparative Study in the Sociology of Religion*, Centre for Migration Studies, Sydney, 1980
Pittarello, Adrian, 'Migrants and the Catholic Church in Australia', *Australasian Catholic Record*, vol. 65, no. 2, 1988, pp. 141–158
Pittarello, Adrian, 'Australian Immigration and the Church', *Australasian Catholic Record*, vol. 70, no. 3, 1993, pp. 305–313
Pollard, John F., *The Unknown Pope: Benedict XV (1914–1922) and the Pursuit of Peace*, Geoffrey Chapman, London, 1999
Praetz, Helen, *Building a School System: A Sociological Study of Catholic Education*, Melbourne University Press, Melbourne, 1980
Richards, Eric, ed., *The Flinders History of South Australia: Social History*, Wakefield Press, Adelaide, 1986
Rogan, Frank, *A Short History of Catholic Education: Archdiocese of Melbourne, 1839–1980*, Catholic Education Office, Melbourne, 2000
Ryder, William, 'The Australian Bishops' Proposals for Vatican II', *Australasian Catholic Record*, vol. 65, no. 1, 1988, pp. 62–77
Rynne, Xavier (Francis X. Murphy, CSSR), *Vatican Council II*, Orbis Books, Maryknoll, NY, 1999
Santamaria, B. A., *Daniel Mannix: The Quality of Leadership*, Melbourne University Press, Melbourne, 1984
Santamaria, B. A., *Against the Tide*, Oxford University Press, Melbourne, 1981
Santamaria, B. A., *Santamaria: A Memoir*, Oxford University Press, Melbourne, 1997
Saunders, Malcolm, 'Opposition to the Vietnam War in South Australia, 1965–1973', *Journal of the Historical Society of South Australia*, vol. 10, 1982, pp. 61–71
Saunders, Malcolm, 'The Labor Party and the Industrial Groups in South Australia 1946–1955: Precluding the Split', *Journal of the Historical Society of South Australia*, vol. 33, 2005, pp. 71–79
Malcolm Saunders and Neil Lloyd, 'Remembering the Past and Hoping for the Future: Why there was no Labor split in South Australia in 1954–1956', in *The Great Labor Schism: A Retrospective*, eds Brian Costar, Peter Love and Paul Strangio, Scribe Publications, Melbourne, 2005
Southerwood, W. T., *The Wisdom of Guilford Young*, Stella Maris Books, Hobart, 1989
Stacpoole, Alberic, ed., *Vatican II By Those Who Were There*, Geoffrey Chapman, London, 1986

Stewart, Ronald, *The Spirit of North, 1903–2000*, St Joseph's College, Melbourne, 2000
Stirling, Alfred, *A Distant View of the Vatican*, Hawthorn Press, Melbourne, 1975
Stock, Jenny, 'The Role of Religion in the 1951 Referendum to Ban the Communist Party: The South Australian Example', *Australian Religion Studies Review*, vol. 11, no. 2, 1998, pp. 38–56
Sutalo, Ilija, *Croatians in Australia: Pioneers, Settlers and their Descendants*, Wakefield Press, Adelaide, 2004
Thompson, Roger C., *Religion in Australia: A History*, 2nd ed., Oxford University Press, Melbourne, 2002
Turner, Naomi, *Catholics in Australia: A Social History*, 2 vols, Collins Dove, Melbourne, 1992
Vodola, Max, *Simonds: A Rewarding Life*, Catholic Education Office, Melbourne, 1997
Weigel, George, *Witness to Hope: The Biography of Pope John Paul II*, Harper Collins, New York, 1999
Wiltgen, Ralph, *The Rhine Flows Into the Tiber: A History of Vatican II*, Augustine Publishing Company, Devon, 1978
Wray, Vamplew, Richards, Eric, Jaensch, Dean and Hancock, Joan, eds, *South Australian Historical Statistics*, Historical Statistics Monograph, vol. 3, History Project Inc., Sydney, 1984

Index

Wakefield Press is an independent publishing and distribution company based in Adelaide, South Australia. We love good stories and publish beautiful books. To see our full range of titles, please visit our website at www.wakefieldpress.com.au.